Painting in America

PAINTING

IN

AMERICA

The story of 450 years

E. P. RICHARDSON

The Detroit Institute of Arts

THOMAS Y. CROWELL COMPANY, NEW YORK

THE GROWTH
OF AMERICA
SERIES

Copyright © 1956 by E. P. Richardson

*All rights reserved. No part of this
book may be reproduced in any
form, except by a reviewer, without
the permission of the publisher.*

Designed by EMIL SILVESTRI

*Manufactured in the United States of America
by the Cornwall Press, Inc., Cornwall, N. Y.*

Library of Congress Catalog Card No. 56-7793

Third Printing

CONTENTS

LIST OF ILLUSTRATIONS

PAGE

COLOR PLATES

Painting in America

THE PROBLEM

PAINTING IS BOTH AN ART AND A CRAFT. IT THEREFORE SHARES BOTH THE UN-predictable nature of the imagination which, like the wind, blows where it wills and the social character of an organized skill in human society. These two elements—the one volatile as air or fire, the other earthbound and practical but, like the earth, stabilizing and life-giving—are always present in art. But nowhere is their mutual action and reaction more striking, their interplay more curious, than in their creation of a new national tradition of painting in America.

The story of both art and craft of painting in America is part of the larger story of how Western civilization, after developing through a thousand years in Europe, spread in the sixteenth and seventeenth centuries in the minds and hands of adventurous men to the western shores of the Atlantic, took root there, and developed in a new series of nations on the American continent. Since the American Revolution of 1775-1783 the United States has been politically separated from Europe; but American culture has continued to live its own life within the greater life of the entire Western world, just as have the national cultures of Great Britain, France, Italy, and every other Western nation.

It is written everywhere, across the story of these past centuries, that we have shared with Europe both a common heritage of the past and the climate of the mind which prevails in each successive age: yet this fact is greatly in need of interpretation. One main purpose of this book is to see how American painting appears when observed within the perspective of Western art, seen as a whole. The mental climate of thought and feeling, and the evolution of forms, familiar in the general history of Western art, have never been brought into relation with the works of American painters. I have tried to tell the story of American painters from their own viewpoint, but in relation also to what was happening in the rest of the world. I do not find that American painting seems less interesting when set beside that of other countries: rather the contrary.

European historians have tended, owing to an understandable but almost total ignorance of America, to limit their sympathies to the American artists closest to European life, especially to such painters as West, Whistler, and Cassatt, who lived in Europe and played an active part in European art. From this limited perspective, however, American painting appears a marginal phenomenon, hardly continuous or abundant enough to be considered.

Perhaps in reaction, recent American writers have often seemed to resent any connection with Europe and have emphasized the opposite end of the scale: the untaught, the naïf, the artists who never studied or journeyed abroad. This produces what I call the *frontier fallacy*,[1] which tries to identify a "truly American" note in our art by identifying it with the sturdy, self-taught independence of the frontiersman. This note exists, and lends its flavor to our history. Yet the imaginative life of a whole nation is a vast chorus of a thousand voices, not to be reduced to a single note.

American culture is neither a raw new product nor a borrowed old one. It is the imaginative life of people who share the common inheritance of Western civilization, but live under new skies and feel novel experiences as well as those that all men share. Regard it, then, as one of the broad national traditions which make Western life so varied and so rich: it will provide both surprises and matter for pride.

Two of its stranger elements may call for brief mention here. It is a curious spectacle, for one interested in the life of forms in art, to see how in the colonial centuries, when life on this continent was months away from Europe and still in its rude beginnings, the forms of European painting still made themselves felt. The rich, splendid, complex forms of Baroque and Rococo painting spread outward from their centers, like ripples on a pool, growing fainter as they crossed the broad Atlantic, changing as they broke upon a distant shore, yet still discernible and recognizable, until they vanished into the silence of the forest.

On the other hand, in the vast, centuries-long migration of people and ideas to the New World, talent sometimes outdistanced both the forms and the skills of painting. Notable qualities of art sometimes appear in painters born in frontier cabins, and equipped with most crude or homespun skills, like Winthrop Chandler, or the anonymous New England or Hudson River painters. Or, side by side with those *naïfs*, one finds another artist, such as West, or Allston, who is a stylist in the extreme forefront of the movement of his times. Skill and perception, imagination and style thus appear in unexpected relations.

[1] Cf. my *Washington Allston, A Study of the Romantic Artist in America*, Chicago, University of Chicago Press, 1948, p. 13.

To tell this story properly, we must follow (1) the first migration of drawing and painting to the New World, among the explorer artists; (2) the gradual transplanting of the skills, the *craft*, of painting from their old home to the New World, and the growth of its supporting institutions; (3) the changes in the direction of attention, or imaginative interest, that prevail from generation to generation; (4) the evolution of the language of painting, which grows and changes like any other language under the drive of new minds and new ideas; (5) the interaction of American developments with those in other parts of the world; (6) the perceptions, talents, works, and fortunes of many gifted individuals.

Most of these will fall into their place as our story develops; but there are a few points I feel a need to discuss further here. Those who do not care for theoretical discussions may go on to Chapter 2. To those who may have the patience to follow me, I will say something about (1) and (2), since they are points which help to separate the experience of American artists from those in Europe.

(1) The skills of drawing and painting have been practiced in America throughout the 450 years since the New World first appeared in history. They came with the first explorers. In the city of Genoa there is preserved a drawing, long attributed to Columbus, which was supposed to have been sent by Columbus himself from Seville in 1502. It appears to be, more accurately considered, a Baroque allegorical sketch; no authentic drawings by Columbus are in existence. Yet he had the reputation of being a good draughtsman, and it is not unlikely that he made drawings of things he saw on his voyages of discovery. Other exploring expeditions were accompanied by trained artists. A painter, Rodrigo de Cifuentes, accompanied Cortes on his expedition into Honduras in 1525. Jacques le Moyne de Morgues, a French artist, came to Florida about 1564 with the Huguenot expedition under Laudonnière. John White, a draughtsman of lively charm, came to Virginia with Raleigh's first colony in 1585 and returned to America in 1587 and 1590. Other explorers, although without professional training, made drawings to illustrate their reports of the vast, wild continent, its coasts, its harbors, its novel men, and beasts, and plants. The craft, or skill, of drawing and painting thus came along with the first Europeans to set foot on these shores. As permanent settlements were made, artists are found at work here well within the lifetime of the first settlers. The history of American painting, from this point, has to do with the establishment of a descriptive skill, first, and then the slow unfolding of the imaginative and contemplative life of the mind that found its outlet through that skill.

(2) Painting is both a language of the imagination and a craft. Only in recent times have these two elements been distinguished within the term *art*,

which originally meant any form of disciplined skill. In antiquity *ars* meant all the works of man as distinguished from the works of nature; in the Middle Ages Dante still used *art* almost as a synonym for industry—there was the art of the wool workers in medieval Florence as there was the art of the gold-smiths, to whose guild the painters belonged. In modern usage the word has come to mean only the arts practiced for pleasure and imaginative communication, rather than utility. The character of painting as an imaginative language has been realized in the theory of art only during the last century or two. Modern criticism, in its pride at this discovery, has tended to underestimate the importance, and the life-giving quality, of the disciplined skill or the *craft* in painting. The ignorance of the theoretician has received support from the industrial revolution, which swept away the crafts of the engraver and, very nearly, those of the illustrator, the decorative painter and designer, and the portrait painter, a disaster which modern theorists accept complacently as a good thing and a confirmation of their view that art exists without relation to anything but the artist's self-consciousness. Only the hard-working scientists, too busy to keep up with esthetic theories and well aware that the human eye and hand can do what the camera cannot (as the camera can do what the hand cannot), continued as a matter of course to use the crafts of the scientific draughtsman and artist.

Before the separation of the artist from the craftsman, which occurred only as a gradual change between the Renaissance and the nineteenth century, stretches "the undisturbed, innocent, somnambulatory production" (to use Goethe's phrase) of ages when the artist worked undisturbed by the worship of his own genius or by the critics' curiosity to peer into his psyche. Art was intended for use or delight, no more. One has only to look at the achievements of those ages to be aware that esthetic self-consciousness is not the all-in-all of art, nor an entirely unmixed good. Perhaps, so far as painting is concerned, the greatness of the period from the fifteenth to the eighteenth century rose partly from the happy balance of the craft and the imaginative elements in its organization.

But painting on this continent is not like the European schools of art which grew up slowly, almost unconsciously, out of an ancient tradition of craftsmanship, stretching back so far that its origins have been forgotten. Painting sprang up here, in the wilderness, wherever men of Western origin settled, where there was nothing to foster it—nothing but the inner urge, a need of the imagination, a thirst in the soul, that demanded satisfaction and created the art, by sheer force of will, while the forest trees still grew around them.

The *art* of painting came to America in the mental inheritance of the race. But the *craft* of painting is a social product and had to wait upon the slow growth of the tiny European settlements into, first, self-sustaining, then

growing and creative organisms. Although painters began coming to America
with the first explorers, the earliest professionally trained European artist to
settle here permanently was Hendrick Couturier, a Leiden-trained painter
who emigrated to the Dutch West India colonies about 1661. A century later,
Benjamin West, the first American-born painter to win an international reputation and play a part in the artistic life of Europe, sailed for Italy. In a period
of a hundred years, the art was native-born. By the eighteen-thirties, to the
eyes of a surprised English visitor, Mrs. Anna Jameson, "the country seemed
to swarm with painters." Yet the first academies and exhibitions were established only in the early nineteenth century; the first serious art schools came
only in the eighteen-seventies; and for representative collections of great
paintings to study, the American artist had to wait until the twentieth century. Both the training of artists and opportunities for self-training were
haphazard until late in our history. Some studied abroad; some learned as ap-
prentices to older men; the majority in early times were self-taught, with
such assistance as they could glean from imported mezzotint engravings or
the few pictures to be seen in their immediate neighborhood. Artists born
under frontier conditions—as many were—learned their skills late, and under
great difficulties. Whatever else it was, American painting during most of
its history was not a highly schooled art. Perhaps that is why we have in recent times tended somewhat to overvalue technical assurance. Certainly, the
lack of a strong, indigenous craft tradition is one of the factors that has
deeply affected American painting.

As a craft, painting lives the life natural to any disciplined professional
skill in human society. A skill requires training; it implies standards of competence; it creates products that must be offered somehow to society; it is
affected by the kind of tasks that society asks it to perform. Some of the elements we must try to trace are: the struggle of artists to create high professional levels of skill in the New World; the gradual establishment of academies
and art schools; the rise of exhibitions, museums of art, art dealers, and of the
journalism of art by which reputation and commercial success are supported.
Over and above this is the life of the imagination, the story of individual talents, of sensitivity and genius. But we must show the two together if we are
to understand how the difficult and subtle skills of the painter's craft were
transplanted from Europe to America, and how a well-trained, self-sustaining
body of artists, with all the institutions of an active artistic life, was created
here.

The slow development of the technical skills and professional organizations of painting meant that, until relatively recent times, American painters
looked to Europe for the great collections of art to study, the leading schools
and teachers of art, and the most accomplished living practitioners of their
craft. As a result American artists have always been intensely curious (sometimes too curious) to know what was going on abroad. Style in painting can

be studied, but it cannot be borrowed; for a style is the organic expression of what the artist has to say. A cross-conflict between, on the one hand, the need of artists to learn the tradition of painting and the best current practice abroad and, on the other, the need to create a vital expression of their own produced a dichotomy in American painting which has endured to the present day. There is of course always a dichotomy in art between inspiration and conscious style—between the appeals of life and of art—but it has taken a special form in America as a result of these historical forces.

Under their influence American artists have tended to fall into two types: (1) Gifted cosmopolitan minds like West, Allston, Whistler, Sargent, Marin, Marsden Hartley, Franklin Watkins, whose art is nourished by and belongs to the international currents of art of their day. This type at its best makes a brilliant personal contribution; at its worst, it constitutes the mass of *pasticheurs* who have characterized Western art since the rise of easy communication, in the past one hundred years, but who are nowhere more numerous than in the United States. (2) Solitary individualists like Winslow Homer, Thomas Eakins, Albert Ryder, Charles Burchfield, Edward Hopper, Ivan Le Lorraine Albright, who are so concerned with finding a personal interpretation of life that they do not fit easily into the current of contemporary painting. This type may achieve a high technical level, although often they have sacrificed ease and fluency of manner in their dogged effort to find an individual interpretation of life. At its best, this type of mind has produced some of our best artists, strong, convincing, idiosyncratic, though rugged in style. At its worst, this type is simply provincial.

There is also a third type peculiar to America and to our historical conditions of the frontier. In the process of settling the continent, as family after family left the old, settled districts near the seacoast to try its fortunes in the wilderness to westward, the population spread itself very thinly through an immense territory. Gifted individuals with the natural endowments of the artist were born in lonely frontier settlements, perhaps as often as in the old and settled regions, but under such conditions that they grew up remote from the established profession of art. Good painters like Charles Willson Peale, Chester Harding, or Francis Alexander, for example, grew to manhood before they heard of the existence of the art of painting. These three, once discovering their vocation, sought teachers and made themselves trained artists. But frontier conditions prevailed over a very large part of this country for a very long period; and not all natural artists were able to find the best training or an opportunity to work in a large city.

Out of these conditions came a kind of artist peculiar to American painting, whom I call the *untrained professional* artist. There were many such artists and, untrained though they were, they were often men of great innate sensibility. The so-called Patroon painters of the early eighteenth century among the Hudson River Dutch; the vigorous and interesting back country painters of New England, especially numerous and prominent in the second half of the eighteenth century; some of the anonymous artists of the nineteenth century, all show fine powers of observation, sense of character, and instinctive sense of style. They were artists in all but their schooling. Some critics and historians have sought to find the essential element in American painting in these artists.[2] I believe that this is an exaggeration: as a serious element in American painting the untrained professionals were a product of the frontier, and vanished with it.

The untrained professionals are only one of a number of types lumped together by the enthusiasm for "primitive" painting or "folk art," which has made so strong an appeal to modern taste. Various names have been applied to this conglomeration: folk art, amateur painting, lay painting, primitive painting, Sunday painting. We need, I venture to say, a more exact appreciation of what we enjoy in these works, and why.

True folk art, in the first place, is an unself-conscious, highly developed, traditional craft. Its makers are not amateurs. They are highly skilled craftsmen. The element of continuity is important: folk art's products follow an ancient and traditional sense of design. They are also *made for use*. Folk art is a skilled handicraft product, made to enrich one's home, or articles of daily use, and intended for the general untrained enjoyment of simple people, rather than for the self-conscious enjoyment of the connoisseur. There are such true folk arts in America—Pennsylvania German handicrafts, the *Santos* of New Mexico, cowboy saddlery, the decoration of Mississippi steamboats, the carving of ships' figureheads and sternboards are folk arts. The simplicity and cheerful pageantry of such unself-conscious traditional arts are refreshing in the hyperself-conscious atmosphere of our world, and exert a very strong appeal. Folk art has its own esthetic and human values, but they are not the same values as those of conscious art. In American painting true folk art is found only rarely.

What is commonly called "folk art" and which forms the bulk of such collections as Mrs. John D. Rockefeller's at Williamsburg or the Garbisch collection in The National Gallery, Washington, is more truly amateur art, which also has its own place and value. Yet exactly what its value is, whether esthetic, or moral, or social, whether the lasting enrichment of society, or only the happiness of the individual producing it, is more difficult to say. The modern mind tends to confuse *creation* with *self-expression:* actually they are quite different things. The value of amateur art is a facet of this question.

[2] Cf. Alan Burrough, *Limners and Likenesses*, Cambridge, Mass., Harvard University Press, 1936; Oskar Hagen, *The Birth of the American Tradition in Art*, New York, Charles Scribner's Sons, 1940; Gordon Washburn, *Old and New England*, Providence, Museum of Art of the Rhode Island School of Design, 1945.

Human society carries its own history within itself. At all times there exist people of all grades of development, from the most highly developed to the most primitive. At the same time that great, civilized, disciplined minds are at work on the most advanced problems of life, the frontiersman lives on among us in the ranger, the cowboy and the forest guide, the eighteenth century planter in the modern educated large-scale farmer, the peasant in the farm laborer, the bandit in the city gangster. A few miles from where I write, an assemblage of the highest technological skills of our time is the collective brain of factories pouring forth the wonderful machines of the twentieth century, while almost within sight of the factory chimneys the descendant of the French-Indian trapper eats muskrat stew in a cabin on the river marshes. The primitive, the child in the life of civilization, we have always with us. Indeed, we carry him within ourselves. Out of this level of human consciousness, too, comes artistic expression. One characteristic of such work is shared with that of the untrained professional. Neither is able to speak the complex and subtle language developed by centuries of conscious art, with its plastic, three-dimensional images, its harmonies of atmospheric color. Both tend to revert to flat, two-dimensional images and patterns of local rather than atmospheric color.

The true primitive, however, speaks as a child in ideographic rather than observed and controlled images. The slightly more sophisticated amateur knows enough to imitate the prevailing manners of art. But much of what is called "primitive" painting in America consists of crudely amateur copies after prints and engravings and demonstrates little but inexperience. Amateur art, in fact, shows innumerable shadings of value, from innate sensibility to fumbling efforts of no artistic interest. It can be compared to popular speech, which is capable of pithy expression and shrewd wisdom, as well as of immense tedium, but is never organized into conscious eloquence or literature.

As a language of the imagination, painting is governed by the *direction of attention* prevailing in the mental climate of its age. The universe is so vast, so complex, so infinite in its interacting life, that no man can grasp more than a trivial fraction of what there is to observe. Let us emphasize this: the artist does *not* paint what he sees. Rather, he sees what he looks for. (This is what is meant by the artist's selecting a *motive*.) Out of the infinite variety of the universe he selects (1) what is paintable, that is, what is within the range of his art; and (2) what interests him as a subject. In doing so, he is governed unconsciously by what not only he, but other artists before him and around him, and the people of his time think should be painted. This has been, in the history of Western art, the religious and historical and literary memories of the race, the interest which men take in one another as individuals or as heroes, and certain aspects of nature in the world around us. In even the greatest ages of art, far more is left unpainted than is painted. The direction of attention, like a searchlight with its sudden revelations and its surrounding wall of darkness, is one of the most important and most mysterious aspects of any history which attempts to trace the work of human minds across any period of time.

The limitations of one small individual view of things are not wholly weakness, however. Selection is necessary. A canvas can contain only so much, and a work of art must have unity of focus. Selection is not only necessary; it is one of the ways by which men achieve *value*. Concentration upon a few motives therefore does not indicate imaginative poverty. To the discerning mind any motive selected—any thing, any moment of life—may be representative in its own way of the cosmos and of eternity.

Although the field of painting covers only a tiny fraction of what might be observed and thought about, it is none the less true that we have inherited from the centuries of Western civilization the richest tradition of experience in the world. It owes its riches not only to the abilities of the countless individuals who have contributed to it, not merely to the quantity of knowledge it has accumulated, but to the historic width and variety of its perceptions of life. "That day is good on which we have the most perceptions," said Emerson. He was speaking for the wisdom of our civilization, which has inherited from its fortunate complexity of sources—Greek rational intelligence and oriental mysticism, the Roman sense of social order and the individualism of our Teutonic ancestors—intuitions of the greatest variety of gifted races, mingled by the slow development of a thousand years into our many-sided awareness of life. We must not expect the art of such a civilization to follow a simple pattern. It is the spirit of polemics, not of history, that forever strives to beat its many-sidedness into a single face.

Mysterious tides move within the direction of attention. In each generation there are artists born to explore the outer world of the real—of nature, as the painter uses the word, to indicate the whole of nature and other men outside himself. And there are those born to explore the inner, ideal world of memory, reflection, and dream. The shining globe of consciousness revolves and, as it moves, one of these halves of our mental world is now more to the front, now the other. All this must be taken account of in our story.

Many of the early passages in the story of painting in America are, too, at the present time very imperfectly explored and documented, many of its biographies unwritten. It is evident that to write such a story in even a cursory way is a vast undertaking and involves the possibility of errors great and small. Anyone in his senses would, no doubt, avoid it. Yet what an interesting problem!

CHAPTER 2

ARTIST-EXPLORERS AND ARTIST-NATURALISTS

ON SUNDAY, OCTOBER 21, COLUMBUS WROTE IN THE JOURNAL OF THE FIRST Voyage:

I . . . went forth with my captains and crews to see the island [Columbus called it Isabella; it has been identified as either Fortune or Great Magna Island] and if the others we have seen were beautiful and green and fertile, this one is much more so; with large groves and deep foliage. Here are large lakes, and the groves about them are marvelous; and here and in all the island, everything is green as in April in Andalusia. The singing of the little birds is such, that it seems that one would never desire to depart hence. There are flocks of parrots that obscure the sun, and other birds, large and small, of so many kinds, different from ours, that it is wonderful; there are trees of a thousand species, each having its particular fruit and all of marvelous flavor, so that I am in the greatest trouble in the world not to know them, for I am very certain that they are all of great value. I shall take home some of them as specimens, and also of the herbs.[1]

This is the first record of an experience which Columbus, and many other men in the two or three centuries following, were to feel. Columbus' discovery of nameless islands in the sea, inhabited by brown naked men and filled with unknown trees and flowers, beasts and birds, had to be described to the world at home. But neither in words nor in painting did a style of art exist capable of dealing with this experience. Columbus' excitement and the poetry of discovery sometimes make themselves felt in the *Letter on the Discovery of America*, but his descriptions end in vague generalizations: the trees are green; the birds are countless; the products of the islands are very good.

We meet here not with a deficiency in Columbus, who was a man of

[1] *The Voyages of Christopher Columbus*, New York, 1892, p. 48.

great ability and intelligence, but with the intense concentration of attention then governing the arts and languages of Europe.

Spain, Portugal, France, the Netherlands, England, the countries looking out upon the Atlantic, which were to carry out the exploration and settlement of America, in 1492 were still medieval countries. Painting and drawing were highly developed in them. But the task of painting had been, up to that date in medieval art, to depict the ideal world of religious faith, the story of Christianity, the lives of the saints. The arts in the medieval world spoke of these ideal subjects in noble, generalized, ideal images. The need for precise and convincing description of this present world had not yet arisen. Early in the fifteenth century, great imaginative geniuses in the commercial centers of Bruges and of Florence had already discovered the world of nature. Jan van Eyck in Flanders and Masaccio in Florence introduced a new vision and technique into painting. They were not realistic in the modern sense. Their subjects were drawn from the world of Faith. But they were also observers of genius, and they cast their images of the ideal world of Scripture in the image of their exact visual impressions—this was how a man really stood or sat, how the light fell through a window—therefore this was how Christ and the money-changer stood, how St. Jerome looked as he worked at his desk. The language of painting never went back to where it was before the early fifteenth-century masters of observation touched it. But this period of realism was brief, and painting soon turned back toward idealism. In the most advanced centers of painting, by 1500, at Rome in the High Renaissance art of Raphael and Michelangelo and in Antwerp among artists like Massys and Joos van Cleve, the task of painting was again, as it had been in the Middle Ages, to illustrate the communal beliefs of men in generalized, ideal images.

The discovery of America occurred when painting was in one of its greatest periods, but Western painting had not yet perfected its double vision —looking inward upon the subjective world of thought, revery, and dream; outward upon the objective world of nature. When Columbus sailed from the port of Palos into the Western ocean, the painting of the ideal world was at the height of its splendor and convincing power; the painting of the world of nature was in its infancy. The key names at the dawn of the new sensibility are Giorgione, who first made his own individual sensibility his subject matter, and Pieter Bruegel, who first gave to the realistic study of nature and his fellow men the stature of great imaginative art. Both of these artists were after Columbus. Thus, for all its power, Renaissance art was ill adapted, or to speak more truly, was not interested in giving us a record or a comment on the discovery of the New World.

During the next two centuries, the sixteenth and the seventeenth, a series of great minds opened a new window upon the infinite reaches of the natural world. This was the age of the rise of natural science. Galileo, Huygens,

Newton, and a host of others discovered that profound significance was to be found not only in the books of authority, but in the exact study of the simple things around them—the falling of a stone, the swinging of a hanging lamp, the beams of the sun's light.

In the arts the world of nature was also discovered. The rise of realism (that is, the objective view of nature) is the parallel, in the realm of imagination and feeling, to the rise of science in the realm of the intellect. There is a tradition that the painter Caravaggio, one of the great pioneers of the new approach to nature at the beginning of the seventeenth century, was criticized by the *cognoscenti* of Rome for not studying Raphael and the antique marbles: that is, for not following precedent and authority. Without saying a word, he drew his critic to the door and pointed to the people passing by in the street: then to prove his point, he took a gypsy from the street and painted her in the act of telling the fortune of a young man. It is hard now to realize what it meant to break away from the noble, ideal subjects of medieval and Renaissance art to paint the passing moment of life. The change in the direction of attention, which Caravaggio symbolizes, was like his contemporary Galileo's break from traditional authorities to direct observation of nature. Caravaggio might have accompanied his silent gesture with the words of Cicero's *Dum tacit, clamat,* that Emerson used to express the significance of each moment of life. Though silent, it cries aloud.

The artists who first practiced a descriptive art in America were only on the fringes of this movement. Their part in it is small; they were modest artisans or amateurs. Yet their reports of an age of geographical discovery must have had a part in the rise of the scientific mind and the new realism of Western art during the sixteenth and seventeenth centuries. Men's thoughts were suddenly confronted with a dramatically expanding world, filled with marvels.

In Florence and Rome there was published in pamphlet form in 1493 a narrative poem by Giuliano Dati on the voyage of Columbus. The title pages of these two rare pamphlets were illustrated by woodcuts which are the first representations of the discovery of America. The title page of the Florentine edition may be taken as the starting point of our story (Fig. 1). The King of Spain sits upon his throne in the foreground while Columbus' ships with swelling sails press across the seas to the new lands of wonder, inhabited by crowds of naked figures. In its decorative felicity, the ease with which it expresses an idea, its naïveté, its grace, this woodcut by an anonymous Florentine craftsman is a charming ideal image in the manner of the past pages of art. It has little sense of fact, but a great sense of idea and of style.

The illustrations of Indians in Amerigo Vespucci's *Letters,* published in 1505-1506 in Italian and German, are likewise wholly imaginary.

The earliest view of a city of the New World is the map or sketch of

Mexico City in 1520 which ornaments Cortes' *Praeclara . . . de Nova Maris Oceani Hyspania Narratio* (Nuremberg, 1524) (Fig. 2). It is, one may suppose, based on an eyewitness description if not a rude sketch of the Aztec city set in fantastic beauty in the midst of its lakes and its terrible temples. Yet it is still an ideograph, handsome and expressive but giving no sense of actuality. The illustrations to Oviedo y Valdes' *Historia de las Indias* (1535) and to the *Historia del Mundo Nuovo* (Venice, 1565) of Girolamo Benzoni, a Milanese adventurer who traveled in the New World from 1541 to 1556, are drawn from some kind of description also, yet their relation to actuality is equally tenuous. Such decorative and imaginary illustrations may be taken as a standard by which to watch the powers of realistic observation and description develop in the first artists who came to America. These early illustrations are products of a great period of art which had no interest in the world of nature for itself, but only as a source of ideas and ideal images.

We may see this all-powerful direction of attention in the career of the first professional painter who came to the New World. In 1525 a painter from Cordova in Spain named Rodrigo de Cifuentes, a pupil of Bartolommeo de Mesas of Seville, accompanied Cortes on his expedition into Honduras. A picture signed by him is preserved in the Academy of San Carlos in Mexico City. It represents a *Martyrdom of Saint Hippolytus*. Other religious pictures and a double portrait, supposed to represent Cortes and his Indian mistress, Doña Marina, are attributed to him. Rodrigo de Cifuentes painted in Mexico what he would have painted had he remained in Spain, that is, the themes normal to High Renaissance art: the ideal world of faith, and the portrait. Of what he saw in Honduras, of the strange Indian cities and their fierce inhabitants, of the army of the conquistadores, he left us no record.

Rodrigo de Cifuentes was not a great or original mind. He was a modest painter-craftsman wholly governed by the direction of attention prevailing in his own society. There was in the sixteenth century no esthetic theory, like that of abstraction today, to persuade such an artist that the remarkable and terrible scenes taking place around him were unworthy of being painted. There was no theory of art for art's sake to tell him that he must turn his back upon all but the purely esthetic in life. Indeed the notion that there was a division between art and the ordinary interests of life would have been looked on in sixteenth-century Spain as incredible. Painting and drawing were not only pleasing things but essential skills of society. The aim of life was Heaven and to the sixteenth-century mind it was more important to teach people the doctrines necessary to the soul's salvation than to establish any other ideas or forms of knowledge. It followed that pictures were to tell the story of Christianity to the Indians and to decorate the churches. Rodrigo de Cifuentes was merely doing what his own age considered the proper work of painting. He was the first of the religious painters of Spanish America, not an observer of Cortes' conquests.

In New France we may see the same phenomenon. The Jesuit missionaries in Huronia in 1638-1640, thirty days' journey inland by canoe from the
last French settlement, had in their bark chapel built like a long house on the
shores of Lake Huron, life-size paintings of Christ and the Virgin, and one
of the Last Judgment, to help them convert the Hurons.[2] The life-size figures
made an especial impression on the Indians, Father le Mercier tells us in his
Relation, but they did not seem to care for paintings with small figures.
When later the great Bishop Laval wished to make the Canadian church
self-sustaining, he founded not only a seminary but an art school to teach
the essential skills for making and decorating churches. His academy at
Cap Tourment on the north shore of the St. Lawrence River below Quebec
(the first art school on the North American continent) and the Séminaire at
Quebec itself were schools of *arts et métiers*. Laval brought a sculptor named
Jacques Leblond dit Latour from Bordeaux and the school in which he was
the leading master taught crafts like joinery, lock-making, painting, wood-
carving, and tailoring. Advanced students in letters and theology learned
crafts also according to their talents. "They quickly respond, and they clev-
erly fashion many small articles not only for current use, but also for the
altars which they decorate with taste and discrimination," wrote an observer.[3]

The arts of painting, sculpture, and wood carving were first established
in the New World to serve the need for an ideal, didactic Christian art.

Yet it was not long before other artists appeared in the New World for
the purpose of observing and reporting. Of these some were trained, some
were amateurs. The leader of an expedition who had to report on the strange
lands he had explored, the Indians, animals, and plants he had seen; the governor who wished to describe the forts he had built, the harbors he had
charted, the battles he had fought—each needed the services of an artist. If the
expedition had taken along a trained artist, so much the better; but if no artist
was available, the explorer or governor used what skills were available, even
his own. In the mid-sixteenth century appeared the first artist-explorers and
artist-naturalists, practicing the art of painting in America long before the
appearance of the seventeenth-century colonial portrait painters. Today, when
the old practical uses for the craft of painting have almost disappeared, we
forget how useful it once was for many purposes. For the first three hundred
years in America it was a skill which flourished far from the studio, on the
decks of ships, in the deep forest, or under the sky. If the explorer-artists were
never men of genius, and sometimes not even very good craftsmen, they are
nevertheless a picturesque and interesting part of our story.

In 1555 a cheerful French Franciscan monk, named André Thevet,

---

[2] Le Mercier, *Relation des Hurons*, 1637, pp. 175, 176; and 1638, p. 33, in *Relations des
Jésuites*, vol. I, 1858. Quoted by Francis Parkman, *The Jesuits in North America*, 1867, p. 201.
[3] Marius Barbeau, "The Arts of French Canada," *The Art Quarterly*, IX (1946), p. 329.

sailed on a French expedition led by Villegaignon to South America. Thevet
was a man probably of modest birth and little education, but he had a passionate appetite for knowledge and a thirst for travel which had previously
led him to spend seventeen years wandering in the Levant. Villegaignon's expedition coasted down the west coast of Africa, then struck across to South
America, where it founded the first European settlement in the bay of Rio
de Janeiro. The expedition was, however, of mixed Calvinist and Catholic
membership and the colony was split by violent and incessant religious controversy. Thevet ignored these theological quarrels and devoted himself, with
a scientific curiosity far in advance of his time, to making notes of the peculiarities of the country and forming a collection of birds, insects, plants, and
the arms and utensils of the Indians, which he carried home to form his *cabinet* of curiosities. Villegaignon, the leader of the expedition, sided with the
Calvinists and was glad to get rid of Thevet when he wished to return home
the next year. In his account of the voyage published by Thevet in 1558 under the title *Les Singularitez de la France antarctique*, he says that on the
return journey he also visited Canada. This statement has been much attacked.
He has been accused of never having seen Canada and of borrowing his account of North America from Cartier. As his attackers were Calvinists, we
may be dealing here with religious rather than scientific controversy. On the
other hand, the sense of scientific fact was not very highly developed in the
sixteenth century and many narratives of the New World freely mixed personal observation with hearsay and other men's information. So Thevet may
have done.

What interests us is the illustrations of Thevet's book, engraved at Ly-
ons, as he tells us, by Flemish engravers brought especially from Flanders.
Most of the illustrations are typically Flemish mannerist work, smoothly skillful and wholly generalized. But interspersed among them are others of birds
and plants and animals done with a shrewd realism that strongly suggests
drawings from life. Was the *Toucan* (Fig. 3) with his wicked old eye, the
first known representation of the bird, engraved from a dead specimen, or
does it reproduce a drawing made from life in America? We do not know.
However, if Thevet made this and other drawings of the same kind reproduced in his book, he was the first artist-naturalist to work in America.

There is no question about Jacques le Moyne de Morgues (d. 1588) who
came to America in 1564 as a member of the Huguenot settlement planted
by Coligny at the mouth of the St. Johns River, Florida. Le Moyne was one
of the few to escape when the Spaniards wiped out the colony in 1565. He
succeeded in reaching England with his drawings, which form a vivid record of what it was like to plant a colony in America. The beautiful copper
engravings from these drawings were made by Théodore de Bry and his sons
to illustrate Le Moyne's narrative, which formed the second volume (1591)
of the famous series of voyages published by de Bry at Frankfort-on-the-

Main. These engravings became one of the chief sources of information about what America looked like. For two centuries they were borrowed and imitated by other engravers to illustrate books on America.

Only one original work with American subject matter from Le Moyne's hand is preserved, an exquisite, precise, fresh-colored water-color drawing on parchment, showing *The Indian Chief Saturiba and the French leader Laudonnière at Ribaut's column* (Plate I), a marker left by a previous French expedition of 1562.[4] In the Victoria and Albert Museum, London, there is, however, a series of exquisite water-color drawings of English flowers, fruits, etc., made by Le Moyne after he reached England. It consisted of thirty-four sheets (twenty-five of which have drawings on both sides) which probably formed part of the artist's working library and were the inspiration of some of the woodcuts in his book on botany, *Le Clef des Champs*, published at Blackfriars in 1586. These drawings show Le Moyne as an artist of acute observation as well as charm of style. He was the first serious student of nature and the first artist of quality to work in the territory that is now the United States.

The second is John White (active 1584-1593) who came to Raleigh's short-lived colony in Virginia in 1585 and returned as governor of the colony in 1587 and 1590. In the British Museum there is preserved an album of sixty-five water-color drawings made by White in Virginia. Many show the life and customs of the Indians; others are studies of flowers and birds, fish and animals of the new land. The album is entitled: *The Pictures of sundry things collected and counterfeited according to the truth in the voyage made by S*[r.] *Walter Raleigh Knight for the discovery of LA VIRGINEA. in the 27th yeare of the most happie reigne of our Souveraigne Lady Queene ELIZABETH and in the year of O*[r] *Lord God 1585.* These drawings also were engraved by de Bry for the first volume of his *Voyages* (1590).

With John White we come to the opposite extreme of art from the Giuliano Dati woodcut. Instead of the general idea, we are given the particular fact detailed with loving interest; in the place of an attractive decorative composition, artistic form is forgotten in an eager curiosity to draw a strange butterfly or "A land Tort [oise] w[ch] the Savages esteeme above all other Torts" (Fig. 4). The world of nature has been discovered, its wonder and delight opened to the eye, and the appetite awakened to "counterfeit it according to the truth." In Flanders a great artistic intelligence like Pieter Bruegel had already learned to weave such exact observations into a great interpretative whole. That was beyond John White. But in his own place he is an artist of significance.

Another governor of a colony who was his own cartographer and amateur illustrator was Samuel de Champlain, governor of New France (1567-

[4] The Peabody Museum of Archaeology and Ethnology, Harvard University, owns a crayon drawing of *Saturioua, a Timuca Chief,* doubtfully attributed to Le Moyne.

PLATE I. Jacques le Moyne de Morgues: *The Indian Chief Saturiba and the French leader Laudonnière at Ribaut's column.* (Courtesy of James Hazen Hyde, New York; color plate courtesy of *Vogue* Magazine.)

PLATE III. Unknown, early eighteenth century: *Adam Winne*. (Courtesy of The Henry Francis du Pont Winterthur Museum.)

PLATE II. Unknown, early eighteenth century: *Magdalena Gansevoort*. (Courtesy of The Henry Francis du Pont Winterthur Museum.)

1636). He was a soldier, explorer, geographer. He surveyed coasts and drew his own charts of them; he fought the Iroquois and drew pictures of his battles to illustrate his reports. The original manuscript and drawings of his first exploring voyage to the West Indies (1599-1601) are preserved in the John Carter Brown Library, Providence, Rhode Island. The drawings for his books on Canada are, except for a manuscript map of the New England coast dated 1607, preserved only in the engravings that illustrate his books on Canada. One of the best shows an attack on an Iroquois fort in *Les Voyages du Sieur Champlain Xaintongeois* (1613), representing Champlain's attack on the Oneida village at Nichols Pond, in central New York state. In this campaign Champlain with his Algonquin allies tried to sweep aside the Stone-Age warriors of the Iroquois, who had not yet been supplied with firearms by the Dutch. Had he succeeded, the history of North America might have taken a different course. The subject of this illustration is thus a historical event of some moment. But as a draughtsman Champlain was only a rude amateur. The movement of figures and the detail which would lend them individual life were beyond his little skill.

A more skillful draughtsman was the traveling Netherlander Laurens Bloch, who made the *View of New Amsterdam* in 1650, which is now in The New-York Historical Society (Fig. 5). Nothing is known of Bloch but the inscription on this drawing, stating that it was drawn on the ship *Lydia* by Laurens Bloch, son of Herman, in the year 1650. The skills of drawing and painting were so widely diffused in seventeenth-century Holland that it is probable Bloch was not a professional but simply a skilled amateur. This is the sort of drawing that must have been brought home to Holland in numbers and supplied Blaue with the information for the border vignettes of the maps in his great *World Atlas*. Another view of New Amsterdam, by a different hand, appears on the Nicholas Jansz Visscher map of *Novum Belgium* (1651-1655); a third view of the little trading post on Manhattan Island is the so-called "Prototype" view preserved in the archives at The Hague. These topographic drawings show how common a certain amateur skill had become in Holland. A few years later Jasper Danckaerts and Peter Sluyter, two Hollanders of the Labadist sect, made a voyage to New York and visited several other colonies, in 1679-1680. Danckaerts kept a journal and illustrated it with his own rude drawings of towns and harbors (now owned by the Long Island Historical Society, Brooklyn).

These drawings show what sort of need there was for the craft of painting in the New World and by what stages it made its appearance. As the North American settlements grew more numerous and important, in the later seventeenth century, the impulse to describe the appearance of the New World became stronger. Among the travelers, soldiers, and priests, French, English, or Dutch, who came out, were some men of inquiring and curious minds who wrote books on their travels. Many of the interesting early vol-

umes on America have illustrations either borrowed from de Bry or simply
invented by the engraver in his European workshop. But others have maps,
topographic views, and scenes of Indian life of more substantial interest.

Two of the most popular and widely read of these narratives of exploration were the *Description de la Louisiane* (1683) and *A New Discovery of a
Vast Country in America, Extending above Four Thousand Miles, between
New France and New Mexico* (1698) by that engaging old liar, Father Louis
Hennepin (1640-ca.1701). Hennepin published the first description of Niagara Falls, whose height he exaggerated greatly. The engraving of Niagara
in his *New Discovery* is the first appearance of a landscape subject that was
to interest artists for nearly two hundred years.

Some readers may wonder if such a fact is of any significance in a history
of art. I believe it is significant. Historically, it is one of the steps in the
rise of landscape painting. Second, it reveals to us the path by which men's
perceptions gradually approached nature. The earliest interest in landscape
to appear in America was a naïve interest in the appearance of some great
natural wonder, or of a famous work of man like a town or harbor. Down
through the eighteenth century this was to be the chief form of original landscape done in America. Nor is this to be dismissed too lightly as raw naturalism or as showing a lack of imaginative power. The topographic landscape or
cityscape was the eighteenth century's great contribution to landscape painting, produced by artists of the importance of Canaletto, Guardi, Bellotto,
Panini, Hubert Robert, and Vernet. The appearance of the topographic
landscape in America belongs to a brilliant chapter in the history of the
imagination.

The French in America produced many of the most interesting observers. Baron Louis de La Hontan, who served in the French army in Canada
from 1683 to 1694, took part in the campaigns of De la Barre (1684) and
Denonville (1687) against the Iroquois and was governor of Placentia in
Newfoundland when the English took it. He published his *New Voyages to
North America* in French, English, and Dutch in 1703 and illustrated his
book by his own drawings, of which the engravings in the English edition,
done as he says under his own supervision, are by far the best. La Hontan was
one of the most amusing and lively, as well as instructive, writers in America.
He was intensely interested in the Indians, whom he observed shrewdly. But
as a draughtsman he was capable of only a childlike sort of sketch. His drawings, when engraved, became a sort of crude diagram.

Le Page du Pratz, who spent sixteen years in Louisiana (1718-1734) and
wrote a famous *Histoire de la Louisiane* (1758), illustrated by his own drawings, was also an amateur of very limited powers. His forty plates are valuable for the information they convey but are engraved from originals which
clearly can hardly have been more than childlike diagrams.

Another French artist-explorer was Alexandre de Batz, a good archi-

tectural draughtsman under Broutin, the engineer who introduced the Louis
XV style into Louisiana. De Batz was active in New Orleans as an architect
and draughtsman from about 1732 until his death in 1759 at Fort de Chartres,
the French fortress near Prairie du Rocher below St. Louis. He has left us
some drawings of Indians, of which that of an Indian warrior with three
Natchez scalps, signed and dated New Orleans, 1732, is typical. It is evident
that de Batz, though a good architect, found it difficult to draw the human
figure.

The crudeness of the draughtsmanship of these three makes all the more
interesting one work by an exact eye and trained hand, labeled *View of the
Camp of Mr. Law's Concession at New Biloxi, coast of Louisiana* by Jean-
Baptiste Michel Le Bouteux (1720) (Fig. 6). What took Le Bouteux, a well-
trained artist, to Biloxi, where the French colonists for the Mississippi landed?
We do not know. He sits in the barge in the foreground in the costume of a
French gentleman of the eighteenth century, drawing a picture of the raw
little frontier settlement in the pine woods that was the foundation of the
fantastic dream of wealth we know as the Mississippi Bubble. His refined and
exact art, like his elegant costume, seems out of place in this pioneer setting.
It was not: for it served a practical purpose. In such a setting the arts had to
serve practical ends, like everything else men did.

The artist-explorer continued as a type as long as there was a frontier,
down to the latter part of the nineteenth century. The later examples of the
type will be touched on, however, as part of the story of their own times. We
will close this chapter on the pioneers of realistic observation in America with
Mark Catesby (1679?-1749), the first notable artist-naturalist to work in
America. A man apparently of little education but of great natural gifts, he
came from England to Virginia in 1712. Slowly the beauty and the wonder of
the wilderness continent drew him toward his vocation. Let him tell his discovery of nature in his own old-fashioned and somewhat crabbed words:

My curiosity was such [he relates in his preface] that not being content
with contemplating the Products of our own country, I soon imbibed a passionate Desire of viewing as well the Animal and Vegetable Productions in their native Countries; which were strangers to *England*. *Virginia* was the Place (I having
Relations there) suited most to my Convenience to go to, where I arriv'd the 23d
of *April* 1712. I thought then so little of prosecuting a Design of the Nature of
this Work, that in the Seven Years I resided in that Country, (I am ashamed to
own it) I chiefly gratified my inclination in observing and admiring the various
Productions of those countries,—only sending from thence some dried Specimens
of Plants and some of the most Specious of them in Tubs of Earth, at the request
of some curious friends, amongst whom was Mr. *Dale* of *Braintree* in Essex, a
skillful Apothecary and Botanist: to him, besides Specimens of Plants, I sent some
few Observations on the Country, which he communicated to the late *William
Sherard*, L.L.D. one of the most celebrated Botanists of this Age, who favoured

me with his friendship on my Return to England in the year 1719; and by his advice, (tho' conscious of my own Inability) I first resolved on this undertaking, so agreeable to my inclination. . . .

With this intention, I set out from *England*, in the year 1722, directly for Carolina; which Country, tho' inhabited by *English* above an Age past, and a Country inferior to none in Fertility, and abounding in Variety of the Blessings of Nature; yet its Productions being very little known except what barely related to Commerce, such as Rice, Pitch and Tar; was thought of the most proper Place to search and describe the productions of.

Here, in the words of a man who took part, are outlined the steps in the discovery of the new meaning of nature. First, there is an intense curiosity and a "passionate Desire of viewing" without any clear purpose; then, by the encouragement of a small group of advanced minds, curiosity is crystallized into a purpose—a science or an art. Nature is not merely a source of a few things good for commerce. Its study is an end to which one can devote one's life, and is a source of values as yet vaguely realized but intensely loved.

Such is the origin of *The Natural History of Carolina, Florida and the Bahama Islands* . . . , London, 1731, written by Catesby after his return to England and illustrated by him with 100 plates, representing what he considered to be 102 species of American birds. With the birds he drew some of the plants associated with them, thus pointing toward the future ideas of the habitat or ecology. The illustrations are not only drawn but engraved by Catesby, for finding that the expense of a good Dutch engraver made publication too costly, he studied engraving and made his own plates. "Which, tho'," he said, "I may not have done in a Graver-like manner, choosing rather to omit their method of cross-Hatching, and to follow the humour of the Feathers, which is more laborious, and I hope has proved more to the purpose."

Catesby's plates, of which the *Ivory-billed Woodpecker* (Fig. 8) is a good example, were crudely engraved but are nonetheless strong, decorative, and beautiful. In their rude images is expressed that "passionate Desire of viewing" which during the sixteenth and seventeenth centuries added a new power and a new dimension to the perceptions of the human race. The awakening of this power in the field of intellect made the seventeenth century a great flowering of genius from Galileo to Newton. In the field of the imagination and feeling, in the arts, the development of the sixteenth and seventeenth centuries was a kindred flowering of genius, exploring the world of nature and of light in one of the greatest ages of Western painting. The artist-explorers who brought their art to America were humble representatives on the fringes, but their artistic as well as their documentary value arises from their share in the growth of Western realism.

CHAPTER 3

SEVENTEENTH-CENTURY DUTCH AND ENGLISH PROVINCIAL PAINTING

THE MEN WHO SETTLED THE FIRST PERMANENT COLONIES ON OUR ATLANTIC coast, in the early years of the seventeenth century, brought with them the arts and skills to which they had been accustomed in their homeland. In the hard conditions of pioneer life, all activities had to be purposeful, designed to serve pressing material or spiritual needs. The Dutch and English settlers, sturdy Calvinists all, felt no need for the religious paintings which were the first desire of the French and Spanish missionaries. But family feeling and personal pride were prominent among these strong-willed people; and among the skills which were a normal feature of seventeenth-century middle class life in both Holland and England was that of portrait painting. It accompanied the earliest settlers to America. More than four hundred likenesses have survived of people born in New England and New Netherlands before 1700. The greater part of these were probably painted in America; yet it is characteristic of painting in the seventeenth-century American colonies that the link between the homelands and colonies is still so close that it is impossible to draw a clear line between works painted on this side of the Atlantic and works painted in Europe.

The colonies on the Atlantic shore of the future United States in which painting was first established were New Netherlands and Massachusetts Bay. Both were trading and commercial settlements, closely connected with their homelands. Vessels were constantly going back and forth, new colonists continually arriving. England, or Holland, was still home; lands, relatives, and friends were still there. The old ties could not easily be severed nor, indeed, was there any desire to sever them. Thus there has come down to us a mass of portraits, some painted abroad and brought over as family possessions (like the *Sir Richard Saltonstall* or the eight family portraits brought over in 1675 by Nicholas Roberts), some painted when a colonist was on a visit home (like *Governor John Winthrop*, painted when the governor visited England in 1649, or Increase Mather's portrait, now in the Massachusetts Historical Society, painted during a visit to London in 1688); others painted in America by artists who were as likely to be transient visitors, perhaps, as permanent colonists. The question to ask is not: On which side the ocean was this picture painted? but, In what form did painting come to America with these first permanent settlements?

Virginia was also settled early, and life at Jamestown (as revealed by the excavations of the National Park Service) attained a degree of comfort and even elegance rather at variance with our notions of the frontier. Yet the portraits which have come down to us of men connected with the colony seem all to have been done in England, until the last decade of the century. According to Dr. J. Hall Pleasants, "there are in existence a number of unsigned portraits, certainly painted in Virginia as early as the sixteen nineties and the first decade of the following century" although no painter's name can be assigned to them.[1] By this date, however, they belong in style to the English provincial Baroque, which is described in the next chapter. John Smith's *The Generall Historie of Virginia, New England and the Summer Isles* (1624) is illustrated by engravings either fanciful or borrowed from de Bry's engravings of John White's work. One seventeenth-century picture from Virginia, however, is the title page, *Indian Wheat—an Indian Jay* which illustrates Edward Bland's *The Discovery of New Brittaine* (1651), an account of an expedition inland from the head of the Appamattuck River. The unknown draughtsman made a sad botch of his bird—its tail is too short and the crest is not shown—yet I think it safe to assume that the man who picked a bluejay and an ear of corn to represent the New World knew his subject from firsthand experience.

In the seventeenth century the cultural center of the Protestant world was The Netherlands which, in the sixty years after the truce of 1614, were at the height of their maritime empire and their intellectual powers. At the end of the century, though losing their supremacy at sea to the English, the Dutch gave a king to England itself. The busy cities of Holland nourished one of the greatest schools of European painting; in contrast, painting in England had no strong tradition, but was carried on chiefly by artists from The Netherlands. It is not surprising that the best painting done in America in the seventeenth century was done in New Netherlands; and that the English colonies, like England itself, were within the ambience of Dutch provincial painting.

At home, in Holland, Dutch artists were giving to the new impulse of realism its first and one of its greatest and most poetic expressions. A new

[1] J. Hall Pleasants, *The Virginia Magazine*, 60 (January, 1952), p. 56.

mentality was in flower, a new poetry of nature and life was being explored with immense vigor and imaginative power. Human character, landscape, the charm of daily life, the beauty of cities, of homes and the objects they contain, were studied by artists with love and enthusiasm, sometimes with genius. But in the far corner of the Dutch empire on the Hudson River only a faint echo of Dutch pictorial genius made itself heard.

When Governor Pieter Stuyvesant came to New Amsterdam in 1647 he brought with him his family portraits, which are still preserved in The New-York Historical Society. The *Reverend Lazare Bayard*, minister of the Walloon Church at Breda, and *Mrs. Judith Bayard* were the parents of his wife Judith. *Samuel Bayard and his Wife, Anna, before the Bayard Homestead at Alphen*, represents his brother-in-law who had married his sister, Anna Stuyvesant, in 1638, and the property they had acquired at Alphen in 1644. These pictures give us a very exact measure of the artistic ideas current in the best level of Dutch colonial life. As one might expect, they represent neither the wonderful plastic and atmospheric style nor the imaginative power of the art created by Frans Hals and Rembrandt in the centers of Dutch culture at Haarlem or Amsterdam. The Bayard portraits were painted in 1636 in Breda, a southern border-fortress town, to which had fled many Protestant refugees from the French-speaking provinces of Flanders. They represent the survival of a simpler, earlier idiom, practiced during the transition from sixteenth-century Dutch painting, and aspire to nothing but a simple naturalism. It is a sober idiom, dry in color. The light falls broadly and flatly on the faces, so that the heads can be modeled by outline, and very simple shadows. The drawing is severely naturalistic; the light and shadow are in a primitive stage of development, not free and plastic as Hals and Rembrandt made them. But the most characteristic trait of this transitional style is that the point of sight is slightly above eye level, so that one looks a little down upon the head, while the lower part of the body is seen in steep perspective. Frans Hals had banished this bird's-eye perspective from the main stream of Dutch painting by 1615; but it lingered on in the work of painters of a provincial town like Breda.

The *Samuel Bayard* group represents a more developed art, for, in the drawing of the figures, the free chiaroscuro, and the fine tonal quality of the landscape, it is a characteristic work of the Dutch early Baroque style. It has been attributed to Gerard Donck, not a great name, certainly, but a competent painter.

Several portraits painted in New Amsterdam in the 1660's have been preserved. They represent no special imaginative power applied to the analysis of human character. They have no esthetic flavor beyond the simple, solid craftsmanship of Dutch realism applied to the painting of the human head. The bust portrait, in armor, of *Governor Pieter Stuyvesant* (Fig. 7) in The New-York Historical Society shows the virtues of this craftsmanship.

It is good direct, solid painting, using a severe color harmony of black, white, and brown to block out the head in broad lights and firm, simple shadows. The sense of character is vigorous and direct and the plastic, atmospheric language of Dutch realism is used in a modest, sober, but competent spirit. Whoever painted this picture observed keenly and knew his business.

We know from documents the names of several of the painters of New Amsterdam. Hendrick Couturier, who obtained burgher rights in New Amsterdam in 1663 by painting a portrait of Governor Stuyvesant and making drawings of his sons, was, so far as is known today, the first professional European painter to practice in this country. He is recorded as a member of the Leiden guild of painters in 1648; in 1649 he moved to Amsterdam; by 1661, or possibly earlier, he had emigrated to the Dutch settlement of New Amstel on the Delaware River, where he was a trader and public official. He also spent much time in New Amsterdam. In 1674 he removed to England, where he died about ten years later. Several portraits of New Amsterdam at this period have been attributed to him, including the *Peter Stuyvesant* and *Nicholas William Stuyvesant* (New-York Historical Society) and the *Jacobus G. Strycker* (The Metropolitan Museum of Art); but in the opinion of experts there is no picture that can definitely be assigned to his hand.[2]

Evert Duyckinck, who came over as a soldier in 1638, opened a glazier's shop and is recorded as a glazier and burner of glass, a limner and painter. Those familiar with painted Dutch glass will respect the knowledge of drawing and color implied. Evert Duyckinck was a craftsman and his son and grandson after him.[3]

Esther Singleton published lists of paintings from documents of this period in *Dutch New York* (1909), which show that the houses of New Amsterdam contained landscapes and other types of painting then found in Dutch houses at home. Except for a few portraits, preserved by family sentiment, nothing has come down to us: at least, nothing that can be recognized. The topographic *View of New Amsterdam* by Laurens Bloch (1650), and the Visscher and "Prototype" views, already mentioned, are the only representatives of the "landskips" that must have existed.

In the seventeenth-century Netherlands, where the names of something like eight thousand artists are known, the knowledge of painting was so common, the curiosity to see far places was so great, it seems surprising that some part of that intense activity should not have overflowed into the New World, beyond these few traces. Dutch painters of skill and fame found their way to Dutch colonies in Brazil or the Indies. But New Amsterdam was very small, and very poor, compared with the East Indies; and the human

---

[2] George C. Groce, *Dictionary of American Painters* (manuscript).

[3] In 1746 his grandson Gerardus advertised that he "continues to carry on the business of his late father deceased, viz: limning, painting, varnishing, japanning, gilding, glazing, and silvering of looking-glass done in the best manner. He also will teach young gentlemen all sorts of drawing and painting on glass."

race is careless, destructive, and governed by fashion in what it keeps or throws away. Very little has come down to us. Yet the important thing is that the craft of painting was established in the New Netherlands province, and by the early years of the next century there were already native-born painters at work along the Hudson River.

Family feeling and personal pride were as common among the strong-willed New England stock as among their Dutch neighbors. The family portraits they brought with them show the same qualities and style as the Dutch provincial portraits. The portrait of *Governor Winthrop* (1649), already mentioned (now owned by the American Antiquarian Society), is a good example of the transitional Dutch portrait style that was acclimated in England: the severe palette, the bird's-eye perspective, the vigorous drawing and sense of character, modified by a little of the flatness of Tudor portrait tradition. It is interesting to contrast this assured, intellectual face with the bluff soldier's face of *Sir Richard Saltonstall*, who landed from the *Arabella* to organize the settlement at Watertown in 1630-1631. This latter, which was certainly brought from England, shows some influence of the growing luminosity of the Dutch painting style that had been brought to England in the first decades of the seventeenth century by Mytens, Honthorst, and Janssens van Ceulen.

The portrait style which was brought to New England was thus a Dutch style transplanted to England. The connections between England and Holland were so close at this time that there was constant coming and going. There were English regiments fighting in the service of the Dutch republic. English books were printed at Leiden and English medical students studied at the University of Leiden. England in turn received numbers of Dutch artists and artisans. At King Charles's court, after 1624, it is true, taste was dominated by the more courtly and elegant art of the Flemish artists, Rubens and Van Dyck. But among the middle classes, from whom the American emigration came, the virtues of Dutch portraiture—sobriety, directness, and forceful statement of character—were more congenial than Van Dyck's elegant artifice.

Of the New England painters in this taste who worked in America, only one can definitely be identified by name. This is Captain Thomas Smith, a mariner, who came to New England from Bermuda about 1650. Sailor though he was by profession, he was also a painter, for Harvard College paid him in 1680 for a portrait of the *Reverend William Ames*. On this basis rests the assumption that a portrait of *Captain Thomas Smith* is a self-portrait (Fig. 10). Indeed it has all the characteristics of a mirror portrait. Smith, if he was the artist, painted in a broad, coarse, vigorous style, cruder than the Dutch idiom he was following, but showing energy and sense of character.

A strong grasp upon the inner life, which is the virtue of all the portraits we have been discussing, was the best characteristic of the Puritan world. One hears its spirit in the verses inscribed on the paper beneath the death's head under Captain Smith's hand:

> Why why should I the world be minding
> therein a World of Evils finding.
> > Then farwell World: Farwell thy Jarres
> > thy Joeis thy Toies thy Wiles thy Warres
> Truth sounds Retreat: I am not Sorye.
> > the Eternall Drawes to him my heart
> > By Faith (which can thy Force subvert)
> To crown me (after Grace) with Glory.
> > > > > T. S.

This is as if some lichen-covered tombstone in a Puritan burying ground by the sea were speaking to us. And indeed, the fighting character, the strong aspiration, the firm belief which made these men memorable is recorded in Captain Smith's face.

The same artist has left us also the likenesses of two other old fighters, *Captain George Curwin* (Essex Institute, Salem) and *Major Thomas Savage* (coll. Henry L. Shattuck), as grim and sturdy as himself. He only failed to achieve an interesting characterization when he painted the smooth pretty face of his own daughter. In this he was typical of New England painting, which preferred character to beauty and which showed a preference therefore for old faces marked by years of life.

In these Dutch and English provinces far from the centers of Western culture there was a strong tendency for the language of painting to revert to two-dimensional patterns. Plasticity and atmospheric color—the qualities of the full coloristic tradition of Western painting—were the creation of supremely gifted artists; to sustain them always requires great and conscious mastery. When the discipline of a good school of painting is absent, or for any reason is not mastered, these are the first qualities to disappear.

Yet the absence of a highly developed style does not necessarily mean the absence of imagination, or instinctive taste, or refined perceptions. There is a group of paintings, done in New England about 1670-75 (of which the portraits of *John Freake* and *Mrs. Freake and baby Mary* (Fig. 9) are the leading examples) that show how sensitive the work of an "untrained professional" can be. An instinctive sense of elegance, sweetness of sentiment, graceful elaboration of linear pattern, fastidious delicacy in the harmonies of the flat color areas are the virtues of this artist—and these are no small virtues. He shows the muted, decorative quality and the delicate, lyrical sentiment which characterize English painting whenever continental influence is removed. Painting like this was found in the provincial areas of England itself deep into the seventeenth century (but not perhaps so late as in New England) as a lingering echo of the style of the Tudor period.

But painting in seventeenth-century New England seldom attained this level. Ordinarily it was closer to the ruder amateur level of John Foster, who made a crude woodcut portrait of *Richard Mather*, thus becoming the earliest wood engraver in the United States, and who also probably painted a number of portraits of New England divines, interesting historically but almost totally devoid of any qualities either of craftsmanship or art.

An echo of medieval England lingers in the two-dimensional patterns of the Freake painter. The Middle Ages lingered on in other ways. The seventeenth-century mind in New England was wrapped up in "a deep sight into the mystery of God's grace, and man's corruption, and large apprehensions of these things . . ." as the Reverend John Norton, pastor of the First Church in Boston, said of his colleague, John Cotton.[4] To these men the world was evil, transient. Only Scripture and the writings of theologians saw truth in a clear light. Often, through the distracting veil of this world, burst those gleams of the miraculous which the learned Cotton Mather industriously collected. In all that concerned a knowledge and perception of nature the seventeenth-century mind in New England was still semimedieval. No art of landscape, based upon a clear affectionate view of nature, nor of genre, based upon delight in the savors of daily life, could grow out of such a mentality. Two of the strongest interests of seventeenth-century painting in Protestant Holland were therefore cut off. Neither was there any desire to create an ideal art. The Puritan vision of the ideal world of faith was embodied only in words, in books, or sermons. To embody it in the mere concrete images of painting was distrusted as "papistical."

Human personality was the only interest of seventeenth-century painting that remained to the New England painter and in presenting character —not beauty nor elegance, but character, bluntly stated—the New England painter found a theme congenial to his modest gifts.

---

[4] John Norton, "Abel being Dead yet Speaketh; or, the Life and Death of Mr. John Cotton" (London, 1658), quoted in Albert Bushnell Hart, *American History Told by Contemporaries*, New York, The Macmillan Company, 1900, I, 335-340.

CHAPTER 4

THE BAROQUE IN AMERICA

IT IS NOT DIFFICULT TO TRANSPLANT INDIVIDUAL PLANTS OR TREES; BUT THE only way to produce a forest is to give it time to grow. So it is, also, with human beings. One can transplant individuals, or small groups of people, fairly easily; but it takes a hundred years for a people to strike roots into a new soil. About a century after the first settlements, that is during the first decades of the eighteenth century, the American colonies began to thrive with a vigorous life of their own. The frontier had been pushed back thirty, forty, even a hundred miles from tidewater. In the settled districts there had grown up the population of yeoman farmers and seamen, led by small groups of merchants, craftsmen, and professional men who were to create the American nation.

The colonies were still remote provinces, far from the active centers of Western life: the cities, courts, exchanges, universities, parliaments of Europe. But they began to be alive, with an existence of their own, in commercial, social, and intellectual activities unknown to the seventeenth century. A new architecture appeared, on Palladian models (the most serene and classical phase of Baroque architecture), adapting the English architecture of Wren and Hawksmoor to simpler American materials and needs. Skilled cabinetmakers and silversmiths replaced the old homemade setting of life with elegant and graceful furnishings, in a colonial version of English contemporary decorative arts.

And, though still remote, the colonies had become polite enough to attract trained artists from abroad. In 1705, an English woman pastellist, Henrietta Johnston, settled in Charleston, South Carolina. In 1708, Justus Engelhardt Kühn, a German painter, was settled in Annapolis, Maryland. In 1711, Gustavus Hesselius, of a distinguished family of Swedish intellectuals, came out with his brother, who was to be the minister of the Swedish colony at

Christina (Wilmington) on the Delaware. Hesselius settled at Philadelphia and became the portrait painter of the colonial metropolis and the Chesapeake Bay region. In 1714, a Scot, John Watson, was established at Perth Amboy, then the seat of the proprietors of New Jersey. In 1726, Peter Pelham, an English mezzotint engraver, settled in Boston. In 1729, a traveled and cultured Scot, John Smibert, came to New England in the entourage of Bishop Berkeley. In 1735, Charles Bridges, an old man who "either by the frowns of fortune or his own mismanagement" was "obliged to seek his bread . . . in a strange land" was painting the children of William Byrd of Westover, and remained a few years in Virginia, painting portraits, before going home to dic in London. In 1750, an eclectic German painter and Moravian missionary, John Valentin Haidt, was sent by his Brotherhood to the Moravian mission founded by Count Zinzendorf at Bethlehem, Pennsylvania. These men brought to America a fresh impulse from various European schools of painting.

In the Dutch settlements along the Hudson, however, there were native painters at work; and in New England and the Middle Colonies, in the first decades of the century, a generation of native-born painters appeared, of whom some were to become famous: at Boston, Nathaniel Emmons (1704), Joseph Badger (1708), John Greenwood (1728), John Singleton Copley (1738); on Long Island, Robert Feke (about 1707); in Philadelphia, James Claypoole (1720) and Benjamin West (1738).

The intellectual climate of this century was very different from that of the seventeenth century. King Louis XIV of France, the Sun King, had risen and set; but the grandiose, aristocratic ideal of life at his court had cast its spell over Europe. England and Holland, the keystones of the grand alliance that had pulled Louis down, were themselves captivated by his splendor. Their eighteenth-century culture was now oriented toward the Latin South, rather than the Protestant North. In Holland, the late seventeenth-century Dutch portrait painters followed the aristocratic Baroque style of the painters of Louis's court; and a new generation of ideal figure painters, like Lairesse, Poelenburch, Van der Werff, were creating a Dutch version of the Italian Baroque. In England, Lord Burlington led the swing of taste toward Palladian architecture. Alexander Pope, rather than Milton, was the leader of English poetry. The odes of Horace, rather than the Bible and the seventeenth-century theologians, were the favorite reading of the educated. The age of English aristocratic education by a Grand Tour to Italy and of English collections of Italian art had dawned. And in the widely read *Spectator* papers Addison created, in the character of Sir Roger de Coverley, a new ideal of the country gentleman and of country life.

This ideal world of aristocratic dignity and polite classical learning, seen in terms of the grandeur and elegance of Baroque classicism, became the ideal world of the early eighteenth century in America. Nor do I imply, by calling it aristocratic, that it was alien, or had no place in America. On the contrary, its political absolutism left behind, it came as a cultural aspiration of great value to the colonies. In place of the Calvinistic belief that this world was evil and man's nature vicious, in place of the menace of hunger and the Indian, it brought an imaginative vision of the dignity and sweetness of life. Houses like Westover and Mount Vernon, for example, are "aristocratic" in the sense that they surround life with an atmosphere of spacious dignity, ease, and grace that increases one's respect for man as man. They did not unfit their eighteenth-century owners for hard work and energetic thinking, nor idealism, nor for meeting risk and hardship. A young master printer in Philadelphia named Benjamin Franklin, polishing his literary style on the model of Addison's *Spectator*, was not sacrificing his good sense to an effete ideal. He was disciplining his natural vitality to the literary virtues of classical lucidity, ease, and economy of means.

In painting, the Baroque style which embodied these ideals was brought to America by two means. There was, first, the migration of painters from England and the Continent which, between 1700 and 1750, brought to each of the little tidewater provincial capitals from Boston to Charleston a more or less well-trained painter. There was another quieter, subtler migration of Baroque style forms to America in the form of engravings. Engravings reproducing portraits, landscapes, and ideal compositions of the most famous Renaissance and Baroque painters of Europe were very popular in Europe in the eighteenth century. We know that many found their way to America. The migration of artists from Europe is such a cardinal fact that it takes first place in our review. A question I shall leave to the taste of the reader is whether the stimulus of engravings upon native-born talents may not have produced even more interesting artistic results.

The Baroque style in painting, which originated in Rome about 1600, had given Europe one of its most glorious centuries of painting. For the first time both the inner and outer worlds of consciousness were explored by a profusion of artists of genius, Italian, Spanish, French, Flemish, and Dutch. The observation of Nature and the world of ideas, realism, and the capacities of decorative style were carried to heights of splendor and power: Caravaggio and Poussin, Velasquez and Rubens, Salvator Rosa, Van Dyck and Rembrandt—the parade of names goes on and on. Within the unity of European culture, varied national schools gave expression to the genius of local temperaments. By the close of the century, however, the fires of imagination had sunk; and Baroque painting had become a rather eclectic, international idiom, practiced by artists of the second rank. It was this late Baroque style, of little imaginative glow, but still of large and handsome decorative qualities, that was brought to America by the artist-migrants in the early years of the eighteenth century.

It took root first in the middle colonies of Pennsylvania and Maryland, brought there by painters from the Continent rather than from England. Justus Engelhardt Kühn, a German artist who had applied for naturalization at Annapolis in 1708, died there in 1717. A creditor's inventory of his estate, says Dr. J. Hall Pleasants, the authority on his career, "indicates that he was a lover of good books, music and clothes, that he was wont to live beyond his means, and that he augmented his income by painting coats-of-arms." [1] He has left us some naïvely charming portraits of the children of the Darnall family, who lived at a plantation called "The Woodyard" in Prince George's County, Maryland. Their elaborate scenic backgrounds of columns, balustrades, and formal gardens are echoes, perhaps, of the formal splendor of German Baroque gardens seen by the painter in his youth; perhaps of engraved Baroque portraits.

Technically, however, Kühn was little better than an amateur; he had no followers. The real founder of painting in the middle colonies was Gustavus Hesselius (1682-1755), a cousin of Emanuel Swedenborg, who settled in Philadelphia in 1711. He was active there and in Annapolis until his death in 1755. In his later years Hesselius devoted himself to organ-building and left portrait-painting to his son, John, who lived until 1778. The two Hesseliuses were thus the principal painters in the area of Philadelphia, the colonial metropolis, for half a century.

Philadelphia was the center, in America, of the eighteenth-century spirit of rationalistic science and classical culture that undermined Calvinism. While the Mather family of theologians were the leaders and representatives of New England's intellectual life, the symbol of Philadelphia is James Logan, the deputy of William Penn. Logan was an urbane scholar; owned a rich classical library; and possessed an interest in natural science that led him to publish, in Latin, essays on reproduction in plants and on the aberration of light, as well as on ancient literature.[2]

Philadelphia also attracted from Boston the young Benjamin Franklin, in whom American rationalism flowered into a new philosophy of natural science and democratic common sense. Franklin was the first American writer of international fame, who wrote in the lucid eighteenth-century style created by Addison. His robust rationalism, his intense interest in this world, his lively sense of pleasure were the antithesis of the somber supernaturalism of the seventeenth century. He was the guiding spirit of the American Philosophical Society, formed in the forties, which for the first time made the

[1] Dr. J. Hall Pleasants, *Two Hundred and Fifty Years of Painting in Maryland*, Baltimore, The Baltimore Museum of Art, 1945, p. 14.

[2] His botanical knowledge was such that his friend Linnaeus named after him a natural order of herbs and shrubs, the Loganiaceae.

world aware of an intellectual life in America. Another of Franklin's foundations was the first American magazine, whose success proved that there was
need for a new kind of secular reading, in addition to religious books.

The existence in Philadelphia, also, of two of the finest American Palladian churches, Christ Church and St. Peter's, indicates the strength of the
Anglican Church in the middle colonies. The English church did not use
painting extensively, as the French and Spanish churches in America did; but
it had no doctrinal distrust of religious painting or of humanistic culture, and
commissions for religious pictures were not unknown.

In this atmosphere appeared a modest colonial Baroque art of narrative
painting on the Christian and classical themes characteristic of the European
Baroque. Gustavus Hesselius was trained in Europe, whether in his native
Sweden or elsewhere we do not know. His models are, however, easily identified. They are the Italianate Dutch painters of the late seventeenth century,
like Gerard de Lairesse and Poelenburch, who enjoyed a great popularity, especially in Germany and Sweden. Hesselius brought the late Baroque portrait
formula to America and painted portraits in Philadelphia and Maryland. But
his great interest for us is that we find him painting, probably in the 1720's,
elaborate Baroque figure subjects such as *Bacchus and Ariadne* (Fig. 11) and
a *Bacchanale*, and, in 1721, a *Last Supper*.

The two classical pictures, which have survived, are the earliest known
paintings by an artist in America of the ideal world of ancient poetry. As
such, one looks at them with interest and respect, however modest their at-
tainments. To see Ovid painted in the American wilderness is, in itself, curious enough. Yet the transmigration goes even further. It seems as if his fauns
and nymphs had suffered another metamorphosis: some look exceedingly like
American Indians! Is this fancy? I think not. The resemblance is faint, but
distinct enough to give rise to amusing speculations. Are we to suppose that
Hesselius' imagery was influenced by the Indians he saw around him? that
perhaps, striving to visualize the graceful nudes of ancient Greece, as he
worked in his modest painting room in Philadelphia, there rose before his
eyes the memory of the handsome, bronzed, naked Delawares who used to
camp on the outskirts of the city, and build their campfires on the lawns of
their friend James Logan's Palladian villa in Germantown? If Hesselius was
the first, he was not the last artist to see a classical dignity in the American
Indian. Or, perhaps, is this a first hint of that great wave of eighteenth-century sentiment, which was to transfer the Arcadian graces and the innocence
of the shepherds in Ovid and Theocritus to the Noble Savage in America?
The dream world created by this sentiment, scientifically absurd though it
was, was to have astonishing artistic fruits, in French literature especially.

These are the works of Hesselius' early years in America, close in style
to portraits that can be dated in the early 1720's. At this time also he painted
a *Last Supper* for St. Barnabas' Church in Prince George's County, Mary-

land, which has become famous as the earliest American religious picture. Charles Henry Hart mistakenly identified this, forty years ago, with a Spanish picture of a stylistic character quite unlike Hesselius, which has since been often reproduced as Hesselius' work.[3] Hesselius' *Last Supper* is lost. A *Holy Family*, of a later period of his life and quite genuine exists, but is unfortunately a very feeble work.

Hesselius is interesting to us as the pioneer of religious painting and classical mythology in American painting. He was not a strong draughtsman nor was he an expressive figure painter. His gifts were decorative. His color is luminous and simple, his drawing large. His ideal paintings and his portraits have the virtue of dignified and rather pleasing decorations for a Palladian interior. Beyond that he could not go.

In his later years he developed other interests, also significant for other aspects of colonial life. In 1735 he painted for the Proprietor, Mr. John Penn, portraits of the two chiefs of the Delaware or Lenni-Lenape Indians, *Tishcohan* and *Lapowinsa*, who had participated in the so-called Walking Purchase, a notorious and unjust purchase of the Indians' Lands. Hesselius made no attempt to give these likenesses the elegance of Baroque portraits. He painted the Indians with a careful realism, as simple men of the Stone Age confronting the representatives of the Western world. The leaders of a dying race look out at us, puzzled and uncomprehending of the hopeless problem of their situation, but preserving an impassive dignity. They are the first successful and convincing Indian portraits by an American painter. Their sober, documentary character I should call the first artistic indication of the scientific realism rising in the intellectual life of Pennsylvania.

Perhaps a little later, Hesselius painted portraits of himself and his wife in old age, which again show the shift of attention from Baroque elegance to simple realism. The face that looks out at us from his *Self-Portrait* (Historical Society of Pennsylvania) is strong and worn, marked by many years and by much experience; but there is still fire there. All his life Hesselius had been a religious seeker, moving from one church to another in search of the light. He is a man who had left behind his adventurous youth in Dalecarlia, his fashionable days as a painter of colonial aristocracy, and was now ending his days as a builder of church organs for the German congregations of the back country. The portrait is a revelation of this complex character.

Hesselius, we may say, founded in Philadelphia a tradition of interest in ideal narrative subjects, of scientific realism, and of mechanical ingenuity, which we shall see appear again in Philadelphia painters of greater powers, in Benjamin West and the remarkable Peale family.

There were other infusions of Continental painting in Pennsylvania. In any large migration of peoples the hazards of fortune are great. Some men

[3] This question is discussed in detail by the writer in *The Art Quarterly*, XII (1949), 220-226.

will meet with success, others not; some seed will fall on good ground, some on barren soil, or be choked by the wilderness. The stories of the artists who came to America (and of their native-born followers, also) are sometimes pathetic, sometimes tragic. They, too, throw light upon the relations between the artist, his craft, and his surroundings. Man is a social animal; and even the artist, solitary and individualistic as he has come to be, exists as part of society and needs its support.

One can hardly suppose that Christopher Witt, who came over in 1704 as a member of a mystical German sect called the "Society of the Woman of the Wilderness" (to which no women were admitted), was a professional painter. His portrait of the leader of that sect, *Johannes Kelpius* (Pennsylvania Historical Society), painted between 1704 and 1708, is the work of an amateur painter, but worth remembering for its early date and for the strange character depicted.

John Valentin Haidt (1700-1780), however, was a typical wandering artist of the eighteenth century. Born in Berlin, he studied there, and afterwards worked in Dresden, Venice, Rome, Paris, and London. In the last-named city he joined a congregation of the Moravian Brotherhood. From that day both his art and his life were devoted to his church. In 1750 he was sent to Bethlehem, Pennsylvania, and there spent the rest of his long life. He painted a great number of religious pictures which were hung unframed (in the Moravian spirit of strict simplicity) on the walls of churches in Bethlehem, Lititz, and Nazareth. There they remained, forgotten, until Mr. Frederick A. Sweet brought them to light in an exhibition, *Colony to Nation*, at the Art Institute of Chicago, in 1949. Haidt was not a good artist. He was a rather distressing example of an uninspiring school, of German eighteenth-century imitators of Dutch painting in general and Rembrandt in particular. He had no followers. His art was a dead end. It is an example of the seed that was lost in the wilderness.

The channel through which the late Baroque reached New England and Virginia was the artistic life of London, which, at the opening of the eighteenth century, was dominated by Sir Godfrey Kneller and his school. Kneller was a typical figure of the international late Baroque. A German by birth, a Fleming by training, he practiced portrait painting in London, with a large workshop in which assistants helped him turn out his multitudinous productions. His interests were limited to portraiture. The virtue of his style was its monumental decorative tone. He was not a very personal artist; but he painted portraits admirably suited to serve as decorations in the great rooms of English country houses. He was an artist much like Romney, some generations later. To appreciate either man, one must see his works hanging as decorations in the architectural setting for which they were intended. Kneller's portrait of *Governor Hunter*, a memorable Governor of the New York

Colony (New-York Historical Society), shows his good qualities—largeness of scale, bold sweeping outlines, large simple contrasts of hue and of tone. He used for portraits a formula of a stiff, upright pose given variety by a Baroque swing of the body and a sideways glance of the eyes, which made them fit admirably into the paneling of Palladian rooms or chimney pieces.

Some Americans of the official class, like William and Jeremiah Dummer, Jr., of Boston, had their portraits painted by Kneller in London. At least two excellent representatives of Kneller's school came to America, Smibert to Boston and Bridges to Virginia.

John Smibert (1688-1751), who spent his life here and whose portraits and gallery of copies of old masters became the cornerstone of a New England school of portraiture, was the more influential. He was a man of forty-one when he landed in America; in eighteenth-century terms, he was past middle age, almost an old man. He had lived in Italy and had practiced art successfully in London. He had come originally from Edinburgh, where he was trained as an artisan; but aspiring to paint, he found his way to London and eventually to Florence. In Italy he met Bishop Berkeley, who persuaded him later to join the faculty of a projected university at Bermuda. On their way to Bermuda in 1729 they put in at Newport, Rhode Island, where Berkeley decided to wait for a parliamentary grant for his university that never came. Smibert meanwhile moved from Newport to Boston. There he held an exhibition of his pictures in the spring of 1730. He married a Boston girl in the fall of the same year, and settled down to become the portrait painter of the little New England metropolis. He built a painting room and gallery at the top of the little town, just below Beacon Hill, and supplemented his portrait painting by keeping a shop to sell English engravings, frames, painters' colors, and other goods of an artistic character.

Smibert was a solid, competent, though somewhat monotonous practitioner of the decorative Baroque style. His life-sized group portraits of *Bishop George Berkeley and his Family* (1729), painted at Newport (Fig. 12), or his full-length portraits, like those of *Mr. and Mrs. William Brown* of Brownhall (Johns Hopkins University, Baltimore), are vigorous monumental painting, handsome and luminous in color, imposing in tone, and admirable expressions of the Baroque ideal of personal dignity and elegance.

He also brought with him a small collection of art, including copies made in Florence of Raphael's *Madonna dell' Impannata*, Van Dyck's portrait of *Cardinal Bentivoglio*, Poussin's *Continence of Scipio*, and other pictures whose identity is now lost; also some casts of ancient sculpture, among them the *Head of Homer*, the *Venus de Medici*, and perhaps the *Laocoön*. This gallery, though modest, was in fact a summary of eighteenth-century taste. By good fortune it remained intact for more than a generation after his death, and served as a school of art for New England.

Like Hesselius, Smibert showed a tendency to develop in America, away from the aristocratic ideal of elegance, toward a plainer, blunter realism. His portrait of *Charles Chambers*, for example, is a study of old age, and displays frankness and power. This tendency toward frank realism has been attributed with some plausibility to the democratic atmosphere of American life. A blunt realism has therefore been singled out, with a great deal less plausibility, as the characteristic note of American imaginative life. It is one characteristic, certainly. The New England portrait of character is in strong contrast to the more decorative and idealized style of portraiture that flourished in London. That realism should be the sole characteristic of our imaginative life, however, is contradicted both by the record of American painting and by the facts of human nature, which are an inextricable mixture of realism and dream, in America as elsewhere.

Even before Smibert, however, there were painters in New England who could use the Kneller style. In 1711 an unknown artist painted the portraits of the *Reverend James Pierpont* and *Mrs. Pierpont* of Connecticut (Yale University Art Gallery), in a large, simple, Baroque style, with a good solid construction and expressive drawing of eyes and mouth. The same artist apparently worked in New York, for his hand can be recognized in a portrait of *Caleb Heathcote* (New-York Historical Society).

And, in 1726, Peter Pelham, a trained English mezzotint engraver, settled in Boston. At first, finding no portrait painter there, he was forced to paint the portraits from which to make his engravings. After Smibert arrived, Pelham seems to have been glad to confine himself to engraving. His *Cotton Mather* of 1727 is the earliest American mezzotint engraving, and a good simple likeness in the Kneller formula.

In New Jersey, John Watson (1684-1762), a Scot, arrived in 1714, bringing a rather modest degree of skill. His miniature portrait drawings are rather sensitive, in an amateur way. Their subjects are people from both the New York and the Delaware River settlements, so they tell us that he must have traveled. His oils are more difficult to identify with certainty; but there are a number of portraits in a curious pale color scheme, done with a coarse stroke like that of a scene painter, which seem to be his.

In the Southern colonies, where plantation life had reached a degree of wealth that was expressed in a handsome Palladian architecture, the late Baroque conception of a portrait as an elegant architectural decoration seemed to find congenial soil, for it struck root in this period and remained the dominant conception of painting until the end of the era of plantation aristocracy, at the Civil War.

Henrietta Johnston (earliest dated work, 1705; d. 1728-1729), the first woman painter in America, practiced the eighteenth-century art of portraiture in pastel in Charleston, South Carolina. Her works are all of small cabinet size, done in a simple, knowledgeable palette of three or four colors, and of a fresh, sweet, delicate character that is most enjoyable in her portraits of young girls; but her men are too girlish to be believable.

The next painter to arrive was Charles Bridges (active in Virginia 1735-after 1740). There are references to him in diaries and other records, but he remains a shadowy figure. Several portraits of the Byrd family have been attributed to him on the basis of a reference to him in a letter of William Byrd. If the *Maria Taylor Byrd* of Westover, Virginia (Fig. 14) represents Bridges' work in Virginia, he was a competent painter of the type of courtly and decorative portrait produced in England by Kneller and his school. It is a sophisticated, decorative performance, refined in color and tone, though not conventional in drawing. Through Bridges or other intermediaries, a school of aristocratic portrait painting sprang up in America. There are many portraits from this period of Virginia life. Unfortunately we still know next to nothing about the artists who produced them.[4]

In 1739, a few years after the death of Henrietta Johnston, a Swiss painter named Jeremiah Theüs arrived in Charleston, South Carolina. Here is his advertisement in the *South Carolina Gazette:*

Jeremiah Theüs, limner, gives notice that he is removed into Market Square, near Mr. John Laurens, sadler, where all gentlemen and ladies may have their pictures drawn, likewise landscapes of all sizes, crests and coats of arms for coaches or chaises. Likewise for the convenience of those who live in the country he is willing to wait on them at their respective plantations.

Theüs was the kind of solid uninspired craftsman one might expect from this notice of his skills. His cabinet-size portrait of *William Wragg* (Fig. 13) is an early work that shows Theüs at his best: a fresh and decorative piece of color; drawing, a little awkward; and of characterization, very little. He could give his portraits an appearance of dignity and repose; and they are pleasing in color, so that they were effective decorations over a mantel or on either side of a sideboard. His later pictures became all too often disagreeably careless. But Theüs was popular and he is said to have accumulated a fortune by his art in Charleston before his death in 1774.

None of these migrants to America were artists of great imagination or artistic power. If they had been, they probably would not have left Europe for these distant colonies. They are more interesting to us historically than artistically. They brought a knowledge of forms, especially the Baroque portrait form, and the solid Baroque painter's craft. They were able to use its coloristic style of solid, plastic forms, rhythmic development of line, simple

---

[4] The most complete study of Bridges to date is that of Henry Wilder Foote in *The Virginia Magazine*, vol. 60 (Jan. 1952), pp. 3-55.

luminous color, effective contrasts of light and shade. They may have lacked
inspiration but they were good craftsmen. And, since painters learn their
craft from pictures, native-born artists could learn from their works how to
put together a handsome decorative composition, large in drawing and luminous in color. The craft is all a teacher can ever give an art student. The
qualities of imagination and poetry are born, not taught. The migrants' artistic importance is that they brought the craft of painting to America.

Another source of knowledge of Baroque forms was the engraving. Line
engraving, as a means of reproducing paintings, developed in the sixteenth
century. In the seventeenth came the mezzotint, far richer in tone. A great
development of reproductive engraving followed. The masterpieces of Renaissance and Baroque art, the portraits of French and English court painters,
were made widely available in engravings, which offered even more effective
examples of Baroque composition than did the work of the migrant artists.
During the whole eighteenth century and through the first half of the nineteenth, until the invention of the camera, engravings were the native American painter's chief source of knowledge of the language of European
painting. Their influence was omnipresent. Today they are lost or forgotten:
it is hard for us to remember that they were everywhere, once, and that their
influence was, in some cases, omnipotent.

The point we must now emphasize is that there were native-born painters even before the arrival of Hesselius and Smibert. The migrants brought
trained craftsmanship; but the impulse to paint was already here.

In the office of the mayor of the City of Albany hangs a full-length
heroic portrait of the first mayor of Albany, *Pieter Schuyler* (1657-1724)
(Fig. 16), which, judging by the sitter's age, must have been painted between
1700 and 1710. The unknown artist was American, not European. Schuyler
was a son of a veteran of the Dutch navy, from the times of Tromp and De
Ruyter, who had settled on the upper Hudson. This Pieter Schuyler's lands
lay forty miles above Albany at Old Saratoga (now Schuylerville), which
was then the border fortress against the French. His commanding character,
his sense of personal responsibility for the safety of the frontier, the degree
to which his military successes, with a small force of colonials, counterbalanced
the failures of the professional English armies against the French in Canada
led Bancroft to call him the George Washington of his time. His portrait is
the work of an unknown artist, who was the first and finest talent of a school
of painters active in the Hudson Valley from the earliest years of the century.
These Patroon Painters, as Flexner (who was the first to recognize their
artistic qualities) has called them, are the earliest significant development of
native-born talent in American painting.

The Schuyler painter evidently learned his conception of the portrait from engravings, for he gave us a composition in the lordly Baroque manner. But his style shows the shift toward the two-dimensional—a flattening of the forms, an emphasis on outline and pattern—characteristic of the "untrained professional." Whoever he was, this painter, he was an instinctive painter and observer. The long, firm outlines of his style, the use of lights and shadows, drawn in long, firm strokes to give relief, the simple color scheme of red, brown, blue, gray, and white—all these are singularly knowing and effective. With limited means, he achieved a monumental decorative power. His grasp of character is no less striking: he makes Schuyler's forceful, intelligent, commanding personality so convincing that, to my eye, this is one of the memorable military portraits in American painting.

The Schuyler painter also painted, I believe, in about the same decade, 1700-1710, an equally impressive full-length portrait of *Ariaantje Coeymans*, a half-length of *Gerardus Beekman* and a *David Davidse Schuyler* (once a full-length but now cut down to a head and shoulders), all preserved in the Albany Institute of History and Art. All are characterized by the same forceful grasp of character and monumental style, the same amused eyes, the same archaic smile. Whoever this upper Hudson artist was, he left us a notable image of the strong character of these Hudson River Dutch pioneers. By comparison, Gerret Duyckinck (1660-ca.1710), active in New York city at the same time, and the only one of the Duyckinck clan whose work can be identified, was a feeble amateur.

In the next generation, in the 1720's and 1730's, there were several painters at work up and down the Hudson Valley. One, who painted several portraits dated in the early 1720's, in a flat, rude, harsh style, has been named by Flexner the "Aetatis Suae painter" from his habit of inscribing the age of the sitter and date on the background.

A still more naïve painter (Flexner's "Gansevoort Limner") is known for his portrait of *Pau de Wandelaer* (Albany), a dreamy youth holding a bird on his finger, against a landscape of Hudson River scenery. In this degree of naïveté, the style has become a completely flat pattern of color areas surrounded by maplike boundaries; but the soft charm of color and the mild poetry of the mood have made this painter deservedly popular. Part of the attraction, no doubt, comes also from the landscape background: the beauty of the famous river, which was to be so celebrated by romantic artists a century later, makes its appearance here timidly like a child making its first bow. The same painter may have done the gentle, attractive portrait of *Adam Winne* at Winterthur, dated 1730 (Plate III).

The delicacy of tone shown by these painters is often surprising. Naïve in technique, they betray nevertheless a sweet, untrained sensibility that is the flower of rustic refinement. This is the charm, for example, of the portrait of *Mrs. Elsie (Rutgers) Schuyler Vas*, dated 1723 (Albany), in its pale, soft grays and browns. (This picture was once connected with the name of Pieter Vanderlyn, who came to America in 1718 from Curaçao, after spending his youth in the Dutch navy.)

Another, gayer style, close to the "artisan tradition," appears in the portrait of *Magdalena Gansevoort* of Albany in the H. F. du Pont Museum, Winterthur, a deservedly famous and popular work, often called "The Girl with the Red Shoes" (Plate II).

The "untrained professional" who, about 1728, did a series of portraits of the De Peyster, Van Cortlandt, Levy, and Franks families, based his compositions upon mezzotint engravings after English portraits by Sir Godfrey Kneller. The portrait of Pierre van Cortlandt shows the oddly charming flavor of his work, mingling naïveté with ducal splendors of park or garden and pet animals, all borrowed from Sir Godfrey Kneller. The pomp and pride of the English Baroque nobility becomes, when transposed to the American wilderness, a quaint dream of the sweetness of life.

These unknown painters of the Hudson Valley, with their bold, flat, effective style, their decorative sense, their varied gifts of mood or character, illustrate a phenomenon that was to appear often thereafter. As the population spread inward into America, people of talent were born without organized institutions to train and support them. Art springs from within human nature, while craft lives in organized society. These artists in the wilderness lacked the developed craft of European painting but they nonetheless found their way to create works of art that have life and flavor. This interweaving counterpoint of imagination and craft, of innate sensibility and knowledge, in the story of American painting is to me one of its sources of interest.

An unknown painter, curiously similar to the Aetatis Suae painter, did a group of portraits about 1720-1722 of the Jaquelin and Brodnax families in Jamestown, Virginia. The coarse, strong, flat style of such painters seems derived from another source than the artist's craft. There was, in fact, an artisan's technique of painting, different from that of the artist, which also existed in the colonies, its simple methods and procedures derived from artisan traditions long antedating the Baroque painter's complex and subtle atmospheric techniques. We catch a glimpse of this other painting skill in a partnership which Gustavus Hesselius formed, late in life, to set up an all-purpose workshop. An advertisement in *The Pennsylvania Gazette* for December 11, 1740, reads:

PAINTING done in the best MANNER, by Gustavus Hesselius, from Stockholm, and John Winter, from London, VIZ: coats of Arms drawn on coaches, chaises, &c, or any other kind of Ornaments, Landskips, Signs, Shew-boards, Ship and House Painting, Gilding of all Sorts, Writing in Gold or Colour, old Pictures clean'd and mended, &c.

One suspects an artisan's training in the case of the Aetatis Suae or Brodnax painters.

There is another native-born painter whose striking portraits and enigmatic career are wrapped in mystery. Robert Feke (ca.1706-1710 to before 1767) was born at Oyster Bay, Long Island, of a family closely connected with Newport, Rhode Island. We know really nothing of his life before 1741. He is said to have been a sailor and, according to a vague tradition, was captured and imprisoned for a time by the Spaniards. When he appears in 1741, it is as the painter of a large portrait group, executed in Boston, of the *Family of Isaac Royall*. It is an ambitious, even daring work for an artist plainly without experience, and leans strongly on Smibert's example. From 1741 until 1750 Feke was active as a painter; he is documented in Newport and Philadelphia. Then he disappears once more and, according to tradition, died in the West Indies. His fragmentary, wandering, adventurous life, his unknown training, show the difficulties and chances awaiting a painter born into a society without an established craft of painting.

Feke was nevertheless a born painter. His full-length of *General Samuel Waldo* (Fig. 15), his *Mrs. Josiah Martin* or his *Self-Portrait* of 1750, which show the maturity of his style, reveal a powerful talent. He was only occasionally a student of character. His portraits interest us by their decorative power, their luminosity, by the bold Baroque rhythm in the flowering folds of his women's costumes, and by the eloquence with which they express the aristocratic ideal of dignity, elegance, and formality. In some of his early work, such as the *Pamela Andrews* (Museum of Art, Providence) and the *Reverend Joseph Callender* (Rhode Island Historical Society), a poetry of fresh, youthful feeling veils the stiffness of the pose. In his more characteristic pictures the vitality of a human life is stated simply and powerfully, but is not analyzed. The mood is one of pride, self-reliance, and repose. Obvious awkwardnesses in Feke's work betray the sketchiness of his training; but he worked with instinctive authority and style, and he gave striking expression to the aristocratic ideal.

In the Middle States and the South there were a few artists in addition to those already discussed.

John Hesselius (1728-1778), the son of Gustavus, painted portraits in Philadelphia, Maryland, and Virginia. We must presume that he learned his craft from his father; yet his early work seems modeled upon the dignified Baroque pose and luminous color of Feke's Philadelphia portraits. His later works, under the influence of John Wollaston, belong to the colonial Rococo style (after 1760).

The painting of Maryland and Virginia, however, is full of unanswered questions. There is a large group of Bolling family portraits, now at William and Mary College, at Williamsburg in Virginia; other portraits are at Washington and Lee College; still others are preserved in their original houses. Evidently there were painters at work among the great tidewater plantations; yet documents are few and attributions hazardous. One Virginia painter has, however, recently been identified: William Dering (fl. 1735-1751), a man of many talents—dancing master, portrait painter, teacher of polite accomplishments—which must have been welcome in plantation life. His portrait of *Mrs. Stith* (ca.1748-1750) (Williamsburg, Brush-Everard House) is a stiff and provincial yet at the same time fairly knowledgeable performance. Much work remains to be done, however, on the artists of the Tobacco Coast. All we can be sure of is that the Baroque portrait of elegance was transplanted to the Southern colonies and flourished there.

In New England the seventeenth-century limner's style persisted apparently down to the arrival of Peter Pelham and Smibert. One painter before Smibert's time is called the Pollard Limner, from an incisive portrait of the hundred-year-old *Ann Pollard*. Whoever this painter was, he showed the New England preference for character rather than beauty, and used the virtues of his archaic style—sharp outline, formalized modeling, striking pattern—with vigor.

About the same time, Nathaniel Emmons of Boston (1704-1740), the earliest native-born painter of the period whom we know by name, broke away from the limner's manner and taught himself to paint in the style of the Baroque portrait. His model must have been engravings, for all his surviving works are small portraits done in black and white.

The next two painters born in Massachusetts, Joseph Badger (1708-1765) and John Greenwood (1727-1792), were young enough to learn from the example of Pelham and Smibert. In spite of this advantage, the Baroque portrait became, in their practice, an iron-tinctured essence of provincial stiffness.

Badger has a historical importance because Smibert's death left him, perforce, for some years the principal painter of Boston. Artistically, he illustrates the rule that it is the limitations of such painters that make them interesting. He was a house painter, self-taught as a portrait painter, and capable of a wooden amateurishness that should damn him forever as an artist. Yet out of the very narrowness of his talent, out of his inability to achieve the solid, beef-and-bone plasticity of Smibert's figures, comes his own peculiar quality. His *Mrs. John Edwards*, the wife of a Boston goldsmith (Fig. 17), is an example of his strangely ghostly style, which gives to his portraits, of the very young or very old especially, a wraithlike charm.

Greenwood is less interesting for his portraits than for his rough humor, which led him to produce the earliest colonial genre painting. His mezzotint engraving (1748) of *Jersey Nanny* (Fig. 18) bears the pointed inscription:

> Nature her various Skill displays
> In thousand Shapes, a thousand Ways;
> Tho' one Form differs from another
> She's still of all the common Mother:
> Then, Ladies, let not Pride resist her,
> But own that NANNY is your sister.

Still more vigorous and satirical is the picture, crudely painted in a curious frosty palette, of *American Sea Captains Carousing in Surinam* (1757-1758) (Fig. 19). It was painted after Greenwood left New England for Surinam, where he spent several years, and is the only surviving work to remind us that our New England ancestors were, after all, compatriots of Hogarth. Greenwood ended his days as a successful art dealer in London.

Such realism was rare in the Baroque period of American painting. The aristocratic ideal of grandeur and repose dominated the imagination of colonial painters. There were forces in colonial life working toward realism: there was the spirit of democracy of the frontier; there was humor; there was the rising spirit of scientific rationalism. Benjamin Franklin gave form and literary expression to all three. But the effect of these forces on painting made itself felt very slowly.

One other aspect of Baroque art has yet to be touched on, that is, its relation with nature. Mark Catesby, the artist-naturalist, has already been mentioned in Chapter 2. He spent the years 1712-1719 and 1722-1726 roaming the forests of the South. But what of landscape painting?

There is a common supposition that landscape painting arises, inevitably and automatically, wherever there are people living among woods, rivers, hills. Nothing could be further from the truth. Landscape painting arises from an imaginative impulse notably rare in the history of civilization. Many great and gifted civilizations have come and gone without ever feeling the peculiar kind of contemplative self-surrender to nature that produces a landscape art. In the seventeenth century Europe had seen the first great outburst in the landscape art of Rome and the Low Countries, but this was followed by a prolonged lull during most of the eighteenth century. The late Baroque had little interest in nature for its own sake. Its urbane and decorative interests transposed the seventeenth-century realistic landscape into the plane of graceful decorations for walls, tapestries, or overdoor panels. Aside from the decorative landscape with figures, it developed as its own contribution the town view or cityscape. Canaletto, Guardi, Bellotto, Panini, Hubert Robert made the cities of Venice or Rome or Dresden themes for enchanting works of genius, while pure landscape languished.

The decorative landscape with figures appeared in America perhaps for the first time when William Clark built a fine Palladian house in the old north end of Boston, about 1712-1714. In the main parlor the eleven wall panels were filled with landscape compositions, some time before the death of Mr. Clark in 1742; four of these still exist, rather crude but effective examples of Baroque decoration of a type more familiar to us in the form of tapestry. Decorative landscapes on walls or overmantels or even on canvas are not uncommon thereafter, generally on a very modest level of craftsmanship; an excellent survey of them has been published by Nina Fletcher Little in *American Decorative Wall Painting* (1952).

I am convinced that the vanished landscapes which we know from documents to have been painted by Justus Englehardt Kühn and John Smibert were of this same generalized and decorative type, and probably also the lost landscapes of Emmons, mentioned with eulogy in his obituary.[5] The realistic study of nature for its own sake had to wait for a later day. The direction of attention during the late Baroque was fixed upon the works of man.

The cityscape, however, appeared in America with William Burgis (documented in New York 1716-1718, Boston 1722-1730, New York 1730-1732). Burgis' imposing drawing of New York, engraved in London by I. Harris, appeared as the rare and beautiful engraving entitled: *A South Prospect of Ye Flourishing City of New York in the Province of New York in America* (Fig. 20). Drawn about 1716-1718, engraved 1718-1721, it is the earliest and most celebrated of eighteenth-century views.

From New York Burgis moved to Boston, where he brought out in 1722 *A South East View of Ye Great Town of Boston in New England in America*, the earliest view of that city and likewise a most handsome engraving. Following this came four more Boston-scapes and a view of Harvard College. In 1728 Burgis married his landlady at the Crown Coffee House, Boston, but by September, 1730, he had deserted her and left the province for New York again, where he did two more New York views of 1730-1732.

There is another handsome series of city views of Boston, New York, and Philadelphia, drawn between about 1731 and 1736 by an unknown artist (the dates are given the authority of I. N. Phelps Stokes, the great iconographer of American cities) but engraved by J. Carwitham and published in London some thirty years later, which Miss Helen Comstock has recently attributed convincingly to Burgis also.[6] This closes the record of the first and one of the most brilliant makers of American cityscapes. Nothing else is known of him but from the record he was one of those roving, adventurous artists in whom the eighteenth century was rich.

[5] Kühn's landscapes are mentioned in the inventory of his estate. Smibert is known to have painted landscapes from a letter of 1749 in which he said: "My eyes has been some time failing me but I'm still heart whole and hath been diverting myself with some things in the landskip way which you know I always liked." As Virgil Barker remarks, the emotional pressure behind these words does not promise much. All three of these men were minds carried along by the current of their times, not bold swimmers against it.

[6] *The Connoisseur*, CXXIV (December, 1949), pp. 116-117.

There is also a *View of Charleston, South Carolina* (ca.1737-1738) by a man named Bishop Roberts (active in Charleston 1735-1739) which was engraved in London by W. H. Toms. Roberts' original water-color drawing also exists, rather crudely executed but exactly observed. In 1735 he advertised in Charleston to do "Portrait painting and Engraving, Heraldry and Housepainting"; in 1737 to paint "Landscapes for chimney pieces of all sizes. Likewise draughts of their Houses in Colours or India ink." [7]

Cityscapes in oil are much more rare. In the possession of the Library Company of Philadelphia is a long narrow canvas representing *The South East Prospect of the City of Philadelphia* about the years 1718-1720. It is signed by Peter Cooper. At either end are the arms of the city and the province; beneath is a descriptive panel identifying various buildings. It seems to be the earliest cityscape in oil from the middle colonies that has come down to us. Its long narrow shape strongly suggests the overmantel of a public room and its crude but effective style is that of an artisan. A similarly rough but decorative view of New York harbor during the last French war is preserved in The New-York Historical Society, called *British Privateers with French Prizes in New York Harbor* (ca.1756-1761). It, too, is artisan's work, executed with the flat colors and conventionalized brush stroke that, in the eighteenth century, were reserved for signs and showboards. It is more spirited work than Peter Cooper's and better deserves the title of landscape. These two show, at least, that the painted cityscape existed in America.

One other canvas exists to throw light on the tastes and interests of this time. In the Peabody Museum, Salem, is a ship's portrait of *The Letter of Marque Ship* Bethel *of Boston, 14 guns.* The *Bethel* was launched at Portsmouth, New Hampshire, in 1748, so that the picture, presumably done ca.1748-1750, is the earliest known painting of a colonial ship. The portrait shows her in two views, broadside on and coming about. It is unsigned and a marine painting of excellent quality, the finest American marine of the eighteenth century—if it is American. But did the proud owner of the *Bethel* sail her to England and commission her portrait of a marine painter in London or Bristol, as later Salem ship owners sent their vessels to Marseilles to be painted by Antoine Roux? It is impossible to say. All we can be sure of is that the cityscape and the ship's portrait appear at this time, expressions of a rational age's interest in man and his works.

The colonial Baroque style came to a natural end about 1750. By that date most of the artists of the Baroque generation had become inactive. Smibert, after painting more than a hundred portraits in Boston,[8] had ceased his activity: in a letter of 1749, already referred to, he complained of failing

---

[7] Anna Wells Rutledge, *Antiques,* LII (1947), 100-102.

[8] Henry Wilder Foote, *John Smibert,* Cambridge, Harvard University Press, 1950, records 102 portraits.

eyesight and spoke of diverting himself with "landskips." Peter Pelham died in 1751. Gustavus Hesselius died in 1755 but had withdrawn from painting in favor of his son some years earlier. The mysterious figure of Robert Feke, after producing seventy portraits between 1741 and 1750,[9] disappeared into the unknown. John Greenwood went to Surinam in 1752, leaving behind some thirty extant portraits and a few engravings.[10] Only Badger and John Hesselius carried on past the midcentury mark. Badger died in 1765 and John Hesselius, who married a wealthy young widow, Mary Woodward of "Primrose Hill," in Ann Arundel County, Maryland, became thereafter more country gentleman than active artist. The Baroque impetus given painting in the decades 1710-1730 had run out and art was waiting for a new direction. This was furnished by the Rococo, brought by a new wave of migrants and developed by a new generation of native-born talents into far greater significance.

But the first half of the eighteenth century established the art of painting as an element in the life of the American colonies. Migrants from Europe, native-born talents, skilled craftsmen, humble artisans, all took part in achieving this. The institutions which form and strengthen an artistic life were still wholly lacking. But the thing planted then, took root.

In retrospect, the native-born painters of the colonial Baroque seem often the more interesting. The migrant painters were competent craftsmen but they were rarely inspired performers. The native-born were poorly trained; their faults are often glaring; their knowledge of European forms was limited. But they became painters because they were driven by the urge of talent and passionate interest. The contrast between their sensibility and their primitive means appeals to our imagination, and gives vitality and personal character to their work.

[9] Henry Wilder Foote, *Robert Feke*, Cambridge, Harvard University Press, 1930.
[10] Alan Burroughs, *John Greenwood in America*, Andover, Phillips Academy, Addison Gallery of American Art, 1943.

CHAPTER 5

THE ROCOCO IN AMERICA

THE GRAND AND SPLENDID FORMS OF BAROQUE PAINTING CHANGED, IN EUROPE, into the lighter, gayer, more intimate final phase known as the Rococo, almost as insensibly as one season of the year changes into another. In France the Rococo appears, in the genius of Watteau, as early as the second decade of the century: by 1730 its luminosity and easy grace were visible in England in the early conversations of Hogarth, in Venice in the decorations of Tiepolo and the cheerful views of Canaletto, in Vienna in the cupola of the Hofbibliothek frescoed by Daniel Gran. By the 1760's, the movement that was to replace it had been born in Rome; but the date of the outbreak of the French Revolution, 1789, serves as a convenient symbol of its close.

In the American colonies, the Baroque portrait style introduced in the first years of the eighteenth century reigned undisturbed until two English painters arrived in the colonies, bringing with them the English Rococo, John Wollaston in 1749 and Joseph Blackburn in 1753. Both were craftsmen-painters rather than artists, practicing their art with skill rather than feeling, using a decorative portrait formula which varied little from one sitter to another. But they brought something of the idyllic note of the Rococo, with its pleasing artificiality and delicate movement, which artists like Highmore and Hudson were practicing in London; their portraits made attractive decorations for the Georgian mansions that were now rising in all the colonies along tidewater; and they spread the new style, Wollaston from New York city southward, Blackburn through the provincial capitals of New England.

The eighteenth century was an age of wandering artists. The motive of their travels was not a search for inspiration (as the romanticists in the nineteenth century were inspired by the dream of Italy) but a search for patrons and commissions. John Wollaston's travels took him not only to the North American colonies but to the fantastic new empire that Clive was winning

49

for England in India. Trained in London, he learned there a solid, competent portrait formula: he was essentially a London "drapery painter," one of those specialists in costume who, in the London studio practice, executed clothes and background on a canvas upon which a "face painter" had done the face. This practice, so contradictory to modern notions of painting, was a legacy of the Van Dyck-Kneller tradition of workshop production, and both Wollaston and Blackburn illustrate its peculiar merits and limitations. Wollaston could paint heads solidly, if somewhat coarsely and without much individuality, but imposing on each a curious mannerism of slanting, almond-shaped eyes, one slightly higher than the other. What his portraits lacked in characterization was made up by his skill in painting laces, silks, and satins (Fig. 22). They require to be seen in the setting of a Georgian drawing-room, for which they were designed. Then, as in the case of his *Mary Philipse* and *Margaret Philipse* in the drawing room of Philipse Castle on the Hudson, one sees how pleasing they are as decorations, large in design, rich and luminous in tone. They give little sense of personality, but within their limits they have charm.

This was enough to win Wollaston immense success in America. He arrived in New York in 1749, as soon as the Peace of Aix-la-Chapelle ending the War of the Austrian Succession had made ocean travel safe once more. He was the first painter of fashion to show himself in that city, and his success was immediate. Before he left the colonies for the last time, he had painted some three hundred portraits (equal to the total production of Smibert, Feke, and Blackburn together) and the example of his bold, coarse, confident pictures was the strongest influence upon colonial painting in the middle colonies and the South before the Revolution. He worked in New York 1749-1752, Annapolis 1753-1754, in Virginia 1755-1757. But in 1757 he secured a position as "writer" in the British East India Company (presumably he had married one of his daughters to an official of the company during a brief visit to London between New York and Annapolis) and in the spring of 1758 he was in Philadelphia, painting portraits, on his way to London. In 1760 we know he was in Calcutta and he presumably stayed in the East several years; he returned, it is said, very rich. In the winter and spring of 1767 he was in Charleston, South Carolina, painting portraits in the liveliest Rococo manner of his career. These were his last works in America. He ended his days in retirement in England.[1]

Joseph Blackburn introduced a somewhat more delicate version of Rococo elegance and artifice into New England (Fig. 21). He arrived at Boston from Bermuda in 1753 and extended his practice from there to Newport, Salem, and Portsmouth, until 1774; when, perhaps finding the competition of Copley too formidable, he returned to England. He, too, was a drapery

[1] The authority for Wollaston is George C. Groce, in *The Art Quarterly*, XV (1952), pp. 132-149.

PLATE IV. John Singleton Copley: *Mr. and
Mrs. Thomas Mifflin* (1773). (Courtesy of
The Historical Society of Pennsylvania;
color plate courtesy of Art Color Slides, Inc.)

PLATE V. Benjamin West: *William Penn's Treaty with the Indians* (1772). (Courtesy of The Pennsylvania Academy of the

Fig. 1. *Columbus' Discovery of America* (wood engraving). (From Giuliano Dati, *The Narrative of Columbus*, Florence, 1493. Courtesy of The British Museum.)

Fig. 2. *Mexico City* (wood engraving). (From Cortes' *Praeclara . . . de Nova Maris Oceani Hyspania Narratio.* Nuremberg, 1524. Courtesy of the William L. Clements Library, University of Michigan.)

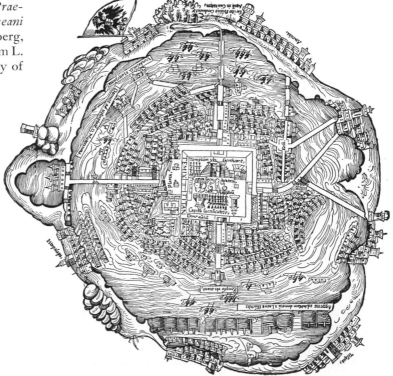

Fig. 3. *Toucan* (wood engraving). (From André Thevet, *Les Singularitez de la France antarctique.* Paris, 1558. Courtesy of the William L. Clements Library, University of Michigan.)

Fig. 4. John White: *A land Tort* [oise] *wᶜʰ the Savages esteeme above all other Torts.* (Courtesy of The British Museum.)

Fig. 5. Laurens Bloch: *View of New Amsterdam,*
1650. (Courtesy of The New-York Historical
Society.)

Fig. 6. Jean-Baptiste Michel Le Bouteux, *View of the
Camp of Mr. Law's Concession at New Biloxi, coast
of Louisiana* (water color, 1720). (Courtesy of the
Edward E. Ayer Collection, Newberry Library,
Chicago.)

Fig. 7. *Governor Pieter Stuyvesant* (ca. 1660-1670). (Courtesy of The New-York Historical Society.)

Fig. 8. Mark Catesby: *Ivory-billed Woodpecker* (copper engraving, hand colored). From Mark Catesby, *The Natural History of Carolina, Florida and the Bahama Islands* ..., London, 1731-42. (Courtesy of the William L. Clements Library, University of Michigan.)

Left: Fig. 9. Freake Limner:
Mrs. Freake and baby Mary
(ca. 1674). (Privately owned.
Photograph courtesy of the
Worcester Art Museum.)

Below: Fig. 10. Captain
Thomas Smith: *Self Portrait*.
(Courtesy of the Worcester
Art Museum.)

58

Fig. 13. Jeremiah Theus: *William Wragg* (ca. 1740-1745). (Courtesy of The Detroit Institute of Arts.)

Opposite page, top: Fig. 11. Gustavus Hesselius: *Bacchus and Ariadne* (ca. 1720-1730). (Courtesy of The Detroit Institute of Arts.)

Opposite page, bottom: Fig. 12. John Smibert: *Bishop George Berkeley and his Family* (1729). (Courtesy of the Yale University Art Gallery.)

Right: Fig. 14. Charles Bridges: *Maria Taylor Byrd*. (Courtesy of The Metropolitan Museum of Art.)

Left: Fig. 15. Robert Feke: *General Samuel Waldo* (ca. 1748). (Courtesy of The Bowdoin College Museum of Fine Arts.)

Below: Fig. 16. Schuyler Painter: *Pieter Schuyler* (ca. 1700-1710). (Courtesy of the Mayor's Office, Albany, New York.)

Above: Fig. 17. Joseph Badger: *Mrs. John Edwards* (ca. 1750). (Courtesy of the Museum of Fine Arts, Boston.)

Right: Fig. 18. John Greenwood: *Jersey Nanny* (engraving, 1748). (Courtesy of Henry L. Shattuck, Boston.)

Fig. 19. John Greenwood: *American Sea Captains Carousing in Surinam* (1757-1758). (Courtesy of the City Art Museum of St. Louis.)

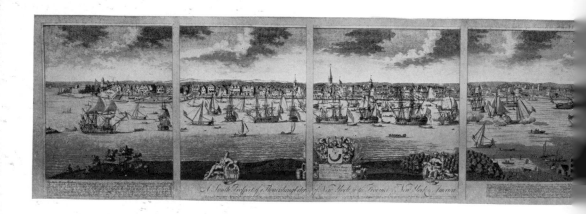

Fig. 20. William Burgis: *A South Prospect of Ye Flourishing City of New York in the Province of New York in America* (engraving, 1716-1718). (Courtesy of Harris D. Colt, New York; photograph courtesy of The Metropolitan Museum of Art.)

Fig. 21. Joseph Blackburn: *Mary Warner* (ca. 1760). (Courtesy of Warner House, Portsmouth, N. H.)

Fig. 22. John Wollaston: *Portrait of a Lady*. (Courtesy of Mrs. Wendell Phillips Colton, New York.)

Fig. 23. William Williams: *Husband and Wife in a Land-scape* (1775). (Courtesy of The Henry Francis du Pont Winterthur Museum.)

Fig. 24. John Singleton Copley: *Mary and Elizabeth Royall* (ca. 1758). (Courtesy of the Museum of Fine Arts, Boston.)

Fig. 25. John Singleton Copley:
Ezekiel Goldthwait (ca. 1770).
(Courtesy of the Museum of Fine
Arts, Boston.)

Fig. 26. John Singleton Copley:
Col. William Montresor (ca. 1772).
(Courtesy of The Detroit Institute
of Arts.)

Fig. 27. John Singleton Copley: *Mrs.
Sylvanus Bourne* (1766). (Courtesy of
The Metropolitan Museum of Art.)

Opposite page, bottom: Fig. 29. Charles Willson Peale:
Peale Family Group (1773). (Courtesy of The New-York
Historical Society.)

Fig. 28. Matthew Pratt: *The American Academy* (1765). (Courtesy of The Metropolitan
Museum of Art.)

Fig. 30. William Dunlap: *The Artist Showing His Picture of a Scene from Hamlet to His Parents* (1788). (Courtesy of The New-York Historical Society.)

Fig. 31. William Bartram: *A Beautiful Fly of East Florida*. (Courtesy of The British Museum, Natural History.)

painter. His works seem today so thin and lacking in characterization that one finds it hard to believe they once seemed fresh, gay and fashionable, and exerted an immense influence.

Yet wherever they went in the colonies, Wollaston and Blackburn found sitters eager to be painted by them and young colonial painters eager to adopt their new manner. In part, their success was one of fashion: they brought the new mode from London to the colonies. Thus they illustrate not only the importance of forms in art but the fact that forms are diffused by means easily forgotten afterward—by men of very modest talent, or by teachers who are not themselves successful painters, or by engravings, small carvings, photographs, or mediocre reproductions. The migration of ideas can be very baffling in the history of art if one forgets how modestly they travel, and looks only for great personalities and obvious sources of influence.

But Wollaston and Blackburn were also in their time an improvement. The Baroque portrait formula introduced by Gustavus Hesselius, Bridges, Smibert, and Feke had become intolerably wooden and dull in the hands of their followers. When one sees a pair of Blackburn's portraits in their fine Rococo frames, like those of *Timothy Fitch* and *Mrs. Fitch* in the dining room of the Pingree House, Salem (now part of the Essex Institute), one discovers the secret of his success. However unsatisfactory as studies of character, his portraits are pretty and graceful decorations compared with Greenwood or Badger; while Wollaston at his most perfunctory was far above the local successors of Bridges. The coming generation of American-born painters studied intently the work of these two migrants. It is not surprising, for they were teachers of the craft of painting.

There were other migrant artists who brought a faint touch of Rococo graces to America without exerting so wide an influence. Lawrence Kilburn (1720-1775), a Danish painter whose name was originally Lorenz Kielbrunn, reached New York from London in 1754. Advertising that he had "just arrived from London" he said that "he don't doubt of pleasing in taking a true likeness, and finishing the drapery in a proper manner, and also in the choice of attitudes suitable to each person's age and sex." Suitable attitudes were his stock in trade and do not seem to have brought him great success, for in his will, drawn in 1770, he described himself as a merchant.

Another migrant painter named Thomas McIlworth, who turned up in New York city in 1757 and was active there and in the region of Schenectady and Albany until 1767, is more interesting. He painted costumes in the Wollaston manner but he observed faces closely and left us a few forceful and convincing likenesses of frontier wardens like the Schuylers and Livingstons and the merchant aristocracy of the river province.

William Williams, an English painter, was active in Philadelphia in 1746-1747 and befriended Benjamin West as a boy. He advertised in the *Pennsylvania Journal and Weekly Advertiser*, January 13, 1763:

William Williams, Being lately returned from the West Indies, desires to ac-
quaint the Publick that he now lives in Loxley's Court, at the Sign of Hogarth's
Head, his former place of residence, where he intends to carry on his Business,
viz, Painting in General. Also an Evening School for the instruction of Polite
Youth, in the different branches of Drawing, and to sound the Hautboy, German
and common Flutes. . . .[2]

Williams was a curious figure of varied talents, as this advertisement implies:
sailor, painter-novelist, musician, and wanderer. He was one of the *petits
maîtres* of the English conversation piece, and of them all perhaps the most
naïve. His conversation pieces painted in America, like the *Husband and
Wife in a Landscape* (Henry Francis du Pont Winterthur Museum) (Fig.
23) are sensitive in color, bold and even impressive in design, and absurd in
drawing to the point of caricature. His most urbane works are the portraits of
William and *David Hall* (Winterthur), the sons of the printer who was Benjamin Franklin's friend and partner. The aristocratic ideal in Williams' hands
becomes a conventional but sweet and flowerlike sentiment. His caricature
of the deformed and eccentric reformer, *Benjamin Lay*, engraved by the
American engraver, Henry Dawkins, shows another aspect of Williams' curious and naïve art. With the Revolution he disappears from the American
scene.

Another migrant, a Scot named Cosmo Alexander, came to Newport,
Rhode Island, about 1765 and worked there until 1772. Of all these migrants,
Alexander was the most interesting observer of character. He painted in a
style almost Whistlerian in its muted delicacy of color and was capable of
subtle characterizations, such as the *Mrs. James Manning* (1770) (Brown
University, Providence), a charming study of a spirited woman. But he arrived too late and traveled too little to have a wide influence in colonial
painting. He did some interesting portraits, and on his return to Edinburgh in
1772 took with him a talented boy of seventeen named Gilbert Stuart, in
whom he had taken an interest. Unfortunately for Stuart, Alexander died
within the year, leaving the boy stranded and friendless in Edinburgh.

But now there were native-born talents pushing forward, who were, for
the first time, to become clearly more important in our story than the migrants. Not all of the native-born were to rise above the level of good competent workmen; but a few had not only talent but individuality and, best of
all, imagination.

A good competent craftsman was John Hesselius (1728-1778), the son
of Gustavus, who worked in Philadelphia, Maryland, and Virginia. He at
first followed Feke's style; later, after Wollaston had left the country, he

---

    [2] Alfred Coxe Prime, *Arts and Crafts in Philadelphia*, Topsfield, Massachusetts, Wayside
Press, 1929, p. 13.

modeled himself so closely upon the English painter's pictures that it is hard
to tell one from the other, except by the coloring and method of lighting.

John Mare, born in New York in 1739, was the brother-in-law of William Williams but formed his style upon Wollaston's portraits in that city,
adopting his ruddy palette and vigorous modeling. Until the Metropolitan
Museum of Art recently discovered his most ambitious work, a *Young Man*
(1767) in frosty blue suit, standing before a claret red curtain and leaning
on a handsome Chippendale chair, Mare had had the odd fate to be best remembered for a painting of a housefly. In 1767 he had painted a portrait
of *John Keteltas* (collection the Misses Wetmore), a bust portrait in a painted
oval of a man with his right hand thrust into his waistcoat. On the white
linen cuff, conspicuous against the dark coat, rests a housefly—the earliest
known American example (as George Groce pointed out) of *trompe l'œil*.
Mare seems to have been active in New York and Albany and is last recorded
in 1795.[3]

In Philadelphia and Boston there were two youths of greater talents,
Benjamin West and John Singleton Copley, who were struggling to teach
themselves to paint in the 1750's from the portraits and engravings available
to them. West imitated Gustavus Hesselius in his portrait, *Jane Galloway*
(ca.1757) (Historical Society of Pennsylvania), and Copley learned what he
could from Smibert and Greenwood. To these youths, Wollaston and Blackburn offered suggestions which they seized on greedily, absorbed, and
quickly transcended.

With West and Copley we come to a new stage in the development of
painting in America. It is an error to believe (although it has often been so
stated) that painting appeared in America because there was a colonial aristocracy that wanted portraits. It was the other way around: painting appeared
because there was an impulse to use the imaginative language of vision, and
the painters adapted themselves as best they could to the world they lived in.
One might say the history of American painting proves that a certain number
of individuals out of the population are born with a predisposition to paint,
as there are a certain number with a predisposition to be professional men or
craftsmen or soldiers. This impulse showed itself very early in the American
colonies and flowed naturally into the kind of painting and direction of attention prevailing. From the first it had to struggle against limitations of environment. Now the time had arrived when talents were to appear too great
to be contained within the limits of colonial life.

John Singleton Copley (1738-1815) was seventeen when Blackburn arrived in Boston in 1755. His mother had married as her second husband
Peter Pelham, the engraver, and Copley grew up in an atmosphere of prints,

[3] Helen Burr Smith, *The New-York Historical Society Quarterly*, XXXV (1951), pp.
354-375.

pictures, and music that must have been helpful to a youth very hesitant and self-doubtful by nature; it helped him find his vocation early and without hesitation. He had studied Smibert's works and the copies of Poussin and Van Dyck in his painting room; he had learned what he could from Badger and Greenwood. But the luster of Blackburn's color, the flash of his textures, the charming artificiality of his poses were both captivating and stimulating. In 1756 he followed Blackburn's style so closely in a portrait of *Jane Browne* (National Gallery of Art, Washington) that he copied even the style of signature the Englishman used.[4] Later in the same year he used one of Blackburn's Rococo poses, a shepherdess with her lamb, in a portrait of *Ann Tyng* (Boston, Museum of Fine Arts). Yet such is the difference between a great talent and a limited one that Copley had already surpassed his model. His Rococo shepherdess in her white dress, seated on a green bank, is more richly painted, more plastic, more effective than anything done by Blackburn.

This is a clear illustration of the relation of forms to imagination in art. Painting is a language; and to use it well one needs to know the language in all its forms. The language itself, however, may be used and passed along by painters of little creative power. Copley, seizing upon the empty Rococo forms of Blackburn, poured into them an imaginative power to observe and to experience reality that filled them with the glow, vitality, and mystery of life. In the ten years after his first contact with Blackburn, Copley created the most brilliant and convincing expression of the aristocratic ideal that American eighteenth-century painting was to produce. His double portrait of *Mary and Elizabeth Royall* (ca.1758) (Fig. 24) (Boston, Museum of Fine Arts) shows two little girls on a couch. One, in a blue dress, holds a hummingbird on her fingertip; one, in white, holds a puppy; swathed around and enframing them, wine-colored and golden draperies flow to the floor. The picture has all the elegance and artifice of Rococo taste, infused with the bright animation of two happy little girls. A second example: his portrait of *John Grey* (The Detroit Institute of Arts) takes a man not overly distinguished in himself, and gives to his image the dignity and decorative grace of life on an ideal plane. Grey was a Boston merchant whose life is interesting mainly for its tragic end. He was a Loyalist, and when the Revolution broke out, removed to England. After a few years in London, he went to India and invested his funds in an indigo plantation and there, living alone in a far land, he was poisoned by a treacherous servant. Copley painted him as a silent, reserved figure, standing against a dark curtain and column, in a portrait notable for its elegance and melancholy.

Copley also made powerful use of another Rococo form which he may have seen in Blackburn but which he undoubtedly studied in engravings, also. This was the portrait of a person in the setting of his daily life—what the

---

[4] Barbara Neville Parker and Anne Bolling Wheeler, *J. S. Copley*, Boston, Museum of Fine Arts, 1938, p. 5.

French call the *portrait d'apparat*. He learned to use this so well that there leaps to the mind's eye, when one thinks of Copley, a crowd of people caught in the midst of life, speaking with characteristic expression and lively gesture —*Mrs. Sylvanus Bourne* (The Metropolitan Museum of Art) (Fig. 27), who has laid down her book for a moment, her face alight with wisdom and good humor, as if to say, "There, the man has sense . . ."; *The Boy with the Squirrel* (private collection) leaning in childish reverie on a table and playing with the chain of a pet squirrel; *Robert Chamblett Hooper* (private collection), the great merchant of Marblehead, seated at his desk examining his correspondence; *Mr. and Mrs. Thomas Mifflin* (The Historical Society of Pennsylvania) (Plate IV) talking pleasantly during an afternoon at home; the shrewd old town clerk of Boston, *Ezekiel Goldthwait* (Museum of Fine Arts, Boston) (Fig. 25) who has swung around in his chair, quill pen in hand, to answer an inquiry or settle a point of discussion; and a crowd of other unforgettable characterizations. Within the discipline of the aristocratic ideal Copley became a penetrating master of human character.

Copley developed a special understanding of old people, rich in character, and of men who work with their minds as merchants, lawyers, engineers do. In force of characterization and economy of means he never surpassed a series of simple bust portraits painted on a brief visit to New York in 1771-1772. One example I am fond of is a portrait of *Col. William Montresor* (The Detroit Institute of Arts) (Fig. 26). Colonel Montresor was the chief engineer of the British forces in America, who had built the famous forts of Sir Geoffrey Amherst's advance into Canada—Fort Edward, Fort William Henry, Fort Ticonderoga, Crown Point—and stayed in the American service until the outbreak of the Revolution, when he resigned and returned to England. Copley painted him leaning on a tree stump, holding a book. Nothing is wasted in this study of a keen, capable, intelligent man; it is a masterpiece of concentrated and imaginative realism. When Copley later painted people of leisure and fashion in London, he was never so happy in characterization: he did not understand them as he did the merchants and professional men with whom he grew up, or the wise old women of Boston.

The effort it cost Copley to create an art of such force and authority, unsupported by any comparable craft or tradition of art around him, is impossible to estimate. He had an instinct, one may say, for the large movement in drawing, for plasticity, for luminous color. He very early learned from Blackburn the eighteenth-century painter's method of painting flesh in three simple tones of green, rose, and cream-white; and he could study chiaroscuro in prints. As one follows his development one sees many unsuccessful pictures, many awkward experiments, that reveal the difficulties through which he struggled. The one quality of the coloristic style he failed to master was atmosphere, although the hard, clear quality of his figures is very handsome in its own way and as uncompromising as his drawing of character. That he was able to achieve a style of first quality, by the standards of any school, in light, form, drawing, expression, far beyond anything in the artistic life or in the pictures around him, is evidence of extraordinary powers.

No one with great abilities is unaware of them. Copley knew he had great talents. He was ambitious. He read, in the books available to him—Du Fresnoy's *De Arte Graphica*, Roger de Piles's *The Art of Painting*, Horace Walpole's *Anecdotes of Painting in England*, David Webb's *Inquiry into the Beauties of Painting*—and he saw, in his engravings of antique sculpture and of the Italian masters, that there was a whole world of art beyond what he had already mastered.

Benjamin West's evolution in Philadelphia was more meteoric than Copley's in Boston. West (1738-1820) had supreme self-confidence: Copley was hesitant, self-distrustful, timid. West gained his first knowledge of painting from the painters he could see in Philadelphia, from William Williams, from Gustavus Hesselius, perhaps later from Wollaston. But West's portrait of the young *Thomas Mifflin* (ca.1758-1759) (Historical Society of Pennsylvania) shows that he, like Copley, had powers that his models lacked. Crude and immature as this picture is in many ways, it has a boldness of composition and luminosity of color such as one does not find in Wollaston. But, happening on a *Saint Ignatius* of the school of Murillo, taken from a Spanish prize ship, West too realized that there were forms of art which he could study only abroad. He determined to go to Italy and, in order to earn passage money, set out for New York, where he thought he could charge higher fees for his portraits. Instead, a group of Philadelphia merchants subscribed the necessary funds. "It is a pity," one of them wrote, "such a genius should be cramped for the want of a little cash." So in 1759 West sailed for Leghorn as the first of a long line of American art students who were to go to Italy to study the great masters of their profession. He never returned.

After three years in Italy, spent chiefly in Rome, where he enjoyed a great social success, he journeyed north to London arriving June 20, 1763. There he met with such encouragement that he remained the rest of his life: Philadelphia could offer no such opportunities for his talents. It is hard now for us to imagine how natural it was that West, meeting with success in London, should stay there. But in 1763 London was the capital of his own country, Pennsylvania was a province of the British crown; Philadelphia was the second largest English provincial city. It was as normal for an ambitious youth to go from Philadelphia to London as to go from Dublin, or Edinburgh, or Bristol.

At first Copley tried a different method of self-improvement. He sent a painting, *The Boy with the Squirrel*, at the urging of a sea-captain friend, to the exhibition of the Society of Artists in London (1766) and wrote to ask

Sir Joshua Reynolds and West for criticism. Reynolds praised it highly but criticized its lack of atmosphere: "A little hardness in the drawing, coldness in the shades, an over-minuteness. . . . If you are capable of producing such a piece by the mere efforts of your own genius, with the advantages of example and instruction you would have in Europe you would be a valuable acquisition to the art and one of the first painters in the world, provided you could receive these aids before its was too late in life, and before your manner and taste were corrupted or fixed by working in your little way in Boston." Copley's response was to paint the portrait of *Mary Warner* (1767) (Toledo Museum of Art) in which he tried to imagine what the aerial richness of color recommended by Reynolds might be. But Reynolds found the second picture less successful than the first; and so did West.

One must try to imagine the deep discouragement of an ambitious young man at finding that he had not understood the suggestions of Reynolds and West but had made his style, apparently, worse rather than better. He had surpassed everything to be seen around:

In this Country as you rightly observe [he had written West on November 12, 1766], there is no examples of Art, except what is to be met with in a few prints indiferently exicuted, from which it is impossible to learn much . . .

It would give me inexpressable pleasure to make a trip to Europe, where I should see those fair examples of art that have stood so long the admiration of all the world. the Paintings, Sculptors and Basso Relievos that adorn Italy, and which you have had the pleasure of making Your Studies from would, I am sure, annimate my pencil, and inable me to acquire that bold free and gracefull stile of Painting that will, if ever, come much slower from the mere dictates of Nature, which has hither too been my only instructor. . . . I think myself peculiarly unlucky in Liveing in a place into which there has not been one portrait brought that is worthy to be call'd a Picture within my memory . . .[5]

West urged him, as Reynolds had done, to study in Europe before it was too late. But in that direction, too, lay difficulties. He wrote to West, January 17, 1768:

I should be glad to go to Europe, but cannot think of it without a very good prospect of doing as well there as I can here. You are sensable that three hundred Guineas a Year, which is my present income, is a pretty living in America, and I cannot think You will advise me to give it up without a good prospect of something at least equel to it . . .[6]

And he begged West to tell him frankly what possibility there was for him to become as successful in London.

The dilemma of the man with a family to support, the craftsman with a

[5] *Letters and Papers of John Singleton Copley and Henry Pelham, 1739-1776*. Boston, The Massachusetts Historical Society, 1914, p. 51.
[6] *Op. cit.,* p. 68.

skill to be learned, and the artist obscurely aware of powers within himself that demanded their rights also, could hardly be more clearly stated than in these letters. Another gnawing sense of discontent is hinted at in an undated and unaddressed draft of a letter (in the Copley-Pelham letters):

A taste of painting is too much wanting in Boston to afford any kind of help; and was it not for preserving the resemblance of particular persons, painting would not be known in the place. The people generally regard it as no more than any other useful trade, as they sometimes term it, like that of carpenter, tailor, or shoemaker, not as one of the most noble arts in the world, which is not a little mortifying to me. While the arts are so regarded, I can hope for nothing either to encourage or assist me in my studies but what I receive from a thousand leagues distance, and be my improvements what they will, I shall not be benefited by them in this country, neither in point of fortune or fame.

In point of fortune or fame. In point of fortune Copley was doing very well: but in point of fame—what was it to be the leading painter of Boston, where people thought his art no more than a trade? Another American, West, had left America for London and become a celebrity, even a favorite of the king. West was famous; Copley no more than the portrait painter of a remote provincial town. Jealousy of West haunted Copley throughout his life.

Ultimately, after seven more years in America, during which he rose to the heights of his American style, Copley reluctantly left America to study abroad. It was a hard decision to leave his home, his pregnant wife, his children, his position. Perhaps he would never have done so had not Boston itself become miserable and insecure. Copley had married into one of the leading Tory families of Boston: his father-in-law was one of the merchants to whom the tea was consigned that was thrown into the harbor by the famous Boston Tea Party. Copley, a gentle, timorous man who hated violence, had friends and sympathies on both sides. He made a great effort, as a man of peace, to bring the two sides together, speaking in raging town meetings, talking with Adams, Hancock, and Warren, arguing with the Tory merchants who had taken refuge in the British fortress in the harbor, and failed. For reward he was several times threatened in the streets of Boston. He did not foresee civil war. But he could see that these civil riots had ruined his profession for the moment. It was better to go abroad, to study and improve himself.

In June, 1774, he sailed for London, on the road to Italy, leaving his family in Boston. He had not decided to leave America. That decision was made for him later by circumstance. He made the Grand Tour of Paris, Rome, Florence, Parma, Mantua, Venice, Amsterdam, Brussels, Antwerp, studying his art voraciously, and writing homesick letters to America. In the meantime the American Revolution had begun; Massachusetts was the seat of war. Boston was no place, he saw, to support a family by portrait painting.

He wrote for his wife to join him in London and settled where fate had directed that he could practice his art and support his family, but his heart was with the colonies.

A disparity had grown up between the talents and aspirations of the artists born in America and the primitive state of their profession. There were neither teachers nor collections of art for them to study in America. There was no sale for anything but portraits. Both Copley and West were too big for their limited setting. They went abroad to learn more of their art, and, in the end, remained there. This has frequently been treated by American writers as an act of deplorable moral weakness, as if they had been untrue to themselves—which is to read the emotions of later times into the eighteenth century. Copley and West loved their native land. When the colonies revolted against the absolute rule of Britain, their sympathies were American. But art, proverbially a jealous mistress, led them elsewhere. The opportunities and rewards for their talents were so much greater in London that they could not afford to come back to America. The careers of other American artists in their own and in the next generation confirm the wisdom of their course. This disparity between talent and environment was to trouble the course of American painting for a long time. In this period, it split the artistic life of America into two.

Benjamin West was born under a fortunate star. In spite of the crowd of talents in London, there was no one to compete with him in the style of historical painting he had learned in Rome. Within five years he had attracted the attention of King George III, and his fame and future were assured. The story of West as a pioneer of neoclassicism and subsequently of romantic painting belongs to the chapters on those movements. But as the first American artist established in Europe he served as a magnet to attract others. Almost as soon as he was settled in London, other American painters came to join him. He was a man of great generosity of character, unfailingly kind and helpful to all young artists who sought his aid. As his career gained momentum, he received commissions for enormous historical canvases in which he could give small parts to assistants. He also became a collector of art, so that his house was a gallery (both of his own pictures and those of greater, earlier masters) which was open to art students. In those days there was no public gallery in London. His studio and home thus became the first effective American art school. Pratt, Delanoy, Benbridge, Stuart, Dunlap, Earl, Wright, Peale, Trumbull, all worked and studied there. It is a mistake, however, to think that they all learned the same thing.

The Americans who came first, in the 1760's, were West's own contemporaries in point of age. When West's father took his son's fiancée, Betsey Shewall, to London in 1764, he was accompanied by a young painter from Philadelphia named Matthew Pratt, who was a relative of the bride. Pratt stayed four years with West, from 1764 to 1768. Abraham Delanoy of New York was there from about 1766 to 1770. Henry Benbridge, of Philadelphia, stayed there the winter of 1769-1770 on his way home from Italy. Charles Willson Peale also was there in 1766-1767.

The effect of these studies in London was not to bring to America West's neoclassic style (which was hardly as yet formed) but the English provincial Rococo style, such as was practiced by the men we think of as the *little masters* of the English conversation piece, like Arthur Devis or Benjamin Wilson. These English artists did not paint with Reynolds' full-loaded brush and rich compositional imagery. Their art was simpler and more direct than that of the great, fashionable portrait painters of London: they drew with precise, clear outlines and painted with clean, fresh, luminous colors, in a style not unlike what the Americans were used to. In fact the painters of this simple and idyllic school, with its combination of realism and delicate formality, were close, in many ways, to American taste. They found their chief patrons among the British merchants, professional classes, and country gentry who were, of all the English, closest in temperament to their American counterparts. When Benjamin Franklin went to London in 1757, one of the things he wished to do was to "get all our little family drawn in one conversation piece"; [7] and he took with him for that purpose likenesses of the members left behind at home. The painter to whom he went, Benjamin Wilson (like Franklin an early student of electricity and ultimately inventor of a rival lightning rod), evidently did not like to work from other men's portraits and persuaded Franklin the group portrait would not turn out well.[8] In its stead Wilson painted the life-sized bust of Franklin which is now in the White House.

The most famous of American conversation pieces is *The American Academy* (1765) (Fig. 28), painted by Matthew Pratt (1734-1805). It represents a group of young American painters working together in West's studio. At the left, West is criticizing a drawing by Pratt; the other two artists have not been identified. This is a typical eighteenth-century conversation piece— a group portrait of figures, represented smaller than life, and engaged in the activities of their daily life. The precise, slightly naïve drawing and the luminous color are characteristic of Pratt. He was not a young beginner at this time: he was thirty when he went to London; he had studied first in Philadelphia under James Claypoole (an active and prominent figure, whose works have been almost totally lost) and had painted portraits for eight years in Philadelphia and New York before going to England. He worked with West during the years 1764-1766, and painted portraits in Bristol 1767-1768 before returning to Philadelphia. After his return Pratt painted a few modest por-

[7] Letter to Mrs. Franklin, November 22, 1757.
[8] Letter to Mrs. Franklin, June 18, 1758.

traits, but found it necessary to supplement these by painting signs. Both Dunlap and Neagle speak of these with enthusiasm, saying that he made Philadelphia remarkable for the beauty and skill displayed in its signs.

Henry Benbridge (1744-ca.1812) was another Philadelphian who did not accomplish as much as one would expect from his talents. Apparently he had studied art first in Philadelphia with Wollaston; in 1764 he went to Italy, where he studied with Mengs and Batoni. In 1768, James Boswell of Auchinleck, traveling in Italy, commissioned Benbridge to go from Florence to Corsica to paint a portrait of General Paoli. He took the portrait to exhibit in London in 1769 and while there introduced himself to Franklin and West. He exhibited a portrait of Franklin at the Royal Academy in 1770. When he returned to Philadelphia, Franklin wrote a letter for Benbridge to take to Mrs. Franklin (July 17, 1770), saying: "If Mr. Benbridge did not from Affection chuse to return and settle in Philadelphia, he certainly might live in England extremely well by his profession." Perhaps on the strength of this recommendation Benbridge was elected to the American Philosophical Society in 1771.

Benbridge brought home a richer, more sophisticated style than Pratt's, capable of large and skillful group portraits like the *Gordon Family* (painted in Philadelphia in 1771). Later in the year 1771 he moved for the sake of his health to Charleston, South Carolina, where, after this promising beginning, he settled down to succeed Theüs as the local portrait painter. He seems to have settled down all too well.

Another life-size conversation piece, by one of West's pupils of the sixties, is the famous *Peale Family Group* (Fig. 29) (1773 with later additions) (The New-York Historical Society) showing the artist giving a drawing lesson to his brother, St. George Peale, who is sketching their mother at the other end of the table. Seven other figures and a dog complete this cheerful and animated scene "emblematical," as Peale said, "of family concord." Charles Willson Peale's pupil and brother, James, subsequently became the most prolific painter of conversation pieces in America.

William Dunlap's little picture of *The Artist Showing His Picture of a Scene from Hamlet to His Parents* (1788) (Fig. 30) (The New-York Historical Society), is one of the most attractive examples of the genre produced in America. William Dunlap (1766-1839) went to London in 1784 to study with West. His autobiography, in his *History of the Rise and Progress of the Arts of Design in the United States* (1834), gives us a lively picture of an idle apprentice in London. Dunlap's career as a painter was, however, divided into two periods, with a long interval between. For a few years after his return he painted in the late Rococo manner of this family group. Then he became interested in the theater and enjoyed a twenty-year career as playwright and theatrical manager, during which he did not paint. When he resumed painting again after the bankruptcy of his theatrical enterprise, it was in another period and style of art. Yet as late as 1823, when he returned to the conversation form in his *Scene from "The Spy" by Cooper* (New York State Historical Association, Cooperstown), he produced a work still of the eighteenth century in manner and form.

Abraham Delanoy (ca. 1740-ca.1790) we know as a pupil of West, and a painter in the somewhat stiff style of the conversation masters, from his portraits of *Benjamin West* and *Mrs. West* (1766) (The New-York Historical Society). He seems to have been by nature a modest follower and a man who had little fortune in life. After his return from England in 1767 he settled in New York, where he found it necessary to fall back upon painting signs and keeping a shop to supplement portrait painting.

With the exception of Peale, the careers of the Americans who studied in London in the sixties with West and returned to try to practice their art in America during the troubled years of the Revolution are fragmentary and meager. One should consider the problem that faced Copley and West in the light of the record of those who returned. The urge toward painting at this moment of our history was far greater in America than were the resources of American society to reward or support its artists.

Other painters were developing who had no chance to go to London and enjoy the benefit of West's encouragement, who show the variations in technique to be expected of the "untrained professional."

John Durand (fl.1767-1782) came of a Huguenot family settled in Connecticut. His training is unknown but he used in his portraits a formula of Rococo elegance such as he might have seen in the work of some one like Kilburn. Like all untrained professionals, he saw in terms of outlines and flat areas of color, rather than of solid shapes surrounded by airy space; yet within his limits he was an artist of innate elegance and style. His best pictures have a crispness of outline, an interest of pattern, and a distinctive frosty color palette that are marks of a truly artistic sensibility. His portrait group of *The Rapalje Children* (ca.1768) (Fig.33) (The New-York Historical Society), a work both charming in its style and diverting in its naïveté, is his most ambitious painting. Like many other American portrait painters, he found it necessary to move from town to town in search of sitters. He is documented in New York city in 1767, in Virginia in 1770-1772 and 1775-1782, and in Milford, Connecticut, in 1772.

Connecticut was to produce a surprising number of painters in the next half century. Winthrop Chandler (1747-1790) was born near Woodstock, Connecticut, and is supposed to have served his apprenticeship to a painter-artisan in Boston. He was trained, that is, in a tradition of craftsmanship which extended from heraldry to house painting, and from limning portraits to japanning and gilding. Chandler's obituary says: "By profession he was a housepainter, but many good likenesses on canvas show he could guide the pencil of the limner." He painted the portraits of his friends and neighbors in Woodstock and, for a few unfortunate and unhappy years, practiced his art in Worcester, Massachusetts. In experience and in training Chandler could hardly have been more limited; yet his innate powers were those of an artist. He had a gift for the *portrait d'apparat*, for color, for vigorous linear pattern, and for seeing character—and those are no small equipment for any artist. His portrait of the *Reverend Ebenezer Devotion*, seated among his books (1770) (Brookline Historical Society), or of *Mrs. Samuel Chandler* (ca. 1775-1785) (Fig. 32) (Col. and Mrs. E. W. Garbisch), seated in her parlor, enframed in a strange arrangement of drapery, are extraordinary pictorial documents. They are works of skill—but it is an unlettered skill; whereas the intuitive sensibility that speaks through them has power. During the past hundred years we have been surrounded by masses of skillful, dull work, done by well-schooled, clever painters with nothing of interest to say: it is refreshing to the spirit to see work like Chandler's, in which the common ratio of skill to content is reversed. "The world was not his enemy," his obituary went on, "but as is too common, his genius was not matured on the bosom of encouragement. Embarrassment like strong weeds in a garden of delicate flowers, checked his enthusiasms and disheartened the man. Peace to his *manes* [spirit]."

The forms of Rococo painting came across the Atlantic, twice-diluted, in the work of uninspired artists and in small black-and-white engravings. A drive to breathe into them the force and conviction of their own life animated West and Copley, as it did the best of the untrained professionals. Pale, attenuated, esthetic spirits did not become painters in America in the third quarter of the eighteenth century, under so many difficulties and in an atmosphere so lacking in art. Only robust spirits impelled by a fierce inner drive did so. The same earnestness and passion that drove them into painting sent some of them across the sea in search of greater knowledge; impelled others to turn a rustic technique, intended for tin trays or inn signs, into an instrument for painting pictures. Their knowledge of the language of painting was very small, their direction of attention painfully limited. Yet in the course of a quarter-century a style which began in an imported artificial charm and decorative grace was transformed into one of deeply felt humanity. That is the achievement of American Rococo painters.

The study of human personality and the portrait form absorbed almost the whole attention of artists. Landscape and still life occur only enough to show that the thought of them was in the atmosphere but that no strong imaginative impulse had been awakened to explore in these directions.

Decorative landscapes continued to be painted. In New England there seems to have been rather a fashion for landscape painting on the wooden panels that surmounted the fireplaces in American parlors or best bedrooms. A number of crude overmantel paintings of hunting scenes or landscapes exist. One overmantel by Winthrop Chandler represents an imaginary city; another by the same artist is a book still life. In the Southern colonies a few painted rooms have survived, with elaborate Rococo decorations in the paneling, like the room from "Marmion," King George's County, Virginia (Metropolitan Museum of Art). But the people who wished such decorations could also get them in more urbane and attractive form from overseas, in the form of painted wallpapers. These were not the familiar, French, printed scenic papers of the early nineteenth century but an earlier form, *painted* in the Rococo style, after engravings after Panini, Lancret, Vernet, and similar artists. A fine example is the painted wallpaper installed in the Van Renssalaer Manor House at Albany in 1768 (now in The Metropolitan Museum of Art). The Jeremiah Lee house at Marblehead was similarly decorated a little later. In the nature of things, other such papers must have been imported and later destroyed.

An interest in landscape views of towns or famous sights also continued to flourish. The finest views of American eighteenth-century subjects were produced in London. *The Scenographia Americana*, a series of twenty-eight views in line engraving, hand-colored in the fine style of that time, was issued in 1768. It is second in importance and beauty, however, to the series of plates called *The Atlantic Neptune*, prepared for the British Admiralty by J. F. W. Des Barres. Des Barres' plates are in aquatint, a medium just then becoming popular, which was to make the last part of the eighteenth century and the first four decades of the nineteenth the golden age of topographic engravings. *The Atlantic Neptune* was a series of views, maps, and plans of the towns and harbors of the American seaboard, issued at irregular intervals from 1763 to 1784. Stokes and Haskell, in *American Historical Prints*, say that the complete set numbers two hundred and seventy-five separate items, including plates and preliminary leaves.

Compared to Des Barres' crisp, handsome plates, the landscape views of engravers working in America, like Henry Dawkins, Thomas Johnston, or Paul Revere, seem rude enough. A significant development was the appearance of the historical print, a symptom of the eventful times and also of the rising national spirit.

Thomas Johnston (ca.1708-1767) of Boston, a painter, engraver, builder of organs, who also did japanning and similar artisan's work, was one of a numerous family of craftsmen. He engraved views of towns but is remembered chiefly for his *A Prospective Plan of the Battle Fought Near Lake George, Sept. 8, 1755*, engraved after a drawing made by Samuel Blodget (1724-1807), a Boston trader and sutler who was present at the battle. This first historical print engraved in America is a throwback to the mediaeval narrative tradition, for it is really four scenes in one. At the left is the "bloody morning scout" in which King Hendrick and Colonel Ephraim Williams were killed, showing the head of the New England column surrounded by the ambushing French; at the right, a view of the attack on Johnson's camp; while across the top is a map of the Hudson River, and inset plans of Fort William Henry and Fort Edward. A generation later, when Amos Doolittle engraved Ralph Earl's drawings of the Battles of Lexington and Concord, he did the four scenes on four separate plates.

Another landmark in the development of the American historical print is a work of that versatile fellow, Paul Revere (1735-1818), silversmith, engraver, frame maker, and craftsman. His engraving of *A View of Part of the Town of Boston in New England and British Ships of War Landing Their Troops, 1768*, was issued in 1770 and bears a dedication to Lord Townshend, the British minister of colonies, which shows that Revere, like most other Americans at that date, was not yet an advocate of independence. Its steep, bird's-eye perspective is somewhat archaic but the print is a great advance, both in drawing and engraving, over Thomas Johnston's view. It is a more significant engraving than the much more famous *Boston Massacre* (1774).

Another topographic artist was a seaman from Cape Cod, Christian Remick (born 1726—active 1768), who sailed in privateers during the Revolution. Remick did a series of water-color drawings of *The Blockade of the Town of Boston* (1768). He advertised that he was prepared to do "Sea Pieces, Perspective Views, Geographical Plans of Harbours, Sea Coasts, etc.," which places him in the honorable tradition of the explorer-artists.

In this period also came the second important artist-naturalist, William Bartram (1739-1823), the son of the great botanist John Bartram of Philadelphia. William was a born plant hunter and artist. In 1755 his father wrote: "Botany and drawing are his darling delight: am afraid he can't settle to any business else." He was self-taught, drawing plants as his father had collected them, by instinct. In 1765 he accompanied his father on a plant-hunting expedition to Florida and made many drawings. After his father's death, he took another long plant-collecting trip in 1773-1777 for Dr. John Fothergill of London, for whom his father had also collected. He ranged on this trip from North Carolina south to central Florida and west to Mississippi, much of the journey through Indian country. A manuscript report to Dr. Fothergill, with thirty-eight drawings bound in with it, is preserved in the British Museum. Fourteen years later he wrote, and illustrated his own drawings, one of the most famous and influential American books of the eighteenth century. *Travels Through North and South Carolina, Georgia, East and West Florida, the Cherokee Country, the Extensive Territories of the Muscogulges, or Creek Confederacy, and the Country of the Chactaws; Containing an Account of the Soil and Natural Productions of Those Regions, Together with Observations on the Manners of the Indians*, published in Philadelphia in 1791, had seven European editions within ten years: London (1792-1794); Dublin (1793); Berlin (1793); Haarlem (1794-1797); Paris

(1799-1801). The charm of its description of tropical forests and the life of the wilderness made it eagerly read by poets like Coleridge and Southey, while its information was welcomed by scholars.

In 1803 Bartram did the majority of the copper plates illustrating his friend Benjamin S. Barton's *Elements of Botany*, the first elementary botanical book written in this country. He also illustrated another more ambitious work by Barton, *The Prodromus of a Flora of the States of New York, New Jersey, Delaware, Maryland and Virginia*, of which Dr. Barton destroyed every copy after five hundred had been printed.

These drawings by Bartram, such as *A Beautiful Fly of East Florida* (the imperial moth and a marsh pink) (Fig. 31) are delicate and exact in line, often quite without composition, but vital and graceful. They have the artless spontaneity of things seen in excitement for the first time.

The Revolution cut across the years in which our art assumed an independent stature. They were years of confusion and of hard decisions. Decades of agitation and war and the exhaustion that follows on the disruption of social and economic life were not favorable to artists. Matthew Pratt, who found it necessary to eke out portrait painting by doing signs, Delanoy, who kept a shop, are typical of how hard it was for artists to make a professional career during these years. "In point of fortune and fame," the rich, continuous production of Copley and West in London confirms the wisdom of their choice.

The difficulties through which our art was then passing were not, however, solely the result of war. The artistic life of Europe was made possible by the efforts of hundreds of years, slowly building up the institutions, skills, and social habits that now sustained it. Artists appeared in this country in the second half of the century who had great talents and great aspirations. More than one short generation, or two, would be required to build the foundations to sustain those aspirations.

Yet, incomplete and confused as the period was, it confirms what had before been only a latent suggestion: that American painting, though closely related to English and Continental painting, had already a character of its own. In the Baroque period, such differences as there were might have been caused by lack of skill or training. In the Rococo age, painters emerged on a level of unquestioned skill; and it becomes clear that a new national temperament and life were finding voice. American painting had not the inherited grace of the French, the gaiety and grandeur of the Italian, nor the aristocratic decorative tone of the English Rococo painting. Yet it had its own integrity. The people of America were something new. They breathed a new air. Their art was that of a strong, earnest, intelligent, middle-class society, somewhat sober and limited in its interests, but thoughtful, and of deep, earnest feelings.

CHAPTER 6

NEOCLASSICISM: THE IDEAL AND THE REAL

THE AMERICAN REVOLUTION CREATED A NEW NATION IN THE UNITED STATES OF America and determined the political separation of the American continent from Europe. Beyond that, in the history of ideas, it was the first act in a profound change that, bursting out violently in France, engulfed the whole of Europe and altered the life and outlook of Western civilization. The American and French Revolutions put a period to the Renaissance epoch. The Western world entered a new phase of its development, a phase in which we are living today.

With the second half of the eighteenth century the aristocratic ideal, having played its part, began to disappear. In France, the country that for a century had enjoyed the intellectual leadership of Europe, a new ideal of society appeared, optimistic, expansive, and most attractive to generous minds. The democratic rationalism of Americans like Franklin and Jefferson was inspired by the ideas of the French encyclopedists, who, inspired in turn by English thought of the period of Newton, Locke, and Hume, put an end to the theory of divine right and the aristocratic ideal of society. As that ideal faded, the eighteenth century's other enthusiasm for the classical world of Greece and Rome grew. Political rebels searching for a new form of government found their model in the republics of antiquity. Moralists searching for a new theory of society to take the place of rank and birth found it in the ideal of *citizen*, the responsible individual member of the *civis* or city-republic of the ancient world. Theorists of art searching for a new form to replace the Rococo found it in the imitation of antiquity. As the radiance of the Sun King faded away, the world of men's minds was illuminated instead by another dream called Antiquity.

As France approached the last quarter of the eighteenth century, a restless urge arose to do away with the old forms of life and to find new ones.

The Western mind was discovering fascinating new intellectual tools in the new-born discipline of history and its companion science, archaeology. The excavations at Pompeii and Herculaneum, begun in the second quarter of the eighteenth century, had opened a world of marvels. The educated classes of Europe had for centuries been educated upon the works of the Greek and Roman poets and historians, who offer the mind a spectacle of human thought unsurpassed in variety, urbanity, and elevation of feeling. Archaeology now resurrected the long-lost physical appearance of that vanished world in enchanting completeness. At the same time, the mental image of the past was transformed by writers like Gibbon and Voltaire who, instead of writing a mere chronicle, used a comparative and critical study of sources to build up a living portrait of civilization.

The rational, skeptical minds of eighteenth-century liberal thinkers had no conception of the unconscious habits, the deep emotional needs and loyalties that bind men to their past and hold society together. Dissatisfied with their world, they thought it an easy thing to change it. In America Jefferson and Tom Paine and Joel Barlow made the same confident appeal to reason and justice as Godwin in England and Rousseau in France. Modern society had become corrupt: why not remodel it upon the image of the antique virtue and simplicity so attractively described by Plutarch?

In the arts also a historical eclecticism, an urge to break violently with the present and set up in its place a historically accurate reconstruction of the past became the new direction. In France a series of powerful talents, beginning with Jacques Louis David in the 1780's and ending only with the death of Ingres in 1867, tried to make modern art the reconstruction of an antique world. In Germany, after the transition figures like Mengs and J. H. W. Tischbein, the friend of Goethe, there came a generation of passionate, idealistic neoclassicists Asmus Jacob Carstens, Joseph Anton Koch, Bonaventura Genelli, and Gottlieb Schick. These artists sought to live in an ideal world where only antique sculpture, Homer and Plutarch, Michelangelo and Raphael existed. The contemporary mind today dislikes anything savoring of imitation and therefore distrusts tradition and the past. To the men of the eighteenth century the past was, on the contrary, a tool of liberation, the key to the future. It is impossible for us to comprehend today how vivid, fascinating, and important the dream of Greece and Rome was to men in the later eighteenth century.

The capital of that dream world was Rome. There antiquity still lived in the beautiful, half-buried, golden ruins which the eighteenth-century painters Panini and Hubert Robert had made familiar. There in the Vatican were the galleries of ancient sculpture which represented, to that generation, the highest achievements of ancient art, culminating in the *Apollo Belvedere*, the *Laocoön*, the Farnese *Hercules*. There a new theory of art was developed in the 1750's and 1760's by a German art critic, Winckelmann, and by the artists Raphael Mengs and Pompeo Batoni, expressing the urge of their generation to transform the arts into an image of classical beauty. Their theory, which swept over Europe as the first of the succession of esthetic dogmas that have characterized our epoch, sounds, in part, strangely familiar to modern ears. It may be summarized as the doctrine of Ideal Beauty. Beauty—ideal, impersonal, universal Beauty—the neoclassic theory held, is found not in the world of nature, but in the mind. Nature, which is diverse and constantly changing, is the object of sensation, a lower form of human response; but Beauty, which is ideal and universal, is the conception of Reason. Art must therefore turn its back upon Nature and create an Ideal Beauty out of the mind.

To this Winckelmann added two other notions, derived from his love of the antique sculpture in the Vatican, which distinguished the neoclassic dogmas from more recent ones. The stable and intellectual elements of art, he said, are drawing and form. These represent the geometry of the mind and are therefore the primary elements of art. Color, which is variable and makes its appeal to the emotions, is secondary. And, since classical sculpture had attained the perfection of ideal nobility, modern artists should model themselves upon antique sculpture. Neoclassic painting, on the continent, rejected the technique of painting in light and color that had prevailed since the Venetian sixteenth-century painters. Drawing and simple local colors [1] became its new technique, while an episode from history, drawn from antiquity and treated in a style based upon Roman sculpture, became its subject matter.

Into the atmosphere of dawning classical theory in Rome plunged Benjamin West, fresh from America, glowing with self-confidence, ambition, and idealism. He was to play an important part in creating the neoclassical style of painting that became in the last years of the eighteenth century the symbol of a new period. He had already painted one historical subject, *The Death of Socrates*, in Philadelphia, and he had come to Europe, as has been said, in search of a narrative art. When he arrived in Rome in 1760, Winckelmann's theories were in the air but had not yet found expression in painting. In 1761 Mengs painted a fresco of *Parnassus* in the Villa Albani, built by Cardinal Alessandro Albani, a famous collector of ancient marbles, to house his collection. The *Parnassus* is considered to be the first painting conceived in the spirit of neoclassicism, but Mengs was so eclectic that the style of his fresco derives quite as much from Raphael as from the antique.

The first painters to achieve a style based both upon classical subjects

---

[1] The clearest definition of the two types of vision and style involved in this change is offered by Woelfflin's use of the terms *linear* and *painter-like*. The painter-like vision sees color and tonal values, and subordinates the sharp delineation of shapes and details to masses of light or shade or of color. Rembrandt and Watteau are examples. The linear vision subordinates radiance of color and richness of tone to a clear and exact delineation of form. The leaders of French neoclassicism, David and Ingres, abandoned the whole Baroque-Rococo style of atmospheric, luminous colors and glazes to work with outline and local colors.

and upon the qualities of antique sculpture were neither German, French, nor Italian but Scottish and American, Gavin Hamilton and Benjamin West. Gavin Hamilton spent most of his life in Florence and his works have passed into obscurity. West, after three years in Italy, migrated to London where his new style made him one of the most celebrated painters of his age.

Lest it should seem that, through nationalist brag, I am claiming priority for West over a greater artist, Jacques Louis David, who is generally thought of as the creator of the neoclassic style, let me quote a French student of the period, Jean Locquin, who points out that Hamilton and West were in advance of David by twelve or fifteen years:

West, who went to study at Rome for three years, 1760-1763, before taking up his residence in London, where he received the title of Historical Painter to the King, painted in 1766, Pylades and Orestes; in 1767, Agrippina . . . with the ashes of Germanicus; in 1769, Regulus returning to Carthage; in 1770, the Oath of the young Hannibal. . . . The choice of subjects, by itself, proves that Hamilton and West are the precursors and initiators. . . . But it is by the general conceptions of the works, by the disposition of the figures *en bas relief*, by the calm and clear ordonnance of the groups and corteges, by the grave rhythm of movements and of draperies, the effort toward exact reproduction of the furniture and costumes of the Greeks and Romans, by the evocation of the forms of antique sculpture, by the laconic energy of expressions, of which Poussin had found the secret, that the English school affirms, at this moment, its superiority.[2]

Agrippina with the Ashes of Germanicus is now in the Yale Gallery of Fine Arts. It fully illustrates Locquin's characterization of the new style. It illustrates also the difficulty we have today in appraising West. The grandeur and solemnity of the conception strike the observer today, as they did in the eighteenth century. The color is excellent, the chiaroscuro interesting. Yet it has also in the figures the woodenness and mawkishness that are the failings of West's art. We, to whom West's good qualities have lost their novelty, are apt only to see his weaknesses; the eighteenth century, to whom his art was all new, found his good qualities fresh and invigorating. This picture attracted the interest of the Archbishop of York, who introduced West to the patronage of George III, upon whose support he rose to fame.

The neoclassic style of West differed in two important respects from the neoclassicism of David in France or the Germans. As Americans are more intuitive than the lucid and logical French, and less given to abstract thought than the Germans, West's neoclassic painting was not so vigorously doctrinaire as theirs, nor did it represent so drastic a break with the past. West

[2] Quoted by Fiske Kimball in *Benjamin West, 1738-1820*, Philadelphia, Pennsylvania Museum of Art, 1938, p. 10, from Locquin's article, "La part de l'influence anglaise dans l'orientation neo-classique de la peinture française entre 1750 et 1780," *Actes du Congrès d'histoire de l'art*, 1921, II, pp. 391-402.

continued to use the coloristic technique of the eighteenth century instead of abandoning glazes and aerial tone for bare earth colors; and his conception of history included not only Greek and Roman history, but the Bible, English history, even recent events. In *The Death of Wolfe* (1771) he represented a contemporary deed of heroism in contemporary costume. His *William Penn's Treaty with the Indians* (Plate V) (1772) was drawn from the history of his own Pennsylvania. Generous, noble, patriotic actions—the antique virtues—whether in ancient or modern life, were his subject matter.

Penn's Treaty is an example of West's large and simple drawing, the pleasing color, and well-handled chiaroscuro which always make his pictures effective decorations, whatever we may think about their sentiment. His portrait of *Sir Guy Johnson* (National Gallery of Art, Washington) and his *Conference of the American Commissioners of the Treaty of Peace with England* (Fig. 37) (Henry Francis du Pont Winterthur Museum) show his monumental powers, in the case of the latter, in spite of its small size.

West was once praised beyond his deserts. Today he is not given credit even for his good qualities: in recent times no American artist has been more scornfully denigrated. His faults of woodenness and mawkishness are obvious. But he has even been appraised as the evil genius of American painting, who led it astray toward everything that painting should not be, especially because he lived abroad and drew our artists' minds toward a false, international current of art. This seems to me absurd. It was inevitable that American painting should enlarge its field of interest beyond the portrait, should take some part in the great movements of neoclassical and romantic idealism that dominated the mental climate of the next seventy-five years, should broaden itself by foreign travel and study. The only thing to be regretted about West is that he was not better; that he did not have the qualities which make an artist live in history, as well as those which make him important in his own day. Yet he is an interesting figure. He was the first American painter to achieve an international reputation. Not until Whistler would another American occupy so distinguished a place in the artistic life of his own day; and such position, while not final, is not won by men of no talent.

Another American to paint the ideal world of antiquity was John Vanderlyn (1775-1852), who was born at Kingston on the Hudson River. His story is typical of the problems of artists in America at that time.

Life began fortunately for Vanderlyn. At the age of twenty he attracted the interest of Aaron Burr who, believing him a genius, paid the expenses of a year of study with Gilbert Stuart in Philadelphia and then five years in Paris (1796-1801). He was apparently the first American artist to study there. From his teacher, Vincent, he absorbed the fine draughtsmanship, the enamel-like color, the firm sculptural style of the French neoclassic school. His early portraits and portrait drawings are admirable (Fig. 36). But he also absorbed the French neoclassic notion that only great, ideal, historical compositions were worthy of an artist: portraits he looked down upon.

On his return to America in 1801, Burr suggested to him that topographic prints of American "sights," like Niagara, would be profitable. Vanderlyn went to Niagara and painted several studies (Senate House, Kingston) which show the falls still surrounded by forests. The Erie Canal had not yet opened western New York to settlement. Also while he was in New York, the American Academy of Fine Arts was formed (1803) and Vanderlyn was commissioned to buy casts of antique sculpture in Europe for its projected gallery. Returning to Europe, he had his views of Niagara engraved in London and spent two years in Paris (1803-1805). At this time he painted his first historical composition, *The Death of Jane McCrea* (1804) (Wadsworth Atheneum, Hartford), done at the request of Robert Fulton as an illustration of Joel Barlow's *Columbiad*. Fulton wanted Vanderlyn to illustrate the poem, whose publication he was managing for Barlow; but Vanderlyn was so slow in executing this first picture that Fulton was obliged to use English illustrators.

Vanderlyn was about to return to America when a gift from another admirer, William McClure of Philadelphia, enabled him to spend three years in Rome (1805-1808). There he did some charming drawings (Fig. 34) and painted his first classical subject, *Marius on the Ruins of Carthage* (1807) (M. H. de Young Memorial Museum, San Francisco). The sentimental melancholy of this subject, representing the fallen Roman hero brooding in exile on the ruins of the fallen city, aroused Napoleon's enthusiasm. Seeing it in the Salon of 1808, Napoleon abruptly awarded it a gold medal. In Paris again, Vanderlyn painted his best work, *Ariadne* (Fig. 35) (1812) (The Pennsylvania Academy of the Fine Arts, Philadelphia), a dignified, handsome picture of monumental size, which is the most successful ideal nude produced by American neoclassicism. In the meantime he was also painting many excellent portraits, which have the discipline of the French style and the vigorous realism of the American. In 1815, at the age of forty, he returned to New York, having spent half his life abroad. He was well trained. His talents had been recognized by Napoleon's gold medal, which shone with great luster in American eyes. Life had gone well for him. But it had not prepared him for the difficulties he must face in the New World. The rest of his life went badly.

The situation of a painter in New York, to one accustomed to the proud atmosphere of art in Paris, was chilling and depressing. There was no Emperor to distribute honors, no Louvre to lend prestige to painting, no Salon to attract the attention of society. The torpid American Academy of Fine Arts, for which he had bought casts twelve years before, was almost dead and its collections were in storage. Colonel Trumbull, who came back from England the year after Vanderlyn's arrival, claimed and secured the only great public commission for historical painting offered in the United States. Congress voted $32,000 to Trumbull in 1817 for four murals for the Rotunda of the Capitol in Washington. Trumbull no doubt deserved the commission, for he had executed a noble series of small pictures of the Revolution and with this purpose in mind had painted portraits of all the principal actors in the War for Independence. Yet Vanderlyn felt himself the better painter and much ill-feeling ensued between the two men. When the City of New York commissioned Vanderlyn to paint a portrait of *General Jackson* for the City Hall, it did not satisfy his feeling of injured pride and neglect.

Vanderlyn had conceived the notion, before returning to America, that panoramas would be profitable in the United States, for they were a popular amusement in the capitals of Europe. Robert Fulton had supported himself in Paris by a panorama, while working on his inventions. Vanderlyn had prepared sketches (1815) for a panorama of Versailles. In 1817 the city council of New York gave him a ten-year lease on a corner of the park, opposite the City Hall; and Vanderlyn, believing himself secure in possession, spent twelve to fourteen thousand dollars of borrowed money in building a rotunda. There he showed his own *Versailles* (Senate House, Kingston) and other panoramas; his *Jane McCrea, Marius,* and *Ariadne,* and the copies of old masters he had brought home from Europe, without too great success. He was never able to pay off his debt for the building even though in the slack winter months he tried taking his exhibition to southern cities, as far as New Orleans and Havana. At the end of ten years the city council abruptly canceled his lease. A ruined and embittered man, Vanderlyn retired to his native Kingston to support himself by painting likenesses that can hardly be recognized as the work of the same man who had produced the distinguished early portraits.

In 1832 he was given a commission for a full-length painting of *Washington* for the federal Capitol. And at last, in 1838, when he was sixty-three, he was commissioned to paint a *Landing of Columbus* for the Rotunda of the Capitol—a commission he had wanted since 1818. He went to Paris to execute it (1842-1844). It was suggested by his enemies (and even by his biographer, Bishop Kip) that French assistants did the work. It is true, at least, that Vanderlyn had forgotten too much, and also remembered too much. James Freeman, the American landscape painter, tells of meeting Vanderlyn at the Cafe Greco in Rome. Vanderlyn said to him: "Thirty years ago I was on this very spot," and, pointing to different seats, observed, "There sat Allston opposite me; that was Turner's corner; here on my left sat Fenimore Cooper; and there, I was told, Sir Joshua Reynolds and West sat.—Thirty years ago, and here I am again; I come back old and broken with my first and last commission from our government for our Rotunda—too late! Too late!" The *Columbus* was an artistic failure.

Unfortunately for Vanderlyn, he had absorbed along with the technique of French neoclassicism its grandiose ambitions, which he was neither able to carry out by his own unaided strength nor to find a foundation for in American society. Monumental paintings imply a monumental architecture which can house them and calls for enrichment. A certain artificiality infects the vast English and French neoclassic canvases that were painted to show at the Royal Academy or the Paris Salon. But, at least, in England West could paint for Windsor Castle, or sell his historical canvases to the English nobles whose great houses had space for large paintings. In France a large picture might be bought by the state from the Salon, or win for its creator a state commission either to decorate a public building or to paint an altarpiece for a provincial church. In America there was as yet hardly any monumental architecture; there was no king or emperor; no owners of ducal palaces; no apparatus of state patronage, no tradition of church art. The neoclassic architecture then taking shape was monumental in feeling but usually not in size. Even the Capitol at Washington, in its older parts, has narrow intercolumniations and small wall areas; yet when Charles Bulfinch assumed charge of its rebuilding after the war, he thought it a huge building. Poor Vanderlyn's bitter, thwarted career is that of a man who wished to paint great historical murals in a society that could not use them.

The purely practical nature of the problem is illustrated by what happened when Benjamin West sent over his *Christ Healing the Sick*, in 1816, as a gift to the Pennsylvania Hospital. There was no space in the Hospital large enough to receive it. A special building, known as the West Picture House, had to be erected for it.[3]

Yet we cannot blame all of Vanderlyn's troubles upon external factors. If he was a great historical painter, as he believed himself to be, how does it happen that in the twelve years from 1803 to 1815, when he was at the height of his powers, he painted only three historical pictures? These are not enough to justify great claims upon society. Instead of pouring out a stream of work, like his European contemporaries, he let the years pass, or turned aside to some scheme for making money. Was Vanderlyn one of those artists whom an all-powerful *direction of attention* forces to look in a direction opposed to their natural gifts? The neoclassic theory was focused upon ideal historical subjects, which he executed slowly and hesitantly. His admirable early portraits suggest that his natural gifts were for an art of observation, rather than fancy. A conflict between what he was born to do and what he thought he ought to do might account both for his small production and his unhappy nature.

Neoclassic painting in its strictest form, as David or Cornelius practiced it, and as Vanderlyn tried to practice it, fed upon the great collections of an-

---

[3] An admission fee was charged to see the picture and fortunately brought in enough to pay for the building and give the Hospital a profit.

tique sculpture in the Vatican, the Louvre, and the British Museum. Removed from those, it could hardly flourish. Vanderlyn's *Marius* is an illustration. The head of Marius was painted from a marble bust in Rome; the body is a pastiche of other ancient sculptures; the temple and ruins were painted from a model constructed in his studio. The method of production was so laborious and tedious that it alone might have been enough to paralyze the man's power to create. Without abundant models, without ancient sculpture and archaeological remains at one's elbow, such art was impossible. The first move of the little academies and athenaeums organized in America after 1800 was to purchase casts of the most celebrated antique statues: but this was not enough. American painters other than West and Vanderlyn experimented with neoclassic subjects. Yet these efforts were of necessity desultory and ineffective.

Antiquity also presented itself, however, to eighteenth-century minds in another guise—their own better selves. Generous and noble actions, courage, self-sacrifice, elevation of character exist in the present as well as in the past. Americans, saturated in the dream of antiquity (as were all educated men in that time), looked on the valor and devotion of their own Revolutionary leaders and heroes as worthy of the legends of ancient Rome. From these thoughts it was only a step to an identification, by analogy, imaginary but none the less moving for that reason, of America as re-enacting antiquity. Jefferson's dream of reviving Greek and Roman architecture as the future national style of the United States is a well-known example: it was a dream with remarkable practical results.

The painters saw about them a world made memorable by courage, patriotism, and devotion, by the antique virtues enacted in their own times. Here were the ancient themes of classicism alive and breathing. The heroic narrative pictures of Copley and Trumbull, the portraits of Stuart and Peale and their contemporaries apply classical vision and its style of firm drawing and clearly lighted plastic forms to subjects from the world of reality rather than of fancy. As a re-creation of the antique past, American neoclassic painting was uncertain, fitful, and unhappy; as a celebration of antique virtues in modern life, it was energetic, profuse, varied, and assured.

Neoclassic realism has, however, received less attention than the ideal narratives. I suppose it illustrates the prestige of the ideal in esthetic theory that the contrived and rather archaeological ideal subjects of neoclassicism, which one admires but does not enjoy, have been elaborately studied; while the vivid and effective works of neoclassic realism, which one both admires and enjoys, are hardly conceived of as even forming a movement.

It is my opinion that neoclassic realism produced in America an admirable national style, full of character and solid in achievement. It is important, if I am right, to describe its chief works and try to delineate its character.

Let us take Copley's development after 1774 as an example. Copley, it will be remembered, had gone to Europe to escape from an environment that limited him to portrait painting. In Italy his first attempt at a new scale was a huge impressive double portrait (now in Boston) of *Mr. and Mrs. Ralph Izard* with a lavish display of classical *objets d'art* as background. As soon as he was settled in London, he turned his gifts for penetrating observation and robust, objective creation to narrative subjects on the large Italian scale. *Watson and the Shark* (Fig. 40) (a composition which exists in several different versions) is an episode in the life of a friend, Brook Watson, who, swimming as a boy in Havana Harbor, had one leg bitten off by a shark. He was rescued, however, by his shipmates and lived to become a great merchant and Lord Mayor of London. The subject had in it the elements of courage and loyalty in a moment of supreme danger that the classical artist wished to honor. And with it Copley also initiated one of the great themes of American painting, the drama of man's struggle against nature, that was to be developed in many forms in nineteenth-century painting.

In the storm of war and revolution then sweeping over the world there was no dearth of themes for a painter interested in such subject matter. Yet art is selection: Copley, as a neoclassic artist, chose themes of heroism and devotion. The emotions of horror, disgust, or rage against mankind which modern novelists selected from World War II were also present in Copley's time, just as heroism and devotion were also notably present in the wars of our time. Copley's choice of subjects illustrates the neoclassical direction of attention, as those of our recent war novels illustrate a different one.

In *The Death of the Earl of Chatham in the House of Lords* (1779-1780) (Tate Gallery, London) he painted the last act of Pitt, a patriot as devoted as Regulus, who used his final strength to denounce in the House of Lords the government's policy toward the revolted colonies (1778). In *The Death of Major Pierson* (1783) (Tate Gallery, London) he chose the self-sacrifice of a gallant officer. These pictures show Copley's growth. He had left America to master the larger language of painting; now he had done so. In dramatic force, in convincing expression of life, in sweeping movement, in monumental disposition of lights and shadows, these are among the remarkable paintings of their times. Not until Baron Gros painted Napoleon's campaign in Egypt, a generation later, was there to be again such dramatically effective narrative painting.

Another important American narrative painter of the period was John Trumbull (1756-1843). Like the other American artists of this century, he was born with a strong innate urge to paint, for which one can see no cause in his environment. He was the youngest son of Jonathan Trumbull, a Connecticut lawyer and patriot who was governor of the state during the Revolution. Mentally precocious, the boy was sent to Harvard to complete his education, entering in the middle of the junior year at age fifteen. His tutor wrote to his father: "I find he has a natural genius and disposition for limning.

As a knowledge of art will probably be of no use to him I submit to your consideration whether it would not be best to endeavor to give him a turn to the study of perspective, a branch of mathematics, the knowledge of which will be at least a genteel accomplishment, and may be greatly useful in future life." His father replied: "I am sensible of his natural genius and inclination for limning; an art I have frequently told him will be of no use to him." The boy, however, went to call upon Copley, whose elegant clothes and fine house on Beacon Hill impressed upon him the dignity of an artist's life. He returned to Connecticut after his graduation in 1773, and attempted painting portraits with homemade materials. The portraits of these early years (before he went to London to study with West in 1784) are those of an "untrained professional" of great natural gifts.

When the war of the Revolution broke out Trumbull served as aide-de-camp to Washington but resigned from the army in anger, in 1776, because of an error in the dating of his commission. Thus early he showed the traits of irritability, suspicion that he was being injured, readiness to demand everything he believed due him to the last small detail, which were weaknesses of character that slowly poisoned his life.

In 1785, after a year of study in London with West, he produced his first independent composition, a subject from Homer: *Priam Returning with the Body of Hector* (Boston Athenaeum). Then abandoning the Homeric wars, he turned to the wars of his own day and the story of the American Revolution. He knew personally most of the men, in America and abroad, who had played the leading roles. Jefferson and Adams helped him select twelve decisive episodes in the War for Independence and the creation of the United States. He resolved to paint likenesses of the principal actors, while they were still living, and to incorporate these into the twelve large narrative subjects, thus making them a historical record as well as works of art. It was a bold, ambitious idea and it was carried out with skill and devotion. Some of the episodes, like the surrenders at Saratoga and Yorktown, unfortunately proved almost impossible to turn into satisfactory dramatic compositions. Yet the eight small studies completed in the next ten years, and the many miniature portraits in oil of the American, British, and French actors in the story (most of which are preserved at Yale University) are both a unique historical record and a notable artistic achievement.

Trumbull was, fortunately, no dogmatic theorist in the neoclassic manner. The painter he admired most was Rubens (whom the neoclassic theorists detested) and he learned much from Baroque narrative painting. The *Death of Montgomery Before Quebec* and his *Washington at the Surrender of the Hessians* (Yale University Art Gallery) show in their spirited action, their composition in depth, their luminous chiaroscuro, and psychological force, how well he had absorbed the lessons of Baroque painting.

Trumbull thought, not without reason, that engravings after his twelve pictures would be popular in America. In England, such patriotic subjects were engraved and the engravings were very popular. West's *Death of General Wolfe*, engraved by Woolett, had proved profitable for the artist; while of Bartolozzi's large engraving after Copley's *Death of Chatham* 2,500 prints had been quickly sold. Trumbull, descended from a family of Connecticut merchants, was highly sensitive to the business side of his profession. Unfortunately, when he returned to America in 1789 he found the country still exhausted from the war and preoccupied with political and economic problems. After a first encouraging reception, interest lagged and subscriptions for the engravings ceased. Deeply discouraged after a few years of struggle, in 1794 he dropped the project and gave up art to accept a diplomatic post in London. When that post came to an end he stayed in London and, taking up painting once more, spent the next years working as a rather unsuccessful portrait painter, in London until 1804, in New York from 1804 to 1808, in London again from 1808 to 1816. When he returned finally to America in 1816 and Congress voted to commission (1817) four of his Revolutionary subjects in heroic size for the Rotunda of the new Capitol in Washington, thirty years had passed since he first conceived the series. His skill had not failed him to the degree that it failed Vanderlyn in 1841. His pictures in the Rotunda are handsome and imposing decorations. Yet they lack the ardor of his youthful work and also lack some of the plasticity. Trumbull, it is not often realized, lost the sight of one eye in a boyhood accident: his work on a large scale reveals a certain flatness that may be the result of limited vision. The large decorations are less brilliant than the small early studies preserved at Yale, as his enemies said loudly at the time, yet they do not deserve the slighting treatment they have usually received.

Trumbull was an artist of great gifts, an excellent colorist, a master of expressive movement and chiaroscuro. His miniature portrait studies made in preparation for the Revolutionary pictures are admirable observations of character. For the dramatic subtlety of expression one might have expected to find in the large pictures, had he executed them during the freshness of his inspiration, look at the row of officers' heads in the foreground of his *Sortie of the British Garrison from Gibraltar* (1789) (Boston Athenaeum) (Fig. 39). I regard a passage such as this as worthy of the greatest Baroque narrative painters. Trumbull was criticized by Americans for painting this picture, which celebrates a British feat of arms. He answered the criticism in his *Autobiography:* he chose the subject, he said, "to show that noble and generous actions, by whomsoever performed, were the objects to whose celebration I meant to devote myself." The statement breathes the spirit of the classical period, with its conscious choice of lofty, healthy, and universal values. It is interesting also that the young Thomas Lawrence posed for the head of the dying Spanish officer in the foreground, whose attitude is taken from the *Dying Gladiator:* the heroism of the ancient world and the images of a modern age were inextricably blended in Trumbull's vision.

The last chapter of Trumbull's long, changeful, gifted, but unhappy life was the most unfortunate. In 1817, the same year in which Congress voted him the first great national commission ever offered an American artist, Trumbull became head of the American Academy of Fine Arts in New York. The story of this institution will be told in its turn; here it is only necessary to say that it was organized to afford New York two things, a gallery of art and an art school. By selling it his own works at high prices, Trumbull ruined the finances of the gallery. And instead of rising to his position as the leading figure of his profession in America, Trumbull became the enemy of his fellow painters and a caustic discourager of the young. The first war between generations waged in the story of American painting was fought by the young New York painters to rid themselves of the incubus of this bitter old man.

The direction of attention of the classical period was focused very largely upon the merits and the rights of the individual human being. Its political revolutions, its ethical and social ideas, its humanistic culture were all expressions of a profound interest in and respect for the individual. This interest made it also one of the rich periods of portrait painting. Nowhere was the art of portrait painting more popular than in America.

The most celebrated portrait painter, and the creator of a distinctive American classical portrait style, was Gilbert Stuart (1755-1828). He began painting portraits in his teens, in Newport, in a very attractive if naïve style. Cosmo Alexander, the Scottish migrant painter, was interested by the talented boy and took him to Edinburgh to study in 1772. Alexander's death left him stranded in Scotland and he worked his way home as a sailor, suffering hardships he never liked to discuss afterwards. He went again to London (1775-1787), where he became eventually a successful portrait painter. But Stuart was a gay, carefree, extravagant fellow. Debts drove him to Ireland (1787-1792) and again from there to America (1793). He returned, he said, to paint the portrait of Washington. He did so in a way which left a profound mark upon our painting.

In London Stuart experimented with the portrait formulas of English painting. He composed portraits like Reynolds, like Gainsborough, even like Van Dyck; he painted people in action, in the setting of life, without setting. But gradually his portraits grew simpler, quieter; an air of remoteness, of detachment from the stir of existence settled over his characters. When he returned to New York in 1793 his portraiture had assumed the bland stillness, the steady unflickering glow of life that were to be his peculiar note.

Washington Allston observed, "Stuart knows how to distinguish very well the accidental from the permanent." It is the permanent and timeless aspect of a human being that Stuart's portraits give us and of which the "Vaughan" type of *Washington* is perhaps the perfect example. All the accessories of daily existence of the eighteenth-century *portrait d'apparat*, all the fleeting gestures and expressions that Copley had used to create a moment of life were eliminated by Stuart. His figures are motionless, without setting, without detail, without gesture: the head is like a bust upon a body like a pedestal. Stuart knew very well what significant gesture was (witness his *Mrs. Richard Yates* in the National Gallery, Washington) and what accessories could do. If he used them, it was to build an individual into a type. His *Washington at Dorchester Heights* (Fig. 43) (1806) (the City of Boston) is a type of Washington as Soldier Hero, as his *Athenaeum* (1796), *Vaughan* (1795), and *Lansdowne* (1796) portraits, or the seated *Washington* of 1797 are types of Washington as Elder Statesman. His portraits of private individuals wear the same remote and timeless air. Almost without exception Stuart eliminated all detail to show the man or woman in his permanent aspect. The bone structure of the head, the glow of life in the skin and eyes, an expression of calm and well-being, an exquisite freshness of color, these were what interested him and all that, in most cases, he allowed to enter the disciplined perfection of his art. After he had created this very personal classical form, he practiced within these narrow limits for thirty years. Not until the 1820's, when the new taste of romanticism was in the air, did Stuart relax the severity of his classical style to use occasionally again a significant gesture or detail.

Charles Willson Peale (1741-1827), the most interesting artist of Philadelphia, is in every way a contrast to the artists we have been discussing. Unlike Stuart, he was not only an admirable portrait painter but a man of generous enthusiasms and fertile intellectual curiosity. If West and Trumbull and Vanderlyn are examples of how the disembodied Ideal of Art could send its enchantment out into remote frontier regions of a new continent to inspire youths with ambition to become an Apelles or a Raphael almost before they had seen such a thing as a picture, Peale came into painting by way of skilled handcraftsmanship. He believed accordingly that any one could paint, that art was only a matter of training and taking pains, a view that must have been irritating to minds filled with Winckelmann's lofty theories of Ideal Beauty. Peale's belief in training made him the organizer of the first art school in America. And his encyclopedic interests, his ingenious, experimental nature illustrate how closely allied the objective, realistic imagination of the artist may be to the interests of the scientist.

Peale was born in Queen Anne's County, Maryland, the son of an educated man who, banished from England for an early misdemeanor, had become a country schoolteacher on the eastern shore of Maryland. His father died when the boy was nine; the mother, with five small children to support, was glad to apprentice this son to a saddler. The boy was a natural craftsman (all his life, he was happiest when working with tools in his hands) and, having an eager, curious mind, not only learned his own craft, but tinkered readily at any other that presented itself—watch and clock repairing, silversmithing, casting in brass. On a voyage down the bay to purchase leather, at the age of twenty-one, he saw at Norfolk some landscapes and a portrait by an amateur artist. The idea of making pictures now took hold of his mind. Getting paint and brushes into his hands, and buying in Philadelphia a book called *The Handmaid to the Arts*, he discovered a natural aptitude for painting. Yet it was not until a Maryland planter paid him ten pounds for portraits of himself and his lady that Peale (married by this time and with a child on the way) realized he might support his family better by this skill than by his other trades. He got a little instruction from John Hesselius in return for one of his best saddles; went to Boston, where Copley lent him a picture to copy; and made such progress that his friends raised money to send him to study in London. There West received him kindly and he spent two years in the metropolis, 1767-1769, learning to paint in life-size and in miniature, and to make etchings and mezzotints, and to cast in plaster. It was characteristic of him that he tried every craft skill within his reach.

He returned to Annapolis, the natural center for a painter born on the eastern shore. But Philadelphia, the colonial metropolis, offered a better field and in 1776 he moved his family there; it was to be home to him for the rest of his long life. The War for Independence drew him into the fighting as an officer of colonial militia, and into politics as a member of the Pennsylvania Assembly, on the extreme democratic side. By nature he was neither soldier nor politician. In 1780 he retired from politics and began his most active years as a painter.

Ardent, hopeful, enthusiastic, affectionate, Peale was a creature of what the eighteenth century called sensibility. His career, told with insight and wit in Charles Coleman Sellers' two-volume biography (1947) is a most entertaining mirror of his age. The generous enthusiasms and hopes of its liberal thinkers, the optimistic rationalism of the philosophers stirred him deeply; the nascent natural sciences appealed to his insatiable curiosity. After Copley's departure in 1774, Peale was the leading portrait painter in the colonies; but his art was only one aspect of his long, indefatigably active, and influential life.

Even during the war he painted numerous portraits, including several of *Washington* and of other distinguished figures. Shortly after the surrender at Yorktown in the autumn of 1781 gave the colonies a feeling that victory and independence were at hand, Peale seems to have realized the historical significance of those likenesses. Adding an exhibition gallery to his studio, he launched on a project of painting the principal leaders of the Revolutionary War, both civil and military, the outstanding diplomats, and the foreign ambassadors to the young republic. By 1784 there were forty-four such likenesses in the gallery. In 1786 a museum of natural history was added. The collection continued to grow, both in works of art and in natural history. It outgrew Peale's gallery; in 1794 it was transfered to Philosophical Hall, the new building of the American Philosophical Society; finally, in 1802, to the upper floor of the State House (now known as Independence Hall). There it remained until the collection was dispersed in the eighteen-fifties, and there some of the portraits still hang today.

As a portrait painter, Peale was one of the earliest and most interesting figures of the neoclassic movement. What he saw and painted best in human beings was not Rococo elegance but healthy strength, good spirits, and intelligence. He drew firmly and crisply, modeling chiefly by means of his clear outlines; light he used very broadly and simply, varying it only for emphasis; his colors were soft, local tones. How he arrived so early and unaided, cut off from artistic contacts, at so interesting a parallel to the neoclassic portrait style worked out in France by David, I cannot explain. By the early eighties, Peale's portraits had lost all traces of Rococo pose or elaboration, and emerged in a severely simple, neoclassic style, never wholly free from naïveté and provincial awkwardness, but cogent, amiable and, at their best, of penetrating candor.

He understood his own strength and limitations. The Ideal World of neoclassic theory, of which he had had a glimpse in Benjamin West's studio, was not for him. Three years after his return to America, he wrote to his old friend, John Beale Bordley (1772):

A good painter of either portrait or History must be well acquainted with the Greesian and Roman statues, to be able to draw them at pleasure by memory, and account for every beauty, must know the original cause of beauty in all he sees. These are some of the requisites of a good painter. These are more than I shall ever have time or opportunity to know, but as I have variety of characters to paint I must as Rembrandt did make these by Anticks, and improve myself as well as I can while I am providing for my support.[4]

The best of the portraits painted in these years can stand comparison, in all but color and the sensuous use of paint, with the best of contemporary work. At thought of Peale, a crowd of strong, open, confident, faces comes into my mind: faces of men capable of founding a new Republic, and of their equally capable and pleasant wives. Memorable faces of *Washington, Franklin* (1785), *John Adams* (ca.1791-1794), *Jefferson* (1791); of his old friend, *John Beale Bordley,* (1790), gentle, wise, and unfailingly kind; of *James Latimer* (1788-1789), aged fighter and patriot; of *Colonel Charles Pettit* (1792), an intelligent lawyer and member of the American Philosophical Society, but

---

[4] Charles Coleman Sellers, *Charles Willson Peale, Vol. 1, Early Life (1741-1790),* Philadelphia, the American Philosophical Society, 1947, p. 113.

Left: Fig. 32. Winthrop Chandler: *Mrs. Samuel Chandler*. (Courtesy of Colonel and Mrs. Edgar W. Garbisch.)

Below: Fig. 33. John Durand: *The Rapalje Children* (ca. 1768). (Courtesy of The New-York Historical Society.)

Fig. 34. John Vanderlyn: *Classical Landscape* (drawing). (Courtesy of the Senate House Museum, Kingston, N. Y.)

Fig. 36. John Vanderlyn: *A Lady
and her Son* (1800). (Courtesy of
the Senate House Museum, Kingston, N. Y.)

Opposite page, bottom: Fig. 35. John
Vanderlyn: *Ariadne* (1812). (Courtesy of The Pennsylvania Academy
of the Fine Arts, Philadelphia.)

Fig. 39. John Trumbull: *Sortie of the British Garrison from Gibraltar* (1789). (Courtesy of The Boston Athenaeum; photograph, Museum of Fine Arts, Boston.)

Opposite page, top: Fig. 37. Benjamin West: *Conference of the American Commissioners of the Treaty of Peace with England* (1783). (Courtesy of The Henry Francis du Pont Winterthur Museum.)

Opposite page, bottom: Fig. 38. Robert Edge Pine: *Congress Voting Independence* (1788). (Courtesy of The Historical Society of Pennsylvania, Philadelphia.)

Fig. 40. John Singleton Copley: *Watson and the Shark* (1782). (Courtesy of The Detroit Institute of Arts.)

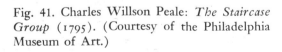

Fig. 41. Charles Willson Peale: *The Staircase Group* (1795). (Courtesy of the Philadelphia Museum of Art.)

Fig. 42. Joseph Wright: *Self-Portrait of the Artist with His Family* (ca. 1793). (Courtesy of The Pennsylvania Academy of the Fine Arts, Philadelphia.)

Fig. 43. Gilbert Stuart: *Washington at Dorchester Heights* (1806). (Courtesy of the City of Boston; photograph, Museum of Fine Arts, Boston.)

Fig. 44. James Sharples: *Moreau de Saint-Méry* (1797). (Courtesy of The Metropolitan Museum of Art.)

Fig. 45. John Wesley Jarvis: *Jacob Houseman* (1809). (Courtesy of The Detroit Institute of Arts.)

Fig. 46. William Jennys: *Mrs. Constant Storrs.* (Courtesy of The Pennsylvania Academy of the Fine Arts, Philadelphia.)

Fig. 47. Ralph Earl: *Roger Sherman* (ca. 1777-1779). (Courtesy of the Yale University Art Gallery.)

Fig. 48. Reuben Moulthrop: *Bradford Hubbard* (ca. 1785). (Courtesy of the New Haven Colony Historical Society, New Haven, Conn.)

Fig. 49. Jacob Eichholtz: *Self Portrait* (ca. 1805-1810). (Courtesy of Mrs. James H. Beal, Pittsburgh.)

Fig. 50. Henry Sargent:
The Dinner Party (ca.
1815-1820). (Courtesy
of the Museum of Fine
Arts, Boston.)

Fig. 51. John Hill, after
Joshua Shaw: *View by
Moonlight, near Fayette-
ville* (aquatint engraving,
1820). (Courtesy of The
Detroit Institute of Arts.)

Fig. 52. James Peale: *Self-Portrait with His Family*
(ca. 1795). (Courtesy of The Pennsylvania Academy of the
Fine Arts, Philadelphia.)

Fig. 53. John Trumbull: *The Surrender of Corn-
wallis at Yorktown* (1817-1820). (Courtesy of the
United States Capitol.)

Fig. 54. John Lewis Krimmel: *A Fourth of July Celebration in Center Square, Philadelphia*, 1819. (Courtesy of The Historical Society of Pennsylvania, Philadelphia.)

Fig. 55. Jeremiah Paul: *Four Children Playing in a Street* (1795). (Courtesy of Arthur J. Sussel, Philadelphia.)

Fig. 56. Pierre Charles L'Enfant: *A View of West Point on the Hudson River* (ca. 1782). (Courtesy of the Library of Congress, Washington, D. C.)

Fig. 57. Charles Févret de Saint-Mémin: *Sha Ha Ka, or Big White, the Mandan Chief.* (Courtesy of The New-York Historical Society.)

Fig. 58. W. R. Birch: *The Sun Reflecting on the Dew, a Garden Scene, Echo, Pennsylvania, a Place Belonging to Mr. D. Bavarage* (stipple engraving). (From Birch's *The Country Seats of the United States*, 1808.)

Fig. 59. Alexander Wilson: *The Little Owl, or Saw-Whet Owl* (pen and water-color drawing). (The Academy of Natural Sciences, Philadelphia.)

PLATE VII. Washington Allston. *The Flight of Flori-mell* (detail) (1819). (Courtesy of The Detroit Institute of Arts.)

also a man with a politician's amiability written in his face; or the artist's brother *James Peale* (1795) painting a miniature. But Peale was profuse and unpredictable. He did silhouettes with the physiognotrace, a machine to record the profile; he painted admirable miniatures; one of his finest works was a life-sized *trompe l'œil*. *The Staircase Group* (Fig. 41) (1795) (Philadelphia Museum of Art), showing his sons Raphaelle and Titian Ramsay Peale going up a narrow stair, was shown at the Columbianum Exhibition of 1795 as a *trompe l'œil*, framed in an actual door frame and with a wooden step projecting out below to complete the illusion.

After 1786 his energies were drawn more and more into his other great activity, the creation of the first American scientific museum. Beginning with a few bones of a mammoth in 1784, his enthusiasm continually enlarged his museum until it eventually filled the second floor of the old State House (Independence Hall) with a collection arranged to show, in orderly fashion, according to the best scientific knowledge of the time, the entire order of nature. Peale's museum was the first in the United States and one of the earliest in the world to pass beyond the primitive stage of a gathering of curiosities, in order to represent a scientific concept. Its greatest achievement was the excavation and mounting of the first mastodon skeleton (1801), of which Peale himself left an amusing record in the painting, *Exhuming the Mastodon* (Peale Museum, Baltimore). Peale's dream of making his institution a National Museum was half a century ahead of its time; the museum had to exist on admission fees. In midcentury, unable to compete with more commercial amusements and Barnum's type of showmanship, it went to the wall and its collections were dispersed. Yet it was, in its heyday from 1800 to Peale's death in 1827, an extraordinary achievement and it entitles the artist to a singular place in our intellectual history.

At the age of seventy-four the old man, whose interest in painting had been secondary for twenty years to the creation of his museum, took up his brushes and colors again, to enter another and in some respects his most interesting period as a painter. In his middle years, his best trait of style was his sensitive, expressive draughtsmanship: now he was interested in light, which he used with true subtlety. His portrait of his brother, *James Peale (The Lamplight Portrait)* (Plate VI) (The Detroit Institute of Arts) was painted in 1822, when the painter was eighty-one years old. It is a subtle composition of half-lights and shadows sensitively observed: one could say without exaggeration, such a composition was beyond the capacity or even the conception of most of the younger American painters at that day.

Peale's *Self-Portrait in His Museum* (1822) (The Pennsylvania Academy of the Fine Arts) shows himself at the age of eighty-one, drawing back a curtain to reveal the institution he had created. Beside him are his painting materials and his tools for stuffing a wild turkey. Behind, the long room of the State House is filled with row above row of box-like dioramas with gilt frames, in which the natural history collections were installed. An ardent naturalist, Peale collected and mounted his own animals, plants, birds, and insects, following the order of classification of Linnaeus. Behind each specimen was a background painted by himself, so that the creature and its setting formed a kind of habitat group. Behind the curtain, at the right, can be seen the mounted skeleton of the mastodon whose excavation and mounting was Peale's most spectacular triumph as a naturalist. And, to make his representation of the universe philosophically complete, there were the double row of portraits above the cases, a gallery of the great men of his day, painted by himself and his sons.

A gifted, ardent, ingenious, practical, idealistic man, who lived to carry out every idea that came to him, from mounting a mastodon to inventing porcelain false teeth, Peale is one of the most entertaining and remarkable characters in our art. During his lifetime Philadelphia was the cultural center of the country. Peale, incessantly active, curious, and alive, was one of figures who made it so.

All of these American neoclassical painters—Copley in his later development, West, Trumbull, Stuart, Peale—worked in a more linear style, more precise in drawing, thinner in pigment, than that of the English neoclassicists like Romney and Hoppner. The Americans seem never to have liked the thick impasto and the generalized, idealizing drawing characteristic of the English school from Reynolds' time. On the other hand, their painting, though firm, was fresh and luminous, a more coloristic style than that of the French neoclassicists.

Around these leaders grew up a school of neoclassic portraiture that is one of the solid and distinctive achievements of American painting. To it belong:

Joseph Wright (1756-1793), son of the first American woman sculptor, who left a few fine, fresh portraits like his *Self-Portrait of the Artist with His Family* (ca.1793) (Fig. 42) (The Pennsylvania Academy of the Fine Arts) and designed the first coins and medals of the United States, before dying in the yellow fever epidemic of 1793.

John Wesley Jarvis (1780-1840), the wit and bohemian, whose portrait of *Jacob Houseman* (1809) (Fig. 45) (The Detroit Institute of Arts) is one of the best examples of the firm, clear, dignified but unpretentious work of the school; and Joseph Wood (ca.1778-1830), at one time Jarvis' partner, and a specialist in cabinet-sized portraits.

James Peale (1749-1831), pupil of his brother Charles Willson Peale, an excellent miniaturist and skillful also in attractive conversation-sized groups like the *Self-Portrait with His Family* (ca.1795) (Fig. 52) (The Pennsylvania Academy of the Fine Arts) or *Washington and His Generals at Yorktown* (Maryland Historical Society).

Edward Savage (1761-1817) who painted the well-known life-sized group of *The Washington Family* (1796, from sketches made from life in 1789) (National Gallery of Art, Washington).

James Sharples (1751-1811) and his family, specialists in pastel portraits in cabinet size, who traveled about the country in a caravan studio in search of sitters. His portrait of the genial French exile *Moreau de Saint-Méry* (1797) (Fig. 44) (The Metropolitan Museum of Art) shows the vitality and decorative charm of his best work.

John Johnston (1752-1818) of Boston, who rose to the rank of major in the army of the Revolution and was capable as an artist of the sensitive portrait of *James Cutler of Boston* (1791) (private collection) in the conversation style.

Edward Greene Malbone (1777-1807), chief of a distinguished group of miniature painters, among whom many others like the English migrant portraitist Robert Field (ca.1770-1819), Charles Fraser (1782-1860) and Benjamin Trott (ca.1790-ca.1841) also did work of first quality.

James Earl (1761-1796), younger brother of the more famous Ralph Earl, who stayed in England longer than his brother and painted with greater suavity but without his power.

Robert Fulton (1765-1815), who gave up painting in the 1790's to become an engineer and to invent the submarine and the steamboat. Both of these inventions were perfected while he was living in Paris (1794-1805) in the house of the American poet, Joel Barlow. To support himself at this time he painted and exhibited the first panorama seen in Paris.

Ezra Ames (1768-1836), the portrait painter of Albany and the upper Hudson River.

Portrait painting was a natural expression of this generation's new perspective upon humanity. The aristocratic ideal of birth and elegance had been swept away by eighteenth-century liberalism. The dignity of the individual had taken its place. The American Revolution had translated this into a new political system. Portrait painting expressed in artistic form this same consciousness of self. Americans of this period look out at us from their portraits, open, confident, cheerful. They believed in themselves and the new nation they had created. Actual events were far from cheerful: revolutions, world wars, economic distress, dictatorships, surrounded them as they surround us. The art of portrait painting expresses the serene faith in their own worth and in the future that carried them through the dangers and convulsions of their time.

From Harrisburg to Pittsburgh, across the mountains in Pennsylvania, is two hundred miles by modern motor road. The fertile lowlands stretch from the tide's edge to Harrisburg, where the Susquehanna River breaks through the mountains. Between that point and Pittsburgh, where the Ohio River begins its journey of two thousand miles to the Gulf of Mexico, lies the great mountain chain of the Appalachians, range after endless forest-covered range, a grim, forbidding barrier stretching fifteen hundred miles from the Gulf of the St. Lawrence to northern Alabama. The tide of population had reached that wall and, in the neoclassic period, began to trickle through three breaks in it—up the Mohawk Valley in New York toward the Great Lakes (where the power of the Iroquois Confederacy, which had held that gate, had been broken during the Revolution); across Braddock's old road through the Pennsylvania mountains to the head of the Ohio River; and through Cumberland Gap along the famous Wilderness Road into Kentucky and Tennessee. But the frontier was still only a hundred miles, or less, from the Atlantic beaches in most of the length of the thirteen states that had gained their independence in 1783. Even the back country of northern and western New England was still in the pioneer stage when the nineteenth century began.

Against this view of a vast historical process, and of the wilderness at the back door of even the oldest colonies, one must try to visualize the movement of the idea and the craft of painting into the interior of the continent. One must not be surprised to find untrained professionals at work in the heart of New England; or portraits painted by them in Connecticut carried westward to towns like Marietta, Ohio, at the gateway to the interior.

Ralph Earl (1751-1801) may be taken as either the most notable of "untrained professionals" or the most unskilled of the professional painters, as you prefer. He was born in one of the hilly interior townships of Connecticut, which were at this time prolific in painters. His early training is unknown. When fighting broke out in the Revolution, he followed the Connecticut troops to Boston and made four drawings of the *Battles of Lexington and Concord* (1775) which were engraved by Amos Doolittle. The four prints are of great historical interest; but Earl's drawings were very rude affairs. In 1779 he was in London studying with West. He stayed in England until 1785 and even exhibited at the Royal Academy in 1783. Yet six years in England made scarcely any impression upon the archaic severity of his Connecticut style.

Roger Sherman (ca.1777-1779) (Fig. 47) (Yale University Art Gallery), painted before Earl's journey to London, already shows his mature manner in essence. The gaunt Connecticut lawyer is painted life-size, in dark red suit and black stockings, seated in a Windsor chair. The figure and chair achieve a maximum effect of pattern against a bare brown background. The effect is one of monumental, rather flat outline and deep tones of red, black, and brown, with only the face and hands as light accents. John Adams, who observed Roger Sherman closely in the Continental Congress, noted in his diary that he was one of those men whose movements are "stiffness and awkwardness itself." Earl's awkward strength of style and the sitter's character combine to make a striking portrait.

Earl was seldom a student of character, neither was he an observer of nature or of light. The most notable characteristic of his work after his return from England in 1785 was its architectonic decorative power, derived partly from the severity of his drawing, partly from the luminosity of his pigment. A painter of such architectural qualities is best understood in his own artistic setting. The village of Litchfield in the hills of western Connecticut was one of the centers of Earl's activity. The architecture of an eighteenth-century New England village achieves there an almost grandiose effect, with immense avenues, and spacious green vistas bordered by white painted mansions of stiff, provincial grandeur. Earl's portraits of the people who lived in these mansions are still preserved in the Litchfield Historical Society, and seem the embodiment in paint of the spirit of the town itself, Earl's elegance and provincialism creating an exact expression both of the limitations and the strength of Connecticut's rural culture.

Connecticut was full of untrained professionals at this period. Richard Jennys (active in Boston in the 1770's; in the West Indies; in Charleston, South Carolina, 1783-1784; and in Connecticut in the 1790's) and William Jennys (active ca.1800-1810) are a confusing family of painters known to have been active in the Connecticut Valley. Both seem to have used rather a muted palette, and to have painted human beings with a kind of rigid, psychological intensity of character that is most convincing (Fig. 46). The sculptured, melancholy face of *Mrs. Constant Storrs* (The Pennsylvania Academy of the Fine Arts), painted by William Jennys, seems like the earnest soul of New England looking out at us from the canvas.

Another Connecticut painter of striking psychological power was Reuben Moulthrop (1763-1814). His grave, thoughtful figures, like the portrait of *Bradford Hubbard* (ca.1785) (Fig. 48) (New Haven Colony Historical Society) look upward from under level brows at the observer. Their bodies are drawn in steep perspective, as if the sight of some old Tudor or Dutch sixteenth-century portrait had helped to form the artist's notion of his art.

All through what was then the back country of the United States, among a vast amount of painted rubbish in the portrait collections of old historical societies, one comes occasionally upon a portrait of surprising power. Some are anonymous. Sometimes the name of the artist is preserved, without any other facts, as is the case of a pair of portraits signed "McKay 1791" in the American Antiquarian Society, Worcester. One anonymous portrait that sticks in my memory is a remarkably vivid character study of a *Captain Nicholson Broughton* (Peabody Museum, Salem), an American naval officer in the Revolutionary War, who, with arms crossed and tousled hair, has an expression of being ready to take on all comers. The Brooklyn Museum owns another striking portrait of *John Vinal* by a New England painter, John Mason Furness (1763-1804), otherwise unknown except for two copies after

Copley. Such artists were most abundant in New England but are not confined to that region. One finds them in New York state and Pennsylvania—
and in the towns along the Ohio River where the population of New England
and the Middle States was beginning to pour over the Alleghenies into the
empty continent.

In the Middle States Jacob Eichholtz (1776-1842) (Fig. 49) of Lancaster, Pennsylvania, represents the art of the back country in contrast to the
metropolis. Like Peale, he came into painting by way of the crafts (he was
a tinsmith before turning to portrait painting) and his work always retained
the flavor of slightly archaic simplicity and severe honesty of spirit that we
associate with the untrained professional. Yet he was nearer to the atmospheric style than Earl, for example—as a young painter he went to Boston
to learn what he could from Stuart and he was a friend of Sully—so that he
occupies a separate niche. His art shows a good sense of character in portraits
of the old, an innocent sweetness in portraits of children, and a hard, clean,
fresh, luminous style that neither fades nor grows dingy—qualities of an excellent craftsman and an unsophisticated, natural sensibility.

These earnest, awkward, but intense statements of an individual life
remind one, as an artistic phenomenon, of the rude strength of Roman ancestor portraits, which were in their time often very awkward in style. Like
the portraits of the Roman republic, the painted portraits of the young
American republic are the expression of a strong, thoughtful people, limited
as yet in their field of interests, but possessed of a great force of self-consciousness. They reinforce the impression, already given by the painting of the
previous quarter century, that American painting was no longer provincial
English. It was the art of a different people, and a different form of life.

Artists continued to be drawn to America from Europe. The confusion
of the French Revolution and the Napoleonic Wars sent many fleeing to the
young republic of North America. The story of the migrant painters becomes
at this time very picturesque and touching: enthusiasts for Liberty, refugees
from the Terror, hapless political exiles, terrified and destitute families escap-
ing from the horrors of the revolt in Santo Domingo, they came for many
reasons, both willingly and unwillingly; some remained, others returned to
Europe. Among them were many of superior talents and intellectual power.
The wonder is that their influence was on the whole so small.

Robert Edge Pine (1730-1788) came from England for the purpose of
painting a historical record of the American Revolution. A painter in the
rich English Rococo style of Reynolds' generation, he was also an intimate
friend of Wilkes and an enthusiast for Liberty. He arrived in Philadelphia in
November, 1784. Robert Morris, who disliked Charles Willson Peale for his
part in Pennsylvania politics, took up Pine, and built him a house and studio

on Eighth Street. Pine died, however, in 1788, leaving only a few competent and luminously colored portraits, and a small unfinished sketch of *Congress Voting Independence* (Fig. 38). This was all he had accomplished of his projected series of illustrations of the Revolution. It was completed, and butchered, by Edward Savage.

Adolph Ulrich Wertmüller (1751-1811), a Swedish artist who had studied in Paris and become a good portrait painter in the French style of the eighties, came to Philadelphia in 1794. There he painted a portrait of Washington which contributes nothing to his reputation. He failed to get enough portrait commissions to satisfy him and in 1796 returned to Sweden. In 1800 he returned to Philadelphia, married a granddaughter of Gustavus Hesselius, and remained here until his death. He seems to have meant little in the artistic life of the United States, except for the notoriety occasioned by his attempt to introduce the French studio nude. His *Danae*, which had been a success in Paris, gave great offense to the provincial prudishness of that day, and achieved only the dubious notoriety of a peep show.

The greater number of migrants were from France. Since Franklin's embassy to France, America had been the fashion among French intellectuals and many travelers came to see the land of Franklin and Washington, among them writers of distinction like Volney, author of *Ruins, or the Revolutions of Empire*. The Revolution sent us other Frenchmen and Frenchwomen as refugees from the Terror in France, or from revolution in Santo Domingo. Later there were refugees from Napoleon, and from the Bourbon restoration. Many of them, thus thrown penniless on our shores, were men of abilities and culture. To support themselves, they turned to whatever occupations their talents and opportunities suggested. Some taught school, others fencing or dancing. Some who had been amateur artists at home became miniature painters. Moreau de Saint-Méry became an influential book publisher in Philadelphia.

Pierre Charles L'Enfant (1754-1825) was neither refugee nor amateur. He was a trained architect and engineer who volunteered in 1777 to fight for the army of the colonies and emerged from the war a major of engineers. His subsequent career belongs to the story of American architecture; yet his skill as a draughtsman left us a few pictorial records of interest, including a panorama in pen and water color of *A View of West Point on the Hudson River* (ca.1782) (Fig. 56) (Library of Congress), which is the only actual drawing of an encampment of the Continental Army I have ever seen.

Charles Balthazar Julien Févret du Saint-Mémin (1770-1852) arrived in New York city in 1793 on the way to Santo Domingo, when the revolution there left him stranded. To support himself he turned to his talent of drawing. His portraits in crayon were done with the aid of a physiognotrace; but Saint-Mémin turned the fixed pose, necessitated by the machine, into an artistic virtue. His profiles have something of the clear, elegant formality of an enlarged cameo (Fig. 57). Saint-Mémin also made topographic views, which he was the first to execute in America in the beautiful medium of aquatint. He taught himself this technique from an article in the encyclopaedia and used it to make medallion-sized miniatures from his life-size crayon portraits. The trial proof sheets of those engraved miniatures are preserved in the Corcoran Gallery and show the excellent technique and decorative charm of this self-taught engraver. In 1814 Saint-Mémin returned to France, where he spent the close of his life as director of the museum in Dijon.

There is a profile in pastel of an *Unknown Man* in The New-York Historical Society, in a more rude and powerful style, without Saint-Mémin's elegance and repose. It is one of the rare works of an ingenious Swiss-Frenchman, Pierre Eugène du Simitière (ca.1736-1784), who had a small semiscientific, semihistorical museum in Philadelphia some years before Peale, and perhaps inspired the latter's project. Du Simitière's notebooks show him to have been of the same kind of ardent, curious, encyclopaedic mind as Peale; but he left comparatively few works of art.

Another French refugee from Santo Domingo, Philippe Abraham Peticolas (1760-1843), found refuge first in Pennsylvania, then in 1805 in Richmond, Virginia. There he painted miniatures, kept a store, and taught music. One of his sons became in turn a popular portrait painter in Richmond.

A mysterious figure named Valdenuit was Saint-Mémin's partner in portraiture for a few years in the 1790's. In St. Louis there are a few attractive portraits by François Guyol, who was the earliest professional portrait painter in that region, active there as early as 1812. His name and neoclassic style are both French.

There were migrant European painters from other countries also. Christian Gullager (1762-1826), a Dane who had studied in Paris under Jacques Louis David, came to America in 1788 and led a wandering life, chiefly painting portraits. A Russian diplomat, Pavel Petrovich Svinin (1788-1839), left some small water colors of street scenes in American cities that are of interest. The Neapolitan artist, Michele Felice Corné (1752-1832) was active in Salem and Boston, where he decorated house interiors with landscapes and, in his spare time, painted ships and marine views.

A number of English painters of decorative landscapes came to America after the Revolution. William Winstanley (active 1795–after 1806) showed the first panorama in America in 1795. George Washington, who seems to have liked landscapes but had little to choose from, bought four of his pictures for Mount Vernon. Washington also bought two views of the *Falls of the Potomac* by George Beck (1748/9-1812), who arrived in Norfolk in 1795. Beck had spent ten years in the Corps of Engineers of the British Army, before resigning to devote himself to landscape painting; and his pictures have at least a topographic interest. Francis Guy (1760-1820), another English landscapist, was a crude painter but more interesting than Beck. Finally,

William Groombridge (1748-1811), who came to America in 1793, and was active in Philadelphia (1794-1803) and Baltimore (1804-1811), brought something of Richard Wilson's sense of tone in landscape, as can be seen in his *Fairmount and the Schuylkill River* (1800) (Historical Society of Pennsylvania).

Two Scots, Archibald Robertson (1765-1835) and Alexander Robertson (1772-1841), established themselves in New York city in 1791 and 1792 respectively, and lived modestly useful lives thereafter as drawing teachers, painters of miniatures, and makers of small topographic views in water color.

It is significant of the growth of a native artistic life, however, that these migrants, although interesting and sometimes attractive figures, were now marginal to the main stream of American painting. The energies and talents of a new American nation had begun to flow into painting. It is the fortunes and difficulties of the American-born artists which now make up the story that concerns us.

Artists in colonial America were lonely figures. In the neoclassic period they became numerous enough to create an artistic life, for the first time, in an American city. The city where this took place was Philadelphia. It was not only the largest city and the first capital, but it had an intellectual life and a humane tradition of culture. It was, to the neoclassic period, what New York became with the rise of the romantic movement, the center of activity and focus of talent.

One aspect of this was the rise of book and magazine publishing in that city. The publishing business brought with it a development of engraving, which had an influence in turn upon the development of landscape. The interest in scenery was still, in the neoclassic period, closely linked to an interest in topographic views of cities, or of famous "sights." The concentration of attention upon human beings, upon their character and their actions, which had characterized the eighteenth century, gradually widened. Men began to look at the earth around them, not solely as the background of their own activities, but as something interesting in itself. After the Revolution, an increasing number of magazines were published in America (apparently we have always been a nation of magazine readers) and there appeared in these, after 1800, a steadily increasing number of landscape engravings. As one looks through their pages, one can watch the topographic interest of the subject slowly recede in importance until the simple contemplation of nature becomes motive enough for an illustration, and the name of the artist is Thomas Doughty or Alvan Fisher.

At about this same time the technique of engraving, which had been very crude, was raised to a new level by a migration of well-trained English engravers, acquainted with both line engraving and aquatint, drawn by the opportunities of the new world. They came to Philadelphia immediately after the close of the War of 1812 and began to lift the standard of reproductive engraving to a good level.

One of the first landscape artists of interest was William Russell Birch (1755-1834), a miniature painter and engraver who settled in Philadelphia in 1794. In 1799-1800 Birch issued a series of twenty-eight plates of Philadelphia, a delightful record of the most beautiful of American eighteenth-century cities. In 1808 he brought out *The Country Seats of the United States*. One plate of this bears a significant title, *The Sun Reflecting on the Dew, a Garden Scene, Echo, Pennsylvania, a Place Belonging to Mr. D. Bavarage* (Fig. 58). Suddenly we are in a new world. It is no longer the country house but a moment in the life of nature itself that interested the artist: and we are on the threshold of the romantic age.

Landscape engraving, in fact, bridges the gap between classicism and romanticism in American perceptions and, in a land where so few paintings were to be seen, formed an influential source of style for many of the early landscape painters.

John Hill (1770-1850), a well-trained aquatint engraver, migrated from London to Philadelphia in 1816. In 1820 he engraved *Picturesque Views of American Scenery* (Fig. 51) after drawings by another migrant, Joshua Shaw (1776-1860), who had come from London in charge of West's picture, *Christ Healing the Sick*. Some scenes of the American Wilderness were depicted in these aquatints, for the first time, in moods of storm and melancholy that foreshadow Thomas Cole. Hill moved in 1824 to New York city (a symptom of the changing importance of the two cities) and there engraved for another topographic watercolorist, W. G. Wall (1782-1864), a portfolio in which a significant name appears for the first time, *The Hudson River Portfolio* (1828).

The prince of American topographical draughtsmen and aquatint engravers was, however, William James Bennett (1787-1844), who also migrated from England in 1816. His nineteen colored aquatints of American cities (issued 1831-1838) were called by I. N. Phelps Stokes the finest series in existence. Bennett's work was done with the transparent realism, the clear lighting and even accent of the classical style, but certainly helped to popularize a taste for landscape that the romantic landscapists were to profit by.

At the same time, wood engraving, to which Bewick had given an entirely new impetus in Great Britain, was lifted to a new importance in the United States by Alexander Anderson (1775-1870). Anderson re-engraved Bewick's cuts (*Quadrupeds* and *Emblems of Mortality*) and was a most prolific craftsman. The New York Public Library has his old scrapbooks, containing something like eight thousand proofs of his wood engravings. He made every kind of illustration, from sheet ballads and business cards to scientific treatises and large Bibles. Wood engraving, which could be printed with the letter press, inexpensive, and capable of producing a large number of impressions, was thus started on its great period in America. It was to have countless and often delightful results in the books and magazines of the nineteenth century. With the rise of wood engraving came the rise of illustration.

The widening of the field of attention brought with it genre painting, which is the art of observation of daily life.

Jeremiah Paul (fl. 1791-1820) is a shadowy figure, known to us by little more than a few uncomplimentary anecdotes in Dunlap's *History*, and one interesting picture. *Four Children Playing in a Street* (1795) (Fig. 55) (Arthur J. Sussel) is sensitively observed and charmingly painted, the warm browns of the background setting off the rose sashes and white dresses of the girls and the fresh-colored faces in a way that shows Paul knew his business as a painter. More atmospheric than Peale's work, with its own objective poetry, it makes us regret that Paul painted so little. Dunlap implies that he was more interested in a life of good cheer than in painting.

Another pioneer of genre painting in Philadelphia was John Louis Krimmel (1787-1821), who arrived in this country from Württemberg in 1810, at the age of twenty-three. Dunlap says that, after doing a few small portraits, he taught himself to paint genre by copying in oil a print of Wilkie's *Blind Fiddler*. He was a modest, genial painter with a pleasant humor, who had time to do only a few good pictures, of which a typical example is *A Fourth of July Celebration in Center Square, Philadelphia* (1819) (Fig. 54) (The Historical Society of Pennsylvania). His career was cut short by accidental drowning at the age of thirty-four.

In Boston another painter also made a beginning at genre. He was Henry Sargent (1770-1845), who had fought as an officer in the Revolution. He visited London in 1793 and received help from both Copley and West but was largely self-taught as a painter. He painted portraits, did a number of large historical and religious pictures, which he exhibited from town to town and, in the same large scale, painted two interesting genre scenes of Boston upper-class life, *The Dinner Party* (Fig. 50) and *The Tea Party* (ca.1815-1820) (Boston, Museum of Fine Arts). They are too large in scale either for the subject or for his powers as a painter, but show nonetheless a sensitive perception of light and a good feeling for architectonic composition. These abilities might have led to interesting results had Sargent been surrounded by an active artistic life in Boston to sustain and encourage him. But Boston had at this time only a fragmentary and disorganized artistic activity and most of Sargent's energies were devoted to other things than painting.

There had been an interest in still-life painting among the artists of the latter part of the eighteenth century. The few pictures of that time which have already been mentioned show that two ideas of still life were in the air—

the decorative grouping of objects on a table, and the *trompe l'œil*. John Mare's *trompe l'œil* fly has already been mentioned, and a shelf of books painted on the paneling of a Connecticut house by Winthrop Chandler. Charles Willson Peale had experimented, after his return from London, with still life in two little pictures now in Detroit.

The catalogue of the Columbianum Exhibition of 1795 lists still-life paintings by William Birch, by Miss Birch, by James Peale, and five still lifes attributed to Copley. A painting of fruit and insects exists, also, probably of about this date, signed by John Johnston, the Boston painter.

The models for these early examples and for those of the first specialists in still life after 1800 were Flemish and Dutch still lifes by the little masters of the early seventeenth century like Van Hulsdonck, Bosschaert, and their compeers. There were such pictures in the colonies. Du Simitière wrote in 1779 to Governor Clinton in Philadelphia, offering for sale a group of Dutch pictures: ". . . pictures chiefly painted in oyl, on boards in black ebony frames highly polished, of these kinds the Dutch settlers brought a great many with their other furniture. . . . I pikt them up in New York, in garrets, where they had been confined as unfashionable when that city was modernized."

Very few still lifes of this early period have been preserved. From about 1810 onward, however, there are many: a Philadelphia school of still life appears, deriving, as did so many other things, from the unpredictable energies of the Peale family. The two elderly miniature painters, James Peale (the brother of Charles Willson) and Raphaelle Peale (1774-1825), Charles Willson's eldest son, were both active painters of still life in their old age. Their pictures followed the Dutch and Flemish model closely; their subjects were a dish overflowing with fruit, and a few other objects, set on a tabletop whose fore edge runs across the bottom of the picture, and lighted from one side. Their still lifes combined precise drawing, bright, clear colors, and simple effects of luminosity. Both uncle and nephew were also skillful miniature painters in the clear neoclassic manner. But Raphaelle was a sufferer from gout, which affected his hands, and furthermore had not been successful as a portrait or miniature painter. His brush was unable, as his father said, to give the "dignity and pleasing effects" which sitters desired. Yet his still life paintings show no weakness or uncertainty of touch, and his fame as a painter now rests on these late works.

The interest of still-life painting lies in the purely esthetic effects of luminosity, color, and texture, and in the love with which the artist approaches his subject. Both James and Raphaelle Peale brought the miniaturist's clarity of drawing and color to their work, but added the cheerful luminosity of oil paint. Both were of the temperament for still-life painters. The gentle, unworldly, retiring James was a perceptive observer, but one who preferred to avoid the world of action and the competition of life. Raphaelle, disabled by ill health and excluded by intemperance from an active and successful life, brought all the warmth of his genial, sensitive nature to his modest little pictures. The works of these Peales, like all good still lifes, have a quiet visual poetry that defies description.

In another larger picture, *After the Bath* (1823) (Fig. 73) (Kansas City), Raphaelle created also a famous *trompe l'œil*. The area within the frame is almost entirely filled by a white linen sheet, strongly lighted, hanging on a rope stretched across darkness; above its edge, against the dark background, appear a bare wrist and arm, obviously of a young girl; below, a bare foot. The subject has made it popular. What makes it a good picture is the intensity with which the light upon the white linen has been "realized" (to use Cézanne's word).

This period also saw the career of one of the greatest of American artist-naturalists, Alexander Wilson (1766-1813). Wilson is an illustration of the power of genius to overcome obstacles. Looked at from another point of view, he is also an illustration of how high a price must be paid by a talent which must create both its own way and its own audience, unaided by either existing traditions or institutions.

Born in poverty in Scotland, Wilson had little education and became first a weaver's apprentice, then a peddler. His sensibility sought an outlet in poetry. In 1792 he published anonymously a narrative poem, *Watty and Meg*. His sympathies were too democratic for that epoch in Scotland, and in 1794 he migrated to Philadelphia. There he supported himself as a printer, weaver, peddler, and finally schoolmaster. He developed also in these years a passion for the great spectacle of nature in this wild continent. In 1802 he went to teach a school at Kingsessing, near the home of William Bartram, where he became acquainted with the naturalist and other members of his circle, including the engraver Alexander Lawson, who later engraved many of Wilson's drawings. These friendships gave direction to his wandering and solitary life. William Bartram not only encouraged Wilson's interest in nature but made him begin to draw, believing this interest would help rid the lonely schoolteacher of his melancholy.

In the autumn of 1804 Wilson set out on a walk to Niagara and back, a journey of 1,260 miles, much of it through wilderness. There was deep snow on the ground before he reached home. He described the journey in a long poem, *The Foresters*, published in *The Portfolio* and illustrated by his own drawings. This was the first of many such journeys. In 1805 he was already at work on the drawings of birds which became his *American Ornithology* (9 volumes, 1808-1814), both text and illustrations provided by himself. It was his ambition to make it not only a complete record of one phase of nature, but the most beautiful book ever produced in America. This was an enormous undertaking for the slender resources either of the man or of the times. He had to discover, study, draw the birds, and to write their descriptions; then sell subscriptions; see each volume through the press; and pay the bills. Alternately, he would set off on foot across half the continent to make his drawings and to sell his subscriptions; then he would return to Philadelphia to prepare another volume for the press.

As an artist Wilson has been overshadowed by his great successor Audubon. The difference between them is not only one of precedence in order of time, but of temperament and artistic period. Wilson drew with a clear, nervous precision. His plates are arbitrarily composed, but with an admirable sense of pattern, as one may see in the plates of *The Nighthawk* or *The Little Owl* (Fig. 59). The cool clarity, the freshness, the objectivity of his art are typical of the American neoclassic taste, of which his book is one of the notable productions.

The successful close of the War of 1812, after a humiliating and disgraceful beginning, set a seal upon our national independence. Peace brought with it an upsurge of national pride and self-confidence. Cities, states, and the federal government gave artists a series of commissions, ordering portraits and historical subjects to dignify their newly built public buildings and celebrate their history. Some of these commissions have already been mentioned. American artists have always, it seems, longed for public subjects and monumental commissions. Only rarely have they been gratified. The impulse toward a public use of art by government has seldom appeared in our democratic society; when it has, the result has so often been an ironic comedy of misunderstanding, artistic frustration, and popular disappointment that it would perhaps be well to take a closer look at this phenomenon. The information to be gained will not be enlivening, but it may be instructive.

After the close of the War of Independence, both Peale and Trumbull set out to tell its story. Peale's gallery of portraits developed into his Museum which, sustained by the energies of the whole Peale family, grew from a private collection in the studio of the artist to a self-sustaining institution. Trumbull's attempt to find a mass market for his engravings of historical subjects, however, failed and in 1794 he abandoned it to take a diplomatic post with Jay's mission to Great Britain. Yet in the same decade Stuart was to score an enormous success with his portraits of Washington. Lawrence Park's monograph lists 111 of Stuart's various likenesses of Washington; G. A. Eisen in his *Portraits of Washington* (1932) lists 175. Americans were evidently more ready to accept portraits of national heroes than paintings of historical events. Or, perhaps, at this date paintings were more popular than engravings: half a century later the situation was to be the reverse.

In the years of peace after 1814 both portraits and historical subjects were commissioned. In 1814 the City of New York commissioned a series of full-length portraits representing the military and naval heroes of the recent war to decorate its beautiful new City Hall. These portraits, which still hang in their handsome neoclassic setting, were an unqualified success. John Wesley Jarvis did most of them; Vanderlyn painted one; and commissions went also to two young men of the next generation, Waldo and Sully.

The partially completed federal Capitol in Washington, burnt by a British naval raid in the most humiliating episode of the war, had also to be rebuilt and redecorated. Colonel Trumbull returned from England in 1815 and offered his sketches of Revolutionary subjects, executed thirty years before, to the consideration of Congress. In 1817 the Congress voted $32,000 to commission four large paintings for the Rotunda under the then unfinished dome of the Capitol. The subjects chosen were, unfortunately, in a pictorial sense perhaps the least interesting of the series. Trumbull painted *The Declaration of Independence* (1818), *The Surrender of Cornwallis at Yorktown* (1817-1820) (Fig. 53), *The Surrender of Burgoyne at Saratoga* (1817-1821), and *General Washington Resigning His Commission* (1824) and installed them in the Rotunda after exhibiting them in various cities. "Public expectation," wrote William Dunlap a few years after, "was perhaps never raised so high respecting a picture, as in this case [of the *Declaration of Independence*]: and although the painter had only to copy his own beautiful original of former days, a disappointment was felt and loudly expressed." The objections of the public were factual: X who was not there is represented, while Y was there and is not in the picture, and so on. Other artists, exasperated by Trumbull's thorny personality, fanned the mood of discontent. When Trumbull had completed four paintings, he was not given a commission to fill the remaining four vacant walls. It has become a tradition to complain of these paintings as total failures. Trumbull, in my opinion, achieved a greater success than he is given credit for: the panels are large in scale and pleasing in color, respectable if not inspiring mural decorations. But his failure to please gave a check to the ambitions and the popular esteem of his profession. When the question of decorating the Rotunda was taken up again in the next generation, it was accompanied by political bickering, carping jealousy, and a preference among politicians for safe mediocrity that have ever since been part of Congress' relations with American painters.

The legislature of Virginia had, in 1784, voted a marble statue of Washington. The commission was given by Jefferson to Houdon, resulting in the dignified statue which has stood since 1794 in the Capital of Washington's native state. Perhaps inspired by this success, the legislature of North Carolina, in 1818, commissioned of Sully a picture of Washington. The artist, without knowing the dimensions of the building, painted a large and handsome historical canvas, *Washington at the Passage of the Delaware*, (Fig. 62), which, when completed, proved too large for any wall in the capitol building and was left on the artist's hands. The ill-fated picture (much superior as a work of art to Leutze's later painting in the Metropolitan Museum of Art) found its way into a Barnum-type museum in Boston and ultimately to the

Boston Museum of Fine Arts. North Carolina had no better success with a commission given to Canova for a statue of Washington: the statue, which arrived in 1820, showed Washington seated, wearing an entirely unfamiliar face and the armor of a Roman general. This odd flowering of the dream of antiquity is known only from an engraving and from Canova's model (a cast of which is in Raleigh), for the marble was destroyed by fire in 1831.

These experiences did not encourage other states to try their luck; and their beautiful neoclassic capitols seem to have contained nothing more ambitious than official portraits. American architects had not yet, in general, created buildings that required or gave scope to mural decoration. It would seem, also, that American life was too individualistic to demand a public art: the portrait, not the mural, was the form instinctively adopted to commemorate public as well as private memories and affections.

Artists had become numerous enough in the neoclassic period to attempt to form, in the larger cities, the kind of institutions characteristic of their art in other countries. The first academies organized in America were, without being aware of it, trying to do several different things. The academies and art galleries of Europe had developed to fill three somewhat disparate needs. The artists themselves had developed the Academy, which was strictly a professional institution. Its original purpose of freeing the artist from mediaeval craft guild restrictions having been gained, it developed into a school to train young students; it also held exhibitions to show its members' work to the public. On the other hand, the layman in the person of the collector and amateur had created the art gallery, an institution which just at this moment reached a crucial point in its evolution. The French Republic had nationalized the magnificent private collections of the kings of France, installed them in the old palace of the Louvre in Paris, and added to them hundreds of paintings and sculptures carried off from the countries overrun by Napoleon's armies. The Louvre, opened to the public as a vast, national museum and treasure house of art, dazzled and enchanted a world hitherto unaccustomed to such public collections. In Napoleon's time it contained also the chief treasures of the few great semipublic galleries that had preceded it—the Uffizi in Florence and the galleries of the Vatican. The effect was decisive: a new kind of institution was born. When the good citizens of American cities along the eastern seaboard began to form academies of art, they were inspired by the Louvre, although they kept the name associated with the artists' professional societies.

Philadelphia, the largest city with the largest group of artists, took the lead. The first move came from the artists who, under the initiative of Charles Willson Peale, formed a society in 1795 called the Columbianum. Its purposes were those natural to a group of working artists—a school and an exhibition. A political quarrel between the American-born artists with pronounced democratic sympathies, led by Peale, and the English-born miniature painters and engravers with British and Tory sympathies split the society before it was more than a few weeks old and it died stillborn. Peale's section of it, however, set up an art school and held a public exhibit in the spring of 1795. It was the first appearance of these two institutions on American soil.

Ten years later, in 1805, the Pennsylvania Academy of the Fine Arts was organized on a different basis. Though formed by a mixed group of artists and laymen, its board of control was dominated by laymen representing the community rather than by practicing artists. This academy had the purposes congenial to the community mind: a public building and a collection of great art.[5] Its trustees organized a permanent gallery by purchasing casts of classical sculpture (which at first cause some embarrassment by their nudity) and after the close of the war acquired paintings by West, Allston, Lawrence, and other contemporaries. The artists in 1810 set up "The Society of Artists of the United States" and in 1811 were invited to hold an annual exhibition in the galleries of the Academy. The Academy subsequently assumed this duty itself, and also that of a school, and has continued to fulfill those three disparate functions until today.

An Academy dominated by laymen was, probably, a necessity of the times; but it presented a new pattern for such an institution. In Europe, academies composed of practicing artists had always been under the patronage of the ruling prince, but otherwise independent. The artists of Philadelphia resented the lay control of their academy and tried at various times to set up their own organizations, but without success.

In New York there were then fewer artists than in Philadelphia. The initiative there came from a few cultured and public-spirited men who represented the layman's interests. The American Academy of Fine Arts was formed in 1802 with Edward Livingston, mayor of the city, as its first president, and DeWitt Clinton, Dr. Hosack, and other public-spirited citizens on its board. The spur to its organization was a letter from Chancellor Robert R. Livingston, then in Paris as United States Minister to France, urging that money be raised in New York to purchase casts of the antique sculpture in the Louvre. The Academy was formed, money subscribed, and Livingston's first purchase of casts arrived in June, 1803. They were exhibited at the Pantheon, a circular building one block from the Battery, originally a riding school, but at that time a museum of curiosities run by the painter, Edward Savage, in imitation of Peale's museum. Later in the same year John Vanderlyn was commissioned to buy other casts in both France and Italy. Vanderlyn

[5] Its organizers stated its purposes as "To promote the cultivation of the Fine Arts, in the United States of America, by introducing correct and elegant copies from works of the first Masters in Sculpture and Painting, and by thus facilitating the access of such Standards, and also by occasionally conferring moderate but honorable premiums, and otherwise assisting the Studies and exciting the efforts of the Artists gradually to unfold, enlighten, and invigorate the talents of our Countrymen."

never lived up to his contract. He went to Paris, bought a few casts, and settled down there, informing the Academy that Benjamin West had told him Paris was the best place to purchase casts.

This Academy led a very fitful life. It was not incorporated until 1808. Robert Fulton lent it two pictures by Benjamin West, *Ophelia* and *King Lear* (the latter now owned by the Boston Athenaeum) which he had bought in London. But it had no permanent home and at various times the collections were put in storage for lack of a place to exhibit them. In 1816 DeWitt Clinton revived it, space was secured in an old almshouse, together with rooms for the Historical Society, the Lyceum of Natural History, and Scudder's Museum; and in the new quarters its first exhibition of contemporary painting was held in the fall of 1816. Annual exhibitions for living artists were thus instituted, and arrangements were made so that young artists could draw from the casts. In 1817 Colonel Trumbull became president.

Boston, like New York, had a very weak and scattered artistic life at the opening of the century. The initiative there came again from the public-minded people of the city, who formed an Athenaeum, an institution which was primarily a library, but providing also a gallery of art. It formed the inevitable collection of casts of sculpture, which included Michelangelo's *Day* and *Night* as well as the masterpieces of neoclassic taste—the *Apollo Belvedere*, *Venus dei Medici*, *Kneeling Venus*, *Laocoön*, the *Fighting Gladiator*, the *Dying Gladiator*, *Antinoüs*, *Diana and Meleager*. Eventually, larger quarters were built and in the new gallery, in 1826, was held the first annual exhibition of painting in New England.

In the South, a group of laymen and artists in Charleston formed in 1821 the South Carolina Academy of Fine Arts, which erected a building and held exhibitions for a few years. There was not enough life either among artists or amateurs to keep it alive, however, and the building was sold in 1831.

Peale's type of museum belongs to another category. Scientific and educational in purpose in the mind of its creator, it was to the general public a place of amusement and a cabinet of entertaining curiosities. Other institutions inspired by it were more frankly entertainment. The Hartford Museum, opened in 1802 by the painter, Joseph Steward, in a room of the Connecticut State House was one of the better examples. In 1819 it was described in its later, enlarged quarters by a Gazetteer as a room "70 feet in length, and . . . neatly arranged, and handsomely filled with several thousand articles; such as paintings, waxwork, natural and artificial curiosities"; it also contained an organ. Among its natural curiosities were the head of a Bengal tiger, a boa, an alligator, and 2,000 shells; among the artificial curiosities were "a spy glass that could see through an inch board."

From this type of institution it was a brief but natural evolution to P. T. Barnum's type of showmanship.

The effort to create institutions to serve the needs of living artists and

to embody the cultural aspirations of American cities had still a long road
to travel. Much had yet to be done before a solution could be found for the
professional problems that forced West and Copley to live abroad, and before Americans could enjoy their share of the wonderful heritage of man's
imagination, perceptions, and skill to which we give the name of arts.

Yet in the neoclassic period American painting assumed a shape and
direction it had never possessed before. It was an age of profuse, varied creation. Its energies went, not as in France and Germany into elaborate, intellectual reconstructions of the past, nor as in England into a last flowering of
aristocratic portraiture, but into the sober study of its own world. Realistic,
narrative, democratic in spirit, it gave this country its first imaginative image
of itself, evolved its own style, and left behind a substantial and distinguished
legacy of good painting.

If American energies and talents flowed less into the recreation of an
ideal past than did those of European neoclassicism and more into depicting
the people and actions our artists saw around them—if, in other words, neoclassic realism outweighed neoclassic idealism—it is a sign that American
painters were at one with their own world. Instead of an artificial and rhetor-
ical art they gave the new American nation so vivid an image of itself, its
great leaders, its heroic actions, that to a very large extent we still see ourselves through their eyes. This I regard as imaginative achievement of the
first order.

CHAPTER 7

ROMANTICISM: THE FIRST GENERATION

THE NEOCLASSIC PERIOD IN AMERICA BEGAN ABOUT 1780 AND CONTINUED UNTIL about 1820; but its last two decades overlap the first romantic generation. Vanderlyn, born in 1776, was the youngest and last of neoclassic painters. The generation born in the decades 1775 to 1794, who made their appearance as artists between 1800 and 1820, belong, with the exception of Vanderlyn, to the first generation of romanticism.

Romanticism was a world-wide movement and one of the most creative periods of Western art. It is a protean thing, this affair we call romanticism. Taking a thousand different forms in a thousand energetic minds, it is like the jinn that filled the sky and refused to go back into the bottle: it defies us to compress it into a formula. One source was the mystical and philosophical movement of thought in Germany. Another was the great flowering of English poetic genius. But its true source was a shift in the direction of attention from the ancient world to other parts of our inheritance, from the clear neoclassic vision of the world to a many-colored and often deeply shadowed perspective. Our Western inheritance is so rich and complex, woven of so many and diverse strands, that it contains within itself a limitless variety of sensibility. Neoclassicism may be defined as a focusing of attention on logic, clear thinking, and the robust, healthy norm of humanity. "Plain sense, measure, clearness, dignity, grace over all—these made the dignity of Greece,"— as Coleridge put it in *Anima Poetae*. Yet it was also a concentration upon order and authority, an esthetic dogma of Ideal Beauty, a preoccupation with antique sculpture and Graeco-Roman mythology at the expense of everything that had happened since the fall of Rome. Among the logical, Cartesian French, among the Germans with their susceptibility to abstract ideas, neoclassicism became an artistic theory so rigid and confining that it perished eventually, as Jacques Barzun put it, "from an excess of abstraction and generality." [1]

In Britain and America theoretical rules were never very powerful. The artist's sensibility remained intuitive and adventurous. The change from one period to the other came as a gradual alteration of the climate of the mind. There was never occasion for a war of styles such as occurred in France between neoclassicists and the men of 1830; for only in France was the problem formal and stylistic rather than intuitive. In Britain, classical purity of outline became the vehicle of Blake's mystical visions; Flaxman found the models and poses for his illustrations of Homer in the streets of London rather than among the sculptures of the Vatican; Lawrence created the romantic portrait of mood, and Turner the landscape of mood, within the framework of the Royal Academy. Among Americans, West was a leader of neoclassicism in the seventeen-sixties and of romantic melodrama a few years later; Copley's dramatic narratives present some revolutionary breaks from tradition; while, on the other hand, Allston had his studio full of casts of classical sculpture and never lost the imprint made by Rome upon his art.

If this intermingling of two movements within the same period of time, and even the same men, seems illogical and confusing, it is not the first time that life and men's dreams have seemed so.

We have inherited the objective, rational spirit of the Greek philosophers whose delight was to explore the world by observation and reason; but also the mysticism of the Orient, whose great representative is Christianity, for which the only true knowledge is foolishness to the wise, and which is founded upon faith's trust in the mystery of God. We are children of the Roman spirit of social order and law, but also of the barbarian warriors' spirit of liberty: heirs of both the feudal code of loyalty and of the Renaissance spirit of individualism. In the rich, fantastic fabric of our inheritance, threads and colors dip beneath the surface for a time but they are not lost. Sooner or later they reappear again in new combinations.

The satisfactions of the mind are order, clarity, a general validity of statement. The satisfactions of the emotions are excitement, intensity, novelty, and change. The art of neoclassicism was that of men with clear logical minds expressing a rational, objective view of life. Their art was lucid and firm, an art of clear outlines and even lighting, whether its subjects were taken from reality or the ideal world. "There are two kinds of taste," said Henry James, "the taste for emotions of surprise and the taste for emotions of recognition." Classicism enjoyed the emotions of recognition. Romanticism, in part, seems a new departure because it turned to those emotions of surprise which have since been so extravagantly exploited. Up from beneath the calm, clear fabric of classical art came highly colored visions of passion, terror, mystery, wonder, horror, and thrilling sweetness. In place of the sunlit mythology of

[1] *Romanticism and the Modern Ego*, Boston, Little, Brown & Company, 1943, p. 82.

Greece, men's imaginations reveled in the violence of the Middle Ages, half seen through the darkness of legend. Instead of the odes of Horace and the couplets of Pope, men read the Oriental romances of Southey and Byron and the medieval romances of Scott. In American literature, after the shrewd, practical wisdom of *Poor Richard* and the framers of the Constitution, came the madness-haunted violence of Charles Brockden Brown, the mysticism of Channing, and the humorous sentiment of Washington Irving.

Romanticism seems to have been peculiarly sympathetic to our temperament. It came early; it unloosed an extraordinarily wide and varied flowering of talent; it lingered as an overtone of sentiment far into subsequent periods. And it assumed, among the hopeful minds of a new nation, a quite different tone from that on the other side of the Atlantic.

In Europe romanticism was a movement of disillusionment and revolt. The romanticists grew up during the turmoil of the Napoleonic wars; they saw the hopeful idealism of the French Revolution vanish in a maelstrom of social uprising, military dictatorship, imperialism, war, and political reaction. Byron expressed for the whole European world the bitterness and melancholy of his generation; Scott expressed its urge to escape into the world of the past.

In America the upwelling of romantic sentiment had no need to break through the hard crust of an entrenched and dogmatic neoclassical art, nor the pessimism produced by universal war, nor Bourbon reaction. The American artist had to struggle against acute material difficulties but not against hostile ideas: his mood was one of poverty and hope.

Part of this poverty, so far as the artist was concerned, came of the renewed westward expansion of the American people. At the moment when, for the first time, a few cities on the Atlantic tidewater had grown large enough to sustain an artistic life, the great migration began again over the mountains into the interior of the continent. Beyond the Appalachians, in 1800, there were scattered pioneer settlements in Kentucky and Tennessee and a few fur-trading posts originally founded by the French at Mackinac and Detroit, Vincennes, St. Geneviève, St. Louis. Beyond these stretched a vast, unknown, unexplored wilderness. While Washington Allston was creating the first landscapes by an American to depict nature as a majestic, beautiful, and terrifying power, Meriwether Lewis and Captain William Clark were leading the first exploring expedition (1804-1806) to reach the Pacific Ocean by overland journey, crossing the immense nameless rivers, plains, and mountain ranges. In the next seventy-five years Americans spread westward two thousand miles across the continent, creating on the march most of the states and cities we now inhabit. Once more the American people plunged into the wilderness, far from the settled eastern coast and its only-just-consolidated society. The artists of the little cities of the seaboard were poor and struggling enough. Now the story of the artist born in frontier con-

ditions was to be repeated three, four, five hundred or a thousand miles farther west. Once more the creation of a skilled craft, a professional point of
view, schools, academies, exhibitions, an artistic life had to be done over
again, among the forest trees, on the banks of the Ohio and the Mississippi,
or on the shores of the Pacific.

Yet this remarkable national experience, coupled with the novelty of our
form of government and society, also affected in a positive way the spirit of
the romantic movement. The new hope for humanity which Lincoln saw in
American democracy was at its hour of dawn and cast its glow over our romantic age. Artists might be scattered and lonely in their vast new land: yet
vastness and newness were stimulating, when they did not overwhelm. The
poetry of their vision of a limitless virgin land, spread out before the mind's
eye, is vividly expressed in Audubon's essay describing how he and his bride
floated in an open boat down the wild Ohio, through the golden forests of
October, to a new home in the West. It breathes in the noble optimism of
Emerson's essays. It set the scale of Whitman's panoramic art.

This experience affected the interests of American romantic artists in
many different ways. The Byronic elements of European romanticism—the
melancholy and disillusionment, the egoism, the willful break with society
and art, the worship of one's own genius, the withdrawal into a little coterie
in opposition to the rest of life—did not appear here. American romantic artists were saved from pouring their energies into revolt. A growing awareness
of art did not break the intuitive harmony between the artist and his world.
New emotions were awakened in the artist's consciousness, the horizon of his
art was expanded; but romantic art retained as its base a sense of kinship with
man and with the earth.

At the beginning of this period, West's studio in London was the leading American art school; but as artists more and more found their way to
France, Germany, and Italy, the old colonial link with England was gradually
lost. The dream of Italy gradually became one of the great imaginative influences in American romantic painting.

The ideal world of the first American romantic painters was created
chiefly from Shakespeare and the Bible. It is difficult for us to realize, today,
how large a part the plays of Shakespeare took in forming the romantic imagination. This was the great age of Shakespeare on the stage of both England and America. All his plays, not a selected few, were acted constantly by
generations of famous players to an insatiable public. The artists went constantly to the theater; their eyes were filled with theatrical images and their
minds saturated with the grandiose and passionately human visions of Shakespeare's imagination. Nothing is more completely out of fashion, at the
moment, than Alderman John Boydell's *Shakespeare Gallery* (issued ca.1780-
1802) yet a whole generation of the best English painters displayed their

imaginative powers in these wildly melodramatic plates. The romantic spirit was born in hyperbole and melodrama.

The Bible was another source of romantic subject matter. After the skepticism of the eighteenth century came a revival of Christianity. It was of special force in America, which had deep-rooted memories of the religious migrations of the seventeenth century. The mere names of Channing, Emerson, Hawthorne, Thoreau in our literature illustrate the strong ethical intuitions, the idealism, the preoccupation with the grandeur or the tragedy of the individual soul that characterized the mental climate of American romanticism. But like these writers the painters were detached from traditional Christianity. They turned to the Bible as a storehouse of imaginative inspiration for art, but not for liturgical pictures: for the churches made little or no use of them. Their religious paintings were made for the layman and the exhibition gallery, not for the altar.

"Poetry," said Byron, "is the expression of excited passion." This was the mood in which the romantic impulse detached itself from classicism. Subject matter of the most dramatic kind demanded a different style, also, from the clear and sculpturesque groupings of neoclassic art. A new mood and a new manner of painting developed together.

One of the first painters to lead the way was Benjamin West. With his usual facility and sensitiveness to new impressions, West, as early as 1777, painted *Saul and the Witch of Endor* (Fig. 60) (Hartford, Wadsworth Atheneum), a haunting masterpiece of protoromanticism, embodying its fantastic subject in highly dramatic effects of color and light. Such subjects gradually become more important in his work. An enormous *King Lear* (1788) (Boston, Museum of Fine Arts), filled with wild turmoil on a heroic scale, is one of his most powerful romantic melodramas. By 1800 this had become the predominant mood of his work.

When artists attempt to paint scenes of madness, terror, frenzied rage, it is inevitable that the stable and intellectual elements of painting (as Winckelmann called them), i.e., line and sculptured form, should become inadequate as tools of expression. The stylistic discoveries of romantic painting in all Western countries were discoveries in the use of light and color to convey dramatic and mysterious tones of feeling. In this respect West enjoyed an advantage through his position in London. On the continent, classicism had brought a technical revolution of style that swept away the use of color, tone, luminosity, atmosphere, the use of glazes—all the elements of the coloristic technique which the romantic painters had later laboriously to rebuild. But in London the old traditions of the craft of painting survived. The movement of light, the radiance of color, the mysterious resonance of tone were normal studio knowledge. The continuity of craft tradition in the London studios was one of the strongest elements in the rise of romantic style.

It was this, rather than the intrinsic greatness of the London artists, which made the French romantic painters study their work so eagerly.

By 1800 West was a painter of international repute. During the brief peace of Amiens he visited France and was received as one of the leaders of European art. And, in fact, he was. The fine sketch of *Death on the Pale Horse* (1802) (Philadelphia Museum of Art), which he exhibited in the Salon of 1802, anticipated by twenty-five years the coloristic style and the drama of Delacroix's *Death of Sardanapalus* whose exhibition in the Salon of 1827 established the French romantic movement.[2] He gave romantic form also to the portrait. His *Robert Fulton* (1806) (Cooperstown, New York State Historical Association) with visionary eyes, seated moodily before a sullen, dark sea upon which a warship explodes at the blast of a torpedo; or the dark glowing sketch of *Franklin Drawing Electricity from the Sky* (ca.1805) (private collection) are portraits of mood, true romantic compositions both in form and feeling.

The subjects of romanticism—excited passions—were in the air. They crop out in most unexpected places. One might perhaps argue plausibly that Vanderlyn's *Death of Jane McCrea* is more romantic than neoclassical. And Copley, the most objective and realistic intelligence in American painting at that age, drew on one of romanticism's most fruitful sources, Spenser's *Faerie Queene*, for the theme of his curious, dreamlike family group called *Una and the Red Cross Knight* (Washington, National Gallery of Art).

There was thus within later eighteenth-century painting a protoromantic movement of fantasy and melodrama. The first generation of romanticism, from 1800 to 1830, inherited its highly wrought mood.

The most important figure of the first romantic generation was Washington Allston (1779-1843), a South Carolinian whose life was spent in Boston, except for two long periods of study and work abroad from 1801 to 1808, and 1811 to 1818.

Allston was a subjective artist; he was the first American painter whose art was an exploration of the visions within his own mind. The long line of American dreamers after him, throughout the nineteenth century—Quidor and Page, Fuller and Ryder, Rimmer, LaFarge, Vedder—show the importance of this visionary direction of our painting, in which he pioneered. He had somewhat the same kind of brooding imagination as Hawthorne, an imagination fed more by memory and reverie than by observation. His work falls into two recurrent moods, each of which was dominant in a period of his life. Before 1818, the predominant mood was dramatic and grandiose, the scale large, the style monumental. After his return to America in 1818 a delicate,

[2] Another sketch, or rather picture, of *Death on the Pale Horse* by West in the Minneapolis Institute of Arts seems to be earlier and is in some ways an even more dramatic composition.

lyrical mood became predominant, his pictures were small in scale, and are best described as images of reverie.

Like many other Southern boys, Allston was sent North to be educated, first at school in Newport, then at Harvard. When he graduated from Harvard in 1800, twenty-five years after Copley's departure from Boston, the craft of painting had not yet recovered from the check given it by the Revolution. An ambitious art student (and Allston was very ambitious) turned naturally to London for training. It was a fortunate choice. In London, where he studied from 1801 to 1803, he learned the coloristic technique of the London studios: the use of underpaint and glazes, of light and color, which was the key to the stylistic development of romantic painting. When he went on to Paris (1803-1804) and Rome (1804-1808) he had an instrument that Continental painting had forgotten how to use.[3] In Napoleon's Louvre and in Rome he discovered what he wanted to do with this technique. Years later he summed up his impressions of the Venetian sixteenth-century painters in a passage so significant that it is worth quoting here:

Titian, Tintoret, and Paul Veronese absolutely enchanted me, for they took away all sense of subject. When I stood before the *Peter Martyr, The Miracle of the Slave* and *The Marriage of Cana,* I thought of nothing but the gorgeous concert of colors, or rather of the indefinite forms (I cannot call them sensations) of pleasure with which they filled the imagination. It was the poetry of color which I felt; procreative in its nature, giving birth to a thousand things which the eye cannot see, and distinct from their cause. I did not, however, stop to analyze my feelings—perhaps at that time I could not have done it. I was content with my pleasure without seeking the cause. But now I understand it, and *think* I understand why so many great colorists, especially Tintoret and Paul Veronese, gave so little heed to the ostensible *stories* of their compositions. In some of them, *The Marriage of Cana* for instance, there is not the slightest clue given by which the spectator can guess at the subject. They addressed themselves, not to the senses merely, as some have supposed, but rather through them to that region (if I may so speak) of the imagination which is supposed to be under the exclusive domination of music, and which, by similar excitement, they caused to teem with visions that "lap the soul in Elysium." In other words they leave the subject to be made by the spectator, provided he possessed the imaginative faculty—otherwise they will have little more meaning to him than a calico counterpane.[4]

This passage, with its conception of a picture as an evocation of reverie, is a perfect description of his own later paintings. At first, however, he was still governed by the grandiose and dramatic mood. His aim before 1818 was to

[3] A number of anecdotes told both by Allston and other painters, revealing the novelty of his technique in the eyes of painters in Paris and Rome, are in my *Washington Allston,* Chicago, University of Chicago Press, 1948.

[4] Quoted from a letter to William Dunlap in *A History of the Rise and Progress of the Arts of Design,* New York, George P. Scott and Company, 1834, vol. II, pp. 162-163.

use the Venetian language of the radiance of light and the resonance of tone, to express visions of the magical, the terrifying, and the mysterious in nature and in the soul of man.

These visions took shape first in a series of landscapes, *The Rising of a Thunderstorm at Sea* (1804) (Fig. 61) (Museum of Fine Arts, Boston), *The Deluge* (1804) (The Metropolitan Museum of Art, New York) and *Diana in the Chase* (1805) (Mrs. Algernon Coolidge, Boston), which lifted American landscape painting from the level of simple topography to that of the dramatic landscape of mood: Nature has become a vision of magical beauty and terrifying power. (The *Diana* was the foundation of a lifelong friendship with the poet Coleridge, with whose art it has a certain kinship.) Nature is no longer a backdrop for human life, but a vast experience of tremendous imaginative meaning within which human life exists as an element.

In Allston's figure paintings likewise the clear light, the objectivity, the calm and repose of neoclassical art gave way to a mood of magic. His early pictures are dramatic and grandiose, as are those of contemporaries like Blake, in England, Prud'hon, in France, Runge, in Germany. Keats, in an early poem, *Sleep and Poetry* (1817), writes of

> Shapes of delight, of mystery and fear,
> Passing along before a dusky place.

These were Allston's visions. He loved to draw from the Old Testament subjects that lay on the border between the known and unknown, where out of the darkness something makes itself felt upon our psychic life. Two of the most famous of these pictures are scenes from the legends of the Jews, *The Dead Man Revived in the Tomb by Touching the Bones of the Prophet Elisha* (1811-1813) (Fig. 63) (The Pennsylvania Academy of the Fine Arts) and *Belshazzar's Feast* (1817-1843) (The Detroit Institute of Arts).

This was new territory for the imagination of American artists to explore. In the *Dead Man Revived* Allston boldly emulated a great altarpiece of the Renaissance then in London—Sebastiano del Piombo's *Raising of Lazarus*, painted at Rome in 1519 in rivalry with Raphael's *Transfiguration*. (Allston was not alone in such ambitions: Turner, in the same spirit, challenged the monumental landscapes of Claude Lorrain.)

Allston ruined his health by overexertion while painting these great canvases of his middle years; he never again recovered his physical strength. Yet when he returned to America in 1818 his work showed no loss of vigor. Some of his most compelling imaginative pictures were done in Boston in the years 1819 to 1821. But in the quiet, literary atmosphere of Boston, without great works of art to challenge his ambition, and without the stimulus of an active artistic life around, the quietism in his nature came to the front. His pictures became small in size, delicate and dreamlike in feeling. *The Moonlit*

Landscape (1819) (Fig. 65) in Boston and *The Flight of Florimell* (1819) (Plate VII) (The Detroit Institute of Arts), drawn from an episode in Spenser, are typical of the images which initiated a new mood of reverie in American romanticism.

At this moment a group of Boston gentlemen raised ten thousand dollars to purchase the large canvas of *Belshazzar's Feast,* which Allston had begun in London and brought, unfinished but already famous, to America. When he unrolled the canvas in his Boston studio in 1821, he showed it to Gilbert Stuart, who suggested a change in the point of sight. It was the great tragedy of Allston's life that he accepted Stuart's advice. It necessitated months of boring, mechanical drudgery, redrawing and repainting the elaborate architecture of the Assyrian king's palace. When at last he was ready to return to the work of creating the intense, subtle, psychological tensions in the figures, his interest in the picture was gone. The mood of his art had changed. He was never able to finish the key figure of Daniel to his satisfaction. In other circumstances, he would have abandoned the picture and gone on to other work. But oppressed by the obligation that the picture had been purchased unfinished, he slaved at a work of which he had lost the thread for eight years, from 1821 to 1829; then laid it aside for eleven years. In 1840 he unrolled the canvas again, and began to work it out in terms of a new and more monumental conception, but died before he was able to complete it. The anguish and frustration of the years 1821-1829 gave his art, once so ardent and inventive, a blow from which it never recovered.

If one believes as I do that the great task of painting in this generation was to transcend the narrow boundaries of the colonial portrait tradition and to enlarge the imaginative field of subjects that painting could deal with, the importance of Allston's aspiration toward the narrative and the monumental in style, toward the heroic and ideal in subject matter, is obvious. The tide of taste afterwards turned against these big pictures, and his failure to finish the *Belshazzar* became to a later generation a symbol of the failure of his art. Certainly great talents, skill, resolution, and stubborn devotion to an ideal of art went into them. It is likewise true (and this is an inexorable law of art) that only the final result, the work of art itself, counts. All else—intention, struggle, moral courage, personal tragedy—are biography; to confuse them with art (however admirable they may be) is illusion. Yet I find in Allston's series of canvases, from the dramatic power and monumentality of *The Dead Man Revived* to the ruined grandeur of *Belshazzar's Feast,* great qualities both of imagination and style. Compared with the steady, assured competence of Stuart's production, which is usually considered the high point of American painting in the early Republic, Allston's production is tragically uneven and small in number. Yet Thomas Gold Appleton, who belonged to the generation which considered Allston a failure, told of a comment by an English visitor who, seeing an Allston and a Stuart hanging side by side in an exhibition at the Athenaeum, said: "This man has accomplished much more perfectly than the other what he attempted; but Allston attempted what the other could not have conceived." [5] It is a judgment with which I should agree.

The aspect of Allston's art most appealing to modern taste is his landscape reveries upon nature. It was his theory, clearly stated in the letter to Dunlap already quoted, that a picture should be full of suggestion: be so rich in overtones of feeling, and so poetic in its use of light and tone, that the observer will find it the starting point for long meditation. His early landscapes, like *The Rising of a Thunderstorm at Sea* (1804) (Fig. 61) (Museum of Fine Arts, Boston), or *The Deluge* (1804) (The Metropolitan Museum of Art) are images of nature as overwhelming power; *Diana in the Chase* (1805) of nature as magically enchanting loveliness; *Elijah in the Desert* (1818) (Museum of Fine Arts, Boston) of the vast silence of the universe, in which man's soul finds itself alone.

As his art grew quieter, so the mood of his landscape changed: after the drama of the early works came in his old age a quieter reverie on the notes of wonder and solitude. To achieve this, in pictures like *The Moonlit Landscape* (1819) (Museum of Fine Arts, Boston) or *The Flight of Florimell* (1819) (The Detroit Institute of Arts), he developed a style of controlled luminosity and deep resonances of tone that set new standards of subtlety and atmospheric richness in American painting. He learned in these pictures to do what he admired in Venetian painting: to work with atmospheric tone which was also light. He thus found his own way to the new mode of perception which, between 1820 and 1830, became the problem of creation for the most advanced minds in painting—for Constable and Corot, Delacroix and Turner. Allston developed his own technique, a use of underpaint and glazes, to create a diffuse glow of color which is both light and tone, filled with many accents, but fused into that over-all unity which, as John LaFarge put it, is the color of your painting.

Allston was not an active teacher: he preferred to live in retirement among his memories and dreams. Yet through the example of his work and through one of his early pupils, Samuel F. B. Morse, who became the first head of the National Academy of Design in New York city, his influence made itself felt. He was the pioneer of an art of mood in America. The note of grave, brooding reverie which he struck became one of the characteristic tones of American painting: in Page and Quidor, Rimmer and Fuller, LaFarge and Vedder, it is heard throughout the nineteenth century. West had created a grandiose narrative art before Allston; it was the subjectivity, the veil of reverie which transforms Allston's pictures into fantasy and dream that was his contribution. The vein of feeling opened by him proved to be a rich one.

He made still another important contribution when, after winning a dis-

[5] "Portrait Painting and Gilbert Stuart," *International Review*, X (1881), 64-71.

tinguished reputation in London, he returned to practice his art in Boston. Stuart had returned, but to practice the art of portraiture, which was already well established here. Vanderlyn and Trumbull had returned from Europe with another, wider conception of painting, but to become bitter, complaining old men, discouragers of the young rather than leaders of a rising profession. Allston's production after his return in 1818 is tragically small: the break in his development made by *Belshazzar's Feast* was never repaired. Yet he remained a courageous, dignified figure, who lived and worked as an imaginative artist, and gave stature to the profession of painter in American life. His dreamlike pictures, his contemplative life in the studio overlooking the Charles, became symbols of new possibilities in American life. As Margaret Fuller expressed it, writing in the first issue of *The Dial* about an exhibition of Allston's work in Boston, "I saw," she said, "that he had not been troubled but possessed his soul with the blandest patience; and I hoped, I scarce knew what, probably the *mot d'énigme* for which we are all looking. How the poetical mind can live and work in peace and good faith! how it may unfold to its due perfection in an unpoetical society!"

In 1816 the Pennsylvania Academy of the Fine Arts purchased Allston's *The Dead Man Revived*. In the same year West sent over from London another large painting, *Christ Healing the Sick*, as a gift to the Pennsylvania Hospital. These two pictures differed, both in style and in the character of their appeal, from Vanderlyn's panoramas or Trumbull's patriotic murals. Their appeal was neither to the curiosity of travel nor to patriotic feeling, but to the strong, fervent, mass sentiment of Biblical piety; and they were in the eloquent, novel, romantic style, full of color, dramatic movement, and mystery.

Other painters were inspired to paint great religious subjects. But, since the churches were not interested in using their skills, and there were no other buildings suitable for large pictures, there ensued one of the most curious artistic experiments in our history: mural paintings without walls, carried about the country as traveling shows in search of their audience. Most of these itinerant murals have disappeared, victims of accidents, neglect, or wear. The best account of them from the artist's point of view is given by the painter-historian, William Dunlap, in his amusing autobiography. As a young man he had abandoned painting for the theater; the ruin of his theatrical ventures sent him back, twenty years later, to portrait painting as a means of supporting his family. In 1822 he turned his hand to religious murals, painting a picture, twelve by eighteen feet, of *Christ Rejected*, basing it on a printed description of West's picture of the same subject. (When West's son brought over the original in 1829 for exhibition, Dunlap good-humoredly says, he painted out the figures corresponding to West's and introduced "others of my own, worse.") He followed this with *Death on the Pale Horse*, also based on West; *The Bearing of the Cross; Calvary;* and finally a subject from the French revolution, *The Attack on the Louvre.* After trying the experiment of showing these himself, he found it more advantageous to hire an agent to do so. The agent would go from town to town, hire a hall, unroll his picture, set it up, advertise, sell tickets, and usually deliver a lecture in the bargain.

At one place a picture would be put up in a church, and a sermon preached in recommendation of it: in another, the people would be told from the pulpit to avoid it, as blasphemous; and in another the agent is seized for violating the law taxing puppet shows. . . . Here the agent of a picture would be encouraged by the first people of the place, and treated by the clergy as if he were a saint; and there received as a mountebank, and insulted by a mob. Such is the variety of our manners, and the various degrees of refinement in our population.

"On the whole," he concluded, "the reception of my pictures was honorable to me and to my countrymen." [6] All these large pictures have, however, since disappeared; as have those of Henry Sargent, once also popular.

Only one of all these itinerant murals has survived. This is the *Court of Death* (1820) (Fig. 68) (The Detroit Institute of Arts), by Rembrandt Peale (1778-1860), based upon a poem by an English clergyman, Bishop Porteus. Peale called this huge picture (11'6" by 23'5") a "Moral Allegory." The scene represents a huge cave, dimly lighted from above, in which Death presides over a gloomy assemblage. Death sits in the center, his foot upon the corpse of a man stricken in the prime of life, to illustrate his power over mankind. The head and feet of the corpse touch the waters of oblivion, to indicate the mystery surrounding the origin and the end of life. On either side of Death are his principal agents. To the right, War, Conflagration, Famine, and Pestilence rush over the fallen warrior and the widow and orphan. On the left, Pleasure presents the cup to Intemperance, behind whom Remorse covers his face with his hands. Next are Delirium Tremens and Suicide; beyond these a group of Consumption, Despair, Fever, Apoplexy, Hypochrondria, and Gout. In front of this panorama of gloom and horror Old Age, supported by Faith, resigned but unterrified, greets the figure of Death.

One might suppose that since the medieval populace gaped at the miracle plays, there had not been an audience sufficiently simple to relish this allegory. A mistake. This Moral Allegory was so well addressed to the taste of Peale's own age that, when he first exhibited it, he earned over eight thousand dollars in a single year. It continued to be exhibited for over half a century. And it is by no means an inconsiderable painting—monumental, graceful in drawing, subtle in its use of light. Although allegory by its very nature

[6] Dunlap's autobiography forms chapters XIII, XIV and XV in his *History . . . of the Arts of Design, etc.*

makes it impossible to draw together the individual figures into the tight psychological unity that convinces, the individual figures in this huge picture are of considerable eloquence.

There is something fantastic, even a little ludicrous to our minds, in the notion of an itinerant mural painting carried about the country and used to point a moral to the simple. This whole episode in our artistic history has been much laughed at and deprecated. Yet as a cultural phenomenon it has also great interest: representing the drive of so many ideals—of art, of piety, and undoubtedly also of entertainment (for it helped fill a gap left by the evangelical churches' prohibition of the theater)—operating in the emptiness of frontier life, that it deserves some remembrance.

The portrait remained the staple of American painting, both as an economic base and as a disciplined craft, throughout the early nineteenth century. The public wanted portraits and would pay for them: and for the most part would pay for no other kind of painting. When artists painted other types of subject matter, it was to please themselves.

The major cities of the Atlantic seaboard had each a little colony of portrait painters: the older men working in the neoclassic idiom; the younger in the newer, more romantic portrait of mood. The names of these portrait painters, solid, competent, pleasing craftsmen for the most part, have a secure if modest place in our history. In Boston there was Stuart's imitator, James Frothingham (1786-1864), and the giant frontiersman, Chester Harding, whose late development places him with the succeeding generation, artistically. In New York, Waldo, Jewett, W. E. West, and Samuel F. B. Morse belong to this generation; and the lively old painter, William Dunlap, our first important active playwright and theatrical producer, also figures as a portrait painter. Sully and Rembrandt Peale, with headquarters in Philadelphia and Baltimore, were the chief portrait specialists in the Middle States. Charles B. King (1785-1862) was active for forty years in Washington, and during summers in his home at Newport. Farther south, there were Edward F. Peticolas (b. 1793, active 1805-1834) in Richmond; the admirable miniature painter, Charles Fraser, in Charleston; and wandering refugees from the northern climate, like Eliab Metcalf (1785-1834). In Kentucky and Tennessee, Matthew Harris Jouett (1787-1827) and Ralph E. W. Earle (d. 1837) were the leading names. Most of these men, when business was slack at home, would travel widely in search of commissions, often going south in the winter to Norfolk, Charleston, New Orleans, or even Havana.

The stylistic development of the portrait was away from the calm, statuesque, clearly lighted neoclassic portrait toward a portraiture of mood. Allston created a highly original portrait form, suggested to him by the gravity and mystery of Titian's portraits. But his mysteriously luminous portraits were done only to please himself, as records of his family and intimate

PLATE VIII. Samuel F. B. Morse: *Congress Hall (The Old House of Representatives)* (1822). (Courtesy of The Corcoran Gallery of Art.)

PLATE IX. Thomas Cole: *The Architect's Dream* (detail) (1840). (Courtesy of The Toledo Museum of Art.)

friendships, and had no effect on the general practice. The chief influence came from English romantic portraiture, especially that of Lawrence: dramatic contrasts of light and dark, a graceful flowing movement in the pose, a new interest in touch or brushstroke, and especially the suggestion of a flash of fleeting expression by the emphasis given to the eyes and the corners of the mouth were its chief characteristics.

Thomas Sully (1783-1872) was the leading portrait painter of this generation in Philadelphia. He was in the United States what Lawrence was in England, the creator of a romantic portraiture of mood, elegant, reflective, tinged with sweetness and melancholy, and immensely popular. His masterpiece is perhaps the full-length of *Col. Thomas Handasyd Perkins* (Fig. 64), the great China merchant and philanthropist, painted for the Boston Athenaeum in 1831-1832. Sully never surpassed the mingled grace and dignity of this figure. In addition to portraits, Sully painted some five hundred subject pictures, historical compositions, and landscapes during his long life. Many of these are what his own age called "fancy subjects" and appear to us exactly that, for romantic sentiment declined easily into the sentimental. Sully was at his best as a portrait painter. His portraits were always large, easy and decorative in style, sometimes highly perceptive (especially in his earlier years), often romantically pretty. The high level of his portraits and their sheer number (about two thousand) make him the dominant figure in his generation of American portrait painters.

A far more complex, puzzling, and uneven figure was Rembrandt Peale, the son of Charles Willson Peale. His early works start from his father's neoclassic style, but have an easy grace that is distinctive. His portrait of *Thomas Jefferson* (1805) in The New-York Historical Society is an admirable example of this phase. In 1807 and 1809 he twice visited Paris to paint portraits of famous men for Peale's Museum. Denon, Napoleon's director-general of museums, is said to have advised him to remain in Paris. "I prefer Gérard to you," he said, "but I prefer your portraits to any others here." His paintings of this period are in a brilliant, luminous style. The *Robert Fulton* (The Detroit Institute of Arts) is an example which makes one understand Denon's advice. Yet in 1812, piqued by criticism of one of his pictures, he abandoned painting. He built the Peale Museum in Baltimore, established the first illuminating gas works in Baltimore, and returned to painting only in 1820, with *The Court of Death*.

A gifted and energetic character like his father, he was a man of great parts. Yet some instability of character seemed to rob him of the fruit of his talents. His "Port-Hole" portrait of *Washington* (1822) (The Pennsylvania Academy of the Fine Arts) was promoted with the enthusiasm of a Barnum. He campaigned energetically to have it accepted as the standard likeness, in place of Stuart's Athenaeum head; by his own statement, he painted seventy-six replicas. At fifty he could still paint such a frank, intense study of character as his own *Self-Portrait* (1828) (The Detroit Institute of Arts) which I never look at without pleasure. Yet he was also capable of painting, in these years, some of the most disagreeably labored, fussed-over, badly colored paintings one can imagine; and the sum total of his life's work is disappointing.

Samuel F. B. Morse (1791-1872), like Vanderlyn, illustrates the tragedy of an observer, a realist by temperament, who was carried away by the theory of an ideal art. "My ambition," he wrote to his father while studying in London, "is to be among those who shall revive the splendor of the fifteenth century; to rival the genius of a Raphael, a Michelangelo, or a Titian." With such dreams filling his mind, he nevertheless only twice attempted large compositions, neither of which have anything to do with ideal beauty!

Morse brought back from his years in London an excellent coloristic technique; yet he wandered unhappily from city to city, up and down the Atlantic coast, in search of portrait commissions, finally settling in 1824 in New York city. He was tormented by the feeling that the only work worthy of a true artist was to create great imaginative compositions. No one ordered such pictures, however; nor did they come out of Morse's own mind. He had time and opportunity, during the intervals between portraits, to paint whatever he wished. Instead of pouring forth a stream of imaginative compositions he sat idle, and felt unhappy.

Congress Hall (1822) (Plate VIII) (Washington, Corcoran Gallery of Art) and *The Gallery of the Louvre* (1832) (Syracuse University, Syracuse, N.Y.), his two large pictures, are vigorous, interesting, sensitively observed examples of documentary realism, and in their own way truly original. He professed great distaste for portrait painting; yet he could paint delightfully observed and sparkling portraits, like *Mrs. Daniel De Saussure Bacot* (The Metropolitan Museum of Art). His travel sketches of Italy (1832-1834) are pleasing in their transparent romantic realism; the pictures painted from them in the studio tend toward an operatic sentimentalism. But, like Vanderlyn, he had not the independence of mind to accept himself, on whatever plane his abilities lay, and to follow his own inner direction.

Ultimately his restless mind turned to scientific invention. The idea for the telegraph came to him on his return voyage from Italy in 1832 and, seizing upon it, he exhibited the unhesitating, self-confident drive of the man who knows what he wants to do with his life. After 1837 his invention completely superseded painting and became the great achievement of his life. Yet he has a place in painting as a romantic realist; in photography, as one of the first Americans to seize upon Daguerre's invention; and in the social history of art, as the leader of the young romanticists of New York city in their revolt against Colonel Trumbull, a story which will be told in another place.

Samuel Lovett Waldo (1783-1861), on the other hand, perhaps illustrates the danger of too little aspiration. Born in Windham, Connecticut (it is extraordinary how prolific of good painters Connecticut was in those days), he painted portraits until he had saved enough to go to London, 1806-1808. West befriended him, as he did many other young Americans. Waldo returned to New York city in 1809 with a large, simple style of portraiture, as good as Sully's at his best, and superior perhaps in perception of masculine character (Fig. 67). Waldo's portraits in New York during the next seven years are observant, fresh, luminous, giving every indication of an admirable talent. In 1816 he took his pupil William Jewett (1795-1874) into partnership. Thereafter they worked in collaboration for almost forty years, turning out a series of solid and competent portraits, but without any of the distinction of Waldo's early work. Perhaps Waldo would have been the better for a touch of Morse's ambition and discontent.

There is one other interesting portrait painter whose life followed a far different pattern. William E. West (1788-1857) was one of the earliest artists to come from the settlements west of the Alleghenies. Born in Lexington, Kentucky, when that region was still the wild frontier, he found his way to Philadelphia to study with Sully; turned up in Natchez in 1818-1819; then set off for Italy. In January, 1820, he was enrolled in the Accademia delle Belle Arti in Florence. In 1822 the Academy of Fine Arts in New York wrote, commissioning him to make a portrait of Lord Byron, who was then staying with the Gambas at Villa Rossa, Montenero, near Pisa. West painted not only Byron but Shelley and Trelawny also (Fig. 66), in a style whose romantic dash and moodiness is worthy of his subjects. West remained abroad eighteen years, in Italy, Paris (1824), and London (1825-1838), where he seems to have spent his happiest and most successful years. After his return to the United States, he lived in New York for fifteen years (1840-1855) and finally died in Tennessee. Most of his work appears to have remained abroad, or undiscovered. His portraits of Byron and Trelawny show a fine, fresh, youthful, romantic talent. Too little of his work is known to show whether that youthful promise was all, or whether an interesting and significant talent is hidden here.

The first annual exhibition of painting, in 1811, at the Pennsylvania Academy of the Fine Arts, contained not only plaster casts of antique statues, portraits, and still lifes, but landscape paintings. The decorative and topographical branches of landscape had been practiced by a number of migrant neoclassic painters from the 1790's on. The first development beyond these is associated, first of all with Allston's landscapes of mood, secondly with the beginnings of romantic realism in Thomas Birch (1779-1851), Alvan Fisher (1792-1863), Robert Salmon (ca.1785—after 1840), and Thomas Doughty (1793-1856).

Thomas Birch was trained by his father, the engraver and miniature painter, William Birch, whose arrival in Philadelphia in 1794 has already been mentioned. Thomas assisted his father in making a famous set of topographic engravings *Views of Philadelphia* (1798-1800).[7] He seems to have painted at least one topographic view in oil at this time, the well-known *Penn's Treaty Tree* in The Historical Society of Pennsylvania. Yet apparently he did not devote himself seriously to landscape until a visit to the Delaware capes, in 1807, is said to have turned his interests to marine painting. He probably studied Vernet's views of French seaports, available in the form of engravings, but his approach was simpler than these, less dramatic, and closer to that of the Dutch marine painters. The War of 1812 inspired him to paint a series of naval engagements, which made his fame. *The "United States" and the "Macedonian"* (1813) (Fig. 69) (Historical Society of Pennsylvania) represents the peak of his achievement: the plastic beauty of the ships, the freshness of the light, and the movement of the water were never better rendered by him, although he continued to paint marines and harbor views for another forty years. He also painted occasional landscapes and winter scenes in which the charm of evening is often keenly felt, though naïvely executed. Birch's art is a very simple, transparent, romantic realism, using light and air to create the calm distances which are the most attractive feature of his work.

A young clerk in a country store at Dedham, Massachusetts, named Alvan Fisher in the year 1811 formed an ambition to become an artist and began to study with a Boston artist named Penniman. In August, 1815, according to an inscription on the back of a drawing in a sketch book belonging to the Museum of Fine Arts, Boston, he took up the profession of landscape painter and began painting landscapes and rural farm scenes. With very little training, even more amateurish than Doughty technically, Fisher is of interest more because he reveals the beginnings of a new sensibility than because of what he produced. The best pictures I have seen by him are a pair of large panoramic views of *Niagara*, dated 1820, which turned up in the hands of a Boston art dealer some years ago (now in the collection of Mr. Arthur Fleischman, Detroit).

A more interesting figure is Robert Salmon, English-born, and reputed to have been a sailor as well as a marine painter in England before he turned up at Boston in 1828. He lived in a rude dwelling on a wharf in South Boston, devoted himself to painting the sea and ships, and was reported to be eccentric. His firm, disciplined drawing, solid and plastic use of light and shadow, and fine sense of air and light reveal, however, a well-trained talent. He is a minor poet of the sea, perhaps, but the large body of marines and harbor scenes left by him are a handsome and pleasing achievement.

Thomas Doughty was born in Philadelphia and began to draw at four-

[7] Another assistant was the engraver, Samuel Seymour (fl. 1801-1823), who turns up later as an artist on Major Long's exploring expedition across the Plains to the Front Range of the Rocky Mountains, 1818-1820. Seymour (with Titian Ramsay Peale, also an artist on this expedition) thus leads the long list of explorer-artists who recorded the opening of the great West. What little is known of him was published by J. F. McDermott in the *Annual Report of the Smithsonian Institution* for 1950.

teen, but at sixteen was apprenticed to a leather merchant. He taught himself to paint, as an amateur, and did not abandon his leather business to devote
himself to painting as a livelihood until about 1820. Like Constable, he began
to paint because of an intense love of nature. He was an enthusiastic hunter
and fisherman, who found something in the wooded hills and lonely streams
of this country that had to be expressed. His art never lost the impression of
its origin. Each of his pictures is built out of the emotion of communion
with nature. Usually, although not always, it contains a solitary wandering
figure—a fisherman casting his line in the lonely river, a hunter with a gun,
or a single traveler on the road—which is a symbol of the artist's own relation
to nature. Like the sage gazing at the mountains in a Chinese landscape,
these little figures say to the imagination: it is good to be here, in this solitary
valley, lingering by this stream, looking at these hills. Whatever else Doughty
lacked as a painter (and he lacked many obvious things), he had this one
gift of uttering the poetry of solitude. He was never a strong or well-trained
painter. His style was monotonous in color and naïve in composition. His
pictures are small, unassuming, easily overlooked among the works of later,
more attractive, more brilliant men. Yet they have, at their best, a very
personal flavor compounded of their luminous skies and gentle solitude. A
picture such as *In Nature's Wonderland* (1835) (Fig. 70) (The Detroit
Institute of Arts) has something of the quality of Bryant's poem, "To a
Waterfowl," and Doughty, like Bryant, was one of the first to see this wild
and lonely continent as a theme of art.

John Izard Middleton (1785-1849), a South Carolinian of a wealthy and
cultured family, introduced another note that was to be important in American romantic landscape, the elegiac landscape of Italy. Middleton's father
died shortly after his birth. He is said to have been educated in England at
Cambridge, and inherited his mother's large fortune, which enabled him to
devote his life to painting. He spent the years 1808-1809 in Italy, traveling
with two Englishmen, one of whom became later a distinguished archaeologist. In 1812 Middleton brought out a book, *Grecian Remains in Italy, a
Description of Cyclopean Walls and of Roman Antiquities with Topographical and Picturesque Views of Ancient Latium*, from his own drawings (Fig.
71). It came out in London at a time when communication between England
and America was interrupted by war, and it seems now to be excessively rare;
but it is interesting as the first appearance of the picturesque as a theme of
American landscape. Middleton spent most of the remainder of his life in
France and Italy and his other works, if any, are unknown today.

The landscapes of the early romantic realists are as direct and transparent in style as they are in sentiment. A simple perspective from near to
far, a development from warm dark foreground to cool blue distance is their
compositional method: their richest development is in range of tone. But

for the uncomplicated, affectionate contemplation of nature which is their source and reason for existence, these means suffice.

One of the distinctive notes of romanticism was a love of the poetry of the actual, the charm of the ordinary experience, the quiet days and simple things of which the world is made. It was a feeling favorable to still-life painting, among other things. Certainly the interest in still life shown by James and Raphaelle Peale grew and flourished in Philadelphia. Raphaelle's younger brother, Rubens Peale (1784-1864), after having spent most of his life managing one or another of the museums founded by this astonishing family, also turned in his old age to still-life painting. After his museum in New York had gone into bankruptcy, Rubens Peale retired to the country to a home on his son-in-law's lands in the mountains of Pennsylvania. There he amused himself by painting a number of ingenious still lifes and pictures like *Two Grouse in an Underbrush of Laurel* (1864) (The Detroit Institute of Arts). Ostensibly it is a study of nature, yet I cannot escape the thought that we are here seeing one of the famous, vanished "habitat groups" of the Peale Museum translated into paint.

One other still life by an artist of this generation deserves mention, *The Vanity of an Artist's Dreams* (1830) (Fig. 72) (Fogg Art Museum, Harvard University) by Charles B. King, already mentioned as a portrait painter. In this picture of a cupboard stuffed with a confusion of painter's properties, from which the eye picks out two bits of lettering—one, the ragged title page of Campbell's *Pleasures of Hope;* the other, a notice of a sheriff's sale— appeared the *thematic* or *story-telling still life,* which Harnett and his followers were to develop later in the century.

Still life also formed part of the attractive popular art of the period. The so-called "theorem" paintings, made with stencils on velvet or silk, were a popular supplement to needlework as a feminine home-art in the early decades of the nineteenth century. Schematic and conventionalized, they are highly decorative and have great appeal to contemporary taste.

The more robust and masculine forms of popular still life—inn signs, the decoration of carriages, fire engines, circus wagons, even locomotives— were unfortunately also more perishable. Occasionally a fragment of this stylized, artisan kind of decoration has survived, faded and weatherworn, in some historical collection, to remind us how bright, gay, and unself-conscious the popular tradition of painted and gilded embellishment must once have been. The name of one such artisan painter, John A. Woodside of Philadelphia (1781-1852), celebrated for his inn signs and fire engines, has been preserved by some decorative still lifes and farm scenes on canvas.

When the romantic sense of wonder was turned upon nature, immense vistas were opened to the imagination. John James Audubon (1785-1851) is a peak in the long line of artist-naturalists beginning with Abbé Thevet. Born of French parentage in Haiti and educated in France, he came to the United States in 1804 and revisited France 1805-1806. Probably his instruction in drawing under David, of which he speaks in his *Journal*, belongs to the year 1802. The rest of his life belongs to the American wilderness. He lived first on Perkiomen Creek, near Philadelphia, but after marrying an American girl, Lucy Bakewell, set out with his bride for Kentucky, where he hoped to live as a frontier merchant. The wilderness, his gun, and his dogs, drew him constantly away from his business. He had already begun to study and draw birds while a boy living with his family at Nantes. In the fertile, teeming wilderness of the New World, to study and draw birds became an uncontrollable passion. The ruin of his career as a merchant was inevitable. The family migrated to Louisiana, where his wife taught school while the idea of basing a new career upon his drawings of birds gradually crystallized.

Philadelphia was the scientific center of the country. In 1824 Audubon took his drawings there. The scientists of Philadelphia, passionately loyal to Alexander Wilson (only ten years dead) refused to accept the newcomer as either scientist or artist. The check was bitter, but also useful.

Audubon had developed his passionate interest in birds in solitude, by instinct. He learned from his cold reception in Philadelphia that there were exacting scientific standards of which he was as yet hardly aware. The hostility of Wilson's successors was a further good fortune for him, for it sent him to England where there was wealth, taste, and interest in nature enough to support him. In 1826 he sailed for Great Britain, with a few letters of introduction and a portfolio of water-color drawings of American birds as his only capital. The story of what he accomplished in the next ten years— of how he won support for his book, found engravers to produce the plates, sold the subscriptions, acted as his own publisher, painted replicas of his pictures to sell for living expenses, wrote the scientific text and the enchanting essays that lighten it, traveled back and forth to America to complete the series of birds, oversaw the engraving, colored the first plates, and finally brought out, in double elephant folio, *The Birds of America, from Original Drawings, With 435 Plates Showing 1,065 Figures*—is one of the most fantastic instances of talent and energy in the history of American art. *The Birds of America* appeared in four volumes from 1827 to 1838; the accompanying text as the *Ornithological Biography* in five royal octavo volumes, 1831-1839. Taking writings and paintings together, it is a monumental work whose like does not exist (Fig. 74).

After *The Birds of America*, Audubon turned to the animals. The first volume of the *Quadrupeds of America* came out in 1845. But the energies which had carried him from New Orleans to Labrador, from England to the upper Missouri River, and which had poured out a ceaseless flood of work, began to fail; this second work is largely the work of his sons Victor and John Woodhouse Audubon. Although it contains some illustrations of great power, the *Quadrupeds* is not the equal of the *Birds*.

It is as an artist, not as a scientist, that Audubon is remembered. Scientists distrust the force of emotion one feels in his great plates: they point out that he discovered few new species and had little interest in classification. But as an artist he drew with a splendid energy of line to which his clear, fresh, water-color tones give handsome support; his oils are only a translation of this technique into the richer medium. His aim was to depict fact—the birds of America, life-size, with scientific accuracy—but his love and enthusiasm for these strange, wild, lovely creatures, his delight in the splendor and mystery of nature, make his pictures the most dramatic ever published of birds. Birds, one might say, are his subjects: but his theme is Nature—wild, grand, multiplex, and infinitely beautiful.

The generation of 1800-1825, the first of the romantic movement, when compared with the preceding neoclassic generation, seems uneven and inconsistent. It had great ambitions and wide variety of interests (too great and too wide, say its critics), remarkable achievements, great failures, great personal tragedies.

This was the character of the period: in England, this was the generation of Blake and Haydon, as well as Lawrence, Turner, and Constable; in France, of Gros, great painter and suicide, and the short-lived Géricault; in Germany of Runge, dreamer of the German past, Caspar David Friedrich, dreamer of the German landscape; and the Nazarene brotherhood in Rome. Idealism, experiment, discovery, the opening of new roads—also roads that led into cul-de-sacs; experiments too personal to be classified as movements, too eccentric to lead further into the century. The world of the imagination was in turmoil. The clear, rational views of man and of nature held by the neoclassicists faded away. The world was seen through a bewildering variety of new perspectives: passion, gloom, mystery, excitement, tragedy, religious faith, sentimentality, love of solitude. These explorations made great demands for technical knowledge upon the artist. The simple vernacular of American painting, unsupported by accumulated craft traditions or examples, could hardly supply the answers. The portrait painters maintained their high, steady level. But the techniques of realistic landscape, still life, and genre were still to be perfected: the sentiment was there, but the means often terribly limited.

The achievement of this generation is best shown by its two great figures, Allston and Audubon. Worlds apart in their temperaments, ambitions, and styles—the one an explorer of the soul, the other of the world of nature—they are alike only in the excitement, the adventurousness, and the poetry of discovery that filled their vision. It was no inconsiderable generation that produced these two artists and had, in addition, excellent portrait painters and the pioneers of romantic realism in landscape.

CHAPTER 8

ROMANTICISM: THE SECOND GENERATION,
1825–1850

AMERICAN PAINTING TRAVELED FAR IN THE FIFTY YEARS BETWEEN 1775 AND 1825. The strong but narrow colonial tradition, whose limitations had driven Copley and West to Europe, was widened and enriched. The neoclassic generation had introduced new forms; the first generation of romanticists had opened new vistas of objective observation and subjective feeling upon nature and mankind. The horizon of painting had been enlarged at the cost of great struggles and personal tragedy to include narrative painting, still life, genre, and landscape, both ideal and real, as well as portraiture. A thriving craft of engraving gave painting an auxiliary of almost incalculable importance both as a means of popular diffusion and as a practical craft foundation.

Painters in 1825 faced a wide choice of paths instead of the single narrow road against which Copley had revolted. Yet the observant old painter, William Dunlap, who had studied as a boy under West in London and had lived into the period of Thomas Cole, although conscious, when writing his *History of the Rise and Progress of the Arts of Design in the United States* (1834), of great changes in the arts since his young days, looked on those as a healthy growth produced by the increasing number of artists and their increased skill: they meant, to him, ascent and progress, not revolution.

Dunlap was correct. To understand the romantic movement as a whole, and especially its course in England, Germany, and the United States, one must not judge it (as we tend to do often) by the quite exceptional course it took in French painting where its belated arrival, its formal and stylistic character, and its revolutionary struggle against neoclassicism came to a furious and dramatic crisis about 1830.

No revolution in style marks the appearance of the second romantic generation in America. Nonetheless the atmosphere of art changed after 1825 in important ways.

The romanticists of 1800 in all Western countries had been linked still to the neoclassicists by their interest in a monumental and ideal art and by lingering classical enthusiasms. Love of the past and rivalry with it were strong inspirations among the first romanticists; they merely changed their minds about which part of the past it was desirable to revive. For the neo-classicists, the antique sculpture in the Vatican and the Louvre had been supreme. The first romantic painters, with equal passion and delight, studied the great European painting of the sixteenth and seventeenth centuries: this was the past which Delacroix, or Turner, or Allston wished to revive and surpass. To the romantic realists of the next generation the tradition of art meant little. They wished to paint what was before their eyes. And if some of the new men—Cole, Page, or Quidor—were also inspired by the past, as we shall discover, they saw it from a different perspective.

There were potent new elements and inspirations in the America of 1825 making for change. The tone of life itself was radically altered. It was not merely that the old leaders of the republic were dying out and taking with them the lingering traces of eighteenth-century elegance and colonial memories of the days when the United States had been part of the Old World. By 1830 the great tide of settlement was pouring westward. About a third of the American people now lived beyond the eastward face of the Appa-lachians. In the vast Mississippi Valley, cut off by the mountains from the eastern seaboard, there had developed a rough frontier society of pioneers, Indian fighters, and river men; its hero, Andrew Jackson of Tennessee, was in the White House, the first president to represent the coonskin democracy west of the mountains.

Even in the settled East, the eighteenth century was out of date. Its elegant clothes and stately manners seemed faintly ridiculous.

> . . . the old three-cornered hat
> And the breeches, and all that,
> Are so queer!

wrote a young wit of Boston in 1831.[1] But more drastic changes were taking place than that from knee breeches to trousers. The plantation aristocracy of Virginia, which provided four of our first five presidents, had lost the leader-ship of the South to the new power of King Cotton in the deep South. In New England and the Middle States, the families which had made their wealth in ships and overseas trade were transferring it now into factories and mines; the perspective of the manufacturer replaced that of the importer from overseas. And now the terrible issue of slavery arose to dominate the

[1] Oliver Wendell Holmes, *The Last Leaf upon the Tree.*

thoughts and inflame the passions of men. Everything seemed to combine to replace the international interests and the classical culture of the past by new and local interests.

There was loss in this but also challenge. Americans, increasingly remote from Europe and from the old traditions of culture, had to create a new imaginative life out of themselves and their vast new land. A passion to know and to understand themselves was one of the great new inspirations of the age. Emerson speaks in *The American Scholar* (1837):

Give me insight into today, and you may have the antique and future worlds. What would we really know the meaning of? The meal in the firkin; the milk in the pan; the ballad in the street; the news of the boat; the glance of the eye; the form and gait of the body;—show me the ultimate reason of these matters; show me the sublime presence of the highest spiritual cause lurking, as it always does lurk in these suburbs and extremities of nature; let me see every trifle bristling with the polarity that ranges it instantly on an eternal law; and the shop, the plough, and the ledger referred to the like cause by which light undulates and poets sing;—and the world lies no longer a dull miscellany and lumber room, but has form and order; there is no trifle, there is no puzzle, but one design unites and animates the farthest pinnacle and the lowest trench.

The generation that matured men like Lincoln and Emerson cannot be said to have failed to meet the challenge. The country also poured its energies into painting, to such a degree that the English critic, Mrs. Anna Jameson, traveling here in 1837-1838, found painters literally everywhere. Most of them were romantic realists, interested to discover and paint the character of what lay before their eyes.

One of their discoveries was the wilderness. To the eighteenth century nature seemed only a background to human life and was most admired when most humanized in gardens or neat plantations, just as human life was admired in its most civilized form, in the classical hero or the polite citizen of the world. In the 1820's a young portrait painter in Philadelphia, George Catlin, saw a delegation of Western Indians passing through on their way to the capital. Twenty years later he looked back upon the impression they made upon him:

In silent and stoic dignity these lords of the forest strutted about the city for a few days, wrapped in their pictured robes, with their brows plumed with the quills of the war-eagle, attracting the gaze and admiration of all who behold them. After this, they took their departure for Washington City, and I was left to reflect and regret, which I did long and deeply, until I came to the following deductions and conclusions.

Black and blue cloth and civilization are destined, not only to veil, but to obliterate the grace and beauty of Nature. Man, in the simplicity and loftiness of his nature, unrestrained and unfettered by the disguises of art, is surely the most beautiful model for the painter,—and the country from which he hails is unquestionably the best study or school of the arts in the world: such I am sure, from the models I have seen, is the wilderness of North America.

"And," he went on,

the history and customs of such a people, preserved by pictorial illustrations, are themes worthy of the lifetime of one man, and nothing short of the loss of my life, shall prevent me from visiting their country, and of becoming their historian.[2]

Thus, instead of the centers of art in London and Paris, the wilderness had become the inspiration of the artist (Fig. 75).

Catlin's career was one expression of a new enthusiasm. Nature, in all senses of the word—landscape, the wild and untamed earth, the life of animals and plants, the instinctive life of primitive men close to earth—came to have a new meaning and fascination.

The appeals of the world of art and of the past were not forgotten. But the perspective was different. London as a center of art lost its hold upon Americans; French classicism also lost its attraction. Italy was now the dreamed-of land of art. Colonies of American artists sprang up in Florence and Rome, which became the training grounds of most of the artists fortunate enough to travel abroad. Düsseldorf on the lower Rhine also attracted American art students. And a new generation of romantic writers had arisen to furnish new subject matter for illustration.

Another and perhaps the greatest change, whose influence upon the arts and crafts and the imagination was all-pervasive, was only at its beginning and hard as yet to assay: its rising impact was not to be felt until the succeeding generation. In the decades 1830-1850, the great technological changes began that were to alter the whole structure of Western life, sweeping away the handcrafts, the ancient foundation of the arts, isolating the artist in society, setting loose incalculable changes.

In 1830 the United States was still a small rural country. Its cities were little seaports, little river ports, little canal ports, facing upon the waterways that were the only easy highways of commerce. These market towns, these clusters of brick homes where the merchants and professions and craftsmen of America lived, were still smokeless. Hardly two dozen miles of railroad had been built in 1830. Beside the waterfalls of New England the factory system was beginning to take shape and a new fuel, anthracite coal, was coming into use; but these two things, which were to alter the face of the land and the life of human beings completely, were still in their infancy. The

[2] George Catlin, *Letters and Notes on the Manners, Customs and Condition of the North American Indians*, New York, Wiley and Putnam, 1841.

setting of life, men's houses, furniture, clothes, utensils, were still the work of skilled handcraftsmen, whose workshops were found in every local center. Most of the population still lived on farms, where men used the scythe and the sickle, and lighted their morning fires with a brand from the ashes piled on the hearth as they had done in Homer's day. Only the steamboat, puffing its way along the vast network of western rivers, and the cotton gin, building the kingdom of King Cotton in the South, had begun the technological transformation of life. Then, in the 1840's, the camera joined them.

In 1825 three landscapes in the window of a New York shop caught the eye of old Colonel Trumbull. He bought one for twenty-five dollars; the others were bought by William Dunlap and an engraver by the name of Asher B. Durand. They had been painted in the Hudson Valley by a young artist named Thomas Cole (1801-1848). The older artists were thus the first to recognize the talent of the man who was to be the most conspicuous and popular figure of the new generation.

Cole's early pictures represented in a crude but dramatic way the untamed loneliness of the American forest. "I well remember," said the poet Bryant in his funeral oration on Cole twenty-five years later,

what an enthusiasm was awakened by these early works of his. . . . The delight which was expressed at the opportunity of contemplating pictures which carried the eye over scenes of wild grandeur peculiar to our own country, over our aerial mountain tops with their mighty growth of forest never touched by the axe . . . into the depth of skies bright with the hues of our own climate; skies such as few but Cole could ever paint, and through the transparent abysses of which it seemed that you might send an arrow out of sight.

Before 1825 Cole had been a wanderer. Born in England, he migrated as a child with his family to the frontier in Ohio. An itinerant portrait painter had given him his first impressions of painting; but he was really wholly self-taught. He drifted to Philadelphia, then to New York. In the scenery of the Hudson River he found, at last, the reason for his life. In 1826 he moved to the village of Catskill, on the west bank of the Hudson, where he made his home for the rest of his life on a bluff looking out upon the blue heights of the Catskill Mountains and the grand river sweeping past below. But he ranged widely on foot over the northeastern states with pencil and sketch-book, from the White Mountains to Niagara, making pencil studies from which he painted in the studio in winter. Partly as a result of this method, which makes an artist rely upon memory, and partly from temperament, Cole's pictures struck a new note of both romantic realism and dramatic mood. Each was a lyric of the wild and solemn beauty of the American wilderness. Their success was immediate and extraordinary. In 1829 Cole was able to go abroad and spend three years in England and Italy. On his return he found himself the most conspicuous figure, after Washington Allston, in American art.

One of the best examples of Cole's treatment of the American landscape is *In the Catskills* (1837) (Fig. 76) (The Metropolitan Museum of Art), a picture which he never surpassed either in imaginative realism or lyric sentiment. It was painted the year after his marriage and is based upon his favorite evening walk along the road leading westward from the village, beside Catskill Creek, toward the mountains and the sunset. Tiny figures of a woman and child in the foreground suggest his own wife and baby. It is a picture large in scale, rich in tone, and suffused with reverie, excitement, and inner happiness. The brushstroke is minute in detail, but the details fall into place in a luminous and spacious whole.

If Cole belongs to romantic realism on the one hand, his mind was also saturated with romantic literature. His artistic attitudes were profoundly literary and his greatest popular success came from paintings that express a mood of sentimental melancholy derived from books.

As his biographer, Noble, put it, Cole wished from the very first to advance "from pictures merely descriptive of wild nature . . . to paint those poetically expressive of himself." (The traditional prestige of the Ideal over the Real shows in Noble's heading of this chapter: "Cole enters upon a higher style of Art.")

We have already felt the touch of the romantic fascination with death in Rembrandt Peale's *Court of Death*. The elegaic note of meditation upon the flight of time and the brevity of human life was a fundamental of the romantic spirit. Remember the somber eloquence of Bryant's *Thanatopsis* (1816):

> Go forth, under the open sky, and list
> To Nature's teachings, while from all around—
> Earth and her waters, and the depths of air—
> Comes a still voice—Yet a few days, and thee
> The all-beholding sun shall see no more
> In all his course . . .
>
> So live, that when thy summons comes to join
> The innumerable caravan, which moves
> To that mysterious realm, where each shall take
> His chamber in the silent halls of death,
> Thou go not, like the quarry-slave at night,
> Scourged to his dungeon, but, sustained and soothed
> By an unfaltering trust, approach thy grave,
> Like one who wraps the drapery of his couch
> About him, and lies down to pleasant dreams.

These emotions were stirred by countless grave voices—Bishop Porteus' *Court of Death*, Young's *Night Thoughts*, Blair's *The Grave*, and re-echoed in the exhortations of a thousand pulpits, The thought of death appeared in countless ways—ranging from the appearance of a new type of cemetery, such as *Laurel Hill* in Philadelphia and *Mount Auburn* in Cambridge, replacing the old-fashioned churchyard, to the popular vogue for mourning pictures, showing a grieving family, or nymph, leaning upon a gravestone beneath a weeping willow. On a higher level, the thought of death is a basic imaginative element in the art of Poe or Hawthorne.

A vaster theme, the death of civilization itself, was expressed in a book which had immense fascination for that day, Volney's *Ruines, ou Méditations sur les révolutions des Empires* (1791). Volney, a French savant and traveler, had spent four years in Egypt and Syria (1783-1787). He had learned Arabic, lived among the Arabs, and had visited the ruins of Egypt and Palmyra. Volney was one of the first European intellectuals to go beyond Italy, or even Greece, and to visit the deserted lands where enormous ruins of vanished civilizations stood in solitude among the sands. His reflections upon these spectacles, embodied in a now forgotten book, were one of the elements in popularizing a new attitude toward the past in the Western world.

It had seemed an easy thing to neoclassic thinkers to revive the forms and the virtues of antiquity, because the ancient world of Greece and Rome was regarded as continuous with our own. The world was very young—after all, had it not been created in 4004 B.C. according to the chronology of Bishop Ussher? Therefore, when Charles Willson Peale in 1801 excavated the first mastodon skeleton, the men of science had to be convinced with difficulty that it represented an extinct species. The notion that the Creator could allow one of his own creations to disappear was at first resisted by even so advanced a mind as Jefferson's. Volney, however, with impassioned eloquence, drew a picture of entire civilizations, dead, vanished, swept away upon the stream of time. The immensities of time past, the immeasurable perspectives of the earth's history are today an accepted part of our consciousness. It is difficult for us to conceive with what resistance and revulsion, with what shuddering awe and fearful delight, such ideas were received by men of 150 years ago.

Cole returned from his years 1829-1832 in England and Italy, not only enriched by memories of European scenery but in love with the haunting poetry of past time. In rapid succession he produced a series of allegories based on Volney's theme of the passage of time: *The Course of Empire*, in five scenes, painted for Luman Reed; *The Departure* and *The Return*, painted for William van Rensselaer; *Past* and *Present*, painted for P. G. Stuyvesant; *The Voyage of Life*, in four scenes, painted for Samuel Ward (Fig. 78); the last, *The Cross of the World*, was left unfinished at his death. These elaborate allegories were undertaken as commissions for some of the most intelligent and discerning men of that day. They were engraved and, in this form, enjoyed a national popularity. There is no question that they were the most popular and successful expressions of Ideal sentiment painted in this generation. Yet they have grave faults in comparison with Cole's landscapes. Cole too often crowded them with a multiplicity of detail, to which he gave neither the breadth of light and shade nor the largeness of drawing required to lift an ideal composition to monumentality. And to our minds, after the heroic vision of antiquity of the neoclassicists and the tragic images drawn from the Bible or Shakespeare by the early romanticists, these melancholy allegories of the flight of time seem sentimental and obvious. The modern vision of the long, dark perspectives of history and life's mysterious drive upward and ever-repeated fall is perhaps only vaguely realized still, yet it makes Cole's imagery seem like the platitudes of a child's primer.

Yet *The Voyage of Life* is a landmark in our cultural history and landmarks, even if of out-moded design, are not to be ignored. Moral idealism, a brooding upon the mystery of time, the image of life as a dream, were very deep currents in the mental life of the nineteenth century. It was Cole's achievement to feel them and to invent images that expressed them so simply and forcibly that, once seen, they are never forgotten.

The image of life as a dream haunted him. He stated it boldly and eloquently in *The Architect's Dream* (Plate IX), painted for the neo-classic architect Ithiel Town. The practical-minded architect did not care for the picture but to the poet's mind of William Cullen Bryant it was a dream-image of the past "such as might present itself to the imagination of one who had fallen asleep after reading a work on the different styles of architecture." It is a striking piece of romantic melodrama and fantasy.

The reverie upon the past is perhaps expressed most sympathetically, for our taste, in what I should call his elegiac landscapes. In 1843, after his second visit to Italy, (1841-1842), he painted a pair of landscapes, *The Roman Campagna* (Fig. 77) and *An Evening in Arcady* (Wadsworth Atheneum, Hartford), which are to my eye at the summit of his art. The one represents the long line of the Claudian aqueduct at sunset, stretching across the plain to the Alban Hills. A solitary goatherd pastures his flock beside it in the rosy evening light. The other is a singular fantasy upon the ancient, inexhaustible theme of the Golden Age, set in the evening of a golden day. Both are large, simple, luminous pictures, rich in the deep cello tones of reverie.

Another artist who made a large contribution to the new taste was Asher B. Durand (1796-1886), by his two careers as engraver and as painter. He was older than Cole and had made himself first the outstanding line engraver of his day before turning to painting as a new career.

Durand was apprenticed in 1812 to the engraver Peter Maverick, in New York city, and in 1817 became his partner. The older man soon became jealous of his young assistant, who thereupon branched out on his own. His contemporary fame as an engraver rested on his large plates after Trumbull's *Declaration of Independence* and Vanderlyn's *Ariadne;* but he also engraved illustrations for more romantic works—Cooper's *Spy* and Allston's *Spalatro and the Bloody Hand*. All through the twenties and thirties, in the pages of the magazines and gift annuals, there appeared numerous smaller plates inscribed "Engraved by Durand," reproducing vigorously and sympathetically the works of Cole, Doughty, Fisher. These engravings, carried through the country in the pages of popular journals, did much to popularize the new landscape school. But perhaps his greatest achievement as an engraver was a projected serial publication called *The American Landscape* (1830) with plates by Durand after American landscape painters (including himself) and text by William Cullen Bryant. Only one number of six plates appeared. The public was not yet ready to support so ambitious a project; but though a financial failure it was an artistic success. The copper line was never used more vigorously by an American nineteenth-century engraver than by Durand in the plates of *The American Landscape*. In feeling also Durand had left topographic inspiration behind and the theme of his plates became the contemplation of nature for its own sake.[3]

By 1830 Durand had also made himself a good landscape painter in oils, although "his pre-eminent talents as an engraver put him in the background as a painter." [4] A few years later Luman Reed, a liberal-minded New York merchant who was the leading patron and friend of the New York artists, encouraged him to leave engraving and gave him the commissions that enabled him to devote himself entirely to painting.

The note of his painting, both in portraits and landscapes, is a romantic realism so simple and transparent as to seem artless, at least to the complex standards of modern taste. *Kindred Spirits* (1849) (Fig. 80) (New York Public Library) is one of his most attractive works and a revealing document for the spirit of romantic realism. It was painted in memory of Thomas Cole in the year after his death and shows Cole, with the poet William Cullen Bryant, standing on a cliff over a stream in the Catskill forest. It is as direct in spirit as Bryant's poetry of nature and although, like the latter, limited in means, it is unforgettable.

Since Durand was trained as an engraver, it is natural that a fine, precise

---

[3] A. B. Durand's brother Cyrus (1787-1868) was also a notable figure in the history of engraving. In the manufacturing boom before and during the War of 1812, he became a very successful mechanic, constructing machinery of all sorts. About 1815 he made for Peter Maverick the first machines for ruling straight and wavy lines for bank notes; the following year he made machines for ruling water lines and plain ovals. It was thus Cyrus Durand who laid the foundation for the excellence of that beautiful though ignored art, American nineteenth-century bank-note engraving, whose tradition is still carried on today, making ours the handsomest of all paper moneys. Cyrus Durand devoted himself thereafter to bank-note engraving but was so skilled a mechanic, says Appleton's *Cyclopaedia of American Biography,* that he was considered capable of working in twenty-two occupations.

[4] Samuel L. Knapp, *Sketches of Public Characters,* 1830.

line and a sense of tone should be the basis of his art; yet he had a painter's eye for light. At first, in the 1840's, he worked in a warm golden tonality. A notable example of that phase is *The Old Oak* (1844) (New-York Historical Society). A massive tree is silhouetted against the sunset over a vast horizon of forest and lake. In the solidity of its composition it showed that Durand had studied the Dutch landscape painters; but in feeling it is the wide, lonely landscape of America.

Durand was one of the first Americans to advocate painting out-of-doors, in face of nature; the practice led him toward luminism. His exploration of space and light drew him ultimately to the airy vacancy of *Kaaterskill Clove* (1866) (New York, Century Association), remarkable for its headlong plunge into green-gold airy space and for its joy in solitude.

Durand showed himself an effective genre painter in *The Capture of Major André* (about 1835) (Worcester Art Museum) and the *Wrath of Peter Stuyvesant* (New-York Historical Society). He did a few allegories in the vein of Cole. But his true gift was for observation. What observation meant to the romantic spirit was, however, poetry. "Nature is a language," said Emerson in his *Journal*, "and every new fact that we learn is a new word; but rightly seen, taken all together, it is not merely a language, but the language put together into a most significant and universal book. I wish to learn the language, not that I may learn a new set of nouns and verbs, but that I may read the great book which is written in that tongue."

In such an atmosphere landscape painting flourished. New York city had the largest group but it was only one of many centers; decentralization was the character of the age. The professional artist, the amateur, and the untrained professional appeared wherever the population spread in its westward course: in raw new cities on the rivers of the interior; in small towns where no artist could earn a living today; in remote corners of the backwoods. It was a period of remarkable flowering of the imaginative impulse, remarkable in its profusion although (understandably enough) not always remarkable in its quality.

In New York city, in addition to Durand and Cole, there was John W. Casilear (1811-1893), who turned to painting in oils after learning engraving under Peter Maverick; the clarity and strength of drawing was the best feature of his landscapes.

Boston's most admired painter of landscape was George Loring Brown (1814-1889), who was apprenticed to a wood engraver but began very early to paint landscape. On his first trip to Europe, in 1833, he studied Claude Lorrain, and his later art is based upon Claude. He returned to Italy in 1840 and lived there for twenty years, becoming the most celebrated of American landscape painters abroad. Nathaniel Hawthorne met him and described him in his *Journal* and *The Marble Faun*: his judgment was that Brown's best trait was a patient, loving study of nature. We would agree with this. To our taste, his romantic realism is to be preferred to his rather grandiose pictures in the vein of Claude Lorrain.

A picture such as *Medford Marshes*, painted after his return to America (Karolik Collection, Boston, Museum of Fine Arts) exhibits two traits which might be considered contradictory—a minute attention to carefully drawn detail, and a broad, enveloping effect of light.

They are not contradictory, however: they are the characteristics of a growing interest in the exploration of light among American painters, which was to assume great importance and which I call American *luminism*. The American luminists' exploration of light was not by means of brilliance and variety of hue (the "broken color" of French impressionism), but by delicate modulation of tone combined with an equally delicate exactness of outline.

Another New England luminist of this generation was Fitz Hugh Lane (1804-1865) of Gloucester. For nearly twenty years Lane earned his living in Boston as a lithographer specializing in views of towns and buildings. He returned to Gloucester after 1847 and devoted himself to marine painting. His use of oil paint was thin and a little meager compared to Salmon's full, solid use of the brush; but the spider-web precision of drawing and delicacy of tone of an example like the *Ships in Ice off Ten Pound Island, Gloucester* (Karolik Collection, Boston, Museum of Fine Arts), shows a sensitive natural artistry.

Another minor poet of light was George Harvey (ca.1800-1878), who after a successful career as miniature painter, bought an estate on the Hudson not far from Washington Irving, whose home he helped remodel. In this rural setting he began to study "the ever-varying atmospheric effects of the American climate." He projected an elaborate album of engravings after his paintings, with text by Washington Irving, but after issuing the first four was unable to continue. His paintings have a miniaturist's smallness of touch, but charm of light.

James Pringle, who came to New York about 1827 from England, was also a painter of light. His painting of *The Smith and Dimon Shipyard on the Hudson* (1833) (Cooperstown, New York State Historical Association Museum) shows the pleasant atmospheric delicacy of which he was capable.

Russell Smith (1812-1896) represented another region and another aspect of the changing face of the country. A pupil of Lambdin, the Philadelphia portrait painter, he turned first to stage design and scene painting for the Philadelphia theater. (Many of his sketches for the stage sets of the romantic drama are still preserved and show an interesting light on the history of the romantic theater.) When he returned to Pittsburgh, his landscapes of the wide rivers and smoking mills of western Pennsylvania are interesting not only as part of the march of landscape painting across the Alleghenies but as documents of the infancy of the industrial era.

In the eighteen thirties colonies of American artists began to collect in the old cities of Italy. Some were students, who remained a few years in Rome or Florence, and returned. Others made Italy their home for years. "Rome seems to have within its walls all that I seek," wrote Paul Akers, the

American sculptor, when he returned to Italy in 1854. Sometimes the painters echoed the same sentiment.

The landscapes of Italy painted by these American artists often rose no
higher than souvenirs of travel. But certain ones, inspired by the clarity of
Italian skies and the harmony of Italian architecture with the earth, achieved
their finest works there.

John Gadsby Chapman of Virginia made Rome his home from 1848 until
his death. He is best remembered, perhaps, as a figure painter and illustrator;
but his landscapes and color etchings of the Campagna are fresh in color
and reveal a sensitive and poetic talent. Other landscape painters of this generation who made Italy their home, in whole or in part, were Christopher P.
Cranch (1813-1892), who also lived for a time in Paris; James Freeman (1808-
1882), who went to Rome in 1836 and spent the rest of his life there, leaving
in two books of reminiscences an interesting record of the life of the American colony; Joseph Ropes (1812-1885); and Miner K. Kellogg (1814-1889),
a restless painter-traveler, who was at one period the companion of Layard in
the Near East, and at another, Hiram Powers' agent in exhibiting *The Greek
Slave* to America 1847-1851, and finally, an art dealer in Paris and London,
who formed the E. L. Holden collection of Italian paintings, now in the
Cleveland Museum.

The romantic realist was deeply and sincerely interested in subject matter. The rise of an interest in nature, as an experience for its own sake, transcended but did not supersede the humbler topographic view. The makers
of views continued to flourish side by side with the painters of pure landscape. Alexander Jackson Davis (1803-1892), a brilliant architect of the
Gothic revival, was a leading topographic draughtsman. Jacob C. Ward
(1809-1891) of Bloomfield, New Jersey, using the new medium of lithography, made views both for W. J. Bennett, the aquatint engraver, and for
other engravers. John W. Hill (1812-1897), the son of John Hill, the pioneer
aquatinter who had engraved Joshua Shaw's landscapes in 1819, was perhaps
the best of the many mid-century lithographers who made those large, bird's-
eye views of towns, public buildings, and private houses, which, mounted on
the wall like maps, decorated nearly every American village inn and place of
business in the mid-century. Nicolino V. Calyo (1799-1884) migrated from
Italy first to Baltimore (1834-1845), then to New York where he painted
town and harbor views. Robert Havell (1793-1878), the brilliant London engraver who engraved the plates of Audubon's *Birds of America* (1827-1838),
followed Audubon to America in 1839. After staying for a time with Audubon, he settled at Ossining, then in 1857 at Tarrytown on the Hudson. He
devoted his life to portraying, in aquatint and oils, the countryside made
legendary by Washington Irving.

The impetus to understand and record the vast spectacle of this new land
appeared also still farther west, where another city was rising on the edge of
the Indian country at the junction of the Missouri and the Mississippi. John
Caspar Wild (ca.1804—after 1844), born in Zurich, trained in Paris, emigrated
first to Philadelphia, where he settled for a few years and painted a panorama

of the city; but about 1840 he arrived in St. Louis. Wild was attracted at once to the great river that formed the focus of the whole interior of the continent, and published in periodical form a series of lithographs, *The Valley of the Mississippi Illustrated*, marked by a sensitive and accurate eye for light and color, whose thirty-four prints are among the rarest of the early views of the mid-continent.[5]

If one great discovery of romanticism was that nature was an imaginative experience valuable for its own sake, irrespective of a notable or picturesque subject, the second, parallel discovery was that the study of the simple, the humble, the familiar in human life was equally rewarding. It was not necessary to seek for moments of antique grandeur or of thrilling drama: "The meal in the firkin; the milk in the pan; the ballad in the street" were also wonderful to the discerning eye. A fresh, varied, attractive school of genre—the painting of human beings in their daily life—was the fruit of this perception.

American life was never richer in materials for the observer of the humors and flavors of life. The country was extraordinarily diverse. Costume ranged from the blue-coated elegance of Philadelphia and Baltimore merchants to the coonskin cap and buckskin shirt of the frontier. Manners were equally picturesque and varied. Local differences had not been flattened out by ease of travel and communication. The New England Yankee, the Southern planter, the Western riverman ("half horse, half alligator, a little touched with the snapping turtle"), the farmer, the frontiersman, and the untamed Indian retained their strong individual character.

One of the first and most characteristic traits of romantic genre was humor mingled with affection; but a strange kind of grand and solemn poetry is also found, as unexpected as it is noteworthy.

The mixture of humor, affection, and graceful style, which makes Washington Irving's descriptions of country life on the Hudson River so enduring, has its parallel in the art of William Sidney Mount (1807-1868). Mount was born at Setauket on Long Island and grew up in nearby Stony Brook, then a pleasant, quiet, rural backwater. In 1826 he was one of the first students in the drawing class opened by the National Academy of Design. His early paintings were portraits and religious subjects, but when an illness sent him back to his home he discovered the charm of the rural life in which he had grown up as a subject for art.

Mount, in Virgil Barker's happy phrase, was an artist singularly at ease in his time. He felt no need to study abroad, no restless craving to see Italy.

---

[5] William Henry Bartlett (1809-1854), whose views of American cities are among the most popular engravings of this period, was an English topographic artist who visited the United States briefly in 1838-1839 to prepare the illustrations for N. P. Willis' *American Scenery* (1840). Bartlett was known in his lifetime only as a water colorist, which suggests that the oil paintings often attributed to him were most probably done after the engravings.

All that he required for his life's work was what he saw around him in his own little corner of the earth. This does not mean he lacked ambition in his art. He worked hard to discipline his hand and brush to an effective and distinguished style. A little water color in the Addison Gallery, Andover, called *The Trying Hour* (1834), representing a woman seated before the fire frying fat, is an example of his power of drawing that makes a figure live and express its inner life by its movement. To expressive drawing he added the charm of luminosity and a transparent simplicity of statement. The result is a series of little pictures that sum up, genially and sympathetically, a moment of life: *Bargaining for a Horse* (1835) (New-York Historical Society), two men talking and whittling beside a tethered horse; *The Painter's Triumph* (Fig. 83) (1836) (The Pennsylvania Academy of the Fine Arts); *The Banjo Player* (The Detroit Institute of Arts), in which the only action is the slight, self-absorbed movement of the musician's figure; *Music Hath Charms* (1847), a more elaborate group of four different people enjoying the music of the banjo; or the famous *Eel Spearing at Setauket* (1845) (Fig. 82). In each of these, a human being or a group of people act a passing moment of their lives before our eyes. They are not isolated figures: their lives are drawn together psychologically into the unity of an action which they feel and share. This is a very rare achievement in genre painting. Minor genre painters make up for its lack by sentimentality or exaggeration or obviousness of anecdote. Mount, like Irving, was never obvious. He was simple, natural, easy, with a lucidity of style that conceals his skill. No better example of his lucidity exists, perhaps, than his *Long Island Farm House* (after 1855) (The Metropolitan Museum of Art), a landscape without figures, notable for its subtle luminosity and for its vivid expression of the exact flavor of a place and a day.

New York city had a number of genre painters who painted the rural life of the East or the streets of New York, although no other of Mount's artistic caliber:

F. W. Edmonds (1806-1863), who was both a bank clerk and a genre painter and attained considerable success in both fields;

Tompkins H. Matteson (1813-1884), born in upper New York state where he was a pupil of an Indian who was famous for his carvings and drawings. Matteson was an engaging if sentimental painter of rural subject matter;

John Carlin (1813-1891), a deaf-mute from infancy, who studied art in Philadelphia, London, and in Paris under Paul Delaroche, became a successful miniature painter in New York city (after 1841) and when photography destroyed the craft of the miniature painter turned to landscape and genre;

Albertus de O. Browere (1814-1887), son of a sculptor, who lived in Catskill from 1841, except for four years of adventure in the California gold rush, a bad landscape painter and better genre painter;

James Goodwyn Clonney (1812-1867), another miniature painter, turned to genre after the daguerreotype destroyed his first specialty and painted fairly effectively in the manner of W. S. Mount.

Charles R. Leslie (1794-1859) of Philadelphia, an artist of great talents, went to England to study, remained there to become a famous painter of anecdotic genre and the biographer of Constable, and belongs to the story of British art.

Jerome B. Thompson (1814-1886), a genial little-master of the inhabited landscape. He had a gift for good-humored, rather prosaic, but lively observation of character, and for making his figures seem at home in a landscape setting. His *Pic Nick, Camden, Maine* (Boston, Museum of Fine Arts, Karolik Collection) and *The "Pick Nick"* near Mount Mansfield (M. H. De Young Memorial Museum, San Francisco) show him as a robust and entertaining painter.

The westward migration of the nineteenth century that peopled this continent and created most of the states and cities of the present United States was a unique national experience which has left its traces upon every aspect of American life. In the years of this generation, our people spread across the eastern half of the continent, pouring along the Erie Canal into the Great Lakes region; crossing the mountains to the Ohio and following the Mississippi and its tributaries into the vast interior of the continent; sweeping around the southern end of the Appalachians into the new states of the deep South. They halted at last at the edge of the forests. Beyond were the open prairies, the great plains, and the mountains and deserts, two thousand miles of Indian territory. A new kind of life and a whole series of technological devices had to be invented before they could live successfully in this new kind of world. The first settlers in the Far West crossed over this treeless country, as over an ocean, by the epic marches of the "prairie schooners" to reach the forest lands of the Pacific Coast.

A whole group of artists made this national experience of the frontier their theme. The greatest is George Caleb Bingham (1811-1879), whose achievement is one of the mysterious phenomena of the age. Born in Virginia, he migrated at the age of eight with his family to the outer edge of settlement in Missouri. He had his first glimpse of an artist in the following year when the genial giant, Chester Harding, passed by in search of Daniel Boone whose portrait he wished to paint. The boy Bingham very early began to copy engravings and to paint with homemade pigments; but he met the obstacles natural to the frontier. To earn a living he learned to roll cigars, worked as a cabinetmaker's apprentice, read law and theology, and possibly never saw another artist until Harding once more traveled through that country and showed him enough of the technique of painting to start him as a portrait painter. Harding himself had little enough training at this time. Bingham's first portraits were in the hard, earnest style of the untrained professional, like an Earl or Jennys of the 1830's, yet they showed also a luminosity that relate them to his mature style.

In 1837-1838 he studied for a few months at the Pennsylvania Academy of the Fine Arts in Philadelphia. There he could learn something of the atmospheric style. There were good pictures by West, Allston, Lawrence, Sully, to be studied and he evidently absorbed their lessons. He painted portraits in Washington for a few years and returned finally across the mountains to his home in Missouri about 1844. The first fruits of his return to the frontier was one of the most original and striking works of its age, *The Fur Traders Descending the Missouri* (The Metropolitan Museum of Art) with its archaic strength of drawing, its strange smoky yet brilliant color, its air of solitude and mystery. Bingham seems to have had, at a very early date in his career, the idea of becoming the painter of what he later described as "our social and political characteristics." He looked around him in his frontier region and saw what was original yet typical in the life of America: a pair of wild *coureurs de bois* coming down the river with their furs from the Rocky Mountains, bound for St. Louis (he painted this a second time, on a different scale, in a picture in Detroit) (Plate X); raftsmen playing cards as they floated downstream (Fig. 85); a steamboat crew camped on a sandbar, guarding the cargo of their stranded vessel; a farmers' shooting match, or a game of checkers at a crossroads tavern. He delighted in scenes of political campaigns or elections, where the crude, vigorous democracy of the frontier brought out the excitement and passions of these country folk, when they met to organize themselves as communities and to decide the issues of the day.

It is interesting that he should have had the desire to make himself the social historian of his own place and people. His subjects, which now seem beautiful and original, were then as commonplace as is the sight, today, of a filling station attendant putting ten gallons of gas in a car or changing an inner tube. But Bingham saw the grand meaning of the commonplace. What is more extraordinary, he was able to create, out of his meager experience of pictures and his own sensibility, a style of great visual poetry—a large and almost archaic severity of drawing, brilliantly luminous, yet smoky in color, and extremely subtle in its gradations of light and air. And over all there is a mood of grandeur and solemnity in his work, as if he would say to his fellows: This is a heroic age.

Bingham's works were engraved and accepted as popular illustrations of frontier life. They were distributed widely, some through the American Art Union, others through Goupil and Company, a branch of a French firm of print sellers established in New York in 1850, that was to develop later into the great art-dealing house of Knoedler and Company.

His best works were done in a period extending not much over ten years. In 1856 he went abroad to study at Düsseldorf, the seat of a German school of literary-sentimental narrative painting which had begun to have a great reputation in America in the fifties—perhaps as a result of the German migration after 1848, perhaps because of the growing fondness for sentimental subjects, or both. His work was there infected to some extent with sentimentality and overemphasis; at least, it did not gain. When he returned in 1859, the Civil War was about to burst upon us. Bingham was a man of strong Union convictions. He threw himself into the political struggle in his native state, became an officeholder, served as state treasurer, 1862-1865, became adjutant-general of Missouri in 1875. These things diverted much of his energy and attention away from his art.

Bingham had a remarkable sense of what was grand, essential, typical. None of the other painters of the frontier could approach him, either in sobriety and freshness of observation or in talent as a painter. He was a part of the life he painted. The other painters of the frontier were Easterners, who were drawn to the West by the lure of the picturesque; and the picturesque was what they painted. None the less, their work forms a valuable and entertaining historical record.

George Catlin (1796-1872) was born in Pennsylvania; his discovery of the Indians in the streets of Philadelphia has already been told. In 1832 he set out from St. Louis to follow the Missouri River into the Indian country, where he lived for about eight years among the Indians (Fig. 75). Afterward he lectured and exhibited his collection of paintings widely in the United States, in London, and Paris; he also wrote voluminously, notably *Illustrations of the Manners, Customs and Conditions of the North American Indians* (1841), which went through many editions. About six hundred of his paintings are preserved in the United States National Museum (Smithsonian Institution), Washington, and others are scattered through the science and art museums of North America. Catlin had talent but was too often hurried and careless in his observation and crude in style, so that his work does not go very deep nor get very far beyond the obvious and picturesque.

George Winter (1810-1876) was a young English miniature painter who, drawn by the lure of the Indian, migrated to Indiana and sketched among the Indian tribes along the Wabash before their removal west of the Mississippi; afterward he remained as a portrait painter in the little towns that sprang up in western Indiana after the Miamis and Pottawottamis had vanished. His Indian sketchbooks have been reproduced by the Indiana Historical Society.

William Ranney (1813-1872) was a self-taught artist, who is listed in New York city directories from 1843 on as a portrait painter. He had a love of adventure that, at the outbreak of the Mexican War, led him to enlist in General Taylor's army on the Texas frontier. He became interested in the adventurous life of the prairie hunters and scouts and devoted himself to picturing their life, as well as similar subjects from earlier days in history. He worked these subjects out carefully in large studio pictures which, though never distinguished in color, have excellent dramatic vigor and action.

Seth Eastman (1808-1875) was an army officer whose service on the frontier gave him an interest in the Indians. While in command of Fort Snelling, at the head of navigation on the Mississippi, he made many sketches of the Indians which were used to illustrate books on frontier life written by his wife; later he illustrated Schoolcraft's monumental, six-volume work on the Indians (1851-1857). A somewhat better painter than either Catlin or Winter, he was an accurate observer and gives us a useful historical record.

Alfred Jacob Miller (1810-1874) was a Baltimore artist who, after studying in France and Italy (1831-1834), was painting portraits in New Orleans when a traveling Scotsman, Captain William Drummond Stewart, passed through and persuaded him to join an exploring expedition into the Rockies (1837). Miller made a series of water-color sketches of the scenery and the Indian life of the West, in the period of the "mountain men" and trappers. In 1840-1842, Miller visited Scotland and painted there a series of large oils for his friend, who had then succeeded to a title and an estate. Miller spent the rest of his life in Baltimore painting portraits and repeating his Indian scenes. His later works lack the freshness of his first sketches from life.

John Mix Stanley (1814-1872) was established in Detroit in 1834 as a portrait painter. He made several expeditions into Indian country, up the Mississippi in 1838, to New Mexico and California in 1842, to Oregon and the Columbia River in 1848. Like Catlin, he exhibited his collection of paintings in the East. Unfortunately, all but five of a large collection on deposit in the Smithsonian were destroyed by fire in 1865. A few works are, however, preserved in Detroit and elsewhere.

These painters, with the exception of Seth Eastman, were "romantic" in the popular sense. They were caught by the color and picturesqueness of Indian life. They were not observers of life and character, as was Bingham, nor even serious scientific students of the Indian, but glorifiers and dramatizers.

For serious studies of Indian character one must turn to the professional portrait painters. The portrait painters of the East occasionally seized the opportunity to paint portraits of a delegation of Indians on their way to Washington. John Neagle, for example, painted *Two Chiefs of the Kansas Indians* (1821) (The Historical Society of Pennsylvania) who were in Philadelphia while traveling as a deputation to Washington. One was Caussetonga, or Big Kansas, described as inanimate and sleepy-looking except on important occasions, but a dreadful opponent. He had a great friendship with Sharitarishe, chief of the Grand Pawnees, and would not sit for his likeness without his friend. Sharitarishe was a distinguished orator, had great energy of character, and commanded deep respect from his tribe. In Neagle's acute character studies one can catch a glimpse of the complex and interesting characters behind the genre painter's costume illustrations.

Another group of portraits, preserved in the colored lithographs illustrating McKenney and Hall's three folio volumes of the *History of the Indian*

Tribes of North America (1836-1844), we owe to the humane and intelligent Quaker, Thomas L. McKenney, who was the founder of the "Indian
Department" of the federal government. As superintendent of the Indian
trade for the War Department for six years, McKenney conceived the idea
of a portrait gallery of the Indians who visited the capitol. He employed
Charles B. King, James Otto Lewis, A. Ford, Henry Inman, George Cooke
and Peter Rindisbacher to paint the portraits, of which one hundred and
twenty were reproduced in the *History*. All but a dozen of the originals
were destroyed in the Smithsonian fire of January 15, 1865; but a set of copies
by Inman is in the Peabody Museum, Cambridge, Massachusetts.

Such portraits, together with the work of the genre-illustrators, give us
something of the substance of that vanished stone age world, so picturesque,
so rich in both the worst and best of human nature, whose history contributes
grandeur and tragedy to the story of the Western migration.[6] These artists
belong to the craft of painting, not to the art. Yet they have their place, even
though a modest one, in the story of what artists have contributed to our history as a nation.

One of the most important social changes of the nineteenth century was
the rapid increase in the reading public. The birth of popular education and
the rise of literacy and political democracy went hand in hand with the rise
of the popular newspaper, the periodical magazine, and the novel. But popular
reading was also illustrated: the graphic arts were transformed to meet a
constantly larger use. Wood engraving began a rapid development. About
1835 lithography took the place of the beautiful but difficult medium of
aquatint; and steel engraving came to supplement, but did not wholly replace,
engraving on copper. The new techniques, if less rich in tone, were more

[6] The Mississippi and the Indian country attracted a number of other artists, both Americans and traveling Europeans, who form part of this story also, at least on its margin. Samuel
Seymour, the Englishman who went on Long's expedition to the Rockies, has been mentioned
in the preceding chapter. James Otto Lewis (fl. 1815-1833) visited Prairie du Chien, at the
confluence of the Mississippi and Wisconsin Rivers, as a government artist in 1825. His paintings are preserved as lithographs in his *Aboriginal Portfolio* (1835-1836). Peter Rindisbacher
(1806-1834), a Swiss immigrant to Lord Selkirk's colony on the Red River, arrived in the
upper Mississippi Valley from Canada, at Fort Snelling in Minnesota, in 1826; in 1829 he was
settled in St. Louis. He made a record in water colors of the Swiss emigrants' journey to the
Red River in 1821 (now in the Public Archives, Ottawa) and after his arrival in the United
States did a series of water colors and drawings of the life of the Sioux and of the prairies and
forests. Charles Bodmer (1809-1893), a Swiss artist, came to the United States with Maximilian,
Prince of Wied, a Prussian officer and naturalist, in 1832. They traveled with a group of
American Fur Company men up the Missouri River in 1833, wintered in the Indian country,
and returned to St. Louis and civilization the following spring. Maximilian published an account of his travels in 1839 as *Reise in das innere Nord-Amerika in den Jahren 1832 bis 1834*,
which was accompanied by an Atlas of eighty-one plates by Bodmer. Bodmer was an excellent
draughtsman and well-trained observer.
The artist-explorer was not found only on land. The navy also took artists along on its
explorations by sea. Alfred T. Agate (1812-1846), a miniature painter and illustrator of this
generation, joined the scientific corps of the Wilkes Exploring Expedition, 1838-1842, as a
"portrait and botanical artist." Many of Agate's drawings are illustrated in Wilkes' *Narrative
of the United States Exploring Expedition* (1844, 5 vols.).

suited than the older media to the larger editions and more rapid printing of nineteenth-century periodicals.

Like the reading habit, the appetite for illustration grew with what it fed on. Engravings reproduced and popularized the painters' work; at the same time the illustrator, the humorist, the satirist flourished. A broadening flood of black-and-white illustration and chromolithography spreads through the last three quarters of the century. The phenomenon is so familiar that we hardly notice it: yet it has both artistic results and social implications of very great interest.

The first notable figure in American illustration was John Gadsby Chapman of Virginia, whose achievement as a landscapist in Italy has already been mentioned. Before settling finally in Rome he lived for twelve years, 1836-1848, in New York city. In addition to producing a large mural of *The Baptism of Pocahontas* (1842) for the Capitol in Washington (the most respectable of the later additions to the Rotunda), he made himself in those years the first important American book illustrator, whose numerous works are scattered through the magazines and gift annuals. But his chief achievement was to make more than 1,400 of the 1,600 illustrations of Harper's *Family Bible* (1846), a landmark of American wood engraving whose wood blocks were engraved with such firmness and delicacy by J. A. Adams that they seem like copper plates. Chapman likewise wrote and illustrated an *American Drawing Book*, which went through many editions. He was the first American illustrator to design and execute his own etchings. One cannot expect the rich use of this medium which was invented later by the painter-etchers of the second half of the century: etching in Chapman's time was used in the manner of copper or steel engraving. One sees his qualities in his *JGC in His Studio* (1881) (Fig. 87) (Richmond, Virginia, The Valentine Museum), a late print, showing the genial old artist at work in his studio in Rome. It is a characteristic example of the mellow, sharp-eyed spirit that makes Chapman one of the most attractive of our romantic illustrators.

David Claypoole Johnston (1799-1865) was born in Pennsylvania and was apprenticed in 1815 to a Philadelphia engraver, Francis Kearny. In 1819 he set up his own workshop and began making caricatures of local celebrities. Threats of libel suits by the angry subjects of his prints, however, made the Philadelphia print- and booksellers refuse to handle his work. In 1821 he turned to the stage instead and became an actor; in 1825 he went with the company from the Walnut Street Theatre to Boston. There he returned once more to engraving and humor. He began an etched periodical called *Scraps* (issued in imitation of George Cruikshank's *Comic Almanack*) which satirized the follies of the day without going into personal caricatures. This time his humor found a better reception. Humor is volatile and quickly evaporates. But Johnston was a lively draughtsman and his humor was comedy of character as well as situation. The drollery of his water-color drawing *The Mili-*

tia Muster (about 1829) (Fig. 84) (American Antiquarian Society), for example, wears very well—at least I can never look at it without laughing. Johnston kept a drawing school in Boston and exhibited genre paintings in the annual exhibitions at the Athenaeum.

A satirist of a different type was David Gilmor Blythe (1815-1865), an artist born on the Ohio frontier and active in and around Pittsburgh, Pennsylvania. He was an eccentric, largely self-taught artist, trying his hand at all sorts of things—wood carving, a panorama, theatrical scenery, verses, painting—with frontier versatility and energy. His paintings were rough, satirical, crude, yet alive, too, with a savage energy that keeps its interest, even after a century. *Art versus Law* (Fig. 86) (Brooklyn Museum) or *Pittsburgh Horse Market* (Mrs. Lucien D. Patten) are examples of Blythe's best level.

Beyond this, however, little else is worthy of mention in the field of humor in this generation. There are a few individual pictures, such as the *First State Election in Michigan* (1836) (The Detroit Institute of Arts) by Thomas M. Burnham (1818-1866), which reflect youthful high spirits and satire, but nothing that represents a sustained talent or an idiosyncratic view of life.

On the subject of illustration we must mention, however, the illustrated magazine and the gift annual, both of which did much to popularize the work of the American landscape and genre painters. *The New York Mirror*, founded in 1826 and edited by Samuel Woodward and N. P. Willis, made much use of the artists and copper engravers. *Graham's Magazine*, *Godey's Lady's Book*, and *Sartain's Union Magazine of Literature and Art* (1849-1852) were still more influential in making the illustration an essential part of the American magazine. John Sartain (1808-1897), who was associated with both of the first two and edited the third, was an excellent English mezzotint engraver who migrated to Philadelphia in 1830 and by his rich black-and-white prints founded a new era of American illustration. There were American-born mezzotinters also, of whom the best was probably John Cheney (1801-1885), famous for his sweet, dreaming young women's heads in gift annuals like *The Token*, *The Casket*, *The Opal*.

But on the most popular level, the lithograph reigned. The great name here is Nathaniel Currier (1813-1888), who was apprenticed as a boy to William S. and John Pendleton, who had imported equipment and workmen and set up the first lithographic shop in the United States in Boston. When John Pendleton established a lithographic shop in Philadelphia in 1829, he took the apprentice along, and again in 1833 to New York city. In 1835 Currier, having served his apprenticeship, established his own shop in New York in association with J. H. Bufford, and brought out his first topical print, *The Ruins of the Merchants Exchange*, after a drawing by Bufford. This was the first of the series of popular lithographic prints on topical, landscape, genre, or sporting subjects, which continued for nearly seventy years. In 1850 he took into partnership an artist, J. Merritt Ives (1824-1895), and after 1857 all the prints issued by the firm bore the imprint "Currier and Ives." Although seldom of very high quality, either as drawings or as lithographs, they form an incomparable storehouse of scenes of American life and the events of the day (Fig. 89).

The need for an ideal art remained. To some extent it was satisfied, outside of painting, by the surprising appearance out of nowhere of an active American school of marble sculpture. The United States, which had had nothing but an interesting though humble and local art of wood carving, and which in 1800 had found it necessary to import Italian marble carvers to carve the capitals of the national Capitol in Washington, suddenly found itself in possession, in the 1830's and 1840's, of a whole school of sculptors, working in the ancient art centers of Italy, producing imposing figure sculpture in marble, and enjoying a most flattering degree of international *réclame*. This is not the place to enlarge upon the story of Horatio Greenough, Hiram Powers, Thomas Crawford, Randolph Rogers, Harriet Hosmer, and the others who once made the American colony in Rome and Florence famous. We are concerned only with the influence that their unexpected appearance may have had upon painting. By the standards of any subsequent period, the popularity of these sculptors was phenomenal. Randolph Rogers sold over a hundred repetitions of his marble, *The Lost Pleiad*, a record that no other American sculptor could equal.

These sculptors produced some excellent busts: confronted with a human head to study, they revealed perception and occasionally real talent. But their principal subjects were in a vein characteristic of the decline of the neoclassic style, when to the neoclassic coldness of style was added a romantic sentimentality of subject (of which Powers' *Greek Slave* is the most famous example). The result was a prodigious production of parlor-sculpture, too white, too sentimental, and too bulky to share even in the revived popularity of nineteenth-century American art. It seems possible to me that the explanation for the comparative absence of ideal subjects in painting at this time is that the sculptors filled and monopolized the field.

Italy, which from 1830 to 1860 was the goal of all American artists wishing to study the tradition of their art, was more helpful to painters than to sculptors, simply because there was no strong contemporary Italian school of painting. The danger for American students going abroad to study is that they may, unless very strong personalities, merely borrow the style they find practiced by the artists of the country where they go to study. Artistic style is, however, not a masquerade dress to be donned at will. It is a disciplined language, both conscious and intuitive, which the artist must use with calculation and with skill to express emotions that rise from the deepest and often the most mysterious depths of his being. The American sculptors who went to Italy from 1830 onward found the second generation of neoclassicism at the height of its success in artists like Thorwaldsen and Gibson. They adopted its manner—its cold artifice, its smoothly elegant finish, its fluent line, its easy rhetoric. These were all qualities fatal to their native talents.

The painters found no strong contemporary school at work in Italy. They found instead a landscape of great beauty, an atmosphere stimulating and congenial, galleries filled with the inspiring masterpieces of their art, a spur of emulation in the companionship of other artists, a soil rich with the creative life of centuries past. Even in an age of predominant romantic realism there were many artists who needed this experience of tradition.

William Page (1811-1885) was the most complex personality and the most original, experimental stylist of this generation. Before he was twenty he had tried the study of law, the ministry, painting, and marriage. The combination is revealing: a brilliant talker, a speculative mind, an impulsive, emotional nature, Page was always an unpredictable and a controversial figure, praised and ridiculed by other artists, attacked and defended by critics. He took up again, through Morse (under whom he studied at the newly founded National Academy of Design from 1826 to about 1828) Allston's interest in Venetian color and monumentality, to which he added his own peculiarities.

One of his theories was that monumental paintings of ideal subjects should be based upon sculpture—in which nature was already transposed into a new key—rather than upon life. It was a theory that had been a dogma of the neoclassicists in Paris and Rome; and it had been held and practiced with great success by some earlier painters like Poussin and Tintoretto. By Page's generation it had become highly unfashionable: Page not only believed it but gave it his own original twist. Another of his beliefs, often bitterly attacked, was his theory of the middle tone: this was that colors attain their maximum resonance at the middle point of the scale from light to dark. To attain this maximum resonance (rather than brightness) he painted, as Allston had done, in a warm deep palette and used a technique of underpaint and glazes. At a time when direct painting and a general lightening of the palette were coming into favor, he painted dark, rich pictures like the *Self-Portrait* and *Portrait of Mrs. Page* (Fig. 81), of 1860 (The Detroit Institute of Arts). This, too, was flying in the face of fashion: yet such works show a capacity for original conception and a style of such rich, solemn, monumental gravity as to set Page completely apart from the mass of nineteenth-century portrait painting and give enduring interest to his art.

These portraits are sculptural but not derived from sculpture. His success in basing ideal subjects upon sculpture is best illustrated by his *Cupid and Psyche* (Fig. 79) (Mrs. Lesslie Stockton Howell) based upon the antique, which the Boston Athenaeum exhibited in 1843 but the National Academy of Design rejected as scandalous; and the strange, solemn *Flight into Egypt,* in which one can recognize as the models, freely treated and animated with a new life, Cellini's *Perseus* and Michelangelo's *Medicean Madonna*.

Page lived most of his life in New York city. From 1844 to 1847 he was in Boston and painted some distinguished portraits; from 1849 to 1860 he lived in Italy, where he was a prominent figure in the American colonies of Florence and Rome. He was never a man to have an artistic following and by the end of his life artistic fashions had so changed that his art fell into obscurity, where it remained until our own time.

The dreaming, brooding tone of Page's work at its best is gravely impressive. It is a tone heard often, hereafter, among the most solitary and original of our artists, and may be taken as one of the characteristic notes of American painting.

A dreamer of another sort, even more solitary, John Quidor (1801-1881), never enjoyed Page's degree of acceptance. A simple, eccentric soul (by the few accounts we have of him), he earned his livelihood as an artisan-painter, doing banners and fire-engine panels in New York city, while his imagination lived in the earlier New York of Washington Irving's books. The odd, humorous characters of Irving's invention were transposed by Quidor's fantasy, however, to another plane. Irving's imagination was genial: Quidor's pictures have a pungent flavor, compounded of riotous, uncouth *grotesquerie* and the remoteness of dreams. Contrary to modern notions of illustration, the dramatic energy of his drawing and his fantastic invention are so unlike the tone of Irving's art that his pictures are more like independent inventions than literary illustrations.

Quidor's gift for caricature makes him at first seem out of place in his age—more like an echo of Old Bruegel's spirit or Jan Steen's—until one remembers earlier romantic humorists like Gillray or Cruikshank. If his works had been bound in as etchings or engravings among Irving's or James Kirk Paulding's pages, they would have given us an American parallel to H. K. Brown's illustrations to Dickens. But they were not engravings, they were paintings: and although the National Academy of Design exhibited them, they seem almost never to have found purchasers. Long before his death in 1881 Quidor was forgotten. In 1942 John I. H. Baur brought together eighteen paintings for the first exhibition of Quidor's work, at the Brooklyn Museum, and we suddenly realized that in this strange compound of humor and dream is one of the original voices of that age.

It is a striking fact that Quidor the craftsman must have used the flat, bright, ornamental colors of the artisan-painter; yet Quidor the artist used the same technique of underpaint and glazes that Allston and Page had used. His earliest works, in the 1820's, use fairly light color and even tonalities. By the 1850's he was working in the deep brown-gold tonality and the vague, soft glazes of *The Devil and Tom Walker* (Fig. 90) (Mr. and Mrs. Lawrence

Fig. 62. Thomas Sully: *Washington at the Passage of the Delaware* (1819). (Courtesy of the Museum of Fine Arts, Boston.)

Fig. 63. Washington Allston: *The Dead Man Revived in the Tomb by Touching the Bones of the Prophet Elisha* (1811-1813). (Courtesy of The Pennsylvania Academy of the Fine Arts, Philadelphia.)

Fig. 64. Thomas Sully: *Col. Thomas Handasyd Perkins* (1831-1832). (Courtesy of The Boston Athenaeum, Boston.)

Fig. 65. Washington Allston: *The Moonlit Landscape* (1819). (Courtesy of the Museum of Fine Arts, Boston.)

Fig. 66. W. E. West: *Trelawny* (1822). (Courtesy of Miss P. Trelawny, New York City.)

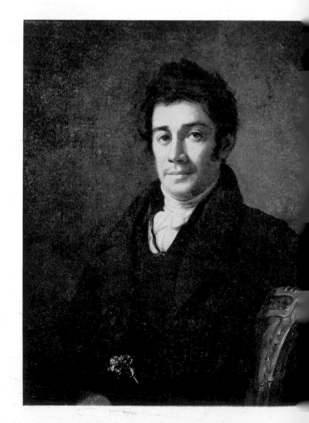

Fig. 67. Samuel Lovett Waldo: *Man with a Watch Fob.* (Courtesy of the M. and M. Karolik Collection, Museum of Fine Arts, Boston.)

Fig. 69. Thomas Birch: *The "United States" and
the "Macedonian"* (1813). (Courtesy of The Historical Society of Pennsylvania, Philadelphia.)

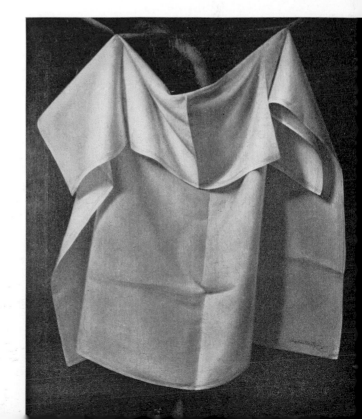

Opposite page, top: Fig. 70. Thomas Doughty: *In Nature's Wonderland* (1835). (Courtesy of The Detroit Institute of Arts.)

Right: Fig. 72. Charles Bird King: *The Vanity of an Artist's Dreams* (1830). (Courtesy of the Fogg Art Museum, Harvard University.)

Opposite page, bottom: Fig. 71. J. I. Middleton: *General View of the Site of the Ancient City of Norba.* (From *Grecian Remains in Italy,* plate 13. Courtesy of the Harvard University Library.)

Right: Fig. 73. Raphaelle Peale: *After the Bath* (1823). (Courtesy of the William Rockhill Nelson Gallery of Art and Atkins Museum of Fine Arts, Kansas City.)

Left: Fig. 74. John James Audubon: *Purple Grackle* (water color). (Courtesy of The New-York Historical Society.)

Opposite page, top: Fig. 76. Thomas Cole: *In the Catskills* (1837). (Courtesy of The Metropolitan Museum of Art.)

Left: Fig. 75. George Catlin: *One Horn. A Dakota (Sioux) Chief* (1832). (Courtesy of the Chicago Museum of Natural History.)

Opposite page, bottom: Fig. 77. Thomas Cole: *The Roman Campagna* (1843). (Courtesy of the Wadsworth Atheneum, Hartford.)

Fig. 78. Thomas Cole: *The Voyage of Life: Manhood.* (Munson-Williams-Proctor Institute, Utica, N. Y.)

Fig. 79. William Page: *Cupid and Psyche* (1845). (Courtesy of Mrs. Lesslie Stockton Howell, West Palm Beach.)

Fig. 80. Asher B. Durand: *Kindred Spirits* (1849). (Courtesy of the New York Public Library.)

Fig. 81. William Page: *Mrs. William Page* (1860). (Courtesy of The Detroit Institute of Arts.)

Opposite page, bottom: Fig. 83. William S. Mount: *The Painter's Triumph* (1836). (Courtesy of The Pennsylvania Academy of the Fine Arts, Philadelphia.)

Fig. 82. William S. Mount: *Eel Spearing at Setauket* (1845). (Courtesy of The New York State Historical Association Museum, Cooperstown.)

Fig. 84. David Claypoole Johnston: *The Militia Muster* (ca. 1829). (Courtesy of the American Antiquarian Society, Worcester, Mass.)

Fig. 85. George Caleb Bingham: *Raftsmen Playing Cards* (1847). (Courtesy of the City Art Museum, St. Louis.)

Fig. 86. David Blythe: *Art versus Law*. (Courtesy of The Brooklyn Museum.)

Fig. 87. John Gadsby Chapman: *JGC in His Studio, Rome* (etching, 1881). (Courtesy of The Valentine Museum, Richmond, Va.)

Above: Fig. 88. James Bard:
*The Hudson River Steamboat
"Rip Van Winkle"* (1854).
(Courtesy of the M. and M.
Karolik Collection, Museum of
Fine Arts, Boston.)

Below: Fig. 89. Currier and Ives:
*"Rounding a Bend" on the Missis-
sippi.* (Courtesy of The Old Print
Shop, New York.)

A. Fleischman). As he grew older, he drew further and further into an ideal world of shadows.

This generation produced few figure painters other than Page and Quidor, who devoted themselves to literary or religious themes. Robert W. Weir (1803-1889) studied in Florence and Rome, 1824-1827, and, a few years after his return home, received the appointment in 1834 as professor of drawing at West Point, a position which he held over forty years. His name as a historical painter is preserved by *The Embarkation of the Pilgrims* (1840) in the Capitol at Washington. But Weir was not at home in this monumental scale and was more successful with illustrations and literary-religious subjects on the scale of cabinet genre.

Luther Terry (1813-1900) of Connecticut, who migrated in 1833 to Rome, was, like Weir, a gentle, unworldly spirit. His religious and historical pictures, like *Jacob's Dream* in the New-York Historical Society, have a larger scale than Weir's, perhaps because he lived in Rome where good examples of monumental painting were on every hand. His works are clear in drawing, tranquil and sweet in feeling. But neither he nor Weir had a very sure color sense; and the world seems quite content to leave their gentle, rather sentimental works resting in their long obscurity.

The tendency away from the monumental interests of the previous generation is very well shown by the second series of decorations in the Capitol at Washington. Trumbull had filled four of the eight panels in the Rotunda (1817-1824). The remaining four blank walls were a mute challenge to complete the set; and in spite of the general disappointment over the first four, in 1834 Congress tried again, voting to commission four artists, each to do a panel. Allston, exhausted by his struggle with *Belshazzar's Feast*, refused even to consider a commission. Eventually the four panels were assigned, in 1836, to John Vanderlyn, R. W. Weir, J. G. Chapman, and Henry Inman; the panels of the first three were installed in 1846. The hostile reception of Vanderlyn's *Landing of Columbus* (1842-1844) has already been described. Weir's *Embarkation of the Pilgrims* (1837-1840) and Chapman's *Baptism of Pocahontas* (1837-1842) were respectable but did not capture the imagination. As one looks at them today, the change in scale and conception between Trumbull's works and these is striking. Trumbull's panels are decorations by a man who had at least some notion of monumental painting. The next three look like romantic book illustrations blown up to gigantic size.

Ill health and the pressure of portrait painting prevented Inman from doing his panel: his subject, *The Emigration of Daniel Boone to Kentucky*, was never carried beyond a sketch. After his death in 1846 there was a scramble for the vacant commission. The artists and amateurs of New York city appealed for S. F. B. Morse, who was, however, at this time wholly absorbed in his telegraph. From St. Louis on the wild frontier came a petition to have the panel assigned to a young painter named Charles Deas (1818-1867), who had made a name for himself by paintings of the Indians. Congress, however, gave the contract to William H. Powell (1823-1879), a young man of twenty-four, whose qualifications were that he hailed from Ohio, a populous state whose congressmen thought that the artists of the Queen City of the West, Cincinnati, should get one of these commissions. Powell went to Paris and spent five years, 1848-1853, on *The Discovery of the Mississippi River by De Soto*, which, although it hangs in the Rotunda and clearly represents a great deal of trouble, has not caused anyone to remember his name. This ended that chapter in the public patronage of painting by Congress.

In still life the daughters of James Peale, Anna Claypoole (1791-1878), Margaretta Angelica (1795-1882) and Sarah Miriam Peale (1800-1885), and John F. Francis (1808-1886) carried on the Philadelphia style of still life without great change, but attaining at their best a shy, decorative charm.

In animal painting also the impetus of the preceding generation carried forward into the thirties and forties. John Woodhouse Audubon (1812-1862) was his father's collaborator in illustrating and writing the *Viviparous Quadrupeds of North America* (2 volumes of plates, 1842-1845; text in 3 volumes, 1846-1854). If he lacked something of his father's dramatic energy and his plates miss the indefinably wild quality of his father's animals, none the less, as Alice Ford rightly says in her recent study of the *Quadrupeds*, John W. Audubon was an animal painter of the first order, although overshadowed by his father's greatness.[7]

Among Charles Willson Peale's children, Titian Ramsay Peale (1799-1885) was distinguished as an artist-naturalist. Trained under his brother Rubens, he rose to be manager of the museum in 1833; in the same year he published *Lepidoptera Americana* and his collection of Lepidoptera is preserved in the Academy of Natural Sciences, Philadelphia.

But he was also a scientific artist of a whole series of expeditions. At the age of nineteen he went on an expedition to the coasts of Georgia and Florida with three pioneer scientists of Philadelphia, William Maclure, Thomas Say, and George Ord. In 1819-1820 he was assistant naturalist and painter on Major Long's expedition to the Upper Missouri and made many of the sketches which illustrate the papers published by members of the expedition. Charles Lucien Bonaparte sent him to Florida in 1824 to collect specimens and make drawings for his *American Ornithology* (4 volumes, 1825-1833), of which Peale illustrated Volumes I and IV. Finally he went as naturalist and artist on the United States Exploring Expedition to the South Seas, 1839-1842, a landmark in Antarctic and Polynesian studies, and wrote and illustrated Volume VIII of the *Reports on Mammalia and Ornithology*. His animal plates have

[7] Alice Ford, *Audubon's Animals: The Quadrupeds of North America*, New York, The Studio Publications, Inc., 1951.

a frosty clarity of color and drawing that gives them a certain decorative elegance, much colder than Audubon's work but distinguished in its own more restrained and objective manner.

An entirely different tradition of animal painting, the sporting picture, also had its first and most distinguished representative in this period. Edward Troye (1808-1874) was born in Geneva, Switzerland, the son of the painter Jean Baptiste de Troye; he anglicized his name to Troye on coming to this country. Troye landed first in Philadelphia, but from 1835 traveled through the South, from plantation to plantation, painting thoroughbred and standard-bred horses. In the 1850's he went to Arabia and the Holy Land, painting landscapes as well as pictures of Arab stallions and mares and Damascus cattle. Troye was a good painter: his sporting pictures have an animation of drawing and a lustrous use of oil paint that remind one of Stubbs or Marshall, the greatest English masters of this genre (Fig. 91).

Yet in spite of the variety of new interests which enriched American painting in this generation, portrait painting remained the staple and main support of the painters' profession. In New York, Boston, Philadelphia, portraits were painted by specialists who carried on the decorative, plastic style and the dignified perception of character established in the early decades of the century. But American portrait painters were at work everywhere, from Bangor, Maine, to Havana, Cuba, and from the old seaports on the Atlantic coast to rough-and-ready towns in the interior hardly emerged from the forest and the ways of fur-trading posts. The sheer bulk of their work makes them difficult to report, for, in great numbers, portraits are monotonous and their merits tend to be lost in the mass.

The significant portraits of the time may be divided into groups: on the one hand those done by professional painters in the great centers, like New York, Boston, Philadelphia, Baltimore, or Richmond, who were distinguished craftsmen and produced a portraiture of solid character and decorative dignity; the work of the untrained professionals; finally, the naïf painters.

In New York city, Henry Inman (1801-1846), a pupil of Jarvis, was looked on in his own time as the leading American portrait painter. He was active in New York city except for three years in Philadelphia (1831-1834) and a visit to England in 1844. Inman was a broad, rapid, direct painter. One of his most attractive portraits is the *Self-Portrait* (1834) (Fig. 95) (The Pennsylvania Academy of the Fine Arts) in a yellow top hat, painted at a single sitting to show three young Philadelphia artists how he worked. Inman was a good-humored man and his genial view of humanity is evident in the calm and amiability of his portraits; that of *Georgianna Buckham and Her Mother* (Boston, Museum of Fine Arts) is an excellent example.

Charles Cromwell Ingham (1796-1863) was born in Ireland and came to New York at the age of twenty-one, having already had a little training at the Royal Dublin Society. He developed a portrait style of elegant outline and enameled color which, though sometimes sentimental, offers a charming treatment for the young girls and pretty women he painted.

After the death of Inman, Charles Loring Elliott (1812-1868) became the leading portrait painter of New York city. He was an excellent observer of character and a painter who used oils in a solid, free, painterly way. His work is interesting and often distinguished, forming an invaluable gallery of the Knickerbocker poets, painters, and celebrities.

William Page's portraiture, the most distinguished of all, has already been discussed.

Cephas Giovanni Thompson (1809-1888) is typical of the many portrait painters of the second rank in New York city. He worked in New York from 1837 until his death, except for seven years in Rome, 1853-1860, where Hawthorne met and liked him; his memory is kept alive chiefly by the enthusiastic mention of him in Hawthorne's *Journal* and the *Marble Faun*.

In Boston also there were men capable of distinguished portraiture. One who belongs by date of birth to an earlier generation was Chester Harding (1792-1866). He has left us a frank and amusing autobiography, the *Egotistography*, which tells a story of the American frontier—the story of a man, born to be an artist, growing up on the western frontier until the age of twenty, in total ignorance of the art of painting. Harding was a genial giant of a man, renowned (like Lincoln) as an axeman, barely able to read, and ignorant of any book but the Bible. Yet having once discovered his art, he made himself an able (if uneven) painter whose portraits have the bluff, objective honesty one might expect. His full-length portrait of the great New England philanthropist, *Amos Lawrence*, (Washington, National Gallery of Art) is perhaps his masterpiece.

Francis Alexander (1800-1881) grew up in equal ignorance of art, in the rugged back country of Connecticut. He managed to get a little training in New York, then settled in Boston, where he learned from Allston's example the warm, resonant tonality and atmospheric depth that make his portrait of the poet *Nathaniel Parker Willis* (about 1830-1835) (Morristown Library, Morristown, N.J.) of his *Mrs. Jared Sparks* (Fig. 96) so attractive. In later life he lived abroad in Florence and gave up painting for the pleasures of collecting other painters' works.

George Peter Alexander Healy (1813-1894) was a precocious youth who established himself as a portrait painter in Boston at the age of eighteen. Having earned enough to take him to Paris in 1834, he went there to spend a year or two in study, and remained sixteen. For the first two or three years he worked in the studio of Baron Gros, where he learned to paint with a good solid impasto and effective use of tone. In 1855 he moved to the new metropolis of the West, Chicago; in 1867 he went back to Europe, living in Rome (1867-1872) and Paris (1872-1892); the last two years of his life were spent in Chicago. Healy's success as a portrait painter was extraordinary: he painted most of the great and famous people of two continents during his lifetime (for he was constantly on the move and even while living abroad, made frequent trips to the United States). His best work was done in the first half of his life, before the influence of the camera made itself felt in a disagreeable dryness of drawing and insipidity of color. At his best, Healy could paint the grace of a young woman, as in the *Mrs. John Church Cruger* (1842) (Fig. 98) (The Metropolitan Museum of Art), or the force of a masculine personality, as in his *John Tyler* (dated 1864 but based on a study of 1842) (The White House), with very happy eloquence. But he was uneven; the bulk of his work is dry and tiresome.

In Philadelphia, John Neagle (1796-1865), who married Sully's stepdaughter, was, with his father-in-law, the chief portrait painter of the city before the Civil War. He was not Sully's pupil. He was apprenticed to a Philadelphia coachmaker, then had a couple of months' instruction from Bass Otis (who, being a scythe maker, had become an artist and at one time a partner of Jarvis); finally, in 1825, he made a pilgrimage to Boston to see Gilbert Stuart. He painted the best portrait we have of the old artist and his admiration for Stuart was a strong influence upon his art: but Neagle was, alas, a monotonous painter.

In Richmond there was a much more interesting personality, William J. Hubard (1807-1862). Born in England, he came to the United States as a boy, and first appeared as a child prodigy, cutting silhouettes "by the hundreds in the Hubard Gallery in Boston" (1825-1826)[8] under the management of a man named Smith. Having received some lessons in oil painting from Stuart and Sully, Hubard left the gallery when he was about nineteen. (The resourceful Mr. Smith replaced him with a boy named Hankes and took the "Hubard Gallery" around the country for another fifteen years.) In 1830 Hubard was in Philadelphia and later he traveled in Italy. A souvenir of this trip is the portrait of *Horatio Greenough in His Studio in Florence*, painted about 1838 or 1839 (Fig. 97) (The Valentine Museum), in which the sculptor, then at the height of his fame, appears as darkly romantic as the hero in a tale by Edgar Allan Poe. About this time Hubard married a Virginian and, in 1841, opened a painting room in Richmond, where he spent most of the rest of his life. His portraits and his few narrative pictures show him to have been an interesting artist, capable of unexpected and original compositions when not bowed down by the monotony of head-and-shoulders portrait commissions.

This generation gave us a strong, firmly drawn and plastic portraiture, whose aim was character. For the most part it was an art of romantic realism marked by an admirable lucidity and directness. William Page, on the other

[8] Swan, *The Athenaeum Gallery*, 1827-1873.

hand, and occasionally Alexander, or Ingham, or Hubard created a romantic portraiture of mood.

The phenomenon of the *untrained professional* continued to lend its distinctive note also. An example of a true and sensitive artist outside the norm of the professional painter's practice is Jeremiah P. Hardy (1800-1888), who had a little training in Boston and New York as a young man, but about 1826 or 1827 returned to his home in Maine and from that time worked as a portrait painter, isolated from the stream of art, in the towns of Hampden and Bangor, Maine. In the Karolik Collection of the Museum of Fine Arts, Boston, are two of Hardy's portraits of his own family. *Catherine Wheeler Hardy and Her Daughter* (Fig. 93) (1842) shows his wife and little girl on a sofa before a window looking out upon the Penobscot River; *Mary Ann Hardy* (1821) shows a little girl in a white dress with a moss rose clutched in one small hand. These pictures have little to do with the atmospheric-plastic technique of Samuel F. B. Morse, from whom Hardy is said to have had a little instruction in New York. Along with a certain flatness and a tentative quality of technique that marks the untrained, his pictures have certain very positive esthetic qualities: very exact observation, expressed in a curiously beautiful quality of outline; luminosity of tone; and a strange mood of loneliness, and melancholy that remind one of another recently discovered romantic soul, Samuel Palmer.

There were a great many other untrained professional portrait painters throughout the country working on Hardy's level of professional skill—too many to attempt to mention—but none who show the same degree of poetry.

But what is really most extraordinary in these decades was the popularity of the visual image. This showed itself most strikingly in the immense wave of portrait painting, yet was by no means confined to it. Painters like Thomas Cole became national figures: his untimely death was spoken of as a public calamity. Illustrated books and magazines became more and more popular. Framed engravings or lithographs were on every wall. Painting was practiced not only by well-trained professional painters in the larger cities, but by the untrained professional, the self-taught, the amateur, in every corner of the land. Housewives, retired farmers, amused their leisure with brush and canvas. The nation poured its energies into painting with astonishing profusion. Nothing is more curious, in a careful survey like Wilbur Peat's *Pioneer Painters of Indiana* (1955), than to see that towns of two or three thousand inhabitants, so newly carved out of the forest that the stumps of trees still stood in the mud of their streets, had resident portrait painters, busy and thriving on the practice of their craft. In sheer mass and enthusiasm, the production of self-taught and amateur painters reached its highest point in the decades from 1825 to the Civil War; although it never quite reached the level of artistic quality attained by the untrained professionals of the preceding fifty years.

A mass phenomenon such as this has the qualities of the popular consciousness from which it sprang. Thousands of pictures have been rediscovered since the revival of interest in popular art, in the past thirty or forty years. A great many are banal, imitative, and of a wearisome monotony: but there are also, in flashes, a gaiety of pattern, and unexpected, frank, shrewd observation; an innocent and childlike freshness of feeling.

Two conclusions may be drawn. One is that the intuitive, undogmatic nature of romanticism produced a very favorable climate for the growth of popular art. Its inspirations rose spontaneously. No esthetic dogma separated the leading professional artists from the interests of the general mass of men; consequently the amateurs and the gifted naïf could feel the strong, warm, magnetic pull of active and gifted minds drawing them generously onward. Romanticism spoke to, and stirred, our whole population as no esthetic or imaginative movement has done since. Secondly, it is clear that painting, after a slow, difficult growth of generations, had struck root. It flourished as a craft; it filled a deep-seated need for the visual image; it was a popular enthusiasm.

It is beyond the perspective of this study to offer a survey of American popular art. This is predominantly an anonymous phenomenon. A great many of even the most interesting canvases are by unknown makers.[9] To give some notion of the character of this phase of American art and of its makers it will fit our purpose better merely to sketch a few of the more prominent figures.

William M. Prior (1806-1873), son of a Maine shipmaster, grew up in the artisan tradition of painting. In 1828 he advertised: "Wm. Prior, fancy, sign and ornamental painting. Also drawings of machineries of every description. . . ." He carried over into portraiture the clean outlines and bold, bright colors of the artisan tradition. His stylized treatment of the human figure is happiest in portraits of little girls, like the *Burnish Sisters* in the Garbisch Collection, who, in stiff dresses and curls, seem like some kind of animated and charming toys. Prior's life was spent in Bath and Portland, Maine, and East Boston, Massachusetts, but intellectually if not geographically remote from the organized world of art. In later days he made a specialty of copies of Stuart's *Athenaeum Washington* on glass.

Ruth Bascom (1772-1848) was a minister's wife of Gill, Massachusetts, who, rather late in life, made a number of profile portraits in pastel, and silhouettes which show a dainty and attractive sense of pattern. The decorative effect of her work was heightened by touches of metal foil.

Joseph H. Davis of Dover, New Hampshire, active in the eighteen-thir-

---

[9] The reader must consult the specialists, such as Holger Cahill, Jean Lipman, Edith Halpert, Nina Fletcher Little, Alice Ford, and the numerous excellent picture books and museum catalogues in the field for a detailed survey.

ties, created a style of portrait in water color, showing figures full length, often a husband and wife, seated or standing in heraldic balance on either side of a table. His work, too, shows an attractive quality of pattern.

Joseph W. Stock (1815-1855), a cripple confined to a wheelchair, was a self-taught painter of Springfield, Massachusetts, who practiced for a time in partnership with a daguerreotypist. He painted portraits, copied prints of famous men, did landscapes and banners.

The artisan tradition of clear outlines, flat bright colors, marked by a strong sense of decorative pattern and naïve drawing, characterizes all these painters. It is the technique whose qualities appeal most strongly to twentieth-century taste. Sometimes, as in the well-known *Miss Tweedy of Brooklyn* (ca.1840) (The Detroit Institute of Arts), the veneered chest of drawers and the flowers are painted with such care as to suggest that its author was a decorator of painted furniture; in an amusing *Sleighing Scene* by M. E. Ferrill (in the same collection), the sleighs are painted so lovingly that Louis Jones suggested the painter was probably a sleigh and carriage painter.

But in the mass of popular painting every kind of technique appeared. The amateur reflects the professional; the naïf, too, is usually inspired by engravings and prints, for nothing is rarer among the unskilled than the ability to create a pictorial composition unaided.

There was also landscape and still life on the popular level. "Theorems," or still lifes on velvet, continued to be an outlet for women's innate decorative sense and skill of hand. The vogue of this form of attractive home decoration, which had begun early in the century, was at its height in the decades 1830-1850.

Landscape is, however, a more difficult problem either to reduce to a decorative pattern or to treat with realism. Men and women and the works of men's hands, like houses and ships, are much more often successfully treated in popular art than the forms of trees, clouds, and running water (Fig. 92).

One painter who applied the artisan's technique to landscape was Thomas Chambers (active in New York and Boston, 1835-1855), who is interesting to modern taste because his flat, brilliant hues, boldly stylized drawing, and two-dimensional nonatmospheric style seem to foreshadow early twentieth-century modes of painting.

James Bard (1815-1897) and his brother John (1815-1856) of New York city, painters of steamboat portraits, show the artisan tradition in its most attractive form. They were twin brothers. James made his first ship portrait of *The Bellona,* a steamboat owned by Commodore Vanderbilt, in 1827. Until John's death in 1856, the brothers worked and signed their pictures together, *J & J. Bard;* but as James outlived his brother by forty-one years, the greater part of the Bard ship portraits are his alone.

Bard's obituary in *Seaboard* says that between 1827 and his death he made drawings of nearly every steamer built or owned around the port of

New York, a total of almost 4,000; and that shipbuilders said they could lay down the plans of a boat from one of his pictures, so correct were they in their proportions.

Some three hundred of his steamboat portraits in oil exist today. They are executed in a flat, gayly decorative artisan style with all that technique's merits of crisp, exact outline and cheerful color. They form the most attractive tribute made by painting to the Hudson River steamboat, a beautiful creation of American technology that, after flourishing for little more than a century, vanished in our own time (Fig. 88).

Another curious and picturesque triumph of popular art in this era was the rise of the panorama, which succeeded the traveling mural. The panorama, as first introduced by Vanderlyn, was really only a large painting by a serious artist; it was static in effect and although it could be moved, it was a cumbersome thing. About 1830 a new kind of panorama was introduced from Europe, consisting of a long strip of canvas wound on two vertical rollers, so that the picture could be unrolled, section by section, to the accompaniment of music and suitable commentary, across any kind of enframement, in any kind of hall or theater. This type of panorama had the interest of narrative, as one scene succeeded another; it was portable; it was accompanied by a lecture, explaining its changing scenes in the purple rhetoric of the romantic stage; and it might be equipped with other tricks of showmanship, such as the real smoke and steam that poured from the model steamboats drawn on a track in front of Leon Pomarede's panorama of the Mississippi. The panorama of the thirties and forties was, in fact, a form of theater, a primitive moving picture. Leon Pomarede, John Rowson Smith, Sam Stockton, Henry Lewis, John Banvard, all were celebrated for their panoramas in their own day. The Mississippi River was a most popular panorama subject: John Banvard advertised his Mississippi panorama as three miles long (it was actually 1,200 feet which is, however, quite long enough) and showed it with great success in this country and abroad.

The style used in painting a panorama was the broad, quick style of the theatrical scene painter, which is what most of the panorama painters actually were. One surviving example is a *Panorama of the Mississippi* (The University Museum, Philadelphia), painted in a coarse stage-scenery style, by John J. Egan about 1850 for Dr. Montrouth W. Dickeson, a Philadelphia physician and enthusiastic archaeologist, who advertised himself as having opened more than one thousand Indian mounds. The panorama took its audience down the Ohio and Mississippi Rivers and included the interior of a limestone cave (with Indian skeletons), a tornado, an Indian massacre, and a scene showing Dr. Dickeson excavating an Indian mound. The doctor himself supplied the commentary in the form of a lecture and showed with it his collection of Indian artifacts. Another panorama of the Black Hills and the

Sioux rising of 1862, painted by John Stevens of Rochester, Minnesota, is owned by the Minnesota Historical Society.

The panorama was a form of educational entertainment, a forerunner of the stereopticon, the magic lantern, the travel lecture with slides, and finally the travel film of today. An attempt has been made to present it as a significant art form, important in the history of painting; but it is actually a theatrical form, a curious anticipation of the motion picture. Its coarse, stylized images were tolerable only as stage effects, and were presently to disappear, replaced by the photograph.

It is a curious evolution, from Benjamin West to John Banvard, from the heroic neoclassic mural of one generation to the panorama, an unambitious but profitable form of amusement. If any conclusion can be drawn, it illustrates the hunger for visual images and the need for entertainment in our hard-working society. The practical ingenuity of the panoramists was able to gratify this need; and the idealism and ambition of artists apparently could not. The panorama is, in this sense, a phenomenon parallel to the rise of the illustrated popular magazine.

In this field of naïve and popular art, however, there are two men who throw light upon deeper bases of popular feeling.

Edward Hicks (1780-1849) was born of Quaker stock in the fertile farming country of Bucks county, Pennsylvania, in the bend of the Delaware River north of Philadelphia. He was a sign and carriage painter by trade. In his trade he learned the artisan's technique of painting, the flat decorative colors and careful lettering and the use of gold leaf; he had also the artisan's attitude toward originality, that to follow a design by some other hand was natural and normal. But his art sprang from his inner life rather than from his craft. He was a kinsman of Elias Hicks, whose teaching split the Quaker fellowship, and was himself an itinerant minister among the Friends. Religious stress made him a dogmatic, contentious, unhappy spirit. The deep emotions of his life—the Quaker dream of peace and the country dweller's simple love of his native land—found expression in his paintings. Many of these were signs for the inns and taverns of Bucks county, compositions taken from prints of well-known pictures—*Washington on Horseback; The Declaration of Independence; William Penn's Treaty with the Indians*—translated into Hicks's own naïve decorative style.

Hicks's popularity today rests largely upon his *The Peaceable Kingdom* (Plate XI) illustrating the prophecy in the book of Isaiah, Chapter 11, of the lion lying down with the lamb. More than a hundred of these exist, often with scriptural texts carefully lettered across the bottom or around all four sides. He painted them to give to his friends as expressions of his simple Quaker faith in the peace of God, and hope for Peace on Earth. He devised stock patterns of all the animal types mentioned by Isaiah (arranging them differently in each picture); and paraphrased Isaiah's prophecy in verses, which he had printed on cards, for presentation with the pictures. Probably no one would be more surprised than Hicks, if he were alive today, to find that these pictures expressing his gentle Quaker piety and intended for his rustic fellow religionists on the farms of Bucks county, a hundred years later fitted exactly the taste of the advanced artists of the 1920's and should become collectors' items in the thirties and forties: yet naïveté, intense conviction, and decorative charm are true artistic qualities and the taste for stylized forms and for the childlike in feeling found an appealing forerunner in Hicks.

If Hicks spoke for the earnest piety of rural America, Erastus Salisbury Field (1805-1900) spoke for its love of the American Republic. He was a rustic portrait painter of the untrained professional sort, in the Connecticut valley. His portraits were no better than a hundred others; the Biblical subjects he occasionally painted were as naïve as Hicks's. But in the 1870's, when the centennial of Independence came around and the Centennial Exposition in Philadelphia became a landmark in American life, the old painter produced his own celebration. On a canvas nine by thirteen feet, he painted a *Historical Monument of the American Republic* (1876) (Springfield Museum of Art), an architectural fantasy so strange, so ingenious, so labored and absurd that it succeeds in expressing, with a genuine and touching eloquence, the love and visions of grandeur that filled his simple mind.

Another sign that painting had struck root in American life was the growth of public institutions devoted to art.

The Pennsylvania Academy of the Fine Arts in Philadelphia was the first to be successfully established. During the two preceding generations, roughly from 1775 to 1825, Philadelphia had been the creative focus of American art. American painting may be said to have taken shape there. In spite of the eminence of Gilbert Stuart in Boston after 1805, and Allston after 1818, it was in Philadelphia that painting passed out of the colonial phase, beyond the efforts of a few, scattered individuals, into that of a lively artistic life and professional organization. It was the home of the activities of Charles Willson Peale and his family, the organization of the first successful Academy and annual exhibitions, the rise of still life, genre, and landscape, the center of the best engravers.

The artists of New York found an effective vehicle for their interests in 1826. This came, by coincidence, almost at the same moment that the opening of the Erie Canal, in 1825, began the transformation of their city. New York had been a small town on a magnificent harbor, until the Erie Canal suddenly made it the gateway to the interior of the continent.

After 1825 New York began to assume an importance in the arts it had never possessed before. The best of the next generation, who were to be the leaders of American painting from 1825 to 1850, were there. The rise of New

York as a port of entry for European goods was paralleled by its rise as a point of traffic in ideas. Journalism and book publishing more and more were centered there, deserting their old home in Philadelphia. In the field of literature Boston was a great center; but the muse of painting for the most part deserted Massachusetts after the death of Allston. The book and magazine publishers carried the engravers with them to New York: and painting, in the second generation of romanticism, was to become very closely linked to engraving. The men, the organizations, and the opportunities in painting after 1825 were increasingly to be found concentrated in New York city.

The American Academy of Fine Arts had been revived in New York city in 1816 with most laudable motives. When De Witt Clinton retired as president in 1817, it seemed natural to elect the dignified, famous Colonel Trumbull, lately returned from London. But it led to trouble. The American Academy of Fine Arts had in its rooms a collection of casts intended to serve not only for public exhibition, but as a school where students might draw from the antique. When that collection was reinstalled in 1816, it was proposed that the galleries should be open for students to draw, from six to nine in the morning. Unfortunately, Colonel Trumbull had employed as doorkeeper a crusty old veteran of the Revolution, who opened the doors when it pleased him to arrive. One morning in 1825, when Trumbull came about eight o'clock, William Dunlap, the keeper of the Academy, interceded for two students who were still waiting outside the locked door. Trumbull was at bottom a kindhearted man; but the slightest sign of complaint or opposition brought out all his morbid readiness to take affront. On this occasion he gave Dunlap the rough side of his tongue; and as for the students, he said, "they must remember that beggars are not to be choosers." This ill-tempered remark touched off a revolt. Some of the artists, led by Inman and Morse, took the side of the students and formed a drawing association to meet in the evenings and to be managed by the artists themselves. This was in November of 1825. All attempts to unite with the Academy were frustrated by Trumbull's pride and violent temper. Finally, in the spring of 1826, the younger group organized themselves as the National Academy of Design, with Morse as president, and held their first exhibition of painting in May, 1826. The group gradually established themselves as the first strong, progressive institution managed wholly for and by artists in the United States. The National Academy of Design attracted all the best of the younger men: for they found in the Academy not only a school but an annual exhibition in which they could make their reputations. The older American Academy struggled on for a few years, but finally collapsed. A fire completed the ruin of the institution; its remaining casts were bid in by the National Academy of Design. An attempt to turn Luman Reed's collection of paintings into a New York Gallery of Fine Arts, supported by admissions, also failed.

New York was thus left without the rudiments of a museum of art.

The result was that a large part of Luman Reed's American pictures, an excellent collection of European painting formed by Thomas J. Bryan, and a large number of Egyptian antiquities all found their way into The New-York Historical Society, as the only institution able to take care of them. The idea of a permanent public gallery of art was not revived until after the Civil War.

In Philadelphia, The Pennsylvania Academy of the Fine Arts carried on its three-part program of school, gallery, and annual exhibition with dignity and success: its school can number Bingham among its pupils, for example. The artists resented its control by laymen and in the 1840's attempted to form a rival organization of their own. After a few years this disintegrated, leaving the field once more to the Academy. But Philadelphia, although still the home of good painters, was no longer the active center of the art.

In Boston the Athenaeum, in 1828, added to its library and its casts of European sculpture an annual exhibition of painting. Boston was an important center of taste and one of the early centers of art collecting. Like the Philadelphia artists, those of Boston resented the layman's control of the Athenaeum and in the eighteen-forties attempted to form an organization of their own, without success. After the death of Allston in 1843 there was in fact a lull in the city's activity in painting. The most promising of the younger men went abroad to live and a generation was to pass before Boston would again be the home of an artist of national stature.

Washington was the capital, but it was a small city with transient population. It attracted a small colony of portrait painters, who satisfied the demand for likenesses of congressmen and government officials but otherwise had, in this period, no strong artistic life. Its importance, both real and potential, lay in its public buildings, which offered almost the only public commissions and large decorative projects known to the American romantic artist. The dismal story of these has already been told.

Some of the small cities also made a beginning: Hartford, in Connecticut, acquired the Wadsworth Atheneum in 1844 as the gift of Daniel Wadsworth. The Albany Gallery of Fine Arts was founded in 1846. The Trumbull Gallery at Yale College, in New Haven, opened in 1832, is a special case. It owed its existence to the enthusiasm of a single individual, Trumbull's devoted nephew-in-law, Professor Benjamin Silliman. Moved partly by a just estimate of the historical significance of Trumbull's life work, partly by sympathy for the man, he raised funds to give the old painter a life annuity, in return for which all works of art in Trumbull's possession were given to Yale. Silliman also secured a grant from the Connecticut legislature which built a picture gallery, designed by Trumbull himself, in a neat Greek Revival style, which must have been not only pleasing to the eye but thoroughly well calculated for its purpose. (It was adopted to other uses in 1867 and torn down in 1901.)

In the West, beyond the Appalachians, new cities were rising overnight along the great riverways. The extraordinary diffusion of the arts meant that artists of some sort were at work in every state, every city, almost every county. But although Cincinnati and St. Louis had little colonies of painters, the artists were on the whole too widely scattered through the vast distances of the interior to create and support institutions of their own.

Distance, lack of population, lack of means, are old, familiar enemies, which Americans have constantly throughout their history used their ingenuity to overcome. The answer for a time, so far as painting was concerned, was found by one original and highly successful device that grew almost overnight into our first national institution of art.

James Herring, an engraver in New York city (remembered otherwise for his National Portrait Gallery in book form), began as a commercial venture what was first called the Apollo Association (1838) and afterward the American Art Union (1842). In essence, it was a lottery, open to all who paid a membership fee, the prizes being works of art. The winners of the drawing, which was held with some ceremony once each year, received one of a number of oil paintings purchased by the Art Union for that purpose; while every subscriber received an engraving made from some American painting of popular interest, such as Bingham's *Jolly Flatboatmen* or Cole's *Voyage of Life*. The Art Union's success was enormous. Its subscribers rose to nine thousand (sixteen thousand in the year that *The Voyage of Life* was distributed) and were found in every remote corner of the land. Before it went out of existence, the Art Union distributed some 150,000 engravings and 2,400 paintings, by more than two hundred and fifty artists. It also published a *Bulletin* and *Transactions*, sent to the members, which may be called the first journals of art in this country. The impact of its activity was very great. It created for the first time a national audience for the artists of America. Philadelphia, Boston, and Cincinnati started Art Unions upon the same lines, which were also successful on a smaller scale.

This prodigiously successful institution was ended by the jealousy of artists. The National Academy of Design, although it did not formally protest, felt that its success was threatened by this rival; certain artists, who felt that they were not so much favored as others, helped initiate a legal suit which led to a court decision, outlawing the Art Union as a lottery. All the Art Unions thus came to an end in 1852; and once again artists were dependent on sales from their studios, or from the three annual exhibits in Philadelphia, New York, and Boston, until the rise of the art dealer's gallery in the second half of the century.

Let us close this chapter by asking how American romantic painting diverged, as a result of its strong local and regional interests, from the general development of romantic painting abroad. In its largest outlines, this was everywhere a period in Western culture of the flowering of romantic realism. The "bourgeois Empire" painters and the Barbizon realists in France, the Biedermeier painters in Germany and Austria, the course of English painting after the death of Lawrence show the same interests—landscape, genre, and portraiture—that flourished in America.

There was, however, in the United States a striking absence of esthetic dogma. American romantic artists were governed by no intellectualized theories of style. There was nothing in America like the war between highly cultured and self-conscious stylists in France, between romanticists and neoclassicists led by Delacroix and Ingres. The relative weakness of literary influences is also striking. There was nothing comparable to the excesses of literary subject matter we associate with the Düsseldorf school, or with artists like Friedrich Kaulbach in Munich, Paul Delaroche and Ary Schaffer in Paris, or the English genre painters in the train of Wilkie and Leslie. A tonic grasp of the significance of the real, the ordinary raw material of life prevailed.

Two trends of style begin to emerge, diverging from those of Europe. The decisive fact there was the re-establishment of the coloristic style in France, which was now to take the lead in Western painting. Inspired by the contemporary English and by the seventeenth-century paintings in the Louvre, the French romanticists of 1830 rewon the coloristic vision and style lost since the neoclassic revolution of the 1780's. Light and color, a rich scale of tone, a broad touch using the pasty, impasto qualities of oil paint—these made the technique of the Barbizon men, of Corot and Daumier and Delacroix, the foundation of the great flowering of French nineteenth-century painting.

In America, however, the decisive influence was that of engraving. Many influential painters like A. B. Durand, J. W. Casilear, or later, J. F. Kensett, were trained as engravers. A more pervasive influence was the fact that there were still no great collections of painting on this side of the Atlantic; and, lacking paintings to study, the painters looked at engravings. A clear, precise quality of outline and delicate minuteness of detail were fundamental to the vision of most American romantic painters, even the luminists.

The other trend, if it can be called such, was the deep, warm, shadowy palette introduced by Allston, which never quite disappeared, but kept cropping up as a love for the grave resonances of the bass tones on the palette (if one may use the expression) in many of the most interesting and original artists throughout the century.

But perhaps the greatest achievement of this generation was in the imagination. Living at a time of great national experiences, they gave this country—as the neoclassicists had done—a large, imaginative vision of itself. Seizing upon its variety of nature and human life, they gave it form. In their enthusiasm for Italy, also, they supplied a fresh stimulus and a sense of the tradition of civilization, which is likewise a necessity for a healthy culture.

American romantic painting was not a revolt against life. It was an art of enthusiasm and delight, of observation and affection, modest, intuitive, undogmatic in spirit, and instinctively at one with the world. The artists had their special skill but they were not walled off by esthetic theory from society. Their task was to take the things lying formless in life about them and give them form in the harmonies of their art; to observe, to clarify, and to express the poetry of their world.

CHAPTER 9

THE CLOSING PHASE OF ROMANTICISM:
THE GENERATION OF 1850.
LUMINISM, NATURALISM, AND SENTIMENTALISM

AMERICAN PAINTING WAS, IN THE TRUE SENSE OF THE WORD, A POPULAR ART in the generation of 1850. Its interests—landscape, genre, portraiture—were those of its public. Its style was simple, transparent, and easily grasped. The esthetic problems that interested painters led toward heightening and deepening the common consciousness rather than breaking away from it. Imaginative painting was surrounded by, and supported by, flourishing crafts of portrait painting, illustration, and engraving. The public appetite for pictures seemed inexhaustible. The style of interior decoration (always a formidable influence) for a brief time called for pictures and more pictures, hanging them in row above row in the drawing rooms of the fashionable and the parlors of the comfortable. If means were not available for paintings, engravings took their place.

It was not the period of our greatest art: but it was the most fortunate period for the artist. Prosperity for a brief moment touched him with its golden wand: he could not only earn a living by the practice of his art; he might even become rich by it. Such a phenomenon, brief though it was, deserves our curiosity.

In the year 1846 an unusual event took place in the organization of Western painting: a landscape painter was elected president of a leading national academy of art; Asher B. Durand succeeded Samuel F. B. Morse at the head of the National Academy of Design in New York. During the development of artists' academies in the sixteenth and seventeenth centuries, the prevailing idealist theories of art had placed landscape in the humble crowd at the bottom of the social scale, with still life, and other minor genres. When the Royal Academy was formed in eighteenth-century England, academic dogma had been softened by the passage of time and transplanting into the undogmatic English temperament. But it would still have been un-thinkable for a landscape painter to hold the post of president: this was re-served for painters of the human figure and history, such as Reynolds, West, and Lawrence. The election of Durand was more than a tribute to his simple goodness of character, more than a sign that social conventions were less powerful in America than in Europe: it symbolized a revolution in values. Two generations of romantic painters had created a faith in Nature that was now triumphant. It was not ill-founded: the history of the nineteenth century is starred with the names of great landscape painters and great objective realists.

The interest in landscape had also a strong, influence upon all other branches of painting, for everywhere in the Western world painters were becoming more and more interested in light. Painting out-of-doors made them conscious of the higher luminosities of sunlight, far up the scales of tone and hue, beyond the sober palette that painters were then using. The movement toward luminism and toward a higher key began first among the romantic landscapists. It produced almost everywhere a break with accepted practice and a war of styles. American luminism presents a difficult and con-fused history in the generation of 1850. Its struggle was, however, not against an external enemy, such as a strong, hostile convention to be overcome, but against its own inner uncertainty. American painters, having not yet formed a strong, coherent national tradition of style, groped their way forward by individual experiments, not all great or even successful, yet tending toward a common goal: Nature, and how she should be portrayed.

Nature is vast beyond the reach of human powers to observe or com-prehend. Any period when men strive to assimilate into art new aspects of this all-embracing and elusive infinity is always a time of flux and variety. But in addition to the search of Nature (as if this were not enough) three other violent sources of change came bursting into the artist's quiet workroom.

One was the influence of the newly risen science of chemistry, which, within little more than two generations, transformed the medium with which the artist works. A great deal has been written about the effect at this time of the science of physics upon painting through the influence of Helmholz' theory of light upon the French Impressionists—an influence, I am convinced, largely exaggerated. The physical theory of light was recondite and abstract, remote from either the interests or the practice of painters. The influence of chemistry was, on the contrary, direct, immediate, and wholly practical, for it offered, instead of the simple earth and vegetable pigments that had been on the artist's palette since painting began, a veritable rainbow of new chem-ical paints of a most attractive gaiety.

The year 1856 is a landmark in the history of the painter's medium. It is the year of the discovery of the first coal-tar color, mauve, by an English chemist named W. H. Perkin, later knighted in recognition of his work as founder of the gigantic, modern, coal-tar dye industry. Chemistry had begun the transformation of the artist's pigments even before this time. Prussian blue, discovered in 1704, was the first chemical color. The early nineteenth century brought in a series of powerful new greens, blues, and yellows: cobalt green and cobalt blue, zinc white (instead of lead white), chrome green and chrome yellow, all early in the century; emerald green in 1814; artificial ultramarine, in 1826, to replace the expensive pigment made of crushed lapis lazuli from China or Tibet; *éméraude* green in 1834; cadmium yellow about 1846 (thirty years after the discovery of cadmium in 1817).

After 1856 a series of sharp new reds and purples flared upon the artist's palette. Mauve was quickly followed by magenta and cobalt violet (1859) and cobalt yellow (about 1861). In the next few years most of the ancient mineral colors and practically all the organic colors gave way to new synthetic products. Some of these proved to be fugitive and quickly faded, others blackened in chemical combination with other pigments, but all were new, brilliant, and irresistibly tempting to the artist's eye.

It was inevitable that artists should experiment with and adopt these colors. For centuries artists had worked with mineral pigments supplemented by a few vegetable colors. Their colors were traditional, well known, and beautiful: but not so brilliant as the new chemical pigments. The harmonies created by the traditional pigments were rich in tone (the range from light to dark) but limited in hue (the range of the spectrum from red to violet). A major revolution took place in the second half of the nineteenth century in the artist's sense of harmony as a result of the study of light and the brilliance of new pigments. The French Impressionists are the most familiar example. Their harmonies reverse the traditional order: limited in range of tone, their pictures became rich and varied in hue. Painting has ever since been swaying and rocking from the shock of this revolution.

In America, where a strong discipline of style had not yet been created, it was inevitable that painters should be not only betrayed by the chemical impermanence of these new colors, but confused by the novelty. The average picture of the sixties was more highly colored than that of the forties. But the harmony was lost. The problem of style was to find a new harmony, balance, economy, among so many novel and confusing possibilities.

The second great outside force was social change. In the United States, as in Europe, the middle of the nineteenth century saw the rise of a new middle class, enriched by the Industrial Revolution. This class made itself felt very powerfully after 1850 in the patronage of the arts. It was building big houses in the new industrial towns spreading rapidly, smoking and dirty, around newly erected factories and railroad stations. It furnished its houses lavishly and it loved pictures. The style of the Crystal Palace Exhibition in England, of the Second Empire in France, and the style of Ulysses S. Grant in the United States [1] are all expressions of a similar phenomenon. This new class of patrons of art was wealthy but untraveled. It represented the simple outlook of an age before rapid travel and communication had begun to break down barriers and dissolve insularities. It was untouched by classical education. Its tastes were simple, pious, and domestic. It valued easily understood subject matter, sentiment and meticulous execution (qualities by no means bad for painting, provided imagination, style, and power are also present), and was prepared to pay lavishly for them. The artists so fortunate as to please it died rich.

In the United States the tastes of this class did not form a barrier like the formidable mass of complacency and prejudice through which the new movement of painting had to struggle in France, nor so suffocating an atmosphere of Philistinism as in England; but it created an atmosphere of sentimentality and liking for the obvious; and it encouraged trivial aims.

(A third external force was the growing influence of the camera.) It was used at first by a few gifted men who made the early days of photography exceptionally interesting. If we (whose eyes are fatigued and whose taste is jaded by the triviality into which the popular amusement of photography has drifted) find so much pleasure in the sober power of fact, the earnest severity of the photographs of David Octavus Hill, Brady, Nadar, and the other pioneer photographers, how must they have impressed the eyes of painters to whom all this was absolute novelty? The question answers itself: we know that painters of every shade of temperament were fascinated and deeply impressed.[2]

If we add to these formidable circumstances the fact that the terrible tragedy of four years of civil war, 1861-1865, cut across the lives of this generation, one may understand why the story of American luminism and naturalism in the years after 1850 is confused and difficult to tell. It does not resolve itself into one or two familiar names or movements but was complex, experimental, diverse, and much of its work was left as unfinished business for the next generation, which forgot all about it.

[1] Although this grave soldier had nothing to do with the artistic exuberance of his age, Grant's eight years in the White House, 1869-1877, represent the high tide of this phase of taste in America.

[2] A notable instance is recorded in Delacroix's *Journal* for May 21, 1853, when after dinner with two friends he tried an experiment upon them. First he made them look at some photographs of nude models, loaned him by Durrieu, "some of whom were poor physical specimens, with parts of the body overdeveloped—not very beautiful to look it." Then he showed them some engravings by Marcantonio, the engraver through whose works three centuries had adored the art of Raphael. "We felt repelled, indeed, almost disgusted, by the inaccuracy, mannerism, and lack of naturalness. . . ." The photographs had spoiled their eyes for the idealized drawing of the High Renaissance.

In 1863 the irritable but highly intelligent James Jackson Jarves, writing on the condition and prospects of art in America, considered landscape to be the one real achievement of American painting.[3] Let us take his opinion as guide and begin with the landscape painters.

There were two main roads of the exploration of Nature. One was luminism, an exploration of light; the other was naturalism, a passionate faith in Nature as the key to art.

Luminism was an intuitive search by American painters for a style of light, growing out of the tonal painting of the thirties and forties. It is an entirely different phenomenon from American Impressionism, which begins twenty or thirty years later. American Impressionism was a struggle to adapt an already perfected style, worked out by the French Impressionists, to a different landscape and a different temperament. Luminism was a struggle to find a style, to express a growing but as yet uncrystallized intuitive vision. American painters (like their colleagues all over the Western world) felt a mysterious tide of interest in light that, in the fifties and sixties, dominated the direction of artistic development. Luminism grew up within romantic realism, gradually altering it more and more into a style of light. I group under this heading landscape painters like Kensett, Whittredge, Sanford Gifford, and a number of others less well remembered.

As an example of the rather delicate bouquet of American luminism let us take John Frederick Kensett (1816-1872). Born in Connecticut, the son of an engraver, he was taught engraving by both his father and his uncle, Alfred Daggett, a bank-note engraver of New Haven; then worked for two years for the American Bank Note Company of New York. His style never lost the quality of clear, delicate line and precise spacing gained from this training. In New York city he met Durand, Casilear, and Thomas P. Rossiter and in 1840 went to Europe with these older men to study the European galleries. He worked for one winter in Paris as an engraver, then went to England to receive a small legacy and, owing to legal complications, remained two years.

"My real life commenced there," he wrote to Henry Tuckerman, the historian of this period, "in the study of the stately woods of Windsor and the famous beeches of Burnham and the lovely and fascinating landscape that surrounds them."

Returning to Paris, he sketched in France for a short time; then with Benjamin Champney, another American painter, made a long sketching tour, on foot, up the Rhine, through Switzerland, to Italy. He took a studio in Rome with Thomas Hicks and lived there two years, making long sketching tours in the summers through southern Italy. Finally, he returned to America

---

[3] Fine Arts Quarterly Review, I (1863), p. 393 ff. The landscapists he mentioned were Cole, Church, Bierstadt, Kensett and Gifford, Colman and Inness, Hunt, Vedder, La Farge, Dana, and Babcock.

by way of Venice and a journey through Germany in the company of George William Curtis, who later was known as editor of the "Easy Chair" in *Harper's Magazine*. When he returned to New York at the end of 1847, his paintings sent from Italy to the exhibits at the National Academy of Design had already made his reputation.

Kensett's European experience is worth recounting in detail because it is typical of a whole generation. The art student of the forties and fifties went abroad not to learn the style of one man, or one school (Düsseldorf was a temporary phenomenon and painters soon learned better), but to learn about art from travel, from pictures, from the life of many cities, and from the landscape itself. A generation later the increase in numbers was to produce great factories like Julian's in Paris for grinding out art students; but in Kensett's time the American art student abroad was on his own in the world of galleries and artists' studios.

Kensett's art required for each picture a fresh observation of Nature. Each picture is based upon its own place, time, and point of view, carefully and exactly observed (Fig. 99). Therefore, although making his home in New York city, he traveled widely in search of new impressions: the Adirondacks and White Mountains; the rocky New England coast; the wide marshes of Long Island; the Catskills and the Hudson River; even the upper Mississippi and the western mountains furnished his subject matter. Yet all his pictures strike a very consistent and personal note. In drawing they are small and precise, in arrangement clear and well ordered, as one might expect from one trained as an engraver. The bright new pigments did not interest him. His painter's eye for light found its tools in delicate aerial tone and transparent depths of space, modulated in simple gradations, rather than in gaiety of hue. Whatever the subject, his works are filled with a sense of solitude and space. The mood is pensive, often tinged with melancholy, but clear and tranquil. His is a quiet art, narrow in range, but sensitive and, to me, delightful.

Worthington Whittredge (1820-1910) represents another type of luminism. He was born on a pioneer farm in the forests of southern Ohio; the abundance of game and the immense numbers of wild fowl, whose cries helped "break the silence and monotony of an otherwise lonesome country," were vivid memories of his boyhood. But he was drawn by some mysterious attraction, like a bee to honey, to Cincinnati, where there were artists. How did this boy in the forest (and others like him) know that he was born to be an artist? His autobiography is amusing reading but offers no answer to this question. His pioneer father would have considered art (had the boy dared mention it) both a sin and a folly.

In Cincinnati he became an excellent landscapist, in style even then possessing an understanding of light as the great source of poetry. He then spent ten years abroad, in Brussels, Paris, Düsseldorf, and Rome, studying the galleries in The Hague, Dresden, Berlin, Antwerp, making sketching trips on foot through the Rhine, Switzerland, and Italy. But he returned doubting the desirability of long foreign study for an American. On the first day after his return to America he went to the galleries of The New-York Historical Society to see Cole's *Voyage of Life* and *Course of Empire* and Durand's *Thanatopsis*. "I may have been a little nervous, I cannot say, but when I looked at Durand's truly American landscape, so delicate and refined, such a faithful if in some parts sombre delineation of our own hills and valleys, I confess the tears came to my eyes." One cannot understand the American romantic landscapists without knowing that they felt such an identification of themselves with their own land and sky.

Whittredge painted broadly and atmospherically, using luminosity and subtle range of tone as his medium; color he used soberly and sparingly. His art is remarkable for a limpid self-effacement; a sensitiveness to the life of nature; an understanding of the character of a place, a season, an hour of the day. In the details of his landscapes, one sees that things are studied and understood, as well as felt. A tree is a strong column that really grows out of the ground and spreads delicate, flexible branches in air (as in *The Trout Pool* in The Metropolitan Museum of Art) (Fig. 100). A corner of the earth, where men have lived for a long time and the sunlight lingers, really has its own warm life (as in *Home by the Sea* at Andover). These are the virtues of the best romantic realism, and not small virtues; Whittredge created, in addition, his own quiet poetry of light, his distinctive note of silence and repose.

On the other hand, as a remarkable example of naturalism, we may take the painter F. E. Church (1826-1900). His landscapes, too, are filled with light, not only of the sun, but of an intellectual vision. Today it may seem that the physical scientists speak in riddles with the harsh, mysterious voice of the oracle. In the early nineteenth century, in the dawn of a new age of knowledge, the vast, unrolling, apocalyptic vision of nature opened by the pioneers of science seemed like one of Church's own early landscapes— the earth at dawn, seen from a mountain top from which one looks out over a sea of mist beyond which the sun is rising, tinging the dissolved wreaths of cloud, and rocks, and trees with rose. It was a heroic and inspiring vision, which Church tried heroically to translate into landscape painting.

Church came from Hartford, Connecticut, a good place for a scientific rationalist to be born. His parents sympathized with his bent toward art and arranged for him to study, first, with two local painters, then with Thomas Cole, who took the boy into his own home at Catskill as both pupil and friend. After Cole's death, Church took a studio in New York city; un-like Kensett and Whittredge, he did not go to Europe until late in life.

From the first he showed a better sense of light and tone than his teacher. He studied skies, and light, and atmosphere, painting wide views of hill and valley, or dawn or dusk seen from some lonely height in the Catskills. He was endowed with a phenomenal skill of hand and, in his earliest pictures, achieved an admirable unity of light and vigor of tone, in spite of an engraving-like sharpness of detail. His *Sunset* (1856) (Utica) and *Morning* (1856) (Albany) are remarkable examples of this phase.

In 1852 appeared the *Personal Narrative of Travels to the Equinoctial Regions of America* of the great German naturalist, Alexander von Humboldt—and in 1853 Church was in Ecuador, living in the same house in Quito where Humboldt had dwelt; copying a youthful portrait of Humboldt he found there; and drawing the great mountain chains and tropical forests of New Granada, which he had found described in that magic book. But Humboldt's earlier book, *Cosmos*, gave him his chief inspiration. This spacious work, now so little read, was a heroic effort, by a mind of liberal culture and large scientific learning, to draw a picture of the earth and of the universe as it presented itself both to scientific knowledge and to the imagination of man. Two English translations of the *Cosmos* appeared almost immediately after the German edition (Volumes 1 and 2, 1845), showing the strength of its appeal to its time. Humboldt devoted an entire chapter in his second volume to landscape painting as one of the important forms of communion with nature. It was his theory that "at periods characterized by general mental civilization, the severer forms of science and the more delicate emanations of fancy, have reciprocally striven to infuse their spirit into one another." [4]

Each portion of the earth, he observed, had its peculiar and characteristic beauty; to apprehend and to reproduce these, "to resolve beneath his touch the great enchantment of nature," is the province of the landscape painter. The grand conceptions which landscape painting owes to the creative power of the mind, were, he knew well, independent of place. But, he could not help speculating, ". . . if the gifted painters of the past, the Carraci, Gaspard Poussin, Claude Lorrain, Ruysdael, could create great works of art from the simple forms of our native European flora, what might not artists of the future do when inspired by the wider horizons, the nobler and grander forms, the luxurious fulness of life in the tropical world?"

Humboldt's speculations, written in his study in Berlin as he mused upon Andean landscapes visited forty years before, became a challenge to the young American in Catskill, New York. They fired him to test himself against that Andean landscape, and to make himself the great artist-explorer of his time. He made two trips to Ecuador, in 1853 and in 1857; in 1859 he went to Labrador to study icebergs; [5] in 1865 he visited Jamaica; and in 1868 he

[4] Alexander von Humboldt, *Cosmos* (trans. by E. C. Otte), London, 1849, II, p. 371.
[5] His traveling companion, Louis Noble, described this trip in *After Icebergs with a Painter* (1861).

went to Europe and the Near East, not to study picture galleries, but the Bavarian alps and the landscapes of Greece, Syria, and Palestine.

His traveling sketches (a profusion of which are preserved at Cooper Union), done in oil on paper, are little miracles of observation, tone and light —often anticipating by twenty years the qualities of Winslow Homer (Fig. 101). Inspired by a passionate quest for knowledge, he really learned his subjects until his mastery of the inner structure and life of each facet of nature—a tree, a rock, a dawn sky, a floating iceberg—is like the knowledge shown by the great Chinese landscape painters. His large compositions, built in the studio from these sketches, are less satisfactory. He aimed to create impressions of the grandeur and awe-inspiring power of nature in *Niagara* (1857) (Fig. 102), *Cayambe* (1858), *The Heart of the Andes* (1859), *Cotopaxi* (1862), *Aurora Borealis* (1865), *Jamaica* (1867), *The Parthenon* (1871). They are all, however, flawed by an overinsistence on detail and a smallness of touch (what might be called the defects of his virtues) and by a weakness of color: forgetting his early simplicity of tone, Church lost himself in a gaiety of color that he could not organize. Yet his *Chimborazo* (1865), which is for me his most distinguished work, is a picture very great in conception, almost very great in execution. Wonderful in its command of detail, it is like a Sung landscape in its effect of the vast panorama of nature and life existing within a greater unity. Though flawed by faults of color and overfine detail, it is a flawed work of genius.

Another painter of this period sought a different solution of the problem of landscape. George Inness (1825-1894) belongs, for the first half of his career, to the period of naturalism and luminism. The other Inness—the painter of vaporous, dreamlike landscapes—is the artist after the age of fifty. Before that there were nearly thirty years devoted to developing from romantic realism to a broad, painter-like naturalism.

Inness was largely self-taught. He was apprenticed first to a map engraver, then studied painting with Regis Gignoux, later was influenced by Corot and by William Page; but the chief sources of his development were his highly emotional temperament (he was epileptic and a religious seeker, who finally found his niche in Swedenborgianism) and his repeated visits to Europe, where he saw a variety of painting and a variety of landscape. He visited Europe in 1847, 1851, 1859, and 1871-1875. The last visit was a turning point, both in popular acceptance and in his own inner life.

Inness' first aim was to give American romantic realism a painterly breadth of touch and richness of impasto. He wished to break away from the linear quality of Durand and Cole, to dissolve outline in atmosphere and color, to achieve the largeness of touch and richness of tint which he was one of the first Americans to admire in the Barbizon painters. The first mature statement of his new style, perhaps, is the *Delaware Water Gap* of 1861 (The Metropolitan Museum of Art); the grandest and most eloquent, the *Delaware*

Valley of 1865 and the heroic-sized *Peace and Plenty* (1865) (Fig. 105) (both in the same museum), in whose mood of joy and calm one can feel the emotions of a sensitive mind at the close of the Civil War. Inness never surpassed these pictures in eloquence or harmony of style. Yet they are exceptions in his work.

In 1859 Inness went to live in Medfield, a little village about twenty miles southwest of Boston in the pleasant but somewhat monotonous rolling landscape of eastern Massachusetts. He found there a countryside of small scale and intimate feeling, more like the landscape around Barbizon than the spacious, deep, all-embracing views preferred by other American romantic landscape painters. He painted there, in the sixties, a whole series of pictures, of which *Harvest Time* (1864) (Cleveland Museum of Art) is typical—intimate in feeling, almost deliberately unpicturesque in choice of subject, exact and naturalistic in vision. Inness' aim was to base the appeal of his pictures not on any special beauty of the scene depicted, but upon esthetic harmonies —breadth of touch, a simple massing of light and shade, and conscious harmonies of color. These are important qualities of style. Yet there was also something lost. The coolness of palette, the depth and freshness of air which breathes from a picture by Kensett, for example, is never found in Inness. The heavy, rather airless quality one finds in the Barbizon painters, like Diaz or Rousseau, whom he admired, marks Inness also. Perhaps it was a result of the change in the artist's palette, brought about by the new pigments. Inness' color sense was not too sure: his palette took on a hot red and yellow, and a sweet, hard blue, which mark the sixties and seventies as a period. He was not alone in this: he shared it with a host of other painters, both famous and forgotten, American and European; but it is a serious obstacle to our enjoyment of his work and has cost him the position in the front rank of landscape painting he was once thought to have.

Within these poles of luminism and objective naturalism inspired by the advance of science, American landscape painting developed for twenty years and more. They were powerful inspirations. The period is a prolific one for landscape painting and variety is its keynote. Neither in technique nor point of view do its artists conform to a pattern.

A painter in whom both inspirations are joined was M. J. Heade (1819-1904). Born in Lumberville, Pennsylvania, he led the wandering life characteristic of these artists, living and traveling over most of the United States, Europe, and South and Central America. From 1866 to 1881 his headquarters were in New York city but in the latter year he settled in St. Augustine, Florida. At that moment the art of painting was becoming centralized in New York city and a painter outside New York was quickly forgotten. Heade disappeared totally, to be rediscovered only in the 1940's.

An intense love of nature and of light were the mainsprings of his art; but his interest in light (which led him to paint brilliantly naturalistic sunsets) was combined with the delicate, precise drawing characteristic of this whole school. In American luminism the study of light was combined with and kept within the bounds of exact linear outline, instead of dissolving outline as it did in French painting. Heade's sense of the mystery and poetry of nature is best expressed, perhaps, in a series of paintings of tropical hummingbirds. In 1860 he met an amateur naturalist, the Reverend J. C. Fletcher, who had spent several years in Brazil. They projected a book on the hummingbirds of South America and went to Brazil together in 1863-1864. The project was defeated by the technical difficulty of reproducing Heade's illustrations in the color processes available at that time. But a remarkable series of pictures (some of which may date from later journeys that took him all over South America) of the vivid little birds in their setting of bright strange flowers and tropical jungle show Heade as an original, poetic observer (Fig. 94).

Sanford R. Gifford (1823-1880) was a luminist who is close to Kensett in the delicacy of his observation of aerial tone and in the pensive mood of his art. He, too, traveled widely in search of subject matter, visiting Europe in 1855-1857 and again in 1868-1869, when he went as far as Athens and the Nile. Whittredge in his *Autobiography* gives an engaging description of how casually Gifford would start off on these expeditions, simply slinging a knapsack on his back, not even bothering to lock the door of his studio. But he was not an artist of the picturesque. His subject was the ethereal delicacy and the wonderful unity of light, shimmering in transparent skies, reflected upon waters, enveloping all things in nature within its radiance (Fig. 103).

If one wonders why the study of light did not lead the American luminists to the same rich, coloristic style that was developing in France, Gifford's method, which is typical, offers an answer. In France, the study of light led painters to direct painting, piling on a thick impasto and dissolving outline in vibrations of color and atmosphere, especially after Daubigny introduced the practice of painting out of doors, and after water color became popular. But Gifford (and indeed all the Americans of this group) continued to make studies from nature either in small pencil drawings, as delicately precise as a steel engraving, or in very small color sketches. The large oils were executed in the studio; and his poetic use of light was held within the control of clean, exact outlines and a thin, carefully applied film of paint. After 1875, when the main effort of a new generation of American painters was to learn the European use of impasto and mastery of the broad, full-loaded brush, the small, exact stroke of the older generation was held to be a sin against art. It is only today, when the stylistic wars of the seventies have faded from memory, that we can again see the painters of 1850 for what they are, interesting and sensitive artists using a style of their own age.

It is impossible to do more than list briefly the crowd of landscape painters of this generation who deserve mention:

Thomas H. Hotchkiss (ca.1834-1869) who died young of tuberculosis in Italy, but whose rare works are those of a sensitive luminist.

George H. Durrie (1820-1863) was a modest, unaffected painter of New England landscapes and farm scenes. Many of his pictures were made into lithographs by Currier & Ives; and in this form his *Winter in the Country, Home for Thanksgiving,* and *Autumn in New England—Cider Making,* have become part of our folk memories of rural America.

Louis R. Mignot (1831-1870) was a South Carolinian who studied with Andreas Schelfout in The Hague (1851-1870) and settled in New York city; his southern sympathies made him leave that city at the outbreak of the Civil War and he died in London.

Richard Clague (1816-1878) a painter of New Orleans who studied in Paris with Ernest Hébert and at the École des Beaux-Arts, and who painted the remote back country of Louisiana or the streets of New Orleans with a fine luminosity and convincing sense of reality. The fruit of his French training was a good solid use of paint.

Joseph R. Meeker (1827-1889) was a student of A. B. Durand and learned from him to draw with minute precision. He settled in St. Louis in 1859 and during the Civil War served as paymaster for the United States Navy. This took him into the deep swamps and bayous of the lower Mississippi. He fell in love with the mystery, the deadly stillness, the pale light of these somber swamps, which became the themes of his art.

Regis Gignoux (1816-1882) was born in France, came to the United States in 1844, and painted rather in the manner of Church.

James Hamilton (1819-1878) of Philadelphia was a marine painter and a sensitive luminist.

Among the naturalists, there was John F. Cropsey (1823-1900), an admirably clear and exact draughtsman but without the delicate, sure control of tone that distinguishes Kensett or Gifford.

There were many other minor painters of naturalistic landscape. For the most part they were men whose qualities are those of a school, rather than of an individual. They interest us by an occasional subject, well chosen and happily observed, rather than by individuality of perception or charm of style. By force of numbers they gradually came to play a large part in the National Academy of Design, and when their pedestrian naturalism fell behind the times the National Academy became their stronghold against change.

William Hart (1823-1894) came originally from Albany (which had a little colony of painters and sculptors in midcentury) but later moved to New York city. He and James M. Hart (1828-1901) are typical school men. They painted straightforward, naturalistic landscapes, usually enlivened with figures or animals, rather detailed in treatment, competently drawn and colored, but neither distinguished nor undistinguished. Their works were the unexciting prose of landscape, which satisfied the taste of the new well-to-do middle class for pleasing, familiar, and undemanding pictures.

David Johnson (1827-1908) in his early years produced a few lucid, hard, exact paintings that impress one by a certain power of statement; but later he fell into dull routine work.

Jarvis McEntee (1828-1891), weak and uneven; James D. Smillie (1833-1909) and George H. Smillie (1840-1921), sons of the old engraver; Albert F. Bellows (1829-1883), influenced by the midcentury English landscapists —all were competent, prosaic, popular landscapists.

James Walker (1819-1889) is remembered for his landscapes of southern life, enlivened by well-observed if thinly painted figures, rather than for his large and very dull *Battle of Chapultepec* in the west staircase of the Capitol at Washington.

A small group of Americans also were inspired by Ruskin's teachings to illustrate his theory of Truth to Nature, trying to present every detail in its exact, precise form and local color.

W. J. Stillman (1828-1901) studied briefly with F. E. Church, then in 1849 went to England, where he met Turner and commenced a lifelong friendship with Ruskin. Stillman's career as a painter was brief, lasting only from about 1850 to 1860. His real medium was words. He was an able and influential journalist, founding a magazine of the arts, *The Crayon,* in New York in 1855 (in which he reprinted Ruskin's writings extensively); and later as the Rome correspondent of the London *Times.*

William Trost Richards (1833-1905), of Philadelphia, was the most productive and consistent Ruskinian naturalist. His minutely detailed wood interiors, in which he tried to represent faithfully every leaf, every roughness of bark, every flower, have an engraving-like fineness of detail; yet his most satisfying works are the marine paintings of his later years, which have a certain largeness of effect.

In reaction, perhaps, to the prosaic literalism of these landscapes, there was a flourishing school of the picturesque. A rich new vein of the strange, the fantastic, and the wonderful in nature was discovered by this generation, in the far western United States. Until nearly the middle of the century the westward expansion had halted at the edge of the prairies; beyond was "the great American desert," a wilderness known only to the fur traders, the mountain men, and the Indians. In the forties began the migration by wagon train across the plains and mountains to Oregon, followed by the Gold Rush to California. These settlements had leaped over, without occupying, nearly two thousand miles of wilderness; until the coming of transcontinental railroads, Oregon and California were isolated. The task of linking east and west by exploring expeditions and railroads was one of the great national undertakings of the mid-century; and a succession of expeditions aroused intense popular interest as they brought to light the spectacular natural wonders of the West.

Albert Bierstadt (1830-1902), was the child of German immigrants from Düsseldorf. He went back to his parents' home city to study painting, in 1853-1856, and spent a winter in Rome with Whittredge, 1856-1857, before returning to the United States. In the spring of 1858 he joined an expedition under General Frederick W. Lander, sent by the federal government to map an overland wagon route to the Pacific. They crossed the high plains along the North Platte and advanced into what is now Wyoming; there Bierstadt left the expedition, spent the summer sketching among the Wind River and Shoshone mountains, and returned to New York.

The pictures done from these sketches, 1859-1863, brought him immediate and sensational popularity. Indeed he deserved it, for these paintings introduced both a fresh talent and a novel and dramatic subject. Bierstadt had learned in Europe a simple, tonal style that is at its best in these early works. The *Thunderstorm in the Rocky Mountains* (1859) (Fig. 104) (Boston, Museum of Fine Arts), for example, is a delightful canvas: simple, luminous, well observed, and full of the poetry of the untouched wilderness.

In the next twenty years Bierstadt enjoyed a popularity and financial reward such as no other American artist has received. A gift for publicity helped, although it did not make him better liked by his fellow artists: when his *Rocky Mountains* was first exhibited in New York, streamers were hung across Broadway to announce the fact. His popularity with the public, however, was immense. His pictures commanded higher prices than had ever previously been paid to an American painter and were extravagantly praised both here and in England; Congress purchased his *Discovery of the North River by Hendrik Hudson* (1875) and *Entrance into Monterey* (1878); he built a thirty-five room stone and marble studio home overlooking the Hudson at Irvington, that was one of the sights of America, visited by traveling celebrities; he grew wealthy, a national hero, decorated by foreign governments. Then the tide turned, as it always does. His house burned in 1882; new fashions in art appeared; in 1889 the committee of New York artists selecting American paintings for the Paris Exposition refused to hang his *Last of the Buffalo* as out of date with the new French ideals of American painting; and the old artist found himself in financial difficulties. The close of his life was a sad anticlimax.

There has recently been a revival of interest in Bierstadt's small sketches. It was his habit from his student years abroad to make numerous sketches which, jotted down rapidly, out-of-doors, have often a pleasant directness, luminosity, and simplicity of tone. In his own generation it was the huge, melodramatic pictures like *The Rocky Mountains* (1863) (The Metropolitan Museum of Art) which captivated the public by their grandiose size and profusion of skillfully observed detail. It is hard for us to see those pictures dispassionately: their romantic melodrama has received too much praise and too much blame. It is my opinion that both praise and blame have been excessive. One misses in Bierstadt's works the deep passion of Church's vision of nature. They are exaggerated in feeling and often marred (in his later years) by his inability to control the hot, bright colors he adopted. Yet there is also something original in Bierstadt which it is snobbish to deny: he is a first-rate second-rate talent.

Thomas Hill (1829-1908), a follower of Bierstadt, settled in San Francisco in 1871. After 1871 he devoted himself chiefly to painting the Yosemite Valley. His early works, painted with the minute detail of Bierstadt, have a certain grandeur of subject, expressed with a naturalism so transparent as to be almost disarmingly naïve. Later, after travels abroad, he adopted a more consciously artistic style of broad brushwork and unified tone, which, however, only reveals his poverty as an artist when attempting to do more than report faithfully the spectacular facts of Western scenery.

Another painter of the picturesque was Samuel Colman (1832-1920). He was a pupil of Durand but formed his style in travels abroad, 1860-1862, and 1871-1875, upon the broad brushstroke and pasty impasto of the Barbizon painters. In 1867 he helped found the American Water Color Society and was its first president. In his own time his fame rested upon his Italian landscapes, done in a mild imitation of Turner; in our time it is his American subjects, such as his paintings of the westward migration, *An Emigrant Train Fording Medicine Bow Creek* (1870) (formerly collection of Hall Park McCullogh) or *Ships of the Plain* (1872) (Union League Club, New York), that, though hot and disagreeable in color, strike us as true and interesting, and keep his name alive.

The appetite for the picturesque was also gratified by landscapes of Italy. The Roman colony of landscapists—George Loring Brown, Christopher Cranch, James Freeman, mentioned in the previous chapter—were at the height of their fame in the third quarter of the century; and some younger men like John R. Tilton (1828-1888) were added to it.

The generation of 1850 was as prolific in genre painting as it was in landscape. The merit of genre painting lies in two things: a poetic intensification of reality and beauty of style. The first is something more than sharp observation; it is an actual intensification or distillation by power of the imagination, which makes an interior of a house in Delft, as seen by Pieter de Hooch, or a glimpse of the orchestra in a Paris theater, as seen by Degas, more memorable than the actual experience of life itself. Contrary to modern theories of art which reduce the representation of nature to the status of senseless copying, this intensification of life is a mark of great imaginative power.

The new generation began with a most promising talent. Richard Caton Woodville (1825-1856) grew up in Baltimore, where he had the advantage of studying good Dutch genre paintings in the collection of Robert Gilmor, an influence which was stronger and healthier than his studies in Düsseldorf after 1845. Woodville drew more expressively than Mount; his color was not only fresh and clear but as solid as that of a Dutch little master. He died, unfortunately, at thirty-five, an age when an artist begins, if he can, to turn youthful brilliance into mature art. Woodville had everything except time. He left a small number of very able pictures, of which *Politics in an Oyster House* (Fig. 107) is perhaps the most completely satisfying.

Eastman Johnson (1824-1906) had, on the contrary, a long lifetime in which to mature his gifts. Born in rural Maine of good family, he had a year or two of training with a lithographer in Boston and at eighteen set himself up as a portrait draughtsman in crayon. In the 1840's, just before the camera appeared to supply portraits after only a two-minute sitting, the portrait drawing or "crayon portrait" became popular. Young Johnson was able to catch a likeness and to give an air of agreeable romantic elegance to his sitters; his success was rapid. He worked in Maine, in Washington, and in Boston, where the poet Longfellow was an influential patron. In 1849 he left America for study in Europe. He settled first in Düsseldorf, but in 1851 went to London to see the Crystal Palace Exposition, and on his return passed through The Hague. There he fell in with another American painter, L. R. Mignot, and stopped for a few weeks to copy a picture in the royal collection; under the spell of Rembrandt and Dutch genre painting he remained three and a half years. He developed in Holland a skillful use of oil, adopting a warm, atmospheric style and subdued tonalities.

The death of his mother brought him home from Europe in 1855. He went first on a visit to Lake Superior to paint Indians and the life of the frontier; worked briefly in Cincinnati and Washington; and sometime between 1858 and 1860 settled in New York city.

The afterglow of romantic humor and sentiment plays upon Johnson's work. Life is pleasant; people are interesting to watch, whether they are the well-to-do inhabitants of brownstone houses of New York, or the Negroes in the South, or farm folk of New England. An early work, *Old Kentucky Home, Life in the South* (1859) (New-York Historical Society), is charming, sentimental anecdote; though it contains too much, and floats on the surface of things, it has always been popular. *Shucking Corn* (1864) (Toledo) shows that he quickly learned to simplify, to let the inner life of his figures speak more quietly, through more natural movements, to work with light and shadow. The *Boyhood of Lincoln* (1868) (University of Michigan) and the *Family Group* (1871) (The Metropolitan Museum of Art) show his mature powers: acute observation; easy and expressive drawing; a warm affection for simple human life.

As a stylist, Johnson's sense of tone was sure and subtle; his mastery of local color was not always true. He is at his best in a black-and-white drawing, like *The Boy Lincoln* (Detroit) or his simpler oils. His warm feeling animates a series of paintings of children playing and of women and children, done at his sister's summer home in Kennebunkport, Maine, in the 1870's: *The Quiet Hour* and *The Little Convalescent* (shown in the retrospective

Fig. 90. John Quidor: *The Devil and Tom Walker* (1856). (Courtesy of Mr. and Mrs. Lawrence A. Fleischman, Detroit.)

Fig. 91. Edward Troye: *Richard Singleton.* (Courtesy of Miss Kate Oglebay, Cleveland.)

Fig. 92. Unknown: *A Street in Brooklyn.* (Courtesy of The Detroit Institute of Arts.)

Fig. 93. Jeremiah P. Hardy: *Catherine Wheeler Hardy and Her
daughter* (1842). (Courtesy of the
M. and M. Karolik Collection, Museum of Fine Arts, Boston.)

Fig. 94. Martin J. Heade: *Orchid
and Humming Bird*. (Courtesy of
The Detroit Institute of Arts.)

Fig. 99. John Frederick Kensett: *River Scene* (1870). (Courtesy of The Metropolitan Museum of Art.)

Opposite page, bottom: Fig. 101. Frederick E. Church: *Housetop in Ecuador* (1857). (Courtesy of the Cooper Union Museum.)

Fig. 100. Worthington Whittredge: *The Trout Pool.* (Courtesy of The Metropolitan Museum of Art.)

Fig. 102. Frederick E. Church: *Niagara*
(1857). (Courtesy of The Corcoran Gallery
of Art.)

Fig. 103. Sanford R. Gifford: *In the Wilderness* (1861). (Courtesy of The Toledo Museum of Art.)

Fig. 104. Albert Bierstadt: *Thunderstorm in the Rocky Mountains* (1859). (Courtesy of the Museum of Fine Arts, Boston.)

Fig. 105. George Inness: *Peace and Plenty* (1865). (Courtesy of The Metropolitan Museum of Art.)

Fig. 106. Alexander H. Wyant: *The Mohawk Valley* (1866). (Courtesy of The Metropolitan Museum of Art.)

Fig. 107. Richard Caton Woodville: *Politics in an Oyster House* (1848). (Courtesy of The Walters Art Gallery, Baltimore.)

Fig. 108. Eastman Johnson: *In the
Fields*. (Courtesy of The Detroit
Institute of Arts.)

Fig. 109. Eastman Johnson: *Two Men*
(1881). (Courtesy of The Metropolitan
Museum of Art.)

Fig. 110. William Morris Hunt: *The Flight of Night* (1878). (Courtesy of The Pennsylvania Academy of the Fine Arts, Philadelphia.)

Fig. 111. William Rimmer: *Pursuer and Pursued* (1872). (Courtesy of the Museum of Fine Arts, Boston.)

Fig. 112. Harry Fenn: *The Battery and Castle Garden.* (From *Picturesque America,* 1872.)

Fig. 113. George Fuller: *The Tomato Patch.* (Courtesy of The Detroit Institute of Arts.)

Fig. 114. James Abbott McNeill Whistler: *Thomas Carlyle* (1872). (Courtesy of The Glasgow Corporation Art Gallery, Scotland.)

PLATE XI. Edward Hicks: *The Peaceable Kingdom*. (Courtesy of Mr. and Mrs. Holger Cahill, New York; color plate courtesy of the Book-of-the-Month Club.)

exhibition at the Brooklyn Museum in 1940) represent the simple domestic feelings of American taste at this time at their uncomplicated best.

In another series of paintings, also done in the 1870's, during summers spent on Nantucket Island, he brought his luminism to its culminating point. In a picture of cranberry pickers, called *In the Fields* (Fig. 108) (The Detroit Institute of Arts), it is not the human warmth that strikes us; the feeling is purely objective—people, place, hour, seen together in the unity of a flood of light. There is no amusing anecdote, only a fine unity of tone and mood. In such a picture Johnson steps out of his period and moves, for a moment, across the threshold of the next period of art, into objective realism.

After the seventies, Johnson went no further with genre; his later years were devoted to portrait painting. These late works have received little attention, for modern taste is not much interested in portraits; yet here also Johnson showed an ability to deepen and mature a familiar, uncomplicated method of observation. His large double portrait called *Two Men* (Fig. 109) (1881) (The Metropolitan Museum of Art) is a distinguished example, so deep and rich in tone, so penetrating in its observation that it lifted the American portrait tradition to a new level of esthetic and psychological power.

In New York city especially but to some extent in other centers flourished, in the third quarter of the century, a large school of genre, anecdote, and historical painters. Easy, skillful, charming, sentimental, they were overrated in their own lifetime and forgotten today when "story telling" is wholly out of fashion.

George W. Flagg (1816-1897) was a nephew of Washington Allston. His precocious talent so impressed Luman Reed that he sent the boy to study abroad. Flagg was a graceful, attractive painter; his *Nun*, which Luman Reed once owned (New-York Historical Society) is a good piece of romantic figure painting, luminous in color and appealing in sentiment; but Flagg lacked stamina as an artist and failed to leave his mark.

John W. Ehninger (1827-1889) was another clever genre painter and illustrator of New York. He made trips abroad and contributed European sketches to the illustrated weeklies; but was at his best with American rural subjects.

James H. Cafferty (1819-1869) was a less skillful painter who exhibited in New York city from 1843 until his death.

Thomas P. Rossiter (1818-1871) made long stays in Paris in the forties and in Rome in the fifties, but New York was his headquarters. His genial, charming little picture called *A Studio Reception of American Artists in Paris* (1841) (Albany) has kept his name alive and green.

Alexander Lawrie, Jr. (1828-1917), a Philadelphian, was a portrait draughtsman and genre painter of pleasant flavor. He worked in Philadelphia 1858-1864, served in a Pennsylvania regiment in the Civil War, and after the war was active in New York 1866-1876, ending his life in a soldiers' home in Indiana.

Frank B. Mayer (1827-1899) of Baltimore was another genre painter of talent. His *Leisure and Labor* (1858) (Corcoran Gallery of Art) is like Mount in its humorous observation, but painted in good solid French technique.

J. G. Brown (1831-1913) in his early works showed himself one of the most gifted figure painters of the period. Unfortunately, when he began to paint the ragged newsboys of New York his pictures were so popular that he was never allowed to paint anything else, and he ruined his talent by repetition.

T. W. Wood (1823-1903) from Montpelier, Vermont, settled in New York city in 1866. His style was hard and factual; his pictures are sometimes very well observed.

Lily Martin Spencer (1822-1902) was born in Marietta, Ohio, and trained in Cincinnati. In the latter city she married a Mr. Spencer and settled later in New York, where she exhibited from 1848 to 1858. Her main field was domestic life and the nursery treated with rather too much sentiment.

Other genre and figure painters of New York were William Morgan (1826-1900); James H. Beard (1814-1893); George H. Boughton (1833-1905); W. J. Hennessy (1839-1917); the writer and painter Cristopher P. Cranch (1813-1892); George H. Story (1835-1923), who was curator of paintings in the Metropolitan Museum of Art from 1889 to 1906.

William H. Beard (1824-1900) must, I suppose, be considered a genre painter, although he painted little moral and sentimental anecdotes acted by animals, in the role of human beings.

Most of these genre painters were drawn to New York city by the greater opportunities offered by the metropolis; but by no means all were there.

Richard M. Staigg (1817-1881) of Newport was an excellent miniature painter, who also produced genre and landscape paintings.

Thomas Le Clear (1818-1882) worked in London, Ontario; central New York state; and Buffalo, as well as in New York. His *Buffalo Newsboy* (1853) (Albright Art Gallery, Buffalo), fresh in color, unspoiled by sentimentalism, is one of the most attractive works of this type in its period.

Charles Caleb Ward (1830-1896), active for some years in New York, spent most of his life painting in his native St. John, New Brunswick.

George C. Lambdin (1830-1896) was a clever, sentimental genre and portrait painter in Philadelphia.

The colony of American painters in Rome included a number of genre painters, who exploited the picturesque charm of Italian peasant life for transatlantic eyes.

George Henry Yewell (1830-1923), a genre painter, lived in Paris 1856-1861 and Rome 1867-1878.

Edward H. May (1824-1887), a painter, illustrator, and writer, lived first in Rome, but is chiefly identified with Paris.

Another group painted the Indian and the frontier. St. Louis, at the meeting point of the rivers that drained the inner continent, was the western metropolis of trade and river travel and headquarters of the American Fur Company. Charles Deas (pronounced Days) (1818-1867) settled there. He was an adventurous young Philadelphian who tried first for the army and, after failing to get into West Point, turned to painting genre and sporting pictures. The sight of Catlin's Indian Gallery (1837-1838) inspired him to go west. In 1840 he set off for Fort Crawford (Prairie du Chien, Wisconsin) where his brother was an officer in the Fifth Infantry. His army connections made it possible for him to travel with army convoys and he ranged up and down the upper Mississippi, the Missouri, and the Platte before settling in St. Louis. About 1848, however, he became mentally deranged with melancholia, and died insane in 1867.

Unlike Bingham, Deas was a painter of excitement and adventure. His subjects were prairie fires, Indian fights, desperate encounters, and similar incidents, whose melodramatic character appeals to us less than Bingham's brooding observation. But melodrama was the mood of the times. In Charles Wimar (1828-1862) it was joined to a Düsseldorf insistence on detail, which he partly threw off after his return from Germany to St. Louis in 1856. Henry Lewis (1819-1904), another of the St. Louis school, made a tremendous panorama of the entire Mississippi, from St. Paul to New Orleans, in two sections each twelve feet high and totalling about thirty-six hundred feet long, with which he made a triumphant tour of Europe. Thus the dramatic spirit came out, in one form or another.

Two other painters of the frontier deserve mention. One was Charles Christian Nahl (1818-1897), born in Cassel, Germany, who worked in New York 1849-1851, then in San Francisco. He threw a curious air of Düsseldorf theatrics over his scenes of the frontier days in California. The other was A. F. Tait (1819-1905), born in England, who became the chief illustrator of sporting and wild west scenes for Currier and Ives.

George Templeton Strong, the New York diarist, was a thoroughly conventional person. When he tells us, therefore, after visiting the National Academy of Design on April 17, 1846,[6] that he disliked Mount's *Eel Spearing at Setauket* (which had been painted for the diarist's father) and praises instead the works of Daniel Huntington and Emanuel Leutze, he is recording not only a preference but a widespread change of taste. The grave mood of meditation upon the past, the slow savoring of the flavor of things gone which romanticism had introduced, had slowly declined into sentimentalism and historical anecdote. The third quarter of the century was the great age of the sentimental historical subject, such as Leutze produced, and the sweet, vague, fancy works for which Huntington was famous.

In certain old families and clubs that dislike change, one still sees the dark, stiffly posed, rather dry portraits of Daniel Huntington (1816-1906). He was a very prominent and well-liked artist at one time in New York,

---

[6] *The Diary of George Templeton Strong*, Ed. by Allan Nevins and Milton Halsey Thomas, New York, The Macmillan Company, 1952, Vol. I, p. 276.

president of the National Academy of Design, and successful in the very literal kind of portrait we associate with the impact of the daguerreotype upon American taste. One would assume, from these portraits, that he was a man wholly without the qualities of imagination or invention. Yet his large, vague pictures based on Bunyan's *Pilgrim's Progress*—such as *Mercy's Dream* (in several versions, the earliest, 1842, in the Corcoran Gallery of Art) and *Christiana and Her Family Passing Through the Valley of the Shadow of Death* (Pennsylvania Academy of the Fine Arts)—and numerous other literary subjects were immensely admired. To our eyes, they seem typical sugar-and-water confections of nineteenth-century sentiment. One of Huntington's famous historical subjects was *The Republican Court* (1861), a costume illustration representing a presidential reception in Washington's time, which found its way via engraving into the national mythology.

Henry Peters Gray (1819-1877) learned in two visits to Italy to admire Titian, but he had none of Page's power to transform his admiration into a personal style. He was, instead, a weak American version of Delaroche or Kaulbach, combining neoclassic figures of *Greek Lovers* (1846) (The Metropolitan Museum of Art) or *Cleopatra Dissolving the Pearl* (1868) with Titianesque color. As Virgil Barker put it, rather devastatingly, Gray's "sweet autumnal spell," praised by Tuckerman, showed that Gray and his admirers confused reminiscence with imagination.

The most prolific painter in this historical vein was Emanuel Leutze (1816-1868), who belongs as much to Düsseldorf as he does to America. Born in Württemberg, he was brought as a child by his family to the United States. In 1841 he returned to Germany to study at Düsseldorf. He remained nearly twenty years, marrying there and making Germany his home.

Düsseldorf has been mentioned frequently in this record: it is time to say something about the qualities of this school, which was once so famous. There was one good painter in Düsseldorf, Schadow, but he had little influence upon the other painters of the Düsseldorf school; their style was formed by the Düsseldorf theater, devoted to German romantic-historical plays, which were, both in subject matter and the style of acting, melodramatic in the extreme. The painters of Düsseldorf specialized in historical and literary illustrations, drawn in laborious detail, colored rather than painted, and conceived in the melodramatic and sentimental style of the romantic theater.

Leutze painted in Düsseldorf a long series of American historical subjects, of which *Washington Crossing the Delaware* is the most famous. The best and the worst thing one can say of these pictures is that they were perfectly adapted to the popular taste of their day. A generation of American school children learned to visualize history in terms of some of his historical compositions. If history were a matter of heroic poses, this might have done no harm.

It was inevitable that such a man would have been commissioned by

Congress to decorate the Capitol. His *Westward the Course of Empire Takes Its Way* in the southwest staircase of the Capitol was commissioned in 1860, the year after his return to America. It was executed with painstaking preparation characteristic of his school—a trip to the Rocky Mountains to study the landscape, a trip to Germany to consult Kaulbach on the best methods of wall painting, resulting in a composition containing a multitude of figures in exalted poses and a multitude of details. I have no intention of denigrating thorough study and information. But Leutze produced a design that is small and mean, rather than monumental; the emotion, such as it is, consists in making the figures pose in excited but unconvincing attitudes.

The same sentimentalism and exaggeration, in greater or less degree, with usually less skill, characterize the other painters of historical anecdote: Alonzo Chappel (1828-1887); Enoch Wood Perry (1831-1915); Junius Brutus Stearns (1810-1885); Peter Frederick Rothermel (1817-1895); Christian Schussele (1824-1879); John T. Peele (1822-1897); W. D. Washington (1834-1870); Robert S. Duncanson (1817?-1872); and the poet-painter, T. Buchanan Read (1822-1872). These men had their reward in their generation and their work has not survived it, except as period pieces.

The popularity of genre was reinforced by the increasing popularity of the illustrated book, the illustrated magazine, the steel engraving, and the lithograph. A new type of magazine appeared in which the illustration was the keynote. *Punch* (1841) and the *Illustrated London News* initiated a new era which was quickly marked by the appearance of American examples. The *Illustrated American News* (1851) was the first, followed by other short-lived journals; then two papers which became national institutions, *Frank Leslie's Illustrated Newspaper* in 1855 and *Harper's Weekly* in 1857. A host of genre painters and illustrators supplied their illustrations.

A new type of monthly magazine also began to appear, which aimed not only at leadership in literary but in political, religious, cultural, and social opinion. *Harper's Magazine* (1850); *Putnam's* (1853); *The Atlantic Monthly* (1857); *Appleton's Journal* (1869); *The Century* (1870); *St. Nicholas* (1873); and *Scribner's* (1887) are the best known. *Appleton's* introduced new standards of illustration, which were to lead to important developments.

The illustrated weeklies created a new type of journalist-illustrator, who traveled about the country making quick drawings of landscapes, city scenes, or news events. Both the illustrator and the wood engraver were, however, pressed for time and developed a method of collaboration which, though efficient, gave rather disappointing results. A typical artist of this type was A. R. Waud (1828-1891), a quick, skillful observer and a principal war artist for *Harper's Weekly* during the Civil War. A large number of his drawings are preserved in the Pierpont Morgan Library, New York city, and in the Prints and Photographs Division of the Library of Congress. But Waud took time to draw only the principal figures and details, roughly indicating how subsidiary parts were to be done, and adding pencil memoranda to guide the "redrawers" who, like the rewrite men on the modern newspaper, put the thing into shape. Such a method did not produce sharp and original observation.

But in magazine and book illustration the standard improved rapidly. It was helped, as in previous decades, by the immigration of skilled engravers from abroad. W. J. Linton (1812-1897), who came to the United States in 1867, was an extremely well-trained engraver. His excellent *History of Wood Engraving in America* (1882) is a valuable source book and critique of the period.[7] His influence was certainly effective in raising the standards of black-and-white engraving on wood. The skill of the engravers, the address of the artists, the growth of publishers, the rise of a vigorous national literature creating an eager reading public—all these factors combined to stimulate a beautiful and interesting period of illustration. Engraving became more delicate and clear in line, richer in tone; illustrated volumes grew more elaborate; gift books, *éditions de luxe*, richly illustrated volumes of travel became more common.

F. O. C. Darley (1822-1888) was the most productive and best known illustrator of his generation. The sheer bulk of his production is impressive. He worked in all media: making outline drawings to be reproduced in lithograph; book and magazine illustrations to be cut in wood; wash drawings to be reproduced in large steel engravings; pencil drawings for bank note engravings on steel. His subjects covered a wide sweep of American life and although his facility sometimes betrayed him into conventionality, he had the qualities of easy composition, variety, and sense of character that are the mark of the true illustrator. His drawings for the novels of Cooper and Dickens, done in the sixties and engraved on steel, are, in the opinion of Weitenkampf, the height of his mature powers.

Another figure that became increasingly common was the artist-author who both wrote and illustrated his own books. Benson J. Lossing (1813-1891), author of the *Field Book of the Revolution* (1851-1852) and *The Hudson from the Wilderness to the Sea* (1866), was a very popular writer who drew the landscapes for nearly all his books. T. Addison Richards (1820-1900) was a landscape painter who wrote and illustrated *The Romance of American Landscape* and other works; David H. Strother, under the name of "Porte Crayon," wrote and illustrated *Virginia Illustrated*. With the increasing popularity of such illustrated books the standard rose.

Another influential illustrator was Harry Fenn (1845-1911), who came to this country at the age of nineteen, like Linton, as an engraver; but he soon became a prolific and active illustrator. He was one of the founders of

[7] Linton, W. J., *The History of Wood-Engraving in America*, Boston, Estes and Lauriat, 1882.

the American Watercolor Society in 1866 and also one of the chief figures in Appleton's great project of illustrating the beauties of the American landscape that resulted in the two massive volumes of *Picturesque America* (1872-1874), edited by William Cullen Bryant (Fig. 112). Its artists included Harry Fenn, Thomas Moran, J. Douglas Woodward, Homer Martin, R. Swain Gifford, A. R. Waud, Casilear, Bellows, and Kensett. W. J. Linton says in his *History of Wood Engraving* that its illustrations were the best engraved in America. Certainly the harmony between the rich, warm blacks of the wood engravings, the silvery steel engravings, and the type face make it an example of nineteenth-century graphic style at its best. Its publication just before the eclipse of the old landscape school also gives it somewhat the flavor of a monument to a period that was about to end.

There were still many portrait painters at work in the third quarter of the century. Nearly every town of any size supported one or more. It would be impossible to mention all their names; and, in most cases, they do not deserve it, for they represent a headlong decline of style.

Eastman Johnson's later career has already been mentioned; he was a portrait painter of penetrating power and admirable style.

Thomas Hicks (1823-1890), a nephew of the Quaker painter, Edward Hicks, was an able portrait painter. His full-length of *Hamilton Fish* (1852) (City of New York), governor of New York and later Secretary of State under Grant, is a dignified and impressively sober work.

W. J. Wilgus (1819-1853) of Buffalo, and Thomas Le Clear, already mentioned as a genre painter, produced interesting portraits.

Jared B. Flagg (1820-1899), a nephew of Washington Allston, had talent and taste but, like his brother, lacked the stamina to leave his mark in his profession.

But the general trend of portrait painting was toward an almost unmitigated dullness of color, pose, and lighting. The costume of the time was dark; the camera's influence encouraged rigid, formal poses; and the mass of portraiture sank to a dull monotony. This was as true of the fashionable Daniel Huntington and Henry Peters Gray in New York as it was of the painters of the provinces.

Francis B. Carpenter (1830-1900) retains a certain interest because he spent several weeks in the White House and wrote a memoir of Lincoln, seen at close range, which is more spirited than the group portrait *The Reading of the Emancipation Proclamation* (1864-1865) (The Capitol, Washington) he went there to paint.

A similar topical interest preserves the name of John A. Elder (1833-1895) of Fredericksburg, Virginia, who studied with Huntington in New York and with Leutze in Düsseldorf before returning to Virginia. During the Civil War he served in the Confederate army and painted portraits of southern generals and war scenes. Yet apart from the interest of their subjects both Carpenter and Elder are very boring painters.

The craft of portrait painting thus sacrificed almost all the merits of oil painting for the hard outline and uniform textures of the photograph, and it retained little more interest of tone or color. It is not surprising that the collector of today prefers portraits painted in the artisan tradition, for this tradition, too, lived on into the third quarter of the century. Its bright, cheerful colors, bold sense of pattern, and untroubled spirit are a pleasant contrast to the dim and melancholy spirit of the prevailing style in portraiture; and some of the artisan painters show charming qualities.

Isaac Augustus Wetherby (1819-1904) is an example of one who joined the western migration. Such training as he had was gained from an itinerant portraitist in Norway, Maine. He developed a graceful and pleasing portrait style—a good example is *Mary Eliza Jenkins* (1843) (Wayside Museum, Harvard, Massachusetts), a naïvely charming portrait of a child—which he practiced first in small communities of New Hampshire and Massachusetts, then in Kentucky, Illinois, and Iowa. When the daguerreotype presented serious competition he became a photographer and in the 1860's abandoned painting entirely.

George W. Morrison (1820-1893) migrated from Baltimore in 1840 to New Albany on the Ohio River, then the largest town in Indiana, became the resident artist of that community, and died there after a long and honored life. He is described as living on a twenty-five acre homesite outside the town and having as his favorite studio, in fair weather, a large oak tree on his grounds. His portraits are both naïve and accomplished. It is evident that he was a man of native taste and skill—a true type of the untrained professional.

A humorous view of western manners appears in a well-known picture of a *Flax Scutching Bee* by Linton Park (1826-1906) (Garbisch Collection, National Gallery of Art). Although the picture was found in Pennsylvania, it represents with uncouth gusto and affection the log cabins and the customs of frontier life.

But formal portraiture, the art of the untrained professional, and that of the naïf or amateur portrait painter could not survive the rising popularity of photography. The camera is one of the inventions of nineteenth-century technology that brought the handcraft period to an end. The craft it destroyed was the craft of portrait painting.

Daguerre's invention of 1837 spread with the speed of Mercury across the Atlantic. Even before Morse returned with the process from Paris in 1839, other Americans were experimenting with it from the printed descriptions. This beautiful little machine was to have an interesting life of its own. But the new invention brought immediate death to the craft of the miniature painter; and within a generation the steady production of portraits in oil, which for two hundred and fifty years had been the staple and mainstay of the profession of painting in America, came abruptly to an end. After the seventies portraits, and often very good ones, continued to be painted, of course. But they were a luxury product only required when, for reasons of prestige, a photograph was not good enough.

Perhaps, from a purely esthetic point of view, the loss will not seem very great, since portraiture on the best level was not wholly extinguished. It is also true that the portrait, as a staple of painting, was neither so exacting nor so inspiring as the religious subjects which were the staple of Italian painting through so many centuries. Yet from the social point of view the change was calamitous. With the disappearance of the demand for portraits painting ceased to be one of the skills for which society had a need, and a pursuit by which a man could earn a steady if modest living in any city of the land. As the portrait painter vanished, there appeared the impoverished bohemian artist, insecure, embittered, earning his living by teaching instead of by the practice of his art, and dependent for the sale of his work upon the whims of fashion. Since fashions in art last only eight to ten years, while the maturing of great art requires a lifetime, the effect upon the artist and upon the art of painting was hideously destructive.

The climate of those decades was not, one would say, favorable to idealism. Yet there were artists who drew their inspiration from the world of thoughts and dreams.

The enthusiasm which greeted an exhibition by George Fuller (1822-1884) at Boston in 1876 shows that there was a public hungry for the note of mystery and sentiment. Fuller as a young man had been an itinerant portrait painter in rural Massachusetts and New York; in 1847 he had a studio in New York, which was his headquarters, but he continued to travel in search of portrait commissions. In 1859 his father and his brother died. Fuller returned to work the family farm at Deerfield in the Connecticut Valley. There, painting only to please himself in the intervals of farm work, he forgot portraits, forgot the careful, undistinguished manner he had shown hitherto, and turned inward into a world of dreams. The pictures he put on exhibit in Boston (because of the failure of his tobacco crop in 1875) were single figures, standing or sitting, painted in a dusky, shadowy manner: wrapped in a twilight veil of reverie, they remind one of Allston's late, dreaming figures. Yet Fuller had none of Allston's skill as a painter. His crepuscular technique was amateurish, and his pictures no longer seem very important—except as they remind us of the strength of this grave, brooding note in American painting. He is more interesting as a phenomenon than as an artist; he survives best in his landscapes (Fig. 113).

The same is true of another dreamer, Robert Loftin Newman (1827-1912), who went abroad to study at Düsseldorf, but instead came in contact first with Couture, then with Millet (1854). He fell in love at once with the

French use of pigment, as have many other American art students since. The art that resulted was, in aim if not in style, very like some twentieth-century movements: for Newman wanted to express subjective feeling through pigment and color, with only vague suggestions of figures. The result is sometimes rather interesting; but unfortunately Newman remained an amateur in his control of oil. The rich use of paint is only a single element in the strong, disciplined French style. Newman, snatching at that alone, is an example of a reaction which was to grow more and more common in the next generation: a superficial impression of some European painter's style developed into a quick, clever improvisation whose weakness time reveals only too clearly.

The most substantial of the men who tried to find a way out of naturalism through study in France was William Morris Hunt (1824-1879). He came of a well-to-do family in Brattleboro, Vermont. His brother, Richard Morris Hunt, became a very successful eclectic architect, famous for transplanting French chateaux to Fifth Avenue, New York, and Newport. Hunt, the painter, first (1846) went to study at Düsseldorf, which was then at the height of its fame; but after nine months left for Paris where he studied under Couture (1847), then with Millet. From these men who were the *avant garde* of painting in the forties Hunt learned a new ideal of poetic figure painting. The means employed by Millet in his transformation of French figure painting were a heavily loaded, broad brush, a warm, shadowy palette, and a vaporous modeling of the figure in rich, glowing color and tone. Hunt, on his return to the United States in 1855, set himself to work out a vision of American art in those terms. He settled first at Newport, then at Boston; there he exerted a profound influence upon New England taste.

Intelligent, enthusiastic, ardent when his interest was aroused, yet impatient of discipline, Hunt had qualities that made him an excellent teacher; but his painting never seemed to grow beyond the tentative promise of a good student. The subjects he found in New England life were either portraits or small, intimate, landscape and figure studies—a quick glimpse of boys bathing in a stream or a game of catch in a field. He treated these in *The Bathers* (Worcester) or *The Ball Players* (The Detroit Institute of Arts), with a simplicity of drawing and a large massing of tone that were a good tonic to American painting. But somehow Hunt was never able to carve out a solid block of life to master in his imagination and to make his own, nor to carry his fine studies to a solid, big conclusion. Compared with his master, Millet, he remained a good disciple, a follower of skill and taste, but nothing more.

Perhaps this was why, when his great opportunity came, he produced his greatest work but broke down under the strain: his first personal achievement as a painter was also his last. In 1875 he was commissioned to paint two murals in the new State Capitol of New York at Albany. He chose an allegoric subject that had interested him all his life, *The Flight of Night* (Fig.

110), from a Persian poem about Anahita, the goddess of Night. it was for him a symbol of the darkness of ignorance fleeing before the light of civilization. Because of bad planning on the part of the builders, the murals had to be executed under great pressure and difficulty in the autumn of 1878; the physical strain, however, was less severe than the fear of failure which tortured him as he worked. The murals were well received but Hunt collapsed, was never able to resume work, and in the next summer died under circumstances that have always been explained as suicide. Within a short space of time the murals themselves were ruined by damp. All that is left is a series of studies, of which *The Flight of Night* in the Pennsylvania Academy of the Fine Arts is the most complete, and a fine version of the central group in bronze. It is a composition of light and movement, large in scale, grave and impressive in its imaginative poetry, the one effective ideal composition by an American painter of Hunt's generation. Beside it the ideal compositions of David Huntington, Leutze, or T. Buchanan Read seem trivial period pieces.

As a center of enthusiasm for French painting in America, Hunt was perhaps of even greater significance than as an artist. He was a picturesque personality and a magnetic talker; his marriage in 1855 to the daughter of Thomas Handasyd Perkins, the great Boston merchant and philanthropist, placed him in a position of influence in Boston. It was Hunt who, as an ardent interpreter of French art, created an enthusiasm for the Barbizon painters, for Millet, Corot, Rousseau, Daubigny, in America even before they were fully accepted in France; it was Hunt who turned the eyes of American students to Paris rather than to Italy and thus began the long period of French influence upon American painters. In the circle closest to him, John LaFarge, William and Henry James were among the young people touched by Hunt's teaching.

A still more complicated case of imaginative power, skill, and amateurism was William Rimmer (1816-1879), physician, anatomist, sculptor, painter; and self-taught in all things. (Not the least curious aspect of this complex man was his belief that he was the son of the lost French Dauphin.) His natural talents were extremely great; but misfortune and tragedy followed his steps, and little is now left of his work.

No one shows more clearly than Rimmer the misfortunes of the imaginative artist who is unsupported by the skilled activity of a craft. The only artistic skill in which he was really trained was that of lithographer. He taught himself anatomy and medicine out of his intense interest in the human figure and, after ten years of practicing medicine in the villages of the back country around Boston, was accepted by the medical profession and issued a formal license by the Suffolk Medical Society. As a sculptor he was not so fortunate. He exhausted himself struggling with granite or clay without knowing the simplest procedures that a month in a workshop would have taught him— how, for example, to use a metal armature to support a figure modeled in clay.

His imagination was haunted by the nude human figure and by wild images of struggle, violence, and exhaustion—"Equestrian battles, wild charges, the rush of banners, armies sweeping up dizzy parapets, the fall of angels, the thunder of demon wings." [8] He was so careless of his pigment that many of his pictures have disintegrated or been destroyed. Yet a picture like *Pursuer and Pursued* (Fig. 111) (1872) (Museum of Fine Arts, Boston) is one of the most passionately convincing and disturbing visions of nightmare painted in this century.

Realistic anatomy, violent movement, imagination, and eccentricity mark all his surviving works in oil or pencil. Rimmer had talent but was never able to channel it into any conventional category nor to fit himself as a craftsman into society. He had few orders for sculpture during a lifetime of effort; he showed his pictures so rarely that, during his life, this side of his activity remained unknown. The only use society could find for his talents was as teacher of artistic anatomy. He began lecturing on this subject in Boston in 1861, with great success: John LaFarge, William Morris Hunt, Daniel Chester French, Frederick Vinton, Frank Benson all testify to his imaginative ability as a teacher. For four years, 1866-1870, he was director of the art school of Cooper Union in New York city. But he was too independent and far-seeing for its trustees and was allowed to return to Boston. There his life continued, harassed, miserably poor, and intensely creative in its own strange fashion, to the end. There is no other ideal artist of the age whose creations are more personal, more difficult to see, or more uneven and impossible to generalize upon: at their best, his hallucinatory visions stare at us from the past like the eyes of the basilisk.

Only one large project of monumental decoration need be mentioned other than Hunt's paintings in the State Capitol at Albany. This was the enlargement of the Capitol in Washington from the designs of Thomas U. Walter, approved by Congress in 1851. This was not a matter of awarding haphazard political plums, like the commission given Powell or the paintings purchased of Leutze and Bierstadt by Congress. The enrichment of the Capitol after 1851 was carried out as a regular part of the building program, in fresco and sculpture, on the initiative of the superintendent of construction, Captain Montgomery C. Meigs of the United States Army Engineers. Constantino Brumidi, a well-trained Italian fresco painter who had fled from Rome after the collapse of the Republic in 1849, offered his services to Meigs in 1854, who saw the appropriateness of the medium and promptly put him to work. Brumidi and the Italian sculptors employed on the Capitol were artists of the last phase of neoclassic taste, as was the Capitol building itself. It was Meigs's misfortune that the artists available to him were rather uninspired. It

[8] Lincoln Kirstein, *William Rimmer*, Whitney Museum of American Art and Museum of Fine Arts, Boston, Exhibition Catalogue, 1946-1947.

is to his great credit that the extensions of the Capitol wings created the only public building of its period in the United States designed and executed, with all its enrichment of form and color and humanistic imagery, as a single consistent whole.

In 1855 W. J. Stillman, the painter-journalist, and John Durand, son of A. B. Durand, founded in New York the monthly magazine in America devoted wholly to the arts, *The Crayon*. Stillman resigned in 1856 because of ill health and the magazine lasted only until 1861. The United States was dependent upon the English *Art Journal* and upon notes and articles in the American literary monthlies for news and criticism of the arts until, in 1875, the firm of D. Appleton and Sons began to issue an American edition of the *Art Journal*.

The Civil War had an effect familiar to us from the wars we have ourselves experienced, of throwing people back upon themselves and their own inner resources, forcing a reappraisal of life and its goals. The war also brought in the North a great growth of industry and manufacture, producing greater concentrations of population and wealth than had ever existed before in our cities. A new period of urban life began and brought, among other things, new civic institutions, new ideals and amenities, as well as grave new problems. The public gallery of art, toward which American artists and art-loving citizens had been making a variety of efforts for three quarters of a century, at last emerged as an institution apart from the Academy, the Athenaeum, or the Art School.

The Metropolitan Museum of Art was organized in New York at a meeting in 1869 called by the art committee of the Union League and presided over by William Cullen Bryant. It was incorporated in 1870; the first group of European paintings was purchased in March, 1871, and exhibited in temporary quarters at 680 Fifth Avenue; and the first Italian Gothic unit of the building in Central Park was under way by 1875, although not opened until the spring of 1880.

Boston took a similar step. A board of trustees was organized in 1870 to build a public museum of fine arts, to replace the exhibition activities of the Athenaeum, and the semiprivate Boston Art Club. Its first building, in the Back Bay, in the polychrome Italian Gothic style advocated by Ruskin, was opened with a collection of Egyptian and Cypriote antiquities, Graeco-Roman pottery, and paintings old and modern, in the winter of 1875-1876. Its paintings included no less than seven pictures by Millet! It also had on loan the private collection of Quincy Adams Shaw, which contained a few important paintings by old masters.

In Washington, the Corcoran Gallery of Art was founded by the private benefaction of the banker W. W. Corcoran, who retired from business in

1854 to devote himself to philanthropy. The first building of the Corcoran Gallery, designed in French Renaissance style by James Renwick, was finished in 1860; but it was occupied by the Quartermasters Department during the Civil War and was not restored for use as an art gallery until 1869.

The Pennsylvania Academy of the Fine Arts in Philadelphia was rehoused in a monumental structure in Ruskinian Gothic style built 1871-1876 and opened as part of the Centennial Celebrations of 1876.

Another museum and school of art grew out of the Centennial year in Philadelphia. The state of Pennsylvania and the city of Philadelphia erected for the Exposition of 1876 an art building, Memorial Hall in Fairmount Park, intended as a permanent building to serve afterwards as a Museum of Art and Industry. The inspiration was the South Kensington Museum in London which had grown out of the profits from the Crystal Palace Exhibition of 1851. Memorial Hall became, in 1877, the museum portion of a new organization, The Pennsylvania Museum and School of Industrial Art, chartered as a state "museum of art in all its branches and technical applications, and with a special view to the development of the art industries of the State, and to provide instruction in drawing, painting, modelling, designing, etc." [9]

The School of Industrial Art portion of this project (now located at Broad and Pine Streets) was opened in May, 1877, the earliest and for long the most important of its kind in the country.

"Industrial Art" was a new phrase in the language of the arts. It was a symbol of a profound uneasiness felt by thoughtful minds at the state of the decorative arts in the nineteenth century. Factory production was rapidly replacing the handcraft skills of the past. The Centennial Exhibition itself had been a triumph for machines, machine-produced and machine-ornamented articles of every description. But the question was: were these mechanically stamped, pressed, turned, molded, and otherwise fabricated pieces of furniture, gas chandeliers, silverware, and tiled fireplaces that filled the exposition halls a good or bad development? What was the place of handcraft, if a machine could cast or carve mechanically a hundred ornaments while the hand was making one? And what use was the Beautiful in an utilitarian age, anyway?

The specter of technology destroying the whole familiar fabric of the arts and handcrafts, rushing mankind forward into an unfamiliar, perhaps uncongenial world, was becoming uncomfortably visible. Where would it lead us? The same kind of debate that rages now, setting nuclear physics and grim necessity over against the humanities and the arts, had already begun to make itself heard—only, at that time, railways and clipper ships instead of atom bombs symbolized the advance of technics. A writer in the first volume of *Putnam's Monthly Magazine of American Literature, Science, and Art*

[9] *Handbook* of the Pennsylvania Museum, 1907.

(1853) used the column headed "Fine Arts" to attack the uselessness of The
National Academy of Design.

Let our artists remember that this is the age of clippers, and turn their talents
into a channel that will pay. It is really one of the saddest spectacles to see so
much good honest effort, so much genius, perseverance and intelligence thrown
away, as the Annual exhibition of our National Academy exposes to public gaze.
Let the Academy institute a wood-engraving department, a glass-staining department, an architectural department, and a calico-designing department, and Art
will flourish here as it did in Rome in the days of Leo X, and as it now does in
France in the days of Napoleon III; for art, literature, and science are nought
unless they minister to the public needs and conform with the popular taste.[10]

To a certain extent we can recognize in the writer in *Putnam's* the voice
of the unimaginative utilitarian; but not wholly—surely there was a challenge
in these new techniques and needs that must be met.

The Philadelphians who organized the Centennial Exposition of 1876 to
commemorate a hundred years of American independence seem to have been
less interested in looking back than in looking forward. The United States
was plunging headlong into the industrial age, changing from an agricultural
to an urban and industrial country. The handcraftsman was rapidly disap-
pearing, apparently forever. Society seemed in the grip of a vast, unpredictable change. Much as people admired the machines in Machinery Hall in the
Exposition, it was impossible not to feel concern about the guidance of this
force. With a touching faith in education, they founded a School of Industrial Art.

Another new element in American artistic life also began to make itself
felt. In 1846 a young man named Michel Knoedler came from France to
establish an American branch of Goupil et Cie., a well-known Paris firm of
engravers and print sellers. He set up a shop dealing in engravings and artist's
materials in Duane Street, New York city. Eleven years later, in 1857, the
name became M. Knoedler and Company. Thus was established a name, still
in existence, that was to become that of one of the famous firms of art dealers
of the twentieth century. At this period, however, it specialized in engravings, particularly reproductive engravings. Other dealers in engravings—Keppel, A. Kohn, Samuel P. Avery, Williams and Company—set themselves up
in New York; Goupil and Vibért, of Paris, set up the International Art
Union in 1849 to capitalize on the popularity of the American Art Union.
John G. Baker, who had lived a long time in Düsseldorf before becoming
Prussian consul in New York, in the same year founded the Düsseldorf Gallery, which for a time was very successful. In 1853 a firm called the Belgian

[10] *Putnam's Monthly Magazine*, I (1853), p. 702.

Gallery was established on Broadway. New York became, little by little, an entrepôt of the European art market: the importation of engravings, then of pictures by the fashionable contemporary painters began.

In 1850, however, a young New Englander, Seth M. Vose, organized the Westminster Art Gallery in Providence, Rhode Island. The main income of the gallery was derived at this time from the sale of art supplies. But Vose, who soon opened a branch gallery in Boston, was a friend of the painters William Morris Hunt and Thomas Robinson, who interested him in *avant garde* French painting—Millet, Corot, Daubigny, Courbet, Delacroix, Rousseau, Dupré, and Troyon. The enthusiasm of Hunt and Vose for the French painters of 1830 made Boston, rather than New York, the center of the taste for the most significant new movements and personalities in French painting.

From 1850 to 1875 painting was, as I said at the beginning of this chapter, in every sense a popular art. Luminism, naturalism, sentimentalism were movements that grew out of or were in touch with main currents in American culture. The artist's achievement, in all but a few cases, clarified and crystallized the intuitive interests of his fellows. In turn, the country came not only to accept but to be proud of its artists and to lavish fame and approval on them. Painters like Church and Bierstadt were exceptionally successful but nearly all painters sold well. When Kensett died in 1872 a sale of the paintings in his studio (600 by Kensett and fifty by other artists) realized $137,715. A generation later Samuel Isham speaks of this sale in his *American Painting* (1905) with wonder and regret: wonder that American painters' work was ever sought after so eagerly; regret that it was not true of his day. Nor is it true of ours.

American painting in this generation was, if I may use the image, like a native apple tree on a New York hillside at the height of its growth, bearing sweet, small, old-fashioned apples. The machine age was cutting at its roots and the next generation of painters had no liking at all for its fruit. They had studied abroad and seen, growing in the rich soil of Europe, a variety of rich, spectacular, and exotic fruits. Returning to this country, they looked with contempt on the poor thing they found here; hacked off its top branches; and endeavored to graft upon it shoots gathered from all the European schools. Some of the grafts flourished; others, less expertly done, died; the tree itself, cut both in root and branch, received a severe shock.

CHAPTER 10

THE ATTRACTION OF EUROPE: AMERICAN
IMPRESSIONISM AND OTHER MOVEMENTS

THE QUARTER CENTURY AFTER THE PHILADELPHIA CENTENNIAL OF 1876 WAS so complex that, for purposes of clarity, I have divided it into three chapters. That this should be necessary or desirable may seem, I suppose, a confirmation of the high opinion the period held of itself, an opinion with which we show a marked tendency to disagree in detail. The generation of the seventies believed, quite sincerely, that it had established American painting for the first time on a basis of good style and that it was extraordinarily rich in talents. We would agree that it made enormous changes in style but are not sure that the results are so brilliant and original as was thought at the time. And while we admire some of its artists greatly, all too often they are artists whom their contemporaries overlooked. Lazarus, not Dives, is now the hero.

The cosmopolitan strain in American painting became dominant in the seventies. Painting in Europe was extraordinarily rich, profuse, and brilliant. It was natural that it should make its influence felt; moreover, Americans played a part in it. That is the subject of the present chapter. Yet there were also great figures who doggedly hewed their art out of native experience: they were so important for our culture that they require a chapter to themselves. Finally, the strain of idealism produced some remarkably interesting figures who demand study in a third chapter.

Before we come to the tidal wave of expatriates in the seventies, there is a solitary, striking figure, earlier and greater than any, who typifies, because in some measure he created, the mood and temper of the last quarter of the century. Many of its most distinctive traits—its cosmopolitan inspirations, its exoticism, its cult of bohemianism and of art for art's sake—were established for English-speaking peoples by James A. McNeill Whistler (1834-1903).

American romantic painters had shown many admirable qualities: delicacy of feeling, warmth, modesty, subtlety. But toward the end, when a pedestrian naturalism became common and sat in the seats of authority, it grew drab and wearisome. The human soul (which painting, in its own fashion, expresses and satisfies) has within it something like one of those cabinets which the last century called a whatnot, whose shelves and compartments were created for all kinds of precious, delightful, and useless things—peacock feathers and shells from the South Seas; marble souvenirs from Italy; corals, and teacups from China. Late romantic painting lacked the exotic; it did not satisfy the need for lovely and arbitrary invention, for the capricious and the exquisite. Who will deny that the mind can suffer from imaginative deficiencies, just as the body can grow weak because of dietary ones? There came a great craving for the exotically beautiful. Whistler, an artist of decorative genius, was born to feel and satisfy that hunger.

Whistler was born in America, the son of an army officer who had resigned from the service to practice civil engineering and, at the time of his son's birth, was employed on the locks and canals of Massachusetts' newfound water power at Lowell. Thus the artist had as background from the beginning the most foot-loose of all the professions, the army and engineering. He grew up abroad, chiefly in St. Petersburg, where his father's profession took him from 1842 to 1849. He had some instruction in drawing at the Academy of Fine Arts in St. Petersburg and at the United States Military Academy at West Point. At the age of twenty-one he returned to Europe, never again to visit his native land. His first two years abroad (1855-1857) were spent as a student in the studio of Gleyre in Paris. His life thereafter was passed in Paris, London, and Venice. During his London years he became such a celebrity and made such an impression upon English society that the English have treated him as one of their own painters. Actually he was a type of the new cosmopolitan age, American in his quick receptivity to new ideas, and in his cleverness at improvising upon them; but belonging to no country except the new cosmopolitan world of art that he helped to create. His career in England (like that of other Americans, such as Henry James or T. S. Eliot, or like the careers of Aldous Huxley and W. H. Auden in America) shows that English and American culture, though separate and to some extent antipathetic, are still in some curious way related; so that certain temperaments, without losing the basic traits of their native air, prefer to live in the atmosphere of the other country.

When Whistler arrived in Paris in 1855, the great flowering of the genius of French painting was just in preparation. The chief figures, at that moment, were still the aged Ingres and Delacroix, great neoclassicist and great romantic. But Whistler's admiration was given to a controversial young painter named Courbet, whose objective realism then seemed to hold great possibilities for the future. He thus ranged himself at once on the side of the objective realists of his own generation, who believed art was something to be made of direct observations of nature, not woven from dreams, or memories, or ideal images.[1] Whistler's early oils use the thick, pasty impasto and deep, warm tones derived from his study of Courbet—like *The Last of Old Westminster* (Fig. 115) (1862) in Boston, *The Coast of Brittany* (1861) in Hartford, or *The Music Room* (1860) (Freer Gallery, Washington). The first *Thames* series of his etchings (1860) also shows him as an objective realist, acute in observation, forceful in statement.

But a characteristic of the restless minds of the new age of which Whistler was typical was the variety of their inspirations. Whistler moved in the sixties from Paris to London, where he gradually refined his own exquisite and entirely personal style from a great diversity of elements. From the Parisian painters he had learned a creamy softness and fluency in handling oil paint. From Velasquez he learned the value of the long line, the cool, empty background, the refined black and silver-gray tonality. He was also one of the first Western artists to feel the wind from the Orient that was later to blow so strongly, and to learn from the Japanese—but not to imitate them, as some later artists did. From Japanese prints he absorbed the quality of two-dimensional pattern that was then so surprising to Western eyes: the exact, unexpected placing of detail within the rectangle of the picture; the clean harmonies of cool, flat tones. Transforming all these into something Whistler's own was an exquisite sense of decoration and a very personal interest in light. His contemporaries, the Impressionists of Paris, were lovers of the sun. Whistler was unique in his passion for twilight and night.

As his search for the pure poetry of sight went forward he found himself more and more isolated not only from the pre-Raphaelites and from the Royal Academicians in London, but from the French Impressionists. His ultimate style, in its refined and muted harmonies, reminds one, curiously enough, of the tonal search of the American luminists whose work he certainly did not know and would perhaps have despised had he known it. His art was, in some respects, the ultimate perfection of the delicate tonal poetry for which American luminism had been seeking.

With his exquisite sense of decoration he refashioned the familiar portrait into a highly personal new form. Spanish painting appears to have aroused his interest in the full-length portrait. (He was not alone in this; Manet, in the eighteen-sixties, felt the same fascination for the sober, reserved, powerful, Spanish idiom.) One of his earliest full-length portraits and a masterpiece of

[1] I use the term *objective realism* for this period in contrast to *romantic realism* for the preceding period. The problem of creation, for the generation of 1870, was to become what Cézanne called Monet, "He is an eye," and added reflectively, "but what an eye!" The romantic realists, however transparent and self-effacing in style, were moved by sentiment. Theirs was an age of great dreams—of freedom, liberty, philosophical idealism, religious faith, which cast a veil of feeling over all. In the realism of the new age the bouquet of tenderness is gone. The objective realists devoted themselves with passion and excitement to exploring the world by the organ of sight alone. They were anti-idealistic; facts were exciting enough.

his first period was *The Woman in White* (1862) (Washington, National Gallery of Art), which was one of the sensations of the Salon des Refusés in 1863, where the new movements in French painting first revealed their strength. It is a brilliant demonstration of a new idiom in painting—light in key, the colors forming broad areas (whose mere breadth was shocking then), without reflections from one to the other, but with long, clean edges, presenting bold contrasts of warm against cool, light against dark, hue against hue.

He went on refining this style, adding, as he did so, new elements of the exquisite, the elusive, and the exotic—the cool, silver-gray tone values of Velasquez and the bright, flat harmonies of the Japanese. Yet what emerges is Whistler's own entirely personal style. To emphasize the quality of formal, decorative harmony he was pursuing, Whistler began to call his works "symphonies" or "arrangements." The *Woman in White* is gravely impressive but static. Whistler went on to add a slight but expressive gesture of the whole figure that creates character and mood with surprising force. What melancholy and self-pity, for example, are implicit in the slouching pose of *Thomas Carlyle* (Fig. 114) (1872) (Glasgow) in contrast to the control and silent force of character of the *Portrait of His Mother* (1871) (Louvre), a picture with a quality of inevitability which its popular fame cannot extinguish. (It reminds one of Degas' terse remark, that a good painting is a platitude.) The same power to strike a clear, single note of character and mood marks other famous full-lengths: the Tanagra-like grace and repose of *Mrs. Leyland* (*Symphony in flesh color and pink*) (1872) (New York, Frick Collection); the nervous glow of the violinist *Sarasate* emerging from the shadows (1885) (Pittsburgh, Carnegie Institute); the intelligence and urbane elegance of the Parisian art critic, *Théodore Duret* (1883) (The Metropolitan Museum of Art).

Landscape he likewise transformed into a formal harmony of tone which he called the "Nocturne," and made a lyric upon the beauty of twilight or darkness. One of the most famous is a study of fireworks at night in an amusement park, called Cremorne Gardens, which he liked to observe from across the Thames. It has the instantaneous quality, the quick accent of a moment of life caught in passing and fixed forever, which Whistler was not alone in seeking—his friends in Paris, Degas and the Impressionists were also masters of it; and so were Winslow Homer and Thomas Eakins—but which is one of the special charms of painting in this last quarter of the nineteenth century. The poetry of glowing spots of light drifting downward in the night sky has never been better observed nor more elusively stated. Whistler called it *Nocturne in Black and Gold—The Falling Rocket* (ca. 1874) (Plate XII) (The Detroit Institute of Arts).

He was very active and productive in the eighteen-seventies. In 1877 he exhibited a group of nine pictures at the Grosvenor Gallery, which included the *Carlyle*, two other important portraits, and four of his most famous and successful Nocturnes. A number of pictures in the group represent the climax of his powers. Unfortunately the exhibition was attacked with insane violence by Ruskin, who wrote of the *Nocturne in Black and Gold—The Falling Rocket:*

For Mr. Whistler's sake, no less than for the protection of the purchaser, Sir Coutts Lindsay [founder of the Gallery] ought not to have admitted works into the gallery in which the ill-educated conceit of the artist so nearly approached the aspect of wilful imposture. I have seen, and heard, much of Cockney impudence before now; but never expected to hear a coxcomb ask two hundred guineas for flinging a pot of paint in the public's face.

Whistler sued for libel. The trial proved a field day for a conservative public's feelings of scorn and hilarity toward an artist of challenging novelty. Although Whistler won the suit (he was awarded a farthing damages), the public sided with Ruskin, and Whistler was forced into bankruptcy (May, 1879). His house and his china, his prints and some of his pictures were sold to pay his debts and in November, 1879, he went off to Venice where he was to retrieve his fortune by a second famous series of etchings, in which he found a new, graphic form for his vision of shimmering, muted light. The decorative impressionism of the Venetian series is a little out of fashion at the moment in the market place, yet it is certainly an original contribution to nineteenth-century graphic art. Whistler's delicacy of touch and subtlety of perception show his art in all its authority in these etchings and in his pastels of Venice.

The Ruskin suit was a tragedy, for it brought out in Whistler the dark side of his nature—his pugnacity, his hypersensitiveness, his readiness to take offense and to indulge in violent, cruel attacks upon those who aroused his displeasure. He became a man at war with the public. Using all his wit and brilliance as a propagandist, he set himself to prove that the artist was a superior being of finer, qualities than ordinary mortals, whose gross minds and dull perceptions were incapable of understanding either the artist or his work. In so doing, he transferred to England and America the war of words between the Bohemian and the Bourgeois then raging in Paris: a war in which insults and scorn took the place of interest and curiosity as the normal relation between the artist and his fellow men.

Whistler's arguments have been repeated by smaller figures until they have almost become the basic philosophy of our world: for still today the artist looks on the layman as a fellow of no perception; and the most generally held layman's belief about art is that if one can understand an artist he can't be a very good one. It is a far cry from this to the concept of the inevitability and universality of great art.

Whistler had no pupils and left no school in the usual sense. His refined, tonal style found fewer followers than the gay palette of French Impressionism. Yet his influence was wide and pervasive through the so-called "esthetic movement" which held that the artistic sensibility was the only thing worth taking seriously in life and nothing but the purely esthetic aspect of things was worthy of being painted. These views gained steadily in importance as the century came to a close. Unfortunately, those whom he influenced lacked the intelligence and style that give strength to Whistler's most fragile creations and what emerged was a weak parody—a pale estheticism combined with a pose of arrogant superiority toward all who were not artistic.

Yet Whistler's achievements—his decorative impressionism, his elegance of style, his sharp grasp of character, his sense of the poetry of night—were real and notable. Born just a century after West and Copley, he took his place like them in the larger world of Western art, with an even wider and more international audience than theirs. He was a great, or if not a great, a consummate artist, who achieved perfection within his chosen range. He scorned the elaborate subjects and sentiments of the English Pre-Raphaelites. He had none of the gusto and love of life, the ardent and unself-conscious love of France which kept the French Impressionists close to earth and makes their art so succulent. He eliminated everything from his art except the expression of a detached, observant eye and fastidious, decorative taste. His aloofness from all that is commonplace and local, his concentration upon style, his preciousness were characteristics of a major artist.

We come now to the esthetic revolution of the seventies. Unlike Whistler's highly personal innovations and discoveries, the series of stylistic changes that now set in was an affair of Movements and Schools.

The Philadelphia Centennial Exposition of 1876 may serve as a convenient symbol of the end of romanticism. The Exposition marked one hundred years of American independence; but its chief effect on the popular imagination was not to solidify an established tradition of the past but to dissolve it. Instead of calling attention to a century of past achievement, it pointed to the new age of machinery rising before us; and it gave Americans their first large-scale glimpse of the arts, the merchandise, and the luxuries of the Old World. Even before the glittering pageant in Philadelphia, artists had felt the swing of the pendulum; a whole generation of art students had gone streaming across the Atlantic to study in Paris, or Holland, or Munich. Within a short time after the Centennial, it was not only the artists, the intellectuals, the dreamers, but all the rich and the fashionable, all the restless people eager to catch they knew not what bubble from life, who succumbed to the fever for going to Europe that Henry James called "the great American disease . . . the appetite for colour and form, for the picturesque and romantic at any price" *(Four Meetings)*. The romantic movement had endured a long time. A reaction was inevitable and, when it came, it was impatient and drastic. The young artists of the seventies could see no good in their elders; they were convinced, without a doubt, that merit in American painting began with them.

In the hundred years before the Centennial the United States had produced a national culture. Its value was not perhaps so much in the greatness of individual talents as in its spontaneous and instinctive character. It was an art without dogma: Art drew its imaginative strength from the general life of mankind. This intuitive harmony between art and life, this oneness of the artist with the society around him was broken in the next period. American society and its artists, and the artists among themselves, fell apart into disconnected and quarreling groups. The last quarter of the century was a period of growth and new knowledge, but also a time of disintegration and destruction. What disintegrated was precisely the unconscious whole. What was lost was the unity of a culture that had been, within its limitations, large and creative. No subsequent generation has been able to rebuild that unity. New artists, new ideas have appeared, but the strong figures stand as isolated individuals or groups, like solitary trees and scattered groves where a forest has been cut down. The forest was gone.

Yet a change was necessary and inevitable. The romantic painters had not achieved the highest levels of style (and style, if not everything in art, is a necessity), while in Europe, especially in France, painting was rising to one of its great points. It was natural that American painters should respond to the technical changes abroad and should strive to learn what they could from their gifted contemporaries. More than this—with the development of railroads and steamships, it had become suddenly easy to go abroad. The romantic artist had dreamed of Italy and the Rhine, but he saw these usually as a mature man who had found himself artistically and knew what he needed. The new generation went abroad as young and plastic students who knew little or nothing of themselves before arriving in Munich or Paris, and who returned home with the idea that the aim of painting was to paint like the teacher they discovered there. The habit of study abroad was no new thing, but a change in its scale and atmosphere became striking in the seventies and continued through the eighties and nineties with ever increasing momentum. Rome, Paris, Venice, Florence, London, Munich, Antwerp, The Hague were simultaneously or successively the training grounds of American painters. In the eighties Paris became the predominant center; but, a little earlier, Munich enjoyed a great vogue.

The failure of the liberal revolution of 1848 in Germany (which Benedetto Croce called the great tragedy of nineteenth-century European history) had brought to America a number of liberal-minded, cultivated Germans who exerted a strong influence upon the middle and far western cities—Cincinnati, St. Louis, Indianapolis, San Francisco—in which they found refuge. Some of them helped direct American-born painters to Munich, which, under the stimulus of its art-loving and prodigal kings, had early in the nineteenth century achieved a new stature in German culture. The first American artist to go there was David Neal, in 1861; then Toby Rosenthal, son of German parents in San Francisco, in 1865; then, in 1870, Frank Duveneck (1848-1919), a child of German immigrants, born in Covington, a suburb of Cincinnati, on the Kentucky side of the Ohio River.

Duveneck was a precociously talented youth. He left school to work as a decorator of Catholic churches and, practicing the skills of the painter-decorator—modeling, carving, painting, gilding—he developed the remarkable facility of hand on which his later reputation was founded. When he went to Munich in 1870 the teaching at the Royal Academy was still in the hands of painters of romantic-historical subject pictures; but a new star was rising in the figure of Wilhelm Leibl, one of the greatest of German objective real-ists, who had learned a broad, brilliant, painterly style from his study of the pictures by Frans Hals and Rubens in the Pinakothek. From Leibl and from the Pinakothek, Duveneck learned what came to be called in America the "Munich style"—a manner of painting that was realistic and atmospheric in vision, dark and warm in tonality, and dashing in its bravura displays of brush-stroke, of broad lights brushed fluently into a dark, red-brown, shadowy ground.

Duveneck returned to America in 1873 and painted portraits in Cincin-nati, then decorated a church in Chicago. At first his work was little seen. In 1875, however, he showed five of his canvases at the Boston Art Club. His novel palette, his unheard-of breadth and facility of brushstroke, created a sensation. William Morris Hunt was enthusiastic; orders for portraits show-ered upon him; he was urged to leave Cincinnati and settle in Boston. He became overnight a national figure. But Duveneck did not settle in Boston. He returned to Munich where, in 1878, he set up his own art school; the following year he moved his school to Florence. He taught and painted in Florence and Venice until his wife's death in 1888. Then he returned to Cincinnati, where he spent the last twenty-five years of his life quietly as the head of the Art Academy.

Samuel Isham had already observed in 1905 that "The canvases that so electrified Boston seem today typical of a school rather than of a distinctly original artist." [2] Duveneck had got hold of a way of painting which looked at once modern and like the time-darkened old masters. As his life unrolled, it became evident that although he had a new palette and brushstroke and a new way of painting the posed model, he had nothing very much to say beyond his technique. *The Turkish Page* (Fig. 116) (1876) (The Pennsyl-vania Academy of the Fine Arts) is perhaps a canvas that gives the best measure of his powers: large in scale, brilliant in its slapdash bravura, painted with real delight in the medium and in the artist's own fluency, it still is a

[2] *The History of American Painting*, New York, The Macmillan Company, 1927, p. 381.

flashy and arresting canvas. But back at home in Cincinnati, without picturesque Bavarian models to paint, and without the surrounding activity of European artists to sustain him, his later life became a long anticlimax to his early fame.

It is worth while to spend this much time upon Duveneck, who is a pleasing and graceful, but on the whole not an important painter, because his story is one that has been repeated over and over again and neither the artists nor the public have yet learned its lesson. The past three quarters of a century have been filled with a succession of such overnight successes. They sweep across the country, each a national sensation (we love sensations and novelties), setting up a shock wave that swings a whole school of imitators, minnow-like, into its train as it rolls across the continent; then fade, like Duveneck. In retrospect, they prove to have been only clever pupils, who caught something of the manner of an able new painter abroad and, on their return home, are mistaken for masters. A new way of painting is always interesting both to painters and lovers of painting: but we have still to learn that readiness to imitate an attractive new style is not the same thing as originality.

A great many other Americans studied in Munich, either at the Academy or with Duveneck—Walter Shirlaw, W. M. Chase, Frederick P. Vinton, Julian Story, Julius Rolshoven, Thomas Dewing, Carl Marr, J. Frank Currier, John W. Alexander, Joseph R. De Camp, Otto Bacher, John Twachtman. But as the brilliant blonde palette of Paris made itself felt, the Munich school faded away. The stronger figures, like W. M. Chase, developed away from its mahogany-dark palette; or, if they did not, they failed to develop at all. The most consistent of the Munich school men (aside from those who, like Rosenthal and Carl Marr, settled in Munich and became really repatriated German artists) were Walter Shirlaw (1838-1909), a fluent decorative painter and designer of stained glass, and J. Frank Currier (1843-1909), a limited but pleasant talent. The Munich manner did not transplant well to America. It did not seem to lend itself either to the American face and style of dress or to the landscape here; and the Bavarian peasant subjects these men brought home have long since lost their novelty and disappeared from the walls of our museums and homes.

Some painters went to Antwerp or to Holland as a midway point between Munich and Paris. Francis D. Millet (1846-1912) is the best known of those who studied at Antwerp; he later settled in England, where his easy, illustrative talent had a good reception. His greatest contribution to American painting was, however, his organization of the mural painting at the Chicago Exposition of 1893, which we shall return to in Chapter 12. In Holland, George Hitchcock (1850-1913) made a reputation painting the tulip fields. Gari Melchers (1860-1932), a skillful figure painter and portraitist, lived for years in Egmond, painting the daily life of the Dutch fishing villages. Melchers was the son of a German wood carver who had emigrated to Detroit. At eighteen, the boy returned to Europe to spend most of his life in Holland, or Paris, or as court painter to the Grand Duke of Saxe-Weimar, returning to America for occasional portrait commissions. In 1914, after thirty-five years' residence abroad, he came back to live in Fredericksburg, Virginia.

Italy was no longer a major center but its timeless beauty still attracted painters. A number of Americans of a variety of temperaments made their home there: Francesca Alexander (1837-1917), a friend of Ruskin and at one time the center of a little Anglo-American cult; W. S. Haseltine (1835-1900), a fine draughtsman and exact naturalist, with something of Sargent's ruthless objectivity; George De Forest Brush (1855-1941), a pupil of Gérôme, who, after making a reputation with life-size Salon paintings of the American Indian, settled in Florence and painted Neo-Renaissance *tondi* of his wife and children which were once to be seen in every American museum; Eugene Benson (1839-1908), Charles Caryl Coleman (1840-1928), and William Graham (1832-1911), painters of the Italian landscape and architecture; and Elihu Vedder, whose career belongs in another chapter.

England, too, had its colony of American painters, not only Whistler and Sargent, but F. D. Millet; Edwin Austin Abbey, the illustrator; George H. Boughton; John McClure Hamilton (1853-1936), an interesting portrait painter who liked to work on the scale of and with the intimacy of genre; and the sharp-tongued Joseph Pennell, the lithographer and disciple of Whistler (1860-1926). But England was an agreeable place of residence rather than a school of style, in this respect at least resembling Venice or Rome.

By far the larger contingent of American students went to Paris. From the seventies on, every French painter who gained prominence, every French movement which appeared collected a number of American pupils and followers: Gérôme, Fortuny, Bouguereau, Millet, Bonnat, Constant, Bastien-Lepage, Carolus-Duran, each had their followers. To keep this chapter from being a mere list of names, I list here some of these students (or in some cases, followers) of the principal teachers in Paris.

1. Pupils of Gérôme and Fortuny: Frederick A. Bridgman (1847-1927); Edwin Lord Weeks (1849-1903); Henry H. Moore (1844-1926); G. H. Mosler (1875-1906); Julius L. Stewart (1855-1920); Alexander Harrison (1853-1930); Thomas Eakins (1844-1916); Abbott Thayer (1849-1921); J. Alden Weir (1852-1919); Wyatt Eaton (1849-1896); Charles Sprague Pearce (1851-1914); George De Forest Brush (1855-1941); Kenyon Cox (1856-1919); Douglas Volk (1856-1935); Robert F. Blum (1857-1903); Percy Ives (1864-1928); William M. Paxton (1809-1941).

2. Of Bonnat: William Sartain (1843-1924); Walter Gay (1856-1937); Henry O. Walker (1843-1929); Edwin H. Blashfield (1848-1936); Francis Petrus Paulus (1862-1933); Frederick P. Vinton (1846-1911).

3. Of Léon Bailly: Louis C. Tiffany (1848-1933).

4. Of Carolus-Duran: John Singer Sargent (1856-1925); Carroll Beckwith (1852-1917); Will H. Low (1853-1932); Birge Harrison (1854-1929); Theodore Robinson (1852-1896); Kenyon Cox; Irving R. Wiles (1861-1948).

5. Of Millet: Wyatt Eaton, pupil; Horatio Walker, follower.

6. Of Bastien-Lepage: W. T. Dannat (1853-1929); Alexander Harrison (1853-1930); Robert W. Vonnoh (1858-1933); Charles Sprague Pearce; Ridgway Knight; Walter McEwen (1860-1943).

7. Of the atelier Julian (Boulanger and Lefebvre, critics): Robert Vonnoh; John H. Twachtman (1853-1902); Childe Hassam (1859-1935); Thomas W. Dewing (1885-1938); Willard Metcalf (1856-1925); Frank W. Benson (1862-1951); Edmund C. Tarbell (1862-1938); Cecilia Beaux (1853-1942); Frank V. DuMond (1865-1951); F. J. Waugh (1861-1940); Percy Ives; Samuel Isham (1855-1914); Gari Melchers (1860-1932); Elizabeth Nourse (1860-1938); Robert Reid (1862-1929); E. E. Simmons (1852-1931).

8. Of Cabanel: Thomas Hovenden (1840-1895); Birge Harrison.

9. Of Benjamin Constant: Mary Cassatt (1845-1926); Theodore Robinson; Henry O. Tanner (1859-1937).

10. Of Claude Monet: Theodore Robinson.

11. Of Bouguereau: Percy Ives; Thomas P. Anshutz (1851-1912); Elizabeth Gardner (1851-1922); Hugh H. Breckenridge (1870-1937).

12. Of E. Frère: James W. Champney (1843-1903).

13. Of Meissonier: D. Ridgway Knight (1839-1924).

14. Of J. P. Laurens: Henry O. Tanner; Frederic P. Vinton.

It is hard for us to realize that had anyone been asked, in the mid-seventies, to name the greatest living French painter, the answer would unhesitatingly have been Gérôme. His taut, disciplined naturalism was an inspiration to Thomas Eakins; but what most of his pupils admired and imitated were his fantastically ingenious and convincing illustrations of history (like *The Gray Eminence* in Boston) or photographically exact scenes of Arab splendor and cruelty, which were once the pride of every fashionable collector. The first American movement to appear in the Paris Salon was an imitation of Gérôme's *orientalism* by painters like Frederick A. Bridgman, Edwin Lord Weeks, or Louis Tiffany.

Then came the life-sized Salon figure picture, generally with a story, which Thomas Hovendon, a pupil of Cabanel, introduced into America. The life-sized scene of peasant life, for which Bastien-Lepage was famous, was practiced with great effect by W. R. Dannat, a pupil of Bastien-Lepage and of Munkácsy in Munich. His *Quartet*, a Spanish peasant scene shown in the Salon of 1884 (now in the Metropolitan) was once a celebrated and is certainly a very clever picture.

In the mid-eighties *pleinairism* was a word of power. It was a movement,

led by Bastien-Lepage, which tried to combine the study of atmosphere and
outdoor light with the exact draughtsmanship of the French academic tradition. In this movement Alexander Harrison, a pupil first of Gérôme, then of
Bastien-Lepage, was one of the important figures. He created a national sensation in the middle eighties, not unlike that of Duveneck's first success, with a
series of paintings of the sea in delicate studies of tonal values—*Le Crépuscule*
(St. Louis), which received a prize of $2,500 at an exhibition in New York
city in 1885; *The Wave* (The Pennsylvania Academy of the Fine Arts); a
second *Le Crépuscule* (Corcoran Gallery of Art, Washington).

All these schools, or tendencies, were based on the French tradition of
rigorous drawing descended from the neoclassicists. Only one French painter,
Carolus-Duran, based his teaching on painting—working directly with the
full-loaded brush, blocking out the figure in tone and color directly on the
canvas. Carolus-Duran took few pupils; but through three of his students,
John Singer Sargent, Carroll Beckwith, and Will H. Low, his direct attack
and suave, sure stroke were to exert a great influence upon American painting.

Finally, in 1888, Theodore Robinson discovered Monet at Giverny and
was the first American to follow the Impressionists, abandoning the French
tradition of drawing entirely for the new technique of light, air, and broken
color, which later so many Americans were to adopt.

But most American students attended the Académie Julian. The influx
of foreign students into Paris in the last decades of the century (Russian,
Polish, English, Irish, American) was so great that it overwhelmed the existing official schools and produced its own institutions, of which this was chief.
The Académie Julian was started as a business proposition by Julian, who
provided a hall and models, hired painters to criticize the students' work, and
collected the fees. The room was always filled to capacity, so that the students
had scarcely elbow room. Cecilia Beaux records in her autobiography that
she had to give up the idea of painting in the class; it was so crowded there
was no room to do anything but draw. Instruction in Julian's thus reverted
to what it had been in the eighteenth century—drawing the human figure;
painting was something the student did on his own at home. As one reads the
monotonous refrain "studied in Paris with Boulanger and Lefebvre" in the
histories of American painters of that time, this is what was meant: Boulanger
and Lefebvre were the chief critics at Julian's.

It was not a bad training, so far as it went. Saturated with hard work
and sense of *métier*, it gave foreign students a glimpse of the French painter's
pride of profession; an opportunity to absorb the atmosphere of a great,
active center of their art; and a sense of belonging to a tradition bigger and
older than themselves. The products of this training became, by the nineties,
the predominant group in America, as the Munich group was in the seventies.
One has only to leaf through the pages of Sheldon's *Recent Ideals of Ameri-*

can Art (1888), which celebrated the triumph of this European-trained generation, to see how firmly people believed that a new and greater era of painting had now begun in America. There is hardly one of the painters described by Sheldon who was not soundly trained; probably none who did not paint at least one good picture. Yet out of the 185 painters Sheldon describes perhaps five are of any interest to us today. (And of these five, three are so treated as to show that their work was quite misunderstood at that time.)

One asks one's self: Why has time taken such a terrible toll of this generation? What was lacking? Not talent, not training, nor opportunity.

What was lacking was a personal point of view. This is what makes an artist, marks him as an individual, sets him apart from the school. The French styles of painting which these American students studied were the outgrowth of long, organic developments. The artists who embodied them were men of personal force, rooted unself-consciously in the life of their native culture. The young students from America, with their native receptivity and openness to new impressions, were able to learn what was teachable in the style of the French painter who was admired at the moment; and did so, often, with surprising rapidity and cleverness. The problem was, upon their return to America, to find something of their own to say with this style.

The landscape painters found that the light was different in America; the trees grew differently; the white farmhouses of New England did not fall into compositions as did the old stone villages of Normandy or Brittany. The figure painters found no picturesque peasants in smocks and wooden shoes driving oxcarts. Instead, they found American farmers in ordinary clothes using the new McCormick reaper and John Deere steel plow. And to many, after their gay student years abroad, America itself seemed dull and insipid. Some of them solved the problem by staying abroad; not because, like Copley and West, they could find a career there that was denied them in the United States, but because they liked the atmosphere of Munich or Paris better than Chicago or New York.

The expatriate element in American art assumed a prominence, in the quarter century after 1875, that it had never had before. Those who returned tended to congregate in New York, where they felt themselves nearest to Europe. New York was the great port of entry for European products, natural and artistic, and the city nearest to Europe in atmosphere. Carroll Beckwith, son of a wholesale grocer in Chicago, spent five years in Paris studying under Carolus-Duran and sharing a studio with Sargent. He returned to Chicago in 1878 but after a short time moved to New York: "I determined to come on to New York, sink or swim, survive or perish, rather than rot in the miserable mediocrity of a western studio," was his way of explaining it. The already predominant position of the city was steadily reinforced, as the European-trained painters congregated there: by the end of the century, the centralization of our artistic life had gone so far that it was almost impossible for an artist to gain a reputation or to secure an audience if he did not live in New York city.

The two major figures of the Paris-trained generation of the seventies were John Singer Sargent and Mary Cassatt.

Mary Cassatt (1845-1926) is one of the few American painters known to European critics and mentioned in European histories of art. As a consequence she has been given, I suspect, a somewhat disproportionate place in the story of our art. Her family lived much abroad, and although she grew up in Philadelphia and studied at the Pennsylvania Academy of the Fine Arts, from 1866 onward her life was spent in Europe. Settling finally in Paris in 1873, she became an admirer and friend of Degas and, through his influence, joined the Impressionist group, of which she became a distinguished minor member. She was a figure painter who learned much from Degas, Manet, and Japanese prints, and developed an admirable manner, large in drawing, broad and luminous in color. What robs her, in my opinion, of the place to which her powerful style would otherwise entitle her, is her excessively unadventurous mind—for the paintings of her mature period are nearly all variations of a single picture, a mother and child. It is hard to see greatness in such monotony of subject. Had her mind been as free and vigorous as her method, she would have been a notable figure in the history of American art.

Her most original work was done in the nineties. Inspired by an exhibition of Japanese prints in Paris in 1890, she put a vigor of outline and color pattern into works like the color print series of 1891, or oils like *Young Women Picking Fruit* (Fig. 124) (1891) or *The Bath* (ca.1892) (Art Institute of Chicago) that make them personal and interesting experiments in style. At about the same time also, following the lead of Degas, she turned enthusiastically to pastel. The dry luminosity of the medium suited her and in it she achieved some of her most brilliant effects. Occasionally one sees a pastel so filled with style and elegance that it seems as if the eighteenth-century French tradition were alive again in this American woman: except that there was an astringent flavor in her vision that places her in the age of Degas. Yet if she achieved style—which is something—it was nonetheless always within territories of art already discovered and cultivated by others greater than she; so that she seems, in retrospect, to be no more than a good painter of the second rank. Perhaps her greatest influence upon American taste was exerted by her success in inducing American friends and relatives to buy the paintings of her friends, the Impressionist painters—an influence of which the Havemeyer collection in The Metropolitan Museum of Art is a notable example.

John Singer Sargent (1856-1925) was born in Florence, Italy, the son of American parents living abroad. His father was a Philadelphia physician who had been persuaded by his wife, a woman of wealth and artistic tastes, to give up his practice to live in Italy. Thus the son came, at birth, into the world of expatriate Americans and into a life of taste and leisure. He had his first artistic training in Florence; but the family wandered foot-loose about Europe until, in 1874, they settled in Paris. There, at eighteen, he entered the studio of Carolus-Duran, a painter of not a great deal of temperament, perhaps, but one of those finely disciplined talents in which nineteenth-century France was rich. Carolus-Duran was not only a brilliant draughtsman but a painter with a very exact control of mass, tone, and line. Sargent, a precocious pupil, emerged from his schooling with perhaps the most thoroughly trained and controlled talent an American painter has ever had. An immense natural facility combined with his exact and lucid vision and dispassionate temperament made him seem to his contemporaries the culmination of American objective realism.

Like Whistler, he settled for a time in Paris. In 1879-1880 he visited Spain and Morocco; *El Jaleo,* in the Gardner Museum, Boston, is a result of this visit. In 1884 he showed at the Salon a full-length portrait of a celebrated Parisian beauty *Madame Gautreau* (now in The Metropolitan Museum of Art), which produced one of those sudden, violent tempests to which the climate of artistic Paris is subject. The lady disliked it; her friends and family disliked it; the critics and public abused it and called its *décolletage* shocking. Taken aback by this unexpected and disagreeable attack, Sargent removed in 1885 to London, which was thereafter to be his headquarters for life. In 1887, however, he came to the United States to paint several portraits. An exhibition at the St. Botolph Club, Boston, was the foundation of a great enthusiasm for his work in America; and this was the first of many visits to Boston. The trustees of the Boston Public Library in 1890 gave him one of the large decorative commissions in their new building of which Boston was so proud. Many friendships also helped attach him to Boston, which became his American *pied à terre,* rather than his family home, Philadelphia.

As a figure painter Sargent seems to solve the most difficult and subtle problems of movement, light, form, with an effortless ease which fascinated his own generation greatly and bored the next quite as greatly, so that one must make a conscious effort, today, to see his true accomplishment.

In his own time, Sargent's instantaneous, photographic vision, which catches the casual movement of life so vividly, seemed startling, even disturbing. One of his most satisfying works, to our taste, is his *Portrait of Robert Louis Stevenson* (1885) (Fig. 117) (Mr. and Mrs. John Hay Whitney). But Stevenson himself, writing to their mutual friend W. H. Low (letter of October 22, 1885), found the picture somewhat disconcerting.

Sargent was down again and painted a portrait of me walking about in my own dining-room, in my own velveteen jacket, and twisting as I go my own moustache; at one corner a glimpse of my wife, in an Indian dress, and seated in a chair that was once my grandfather's; but since some months goes by the name of Henry James's, for it was there the novelist loved to sit—adds a touch of poetry and comicality. It is I think excellent, but is too eccentric to be exhibited. I am at one extreme corner; my wife, in this wild dress, and looking like a ghost, is at the extreme other end; between us an open door exhibits my palatial entrance hall and a part of my respected staircase. All this is touched in lovely, with that witty touch of Sargent's; but, of course, it looks dam queer as a whole.[3]

Sargent was at his best in this type of composition (which the French call the *portrait d'apparat*, the portrait of a person in his natural setting): he was, I think, a genre painter by natural gifts, and a painter of fashionable portraits only because his conventional habit of mind did not allow him to refuse to do the kind of thing people wanted of him.

His best period was in the first years after the Spanish visit of 1880, when, under the influence of Velasquez, he worked in a dark, rich palette, using strong contrasts of tone. All his gifts are at their best in the picture of the *Four Daughters of Edward Darley Boit* (1882) (Museum of Fine Arts, Boston). The four little girls in a vast, dim interior have the informal ease of children at home, as if caught by a snapshot; yet the picture has also the comprehensive grasp of a whole phase of life that only an artist's mind can convey. This picture and others of the same type—the two portraits of *Stevenson* (a second, of 1884, is in the Taft Museum of Cincinnati); *Mrs. Charles Gifford Dyer* (Fig. 123); the *Mrs. Paul Escudier* (1886) (private collection, Chicago) standing, a shimmering note of life, in a shadowy room; the *Judith Gauthier* (1884) (Detroit)—show Sargent's rich, sure sense of tone. When he shifted later to the blonde impressionist palette his sense of hue was neither so sure nor so pleasing.

Another thing that makes one uneasy with Sargent is that he was betrayed by his own facility. Like other artists of extreme virtuosity—Sir Thomas Lawrence, Raphael, Picasso—he was at his best before he was thirty, while his emotions still had the freshness of youth. After that there were no new problems; no difficulties to struggle with; nothing but repetition and boredom. He continued to produce distinguished things, when his emotions were interested; but too much of his late work repels us by its cold, bored brilliance. And even in his earlier work—in, for example, such a beautifully exact study of twilight and the rising moon as the *Luxembourg Gardens at Twilight* (1879) (Minneapolis Institute of Arts)—there is something in the quickness of the clever brushstrokes, at once dashing and unsubstantial, that leaves the spirit unnourished and the eye unsatisfied.

In later life Sargent found refuge from his own success as a fashionable portrait painter in painting landscapes in water colors, creating a peculiarly

---

[3] *The Letters of Robert Louis Stevenson*, edited by Sidney Colvin. New York, Charles Scribners Sons, 1911, vol. II, p. 289.

PLATE XII. James Abbott McNeill Whistler:
*Nocturne in Black and Gold — The Falling
Rocket.* (Courtesy of The Detroit Institute of
Arts.)

PLATE XIII. Winslow Homer: *Country School* (detail) (1871). (Courtesy of the City Art Museum of St. Louis.)

Fig. 117. John Singer Sargent: *Robert Louis Stevenson* (1885). (Courtesy of Mr. and Mrs. John Hay Whitney, New York; photograph courtesy of The Metropolitan Museum of Art.)

Fig. 118. William Merritt Chase: *In the Studio* (1880-1883). (Courtesy of The Brooklyn Museum.)

Opposite page, top: Fig. 121. John Henry Twacht-man: *Sailing in the Mist.* (Courtesy of The Pennsylvania Academy of the Fine Arts, Philadelphia.)

Fig. 119. Thomas Wilmer Dewing: *A Lady in Yellow* (1888). (Courtesy of The Isabella Stewart Gardner Museum, Boston.)

Fig. 120. Theodore Robin-son: *Girl at the Piano.* (Courtesy of The Toledo Museum of Art.)

Fig. 122. Childe Hassam: *Southwest Wind* (1905). (Courtesy of the Worcester Art Museum.)

Fig. 123. John Singer Sargent: *Mrs. Charles Gifford Dyer* (1880). (Courtesy of The Art Institute of Chicago.)

Fig. 124. Mary Cassatt: *Young Women Picking Fruit* (1891). (Courtesy of the Carnegie Institute, Pittsburgh.)

Fig. 125. George Inness: *Grey Day,
Goochland* (1884). (Courtesy of
the Phillips Collection, Washington, D.C.)

Fig. 126. Homer Martin: *The Harp
of the Winds* (1895). (Courtesy of
The Metropolitan Museum of Art.)

Fig. 127. Winslow Homer: *Prisoners from the Front* (1866).
(Courtesy of The Metropolitan
Museum of Art.)

Opposite page, bottom: Fig. 129. Winslow
Homer: *Springtime in Virginia* (water
color). (Private Collection, Detroit.)

Fig. 128. Winslow Homer: *Long Branch, New Jersey* (1869). (Courtesy of the Museum of Fine Arts, Boston.)

Fig. 130. Winslow Homer: *Huntsman and Dogs* (1891). (Courtesy of The Philadelphia Museum of Art.)

Fig. 131. Winslow Homer: *Saguenay River, Lower Rapids* (water color, 1899). (Courtesy of the Worcester Art Museum.)

Fig. 132. Thomas Eakins: *Sailing* (ca. 1874).
(Courtesy of The Philadelphia Museum of
Art.)

Fig. 133. Thomas P. Anshutz: *Steel-workers' Noontime* (before 1884).
(Courtesy of Mr. and Mrs. Law-rence A. Fleischman, Detroit.)

Opposite page: Fig. 134. Thomas Eakins: *The Pathetic Song* (1881). (Courtesy of The Corcoran Gallery of Art.)

Below: Fig. 135. Thomas Eakins: *The Gross Clinic* (1875). (Courtesy of the Jefferson Medical College, Philadelphia.)

Fig. 136. John Frederick Peto: *The Poor Man's Store* (1885). (Private Collection, Newport, R. I.)

Fig. 137. John Haberle: *Grandma's Hearthstone* (1890). (Courtesy of The Detroit Institute of Arts.)

Fig. 138. A. B. Frost: *I am Here for a Purpose*. (From "The Squirrel Inn," *Century Magazine*, June, 1891.)

Fig. 139. Thomas Nast: *Can the Law Reach Him?—The Dwarf and the Giant Thief*. (From *Harper's Weekly*, January 6, 1872.)

Left: Fig. 140. Elihu Vedder: *Ideal Head* (1872). (Private Collection, Detroit.)

Opposite page, top: Fig. 142. John LaFarge: *Athens* (1898). (Courtesy of The Bowdoin College Museum of Fine Arts.)

Left: Fig. 141. John LaFarge: *Greek Love Token* (1866). (Courtesy of the National Collection of Fine Arts, Smithsonian Institution, Washington, D.C.)

Opposite page, bottom: Fig. 143. Albert P. Ryder: *Siegfried and the Rhine Maidens*. (Courtesy of the National Gallery of Art, Mellon Collection, Washington, D.C.)

Fig. 144. Elihu Vedder: *The Lair of the Sea Serpent* (1864). (Courtesy of the Museum of Fine Arts, Boston.)

Fig. 145. John LaFarge: *The Strange Thing Little Kiosai Saw in the River* (1897). (Courtesy of The Metropolitan Museum of Art.)

positive yet liquid style, of which the *Piazzetta* (The Brooklyn Museum) is a good example. In his water colors everything flows and swims in the vibration of dazzling summer light. His manner is so personal that one either likes or dislikes it; no middle ground is possible. He also produced large mural decorations in the Boston Library and also the Museum of Fine Arts, of totally different quality, and much criticized for the wrong reasons; but the discussion of these belongs to Chapter 12.

The American painters who remained in Europe—with the exception of Whistler, Sargent, and Cassatt—do not seem to have made a strong or lasting contribution to American imaginative life. At least, they are not remembered.

Those who will read Sheldon's *Recent Ideals of American Art*, or the wiser views of the period in Sadakichi Hartmann's *A History of American Art* (1902), and Samuel Isham's *History of American Painting* (1905) will find the names of the expatriate painters of the last quarter of the nineteenth century, both the few who are remembered today and many who are forgotten. I am not sure that all these deserve their present oblivion. The foreign flavor which was once the key to their success now works as strongly against them.

It is not hard to see how some artists of that period, like Walter Gay, for example, well launched upon the current of a flourishing European center, enjoying recognition and surrounded by a rich artistic life, should have decided to make their headquarters in Europe, and to keep in touch with America by occasional visits or by contact with American travelers. There is certainly no reason why an artist should not go where his work calls him or live where he can pursue his profession to best advantage.

But over and above these reasons, the atmosphere of the period was saturated with the pleasure of "going abroad." Western culture was enchanted by the novelty and enthusiasm of a great technological revolution. The era of easy transportation and communication opened by the railroad, the steamship, the telegraph, the telephone, the daily newspaper and monthly magazine had created a new kind of world, obliterating distance and physical barriers. In every Western country, England, France, Italy, Germany, as well as in the United States, the old rather simple but highly developed national culture gave way to a new cosmopolitan life.

Cosmopolitanism on this gigantic scale was a new thing. Culture has always been a thing of ideas which know no frontiers. But it is also a thing of feelings which require depth of experience, and of knowledge which requires mastery of carefully studied and thoroughly understood material. Easy travel opened the whole world—not only Europe, but Egypt, India, the Far East— while the busy camera brought the marvels of the world to those who stayed at home. It was inevitable that the age should delight in these thousands of fresh, exotic, intoxicating new impressions. The danger for the artists was that they might substitute the easy excitements and discoveries of the tourist for the perceptions of the artist.

Whether or not one enjoys Whistler's fastidious decorative elegance or Sargent's brilliance and cool detachment (and there are many people today who do not), they were very substantial and powerful talents, who took a front rank in the artistic life of their own day. But the cosmopolitan movement, on the whole, as we look back upon it, dwindles in the perspective of time.

A good place to study its character is in those ground floor rooms of the Gardner Museum in Boston that everyone hurries through on the way to the great things upstairs, but which are nonetheless worth lingering in if one likes to savor the erratic wanderings and strange revolutions of taste. One sees there a collection formed in the eighties and nineties, preserved unaltered: the major and the minor, the enduring and the transient, left hanging together without any of time's ruthless editing. It is a curious experience to find one's self transported back into the intellectual atmosphere of that day, which was so confident of its own superiority to the old, provincial, romantic America. The dominating impression is not one of richly flowing creation, but of a rather self-conscious estheticism. Its pictures are slight little exercises in taste and skill; little landscapes, little still lifes, little figure compositions of no particular subject, chosen for an opportunity to display the artist's impressionist palette and fastidious taste. Secondary, though ever present in the background, is the note of souvenirs of foreign travel as something to be displayed a little proudly. As a whole there seems a general thinness and lack of blood. This painting, one feels, had become an exercise in taste and talent rather than a vehicle for creative passion and power.

The painters who brought their new techniques back to their own country seem to have chosen the more difficult yet the better part, if one may judge by the fact that more of their names have survived. Yet their return to this hemisphere was not easy. To the young students who began returning in the seventies, their eyes filled with the facile charm of Munich brushwork or the elaborate theatrical brilliance of the Salon, the exhibitions of the National Academy of Design seemed niggling in handling, woolly and insipid in color. The older American art, they felt, was stuffy and out of date. A war of generations broke out. The new men founded the Society of American Artists in 1877 in competition with the National Academy of Design. The New York Etching Club (1877) and the American Watercolor Society also gave them space to exhibit and the *American Art Review*, founded in Boston in 1880, a journal to support them. In the first exhibitions of the Society of American Artists, the Munich-trained men were predominant, but in the eighties and nineties the Parisian technique and palette came to the front.

The most influential figure among those who returned to this side of the

Atlantic was W. M. Chase (1849-1916) and his story is instructive. Born in Indiana, he studied with local portrait painters in Indianapolis and in New York at the National Academy of Design; then went to St. Louis, where his family had removed. In 1872 some businessmen of that city, impressed by his talent, raised money to send him abroad. When asked if he would like to go he replied, "My God, I'd rather go to Europe than go to heaven." A St. Louis painter recommended Munich, so Chase went there. He remained five years and had great success: Piloty, his teacher, even selected him to paint the portraits of his five sons. Chase's pictures in his Munich period are less flamboyant than Duveneck's and are painted in a luminous gray and brown tonality that is pleasing. (He also began to paint the still lifes of fish, which were to be one of his great successes.) In 1877 he spent nine months with Duveneck in Venice. Then, in 1878, the newly organized Art Students League invited him to New York as teacher of its painting class. He returned with a halo of European success and a large collection of pictures and curios, which he installed in a spacious studio at 51 West 10th Street that became a noted meeting place for the artists and students of New York. His paintings that show its interior, like *In the Studio* (Fig. 118) (1880-1883) in the Brooklyn Museum, or one in Pittsburgh, are revealing documents of the taste for artistic "atmosphere," by which was meant a picturesque ensemble, exotic bits and pieces, and decorative souvenirs of travel.

Chase was an eclectic painter. His work at various times is close to Duveneck, to Fortuny, to Boudin, to Manet, or to Sargent. During the eighties he abandoned the grays and browns of Munich for the blonde palette of Paris and the facile brushstroke of Sargent. He worked with great rapidity, so that he was able to keep up a large production of portraits, still lifes, and landscapes and at the same time to teach great numbers of students. A story told by Charles W. Hawthorne illustrates his facility; Chase used to advise his landscape classes at Shinnecock, "Take plenty of time for your picture; take two hours if you need it." As a painter, Chase was a man of talent rather than power and conviction; but as a teacher he was a man of extraordinary effect. Probably no other American has ever taught so large a number of pupils. Through his influence, before the end of the century a composite technique of the bright impressionist palette and the dashing brushstroke of Sargent had become the vernacular of American painting.

The broken color of Monet, which Theodore Robinson (1852-1896) brought home, had a much lesser influence, perhaps because Robinson had not the health to be a vigorous leader. By nature he was a realist. His early works, like the *Girl at the Piano* (The Pennsylvania Academy of the Fine Arts; a different version in Toledo) (Fig. 120) are in a dark, warm, tonal style and attractive in their direct, modest observation. In Baur's sympathetic monograph one can read the story of his vain struggle to adjust the impres-

sionist technique to the different light and larger scale of the American landscape before ill health brought his sensitive but slender talent to an end.

Childe Hassam (1859-1935), trained in Boston, was an interesting luminist even before he went to France. His early tonal style, shown in a picture
like *Columbus Avenue, Boston, Rainy Day* (1885) (Worcester Art Museum), owes something to Whistler, perhaps, in its soft grays, but nothing
yet to Paris. In 1886, at the age of twenty-seven, he went abroad and joined
the army of students at Julian's; but it was the touch and palette of the late
Monet that he brought home. Almost alone among the American impressionists, Hassam has the quality of uncomplicated happiness that makes his French
contemporaries so delightful. His *Southwest Wind* (Fig. 122) (1905)
(Worcester Art Museum) is an admirable example of his later style. It is
simply a row of poplar trees with the the wind ruffling their leaves and turning up the silver undersides, and behind them glimpses of some white buildings and the sea. Flooded with a clear white noonday light, it is a piece of
summer wind and sun and freshness translated into art. His later years, unfortunately, showed a sad deterioration from this fresh and easy style.

The most conspicuous reaction of American painters to impressionism
was, however, something quite different. They turned the new color harmonies and the atmospheric touch of French painting into a muted, decorative, luminist style. This took place so spontaneously, in so many forms,
that it must represent a mood or movement of importance in our culture and
worth our while to analyze.

The subdued color harmonies and muted quiet of Whistler's portraits
and Nocturnes are a highly individual but, in this context, not an isolated
phenomenon. They form part of the mood of quietism (not unlike that of
Allston in the eighteen-twenties) to which American taste now returned.
One can see it in artists as original and diverse as Whistler, Inness, and
Twachtman.

In 1870 Inness' dealers, Williams and Everett of Boston, sent him abroad,
thinking a change of subject would help the sale of his pictures. Inness spent
most of the years 1870-1875 in Italy and found, in the landscape around
Rome, not only popular success but the beginning of a new development.
While in Italy, surrounded by Italian art, he achieved the most monumental
of all his works in a brooding picture called *The White Monk* (1874). After
his return he became increasingly a painter of mood; his subjects dissolved
into soft, muted, shimmering color. These late, dreamlike, light-saturated
landscapes were immensely popular in his own time, which considered them
the highest achievements of American landscape painting. We are apt to
prefer his objective earlier works; and even on this basis there are few who
would contend today for the lofty position once given him.

His later pictures, with their mystical mood and soft veils of color, belong essentially to American decorative Impressionism, although Inness ar-

rived there by his own quite original path. The vague, subjective poetry, the spongy softness and glow of pigment that mark these late works are outstanding examples of that movement. The extravagant popularity of these pictures at the close of the nineteenth century reveals, in fact, a striking change in taste. After 1875 a revulsion against naturalism took place and many artists, together with a large segment of their public, turned toward a Tennysonian, trance-like idealism, in which the note of reality, like the echo calling, grew ever fainter (Fig. 125).

Inness was not the only painter who began in the older landscape school but developed into this kind of Impressionism of mood. Alexander H. Wyant (1836-1892) and Homer Martin (1836-1897) followed similar paths—and, on a lower level, so did Thomas Moran (1837-1926), whose dramatizations of grandiose western scenery were very popular.

Wyant also was a self-taught painter. The stylistic revolution of the seventies divides his work into two separate chapters. His early style was an objective, romantic luminism in which he subordinated his own personality to the grand tranquil vistas of nature. His *The Mohawk Valley* (Fig. 106) (1866) (The Metropolitan Museum of Art) is an example of this first phase, when he painted chiefly the landscapes of New England and New York.

In 1873 Wyant joined a government expedition to Arizona and New Mexico, thinking to study and live out of doors. But exposure and fatigue, aggravated by the harshness of the leader of the party, brought on an illness that led to the loss of the use of his right arm. He had to teach himself to paint again with his left hand. The enforced pause in his work produced a change of style. His later work shows the influence of Corot and Rousseau, in that, instead of great vistas, his subjects became small, intimate glimpses of nature. His interest in light and atmosphere was expressed in subtle relations of tone, rather than the bright hues of Impressionism; but he used broken color also to form simple dominant color chords, filled with their own grave, gentle, pensive music.

Homer Martin's career was also divided into two chapters. In the first he was a romantic luminist, painting the mountains and lakes of the Adirondacks, using a somewhat monotonous palette of grays and browns, but achieving at his best something of Kensett's aerial poetry.

The sight of some of Corot's pictures, then just beginning to be imported, sent him abroad in 1876; he returned to France in 1879 and remained until 1887, living mostly in Normandy and Brittany. He learned from the Impressionists their new handling of paint, their soft shimmer of color, although he never adopted their high-keyed palette. *The Harp of the Winds* (Fig. 126) (1895) (The Metropolitan Museum of Art) is the work by which Martin impressed himself on the American public. This canvas, once one of the best known of American paintings, has suffered terribly from overfamiliarity; but looked at again without prejudice, it deserves the place it held in the affections of the nineties. Its gentle lyricism, veiled in atmosphere and softly shimmering light, its grave, quiet melancholy "sobering but not saddening," as Isham said, can still exert their authority on a sympathetic observer and make one realize that Martin was, if not a great, certainly a true and sensitive artist.

In 1895 a group of New York and Boston painters exhibited together, under the name of the Ten American Painters. The Ten were: Thomas W. Dewing (1851-1938); Edmund C. Tarbell (1862-1938); Frank W. Benson (1862-1951); Joseph De Camp (1855-1923); J. Alden Weir (1852-1919); John W. Twachtman (1852-1902); Willard L. Metcalf (1858-1925); E. E. Simmons (1852-1931); Childe Hassam (1859-1935); and Robert Reid (1862-1929). After Twachtman's death in 1902, Chase took his place. As a group The Ten formed a kind of academy of American Impressionism. But some of them were more than this.

Dewing was one of the most original. His small pictures of women seated in cool dim interiors, very precisely and delicately drawn and sensitive in tone, are good examples of the quiet, dreamlike poetry for which the painters of the nineties were seeking (Fig. 119).

Twachtman, like Theodore Robinson, began with a warm, deep-toned palette. Gradually, under the influence of French painting, his color grew light and cool; and his interest in light and atmosphere took a direction that was to be characteristic of American quietism. He preferred slight, intimate little glimpses of nature and, eliminating depth almost entirely, transposed his subjects into a vague shimmer of color so soft it seems to float on the surface of the canvas. *Sailing in the Mist* (Fig. 121) (The Pennsylvania Academy of the Fine Arts) is one of the most attractive examples of this gentle, evanescent style—a delicate soap bubble of blues and whites like a Debussy étude in paint.

There were other painters of quietism who did not belong to the group of Ten: Dwight W. Tryon (1849-1925), whose muted landscapes have their own, gently lyrical, quality; F. Hopkinson Smith (1838-1915), a graceful writer and attractive water colorist, whose work is under a passing cloud of forgetfulness; Dodge MacKnight (1860-1950), who dominated Boston watercolor painting for decades; Robert W. Vonnoh (1858-1933), a skillful Impressionist figure painter and portraitist; Wyatt Eaton (1849-1896), a portrait painter of fine gravity and dignity. They are all painters in whose work one can find pleasant qualities of perception and refinement of style.

The tendency to give a decorative and quietist direction to Impressionism began with Whistler; his example if not his style no doubt had much to do with the prevalence of the trend toward the close of the century. The similarities between Whistler's Venetian pastels, for example, and the intimate, fragile motifs which Twachtman chose from nature, developing them into stylized patterns of colors and brushstrokes, cannot be wholly accidental

—although one could never tell Twachtman a follower or imitator of Whistler.

Two other influences were at work. After the naturalism of the generation of 1850, a reaction was to be expected. Whistler, Inness, Wyant, Martin represent a return to the subjective: they were interested in what they could read into their subject, in the constructions of lyrical sentiment and decorative harmonies they could make from it, not in revealing the objective character they could discover there. The reaction to Impressionism took a different form among Americans but it was a reaction one can see also in French and German painting of the nineties.

There is, also, a phenomenon made familiar by its repetition in every period of art. In the history of every new impulse one finds first a vigorous, exploratory generation of pioneers, full of courage and imagination, who discover a new vision of life and create a style to express it. The second phase is that of the second generation, who turn the new style into a primarily decorative impulse, a thing of taste and charm, rather than discovery and power. One can see this tendency at work among the Ten. The artists who came to maturity in the nineties were the epigoni of Impressionism, interested in the esthetic rather than the vital.

Both tendencies combined, however, to bring the nineteenth century to a close on the note of gentle lyricism and delicate, muted harmonies.

The achievements of this quarter-century are just far enough away to be difficult to estimate fairly. They are not close enough to art today to be felt as vital, nor distant enough to be interesting as history. Yet one can perhaps draw certain conclusions from facts that are not likely to be distorted by our admittedly imperfect perspective.

Judged by the development of the institutions of art, painting grew increasingly popular. The art museum, born in the seventies, developed rapidly in the atmosphere of the new age. Boston, New York, Philadelphia, and Washington having led the way, after the Centennial other cities followed. The Art Institute of Chicago was founded in 1879 (its first building opened in 1882; its first annual exhibition of painting held in 1889). In the same year St. Louis, under the aegis of Washington University, founded a school and Museum of Fine Arts which was forty years later to become the City Art Museum of St. Louis. In the next decade came Cincinnati (1881); Detroit (1885); two benefactions by individuals to their cities, the Crocker Gallery in Sacramento (1885) and the Layton Gallery in Milwaukee (1888); and the great archaeological museum, The University Museum, Philadelphia (1887).

The nineties were still more active in creating museums. Chicago was rehoused in its present building, created as part of the World's Columbian Exposition (1893); the Walker Art Gallery, a small but ambitious neoclassic structure, was given to Bowdoin College (1894) to house a collection formed by James Bowdoin at the beginning of the century; the Carnegie Institute was opened in Pittsburgh (1895; its first international exhibition of painting, 1896); the M. D. De Young Memorial Museum, San Francisco (1895); the Fogg Museum, Harvard University (1895); the Worcester Art Museum (1896); the Brooklyn Museum (1897); and the Cooper Union Museum of the Arts of Decoration (1897).

By the close of the century, an art museum was an accepted part of civic life in our major cities; in many others there were art associations, art clubs, and exhibition societies that were to develop into art museums later. The Pennsylvania Academy of the Fine Arts, The Corcoran Gallery, in Washington, the Art Institute of Chicago, and the National Academy of Design in New York held national exhibitions of painting and the Carnegie Institute had launched an ambitious program of international exhibitions.

The art schools of the country were also put on a better basis. Thomas Eakins, returning from Paris in the seventies, reorganized the old school of the Pennsylvania Academy of the Fine Arts in Philadelphia. In 1875 the National Academy of Design in New York city closed its art school for lack of funds. L. E. Wilmarth, its instructor, and the student body organized the Art Students League as a drawing and sketch class. The National Academy reopened its school in 1877 and Wilmarth returned to take charge. But in October, 1877, the Art Students League also reopened with Walter Shirlaw teaching painting, Jonathan Hartley sculpture, and F. S. Church composition. In 1878 W. M. Chase began his famous painting class; Shirlaw took composition; and Hartley sculpture. The new movement thus had an art school of its own with an aggressive leadership, and in the Society of American Artists (1877) an organization for its exhibitions.

But, alas, the same wind of change that gave the American Impressionists their sense of superiority encased in their experience of European travel also deprived them of their livelihood. As Samuel Isham said, "When the younger men went abroad to study, painting was a lucrative profession; when they returned, they found it was not possible for a man to live by it, even if he were talented, well taught, and hard working." What had been a secure and established profession in the third quarter of the nineteenth century became, in the era of Ward McAllister and The Four Hundred, a poverty-stricken and insecure pursuit—as it has remained ever since.

There were many reasons for this disastrous change. The disappearance of the portrait as a staple (except in its most fashionable and official forms) was one. Another was that the new generation of painters were, many of them, still immature when they returned from their studies abroad and had little to offer except "studies" or "sketches" exhibiting a new kind of brush work, or perhaps one big "salon" picture they had executed in Paris. But chiefly it was because the artists' more wealthy patrons had also been affected by the taste for foreign travel. They too had seen the Salon and had learned to admire the fashionable painters of Paris—Meissonier or Bouguereau or Cabanel—and the Paris-trained Americans did not seem so glamorous or desirable as the originals. When, for example, Jasper Cropsey (who was a well-considered, but never one of the most popular painters in the generation of 1850) wished to go abroad in 1856, he held a sale of the pictures and sketches in his studio and realized over $8,000. The editor of *The Crayon* wrote: "We believe that in no other country will the same class of pictures bring so high prices as here, especially if they are painted by American artists." Twenty years later, the wealthy patrons of art were paying record prices for Rosa Bonheur and Meissonier, or timidly buying a Corot; the man with a few hundred dollars preferred Toulmouche or Merle or some other forgotten French painter with an agreeable aroma of Paris; while the American imitators simply did not sell. Earlier in the century, Samuel F. B. Morse had warned his students at the National Academy of Design that if they studied abroad they would return to a country that, being without sympathy with their foreign tastes, would ignore them.[4] This now came true. The patrons of conservative tastes remained faithful to the older men of the National Academy of Design, while the patrons of advanced tastes preferred to buy European paintings rather than American. Yet although it became impossible for artists to sell their pictures, the demands to study painting multiplied. Art schools and painting classes were springing up; everywhere there were students eager to attend painting classes; and teaching, rather than the practice of his art, became the economic support of the painter.

The taste of American collectors, in short, had developed along the same lines of eclecticism and cosmopolitanism followed by the interests of the painters themselves. Collecting art now rapidly became a mark of foreign travel and an expression of pride in the new-found industrial wealth of America. It was a matter of national pride that Mr. A. T. Stewart paid to Meissonier, for his picture called *Friedland, 1807*, the sum of three hundred thousand francs (sixty thousand dollars) and that Mr. William H. Vanderbilt afterward paid fifty thousand dollars for *The Arrival at the Chateau*, by the same artist. The leaders of society in New York were also leaders of the new spirit of collecting, which dreamed only of Rosa Bonheur, of Bouguereau, or Meissonier; or, if slightly more old-fashioned, of Meyer von Bremen, Knaus, Achenbach, Koek-Koek, Van Marcke. And what the wealthy of New York did, the United States did.

The rise of the art dealer as an intermediary between the artist and the public had begun with the midcentury and developed steadily. By the nineties New York had a large group of dealers' galleries, some of which are remembered, others forgotten: S. D. Avery, T. S. Blakeslee, Boussod-Valadon,

---

[4] Quoted by Frank Jewett Mather, *The American Spirit in Art*. New Haven, Yale University Press, 1927.

Frederick A. Chapman, L. Crist Delmonico, Durand-Ruel, Frederick Keppel, Knoedler, Charles W. Kraushaar, William Macbeth, Julius Oehme, William Schaus, Arthur Tooth, H. Wunderlich, Cottier, The American Art Galleries.

Some of these sold the best European art, some the best American. Others sold the fashionable pseudomasters of the day. It would be idle to generalize as if these galleries were all alike.

Nevertheless, the monument of the period is a book called *Treasures of Art in America,* in three volumes, by Edward Strahan (Philadelphia, 1886), which records the glories of the Astor, Vanderbilt, Stewart, and Wolfe collections of New York, and other collections from Montreal to Cincinnati, from Philadelphia to Sacramento. A French observer, René Brimo, who wrote an acute book on the evolution of taste in the United States, comments on the monotony of these collections: they all contained exactly the same artists, differing only in the number of pictures that represent each artist.[5] He attributed this to the spirit of democratic uniformity prevailing in this country. It seems, rather, the earliest of those waves of uncritical snobbism, so typical of this country, which have marked the subsequent history of collecting in America.

But if collecting by vogue appeared, there were also collectors of the true mettle, who find in works of art an answer to the inner needs of one's imagination and temperament. It is enough to mention a few names, such as Quincy Adams Shaw, Isabella Stewart Gardner, Henry G. Marquand, Benjamin Altman, J. P. Morgan, Henry Walters, W. L. Elkins, John H. McFadden, George Gunsaulus, John G. Johnson, James E. Scripps, all of whom began, in the last quarter of the century, to bring to America some share in the great artistic heritage of our civilization; and to whose discrimination and devotion we owe a lasting debt of gratitude.

Yet for most American artists it was a time of great difficulty. They were the beggars at the feast, picking up the crumbs that fell from the tables where the European painters of fashionable reputation were feasting.

There were other destructive aspects of the period. The handcraft skills and traditions lost ground steadily before the machine; the factory, rather than the craftsman's workshop, became the source of more and more of the things with which the American people lived and furnished their homes. This was not in itself bad. Machine production can be beautiful as well as economical and useful. Many years had to pass, however, before the problem of machine design was to be grasped or mastered.

As the camera had destroyed the crafts of miniature painting and portraiture, the photoengraving process in the nineties destroyed the craft of wood engraving, which had made the two preceding decades the golden period of American illustration. A new type of magazine also appeared,

[5] René Brimo, *L'Evolution du Goût aux Etats-Unis,* Paris, James Fortune, 1938.

cheaper than the famous monthlies, addressed to a less sophisticated public, and with them the art of the illustrator began to decline.

Worst of all, the American intelligentsia lost its self-reliance. The great lesson which Emerson had taught the romantic period was that poverty and rude setting were not obstacles to the inner life: it was possible to be a thinker and an artist in an unknown American village. At the end of the century, European experience had become the prop of everything; the cosmopolitan generation had become ashamed, not only of the provincialism of their parents, but of themselves. Henry Adams, after reading Henry James's biography of the sculptor, W. W. Story, in 1903, wrote to James:

The painful truth is that all of my New England generation, counting the half century, 1820-1870, were in actual fact only one mind and nature. . . . One cannot exaggerate the profundity of ignorance of Story in becoming a sculptor, or Sumner in becoming a Statesman, or Emerson in becoming a philosopher. Story and Sumner, Emerson and Alcott, Lowell and Longfellow, Hillard, Winthrop, Motley, Prescott, and all the rest, were the same mind,—and so, poor worm, was I. God knows that we knew our want of knowledge! The self-distrust became introspection—nervous self-consciousness—irritable dislike of America, and antipathy to Boston. . . . Improvised Europeans, we were, and—Lord God!—how thin! [6]

The mark of culture became a nervous, apologetic attitude about America; self-reliance gave way to the kind of groveling colonialism represented by Charles Eliot Norton's remark to his class at Harvard in the nineties, quoted by Ferris Greenslet, "There are handsome landscapes in our country but in America even the shadows are vulgar."

Thus, the period of eclectic cosmopolitanism was marked both by growth and decay. It created a greater knowledge of the world of art, a wider experience, some brilliant individual achievements. But it lost ground in respect to the harmony between the artists and society, in self-knowledge, in the disintegration of the handcrafts, and in self-reliance.

[6] *Letters of Henry Adams*, 1892-1918, ed. Worthington Chauncey Ford, Boston, Houghton Mifflin Company, 1938, p. 414.

CHAPTER 11

OBJECTIVE REALISM: THE INDEPENDENTS

ONE OF THE REVEALING SIGNS OF WEAKNESS IN THIS GENERATION IS THAT IT ignored many of its own best painters because they were too independent, too original, too far removed from cosmopolitan taste and the fashionable modes of painting. In this chapter I shall try to tell the story of the independent painters, for whom the first task was to see life from their own point of view in space and time, and whose technique grew out of their personal vision.

Underlying the closing decades of the nineteenth century—whether we are dealing with solitary individualists in America or gregarious students in Paris and Munich—was the mental climate of objective realism, the climate of the age of science. The giant Corliss steam engine that had formed the famous central feature of the Hall of Mechanics at the Philadelphia Exposition of 1876 was a symbol of the new age, preoccupied with the study and mastery of nature, and the discovery of new techniques to control and use its infinite forces. The organization of society changed with the rise of modern technology and the climate of the mind changed with it. The simple life of an earlier, agricultural America gave way before the rise of giant industry and finance capitalism, the growth of great cities and of social classes, all the gathering phenomena of modern mass civilization. There arose now in Western civilization a curious new line of prophets like Comte, Proudhon, and Marx, who promised to redeem the world by economics. In philosophy, Herbert Spencer created an image of the universe as a vast machine and fastened the notion of mechanistic determinism on men's minds. Schopenhauer made pessimism easy and fashionable. Nietzsche cried that the values of the good, the true, the beautiful, which have ruled over civilization for thousands of years, are illusory—there is only the will to power. The dream of the freedom of peoples (which had animated the liberal minds of the early nineteenth century), the "religion of liberty" in Croce's phrase, faded before the *real-politik* of Bismarck and the cynical partition of Africa.

Not Jefferson, or Emerson, but Darwin now offered the great challenge to the mind; as once Gibbon and the first archaeologists had conjured, from beneath the soil of Italy, a pageant of classical antiquity to astonish and fascinate mankind, so now a still more vast vision of life arose. In these later decades of the nineteenth century it was paleontologists like O. C. Marsh and Cope, picking up stones in the cuttings made by the transcontinental railroads across the vast, empty plains of Nebraska, who conjured from the old bones of the earth the story of ancient life that Darwin had inferred in the *Origin of Species*—dinosaurs; saw-toothed, reptilian birds; the fossil sequence of the horse, developed with such beautiful logic and coherence from its five-toed ancestor. Biology, geology, physics, chemistry, and economics guided the thought of the age. Life seemed no longer a problem for reason, as the men of the eighteenth century saw it; or for feeling, as the romanticists believed: in place of the Enlightenment, or Transcendentalism, came an overmastering appetite for cool observation of fact.

In the creative imagination, objective realism was the main stream of the arts. But true art, even when devoured by a passion to observe and record, is still poetry. Now it was the poetry of light and of nature studied with passionate intensity that haunted the imagination of the Western world, both among the Impressionists and the independent or isolated painters.

So strong is the kinship of these independents in some instances to American romanticism, in the grave and brooding note of their work and in the dark, warm tones of their palette, that it is tempting to consider them as a continuation of romanticism. The afterglow of romantic feeling lingers upon them; but the greatest and most typical figures, like Winslow Homer and Thomas Eakins, belong nonetheless to objective realism.

Their independence did not mean that they turned their eyes away from what was going on in their art elsewhere. Each of them studied or traveled abroad. Both Homer and Eakins show in the luminosity and monumental simplicity of their work that they were working their own way toward the coloristic style that was flowering at that moment in France. But their point of departure was from American experience, rather than European, and they arrived in consequence at their own independent results. Subject was more important to them than a new way of putting on paint. Their styles grew out of the effort to realize their subjects; and their subjects were the landscape and the human life among which they were born. In this sense they did continue the spirit of Emerson's "What would we really know the meaning of? The meal in the firkin, the milk in the pan, the ballad in the street. . . ."

Winslow Homer (1836-1910) was the only one of the great independents to achieve recognition in his lifetime. In spite of severe criticism caused by his lack of "finish," his early works made their originality felt; and his late

paintings of the sea became almost a national epic. Yet as late as 1908 a writer
in the *International Studio* expressed angry resentment of his lack of suavity:
"There is none who, from the technical standpoint, commonly paints more
hatefully than he, and yet at the same time none who, as a rule, produces
greater pictures." [1]

His work falls into two periods: an early manner before 1881 and a later
phase from 1881 to 1910, when he lived at Prout's Neck on the coast of
Maine.

Homer learned his art, not from schools, but from making illustrations
for the pictorial weeklies. He was born in Boston of a family that had been
in Massachusetts for almost two centuries. At nineteen he was apprenticed
to the leading Boston lithographer of the day, John H. Bufford, but after
completing his two-year apprenticeship he left the shop. For a few years he
made illustrations for *Ballou's Pictorial* in Boston. In 1859 he moved to New
York city. *Harper's Weekly* offered him a position as a staff artist. "I declined
it," he said later, "because I had had a taste of freedom. The slavery at Bufford's was too fresh in my recollection to let me care to bind myself again.
From the time I took my nose off that lithographic stone, I have had no master; and never shall have any."

He became for the next seventeen years a free-lance illustrator, chiefly
for *Harper's Weekly*. His illustrations were not tied to the printed text. He
was free to choose his subjects wherever he could find pictorial value, in the
streets of New York, in fashionable life at Long Branch or Newport, at an
Adirondack farm, or among boys playing on the rocks around the harbor of
Gloucester. The process of woodblock reproduction used in book illustration
and the monthly magazines was now improving in subtlety and refinement
but the black-and-white woodcuts of the pictorial weeklies in Homer's time
remained crude and harsh. He learned to work, however, with clear-cut outlines and broad planes that made the most of his medium; as one turns over
the pages of *Harper's Weekly* for the sixties and seventies, Homer's illustrations stand out, not only by their freshness of observation, but by their
sweeping energy of line and effective massing of lights and darks. During the
Civil War he went south with the Union armies and made many drawings
for *Harper's Weekly;* during the war, in 1862, he did his first painting in oil.

His early oils, inspired by wartime scenes, are sober in color, but show
the discipline of his work as an illustrator in their grasp of character, their
simple expressive drawing, and their breadth of tone. The masterpiece of
this phase is *Prisoners from the Front* (Fig. 127) (1866) (The Metropolitan
Museum of Art). It shows a Union officer examining a group of Confederate
prisoners in the midst of a devastated Virginia landscape. In its contrast between the pale, earnest, civilian-in-uniform on the one side, and on the other
the haughty, graceful cavalier-officer, elegant even in his rags, it tells us all

[1] Leila Mechlin, *International Studio*, XXXIV (1908), cxxv.

one needs to know about the two temperaments which were at war in that conflict. It was exhibited at the National Academy of Design in 1866 and created a sensation—for it was the most powerful and convincing painting that had come out of that terrible national experience—and made its author famous. It was one of the pictures sent to represent American painting in the Paris Exposition of 1867, where its fidelity and power were recognized by both French and English critics. Although Homer could be criticized and attacked after this, he could not be ignored.

From his very first essay in oils, Homer was launched upon the study of light. In 1867-1868 he went to France for a few months, looked at the Louvre, painted a little in the country, enjoyed Paris, and returned home. The composition of one or two small pictures done after his return show that he may have looked at Degas, the French painter nearest him in spirit, but otherwise he went his own way, not in ignorance but in complete independence of other men's work. As Lloyd Goodrich put it, "Homer looked more at nature than at other art, painted by eye rather than by tradition." [2] Homer's exploration of light took him in a different direction from French Impressionism. His long discipline in black-and-white made itself felt: instead of dissolving outline and form into a vibration of light and color, he developed luminosity within a construction of clear, firm outlines and broad planes of light and dark (Fig. 128 and Plate XIII). After he began to use water color his treatment of outline became more fluid and subtle; but he never lost the large, monumental quality of his early style in all his later delicacy of nuance and aerial color.

Water color, which he began to use in 1873, was a medium congenial to his gifts and he gave it an unprecedented authority. Homer had retained from boyhood a love of outdoor life. Water color enabled him to work out of doors; not merely drawing, but painting, in light and color. From the first, he used the medium boldly: *The Sick Chicken* (1874) (Mrs. Harold T. Pulsifer) or *Children on a Fence* (1874) (Lawrence Art Museum, Williams College), though tiny in actual size, are drawn with monumental simplicity and saturated in sunlight; the image is constructed of a few strong, luminous tones, laid down on the paper with the precision of a well-tuned chime of bells.

Until 1874, however, Homer continued to work for *Harper's Weekly* while slowly perfecting his painting. One can watch his eye grow gradually keener and more sensitive to nuances of light, his sense of movement more expressive, his grasp of character deeper. His interest was in human life, out-of-doors under the sky and in sunlight; he liked the simple and unaffected flavors of humanity and showed almost a Dutch genius for the beauty of the ordinary and the everyday. He painted these flavors—the Negroes in the

[2] *American Watercolor and Winslow Homer*, Walker Art Center, Minneapolis, in collaboration with the Detroit Institute of Arts and the Brooklyn Museum, 1945.

South (Fig. 129), soldiers in camp, children on farms, woodsmen in the Adirondack forests—with keen perception and an utter lack of sentimentality. Many of his early pictures of children and young girls show great delicacy of sentiment, without any of the oversweetness that spoils so many nineteenth-century genre paintings; others, like the *Camp Fire* (1881) (The Metropolitan Museum of Art), noteworthy originality not only in its study of firelight and flying sparks, but in its treatment of the masculine world of outdoor life that Homer was to make peculiarly his own.

His early pictures are almost always small in size and large in style, observed with a freshness of eye as delicious as the smell of pine woods to one who, stepping off a train at a remote station, unexpectedly smells that cool fragrance. Our taste, which prefers the simple to the elaborate and the sketch to the finished work, has recently discovered Homer's early pictures and finds them often more pleasing than the larger, more ambitious, and more familiar late compositions that were admired a generation ago. But a taste for his later works will return with another spin of the wheel; and I am not sure that we should value his early work so much if the late pictures were not there, to set them off by contrast, and to lend them their grave authority.

Homer did some of his greatest works in the seventies; yet, although his ability was recognized, his works did not sell. Even to Henry James, perceptive critic of painting though he was, they seemed "damnably ugly." Lloyd Goodrich, in a perceptive and authoritative biography of Homer, believes that Homer became deeply discouraged at his failure to earn a living, not only from a natural pride in art, but because he was in love and had lost hope of being able to support a wife. In 1881, at the age of forty-five, he made a clean break and went abroad for the second time, not to one of the famous cities where tourists and art students flocked, but to the bleak North Sea coast of England at Tynemouth. There he lived and painted for two years in solitude. On his return to America, he abandoned New York and settled at Prout's Neck, a lonely spot on the granite coast of Maine. The scale of his work changed: he painted larger pictures; his subjects became the sea and the contest between man and the forces of nature. Copley had introduced this theme into American art, in *Watson and the Shark;* Allston had painted it, in *The Deluge* and *The Rising of a Thunderstorm at Sea;* other artists had touched upon it; but with Homer it reached new magnitude. At first his marines were consciously heroic in theme: *The Herring Net* (1885) (Art Institute of Chicago); *Undertow* (1886), *The Life Line* (1884) (Philadelphia Museum of Art); *The Fog Warning* (1885) (Boston) and *Eight Bells* (1886) (Addison Gallery, Andover). These subjects of men at work, and in danger, are monumental in scale, painted with rather liquid color and a broad atmospheric touch, yet with solidity and great plastic strength. In the nineties he began a series of pictures in which the theme is the power and loneliness of the sea itself. Famous examples are *The Northeaster* (1895) and

Cannon Rock (1895) (both in The Metropolitan Museum of Art) and *East-ern Point, Prout's Neck* (1900). Throughout these years it was his habit, also, to get away from Prout's Neck on a long trip each year. He visited the Caribbean and explored the Adirondacks and the Canadian forest. The water colors, done out of doors on these journeys, are among his finest works, painted with the force and authority of oils (Fig. 131). He never was con-fused by the fluidity of water color into treating it as a sketchy, accidental medium; on the contrary, he gave it great solidity and strength. Some large oils also came out of these later experiences in the forest. His *Huntsman and Dogs* (1891) (Fig.130) (Philadelphia Museum of Art), in which excited dogs and sullen, silent hunter seem completely part of the vast solitude of mountain and forest, is one of the great imaginative treatments of the wilder-ness in American art; *The Fox Hunt* (1893) (Pennsylvania Academy of the Fine Arts), showing a flock of starved crows attacking a fox plowing through deep snow, is a notable image of the struggle for life in the harsh northern solitudes.

Homer's achievement was to create his own vision of the world and a style to express it. It was an imaginative vision of nature, and of man's life as part of nature, that is one of the original creations of the age. It is also one which embodies deep, national memories of the wilderness and the pioneer, so that, for Americans, a stream of our emotional inheritance seems to flow through his work and his pictures have for us the eloquent overtones of a national heritage, as Reynolds and Gainsborough have for the English, or Watteau or Delacroix for the French.

Thomas Eakins (1844-1916) was born in Philadelphia and spent his life there. He was trained at the Pennsylvania Academy of the Fine Arts and in 1866 went to Paris, enrolling in the Ecole des Beaux-Arts under three teachers, Gérôme, Bonnat, and the sculptor, A. A. Dumont. The chief influ-ence upon him was Gérôme, to whom he became a favorite pupil. He worked so hard under Gérôme that he fell ill and went for seven months to Spain, to seek a change of climate. There he painted few pictures but learned much from the great Spanish realists, Velasquez and Ribera. When he returned to Philadelphia he had absorbed the disciplined French understanding of the human figure and Gérôme's love of precise, factual statement; but instead of devoting his knowledge to factitious reconstructions of history in the man-ner of his teacher, he turned a trained objective eye upon his native city of Philadelphia, studying its people, its life, its sports and recreations, its home life, its scientific interests—but especially the character of its men and women. Not since Copley had an American portrait painter shown so searching a penetration into character as Eakins in his Philadelphia portraits.

Eakins apparently felt none of the difficulty in settling down experienced by many other American students on their return from Paris. He plunged immediately into the familiar life of his own family and friends, painting the sports they enjoyed, like rowing on the Schuylkill River, shooting reed-birds in the river marshes, sailboating on the Delaware; or composing genre pictures of his father watching two old friends play at chess, or of family music at home with a few friends. These are impressive creations both in force of style and depth of feeling. They show a marked command of expressive movement—the movement that reveals the inner life of the figure that moves —and great subtlety in the use of light, although not at all the same use the Impressionists were developing.

Eakins was interested in light; but his studies of the old masters, especially Rembrandt and Ribera, had turned him away from the upper end of the color scale where the Impressionists were at work, toward a Rembrandtesque warmth and depth of tone which, at their best, seem completely appropriate to the silent intensity of his portraits. His interests and habits of thought were very like those of the scientists and university professors among whom he found his best portrait subjects. Eakins had a scientist's liking for fact. He studied anatomy at the Jefferson Medical College; he kept a blackboard in his dining room so that if one wished, one could illustrate the conversation at dinner by a diagram or a few equations. His scientific interests culminated in *The Gross Clinic* (Fig. 135) (1875) (Jefferson Medical College, Philadelphia), which represents one of the outstanding surgeons of the day, and a dominating figure in the medical college, lecturing to a class during the performance of an operation.

Dr. Gross was one of the leading teachers and pioneers of surgery in Philadelphia, a city that has always been one of our great centers of scientific research. The tall, magnetic figure of the doctor dominates the complicated group; he pauses, scalpel in hand, to speak to an amphitheater of students. A single figure, the patient's mother who covers her eyes in horror, brings out by contrast the objective atmosphere of calm scientific skill and intelligence. It was Eakins' vision of the heroic world of science: he put into it everything he had of knowledge, skill, ambition, and power. It is a huge picture. The figures are life-size, painted with somber richness of tone and dramatic lighting. Eakins himself was never to surpass this work of his young strength, nor was another artist to make such an effort to bring the world of science or technology into art in the United States until Rivera painted his frescoes of mass production in Detroit in 1932, fifty-seven years later. But Eakins was too bold for his times. The picture was refused admission to the American section of the Centennial Exhibition (although the jury accepted five other works by him) and he was able only with difficulty to have it hung in the medical section. The public rejection of this masterpiece of his early manhood, his failure to win recognition and support for work of such power, were a defeat from which Eakins' art never recovered. He continued to paint admirably— indeed some of his best smaller pictures were painted in the eighties and nineties—and he did one other big medical group, *The Agnew Clinic*, in 1889. But his art was never again quite so powerful or so ambitious.

In 1876, when the Pennsylvania Academy of the Fine Arts moved into its new building, its famous old art school was still taught by the aging Christian Schussele (whom we mentioned as a sentimental figure painter in Chapter 9). Eakins, a born teacher, became his assistant and, after Schussele's death in 1879, took over the professorship of drawing and painting. The change was a revolution in the teaching of painting. Eakins subordinated drawing from casts to the study of the nude human figure in the "life class." The most searching and severe teacher in America, he made his pupils concentrate on mastery of the living figure, lecturing to them on anatomy and teaching them also to model in clay as a discipline in plastic feeling. He taught his students to *draw with the brush* in light and tone, and founded a teaching tradition so solid that it survived his own dismissal and, through his assistant and successor Thomas Anshutz, nourished a surprising number of the best American painters of the early twentieth century. But again Eakins was too drastic and too tactless; his career as a teacher at the Academy came to an end in 1886.

The sober severity of his work may be seen in his dusky, luminous landscapes, such as *Sailing* (Fig. 132) (ca.1874) (Philadelphia Museum of Art); the Rembrandtesque gravity and intensity of his portraits, in *The Writing Master*, a portrait of his father (1881) (The Metropolitan Museum of Art); the psychological depth and dignity of his genre, in *The Pathetic Song* (Fig. 134) (1881) (Corcoran Gallery of Art, Washington). Yet as he grew older the rebuffs and disappointments of his career drove his sensibility back upon itself: his art did not grow richer with age, as one would hope, but narrower and drier. His objective imagination had to feed upon the outer world, but the outer world rejected him. Gradually the sap and vigor went out of his work and his later life was passed in obscurity.

In fairness to his contemporaries, one must say that the fault was not wholly with society. Eakins was a blunt, independent man, careless in appearance, careless of opinion, and sometimes exceedingly tactless. His teaching, indeed his whole concept of painting, centered upon the nude figure. His attitude toward the nude was that of an anatomist. But in dealing with his public he alienated sympathies needlessly. It was inviting trouble to ask the Philadelphia society women, whose portraits he painted, if they would pose for him in the nude. A quarrel over his insistence on the naked male model in classes for women students eventually caused his break with the Pennsylvania Academy. But it is a great pity, from every point of view, that we were not able to make better use of such a talent.

Yet it is a mistake to think of Eakins as an isolated figure in Philadelphia: he was isolated, it is true, by matters of tact and in degree of ability; yet at the same time he is typical of something basic and enduring in the atmosphere of that city of Franklin and Bartram and the Peales. (The Peale tradition indeed was more than atmosphere, for Eakins was a boy of sixteen when Rembrandt Peale died in 1860. The old painter had lingered on, the last living artist who had seen and painted George Washington, until he was almost as great a curiosity as the Peale mastodon; while Rubens Peale was still painting semiscientific pictures like the *Two Grouse* in the eighteen-sixties.) A passion for the actual, a Dutch sense of the poetry of fact, seemed native there. This is more often realized, perhaps, in the history of American science, where Philadelphia is written large throughout the century, than it is in the arts; for its artistic talents in the later nineteenth century showed a tendency to leave home for greener pastures elsewhere. But I think it is not wholly fanciful to find something forthright and ruthless in Sargent's powers of observation, something downright, too, in Mary Cassatt's way of seeing, that are close to Eakins and to the predominantly scientific-artistic character of the city. (It is true that Poe had written *The Fall of the House of Usher* while living there; but Poe was an exotic anywhere. We are closer to the literary character of the city in Walt Whitman, who lived just across the river and was a friend of Eakins; or in the subtle quiet realism of Frank R. Stockton; or the massive scholarship of Horace Howard Furness, the editor of the Variorum Shakespeare.)

There were other painters, too, around Eakins. In 1881 he acquired, as assistant in his painting classes, Thomas P. Anshutz (1851-1912), a young painter from Kentucky who had studied at the Academy and in New York, and in Paris with Doucet and Bouguereau. Anshutz had never had the attention he deserves, either as a painter or teacher. Cecilia Beaux describes him in her autobiography as adored by his students, but painfully inarticulate on the only occasion he visited her studio. But as a teacher at the Academy he carried on Eakins' firm plastic tradition of form and tone and left his mark upon the twentieth century.[3] As a painter, his masterpiece is the *Steelworkers' Noontime* (Fig. 133) (before 1884) (collection of Mr. and Mrs. Lawrence A. Fleischman, Detroit), a little jewel of solid, knowledgeable, and sensitive painting.

Another teacher at the Academy was Thomas Hovenden (1840-1895), a genial Irishman who had studied at Cork, at the National Academy of Design in New York, and with Cabanel in Paris (1874-1880). On his return to America he worked first in New York but taught at the Pennsylvania Academy and gradually became associated with Philadelphia rather than New York. A magnetic teacher much respected by his students (among whom was Robert Henri), he is remembered today for one picture in the life-sized Salon tradition but nonetheless a well painted piece of realistic genre, called *Breaking Home Ties*, that was the popular favorite in the World's Columbian Ex-

[3] One of John Sloan's early etchings, *The Anatomy Lesson*, represents a lecture by Anshutz.

position at Chicago in 1893. Isham thought Hovenden might have grown to be one of our best genre painters if he had not, with characteristic generosity, sacrificed his life to save a child from under a railroad train.

Another earlier artist who represents the Philadelphia spirit of severe and searching realism was the landscape painter, William S. Haseltine (1835-1900). He, however, left Philadelphia and settled in Rome in 1867 (the year after Eakins went to Paris) and spent the remainder of his life in Italy.

A third example is the forgotten William Brooke Thomas Trego (1859-1909), a pupil of Eakins at the Academy 1879-1882, then of Fleury and Bouguereau in Paris. Trego was so crippled that he could only hold his brush between the palms of his hands, moving it by moving his whole body. In spite of, or perhaps because of his physical limitations, he became a painter of dramatic battle scenes, and did for the Civil War what Remington was later to do for the Indian campaigns of the great plains.

A different development of this ruthlessly factual imagination was a Philadelphia school of still life, led by William M. Harnett, whose rediscovery has been one of the adventures of modern art criticism. I call it the Philadelphia school of still life, because, so far as it has a source in tradition, it grew out of the still-life style of the Peales and out of the wordless, instinctive love of fact, Dutch in its unspoken intensity, which formed the atmosphere of the city.

William Michael Harnett (1848-1892) was brought from Ireland to Philadelphia at the age of one year. He began at seventeen to learn the engraver's trade and supported himself by engraving silver in Philadelphia and New York until the age of twenty-seven. He also studied drawing in night classes, first at the Pennsylvania Academy of the Fine Arts, later in New York city at the National Academy of Design and Cooper Union. He turned to oil paint only in 1875 and when, in the following year, a depression in the silver engraver's trade threw him out of work, he went back to Philadelphia and took up painting still life as a career. The still lifes of his first period (Philadelphia, 1876-1880) derive in style from the pictures done by James and Raphaelle Peale fifty years before, but are harder and more illusionistic in approach. They are tight, dry little compositions of objects piled at the edge of a table, like the Peale still lifes in composition, but notable for a personal choice of subjects: the smoking scene still life (built around a pipe, beer mug, and newspaper); the writing table still life (books, papers, and quill pen the principal elements); and *trompe l'œil* paintings of paper money (old, worn bills of American paper money of the Civil War period, whose worthlessness is indicated by the name "shinplaster" popularly applied to them). These pictures sold well enough to enable him, after four years, to make the trip abroad that was then the goal of every American art student. Harnett lived in Europe six years (1880-1886), chiefly in Munich, and supported himself by his painting. The interests of contemporary European painting affected him little. There is evidence in his work that he admired Meissonier; he acquired a taste for gaudy Munich bric-a-brac; and, more happily, he learned a richer, more painterly use of his medium by studying the seventeenth-century Dutch.

When he returned to America, he settled in New York city. In this last period (1886-1892) he returned again to his own themes of simple, humble, everyday things: but with a difference. Now he was a master of luminosities and textures, which he could sustain with remarkable intensity throughout compositions of great size, up to nearly six feet by four in dimension (Plate XIV).

Sometimes the major works of his last period are compositions in depth; *The Magic Flute* (1887) (collection John S. Newberry, Jr., Detroit) is an example. More often, they were *trompe l'œil* compositions of objects hanging on a painted, wooden door: *The Old Violin* (1886) (collection Mrs. Charles F. Williams, Cincinnati); *The Faithful Colt* (1890) (Hartford, Wadsworth Atheneum); or, *Old Models* (1892) (Boston, Museum of Fine Arts) are characteristic and famous. These pictures are painted with such love for the objects represented and such delight in the process of painting that the exhilaration in the painter's heart gives them not only a convincing life but a haunting mood of mystery and joy.[4]

John F. Peto (1854-1907), Harnett's friend and disciple, made still life a gentle poem on the "fantasticality of the commonplace and the pathos of the discarded," to use Frankenstein's happy phrase. His youth was spent in Philadelphia where Harnett was the strongest formative influence upon him. (Apparently they knew each other well before Harnett left Philadelphia for Europe.) The better part of his life, from 1889 to 1907, was lived in a little summer resort, Island Heights, on the seacoast of New Jersey. There Peto gradually lost touch with the world of art and, long before his death, was so completely forgotten that Harnett's name was forged upon many of his best canvases. His very name disappeared until Alfred Frankenstein, beginning a study of Harnett in 1947, discovered, to the surprise of everyone, another artist in total eclipse behind Harnett.[5]

Peto took over Harnett's concentration upon still life and many of his motifs; but his temperament was very different. His individual style matured in the eighties and nineties. It is based upon harmonies of softly muted luminosities; but his work is neither so lustrous nor so forceful as Harnett's, gentler, more atmospheric, and more relaxed. Peto is uneven in quality, as one would expect from his long isolation; yet his best works, like *The Poor Man's*

---

[4] The essential study of Harnett and his school is Alfred Frankenstein, *After the Hunt, William Harnett and Other American Still-Life Painters, 1870-1900*, Berkeley, University of California Press, 1953.

[5] The story of this scholarly detective work is told fully in *After the Hunt*.

Store (Fig. 136) (1885) or *After Night's Study* (The Detroit Institute of Arts), have a touching and appealing quality that is indescribable, since it is a purely visual sentiment. If Harnett is a master of textures, Peto is a poet of soft, dusky luminosities.

A third notable figure in this school of still life was John Haberle (1856-1933). Unlike Harnett and Peto, he was not a Philadelphian; he was born and spent his life in New Haven, Connecticut, where, before becoming a painter, he worked as a preparator on the staff of the great paleontologist, O. C. Marsh. Mr. Frankenstein has found no evidence that he made scientific drawings for Marsh; yet scientific precision and objective reality inform his work as an artist. Haberle was the greatest illusionist, the most uncanny prestidigitator in *trompe l'œil* effects, of this generation of still-life painters. He is famous for his skillful *trompe l'œils* of paper money and other compositions using scraps of paper. His most ambitious work is a picture of the fireplace of an old-fashioned farmhouse. Logs burning and kettles boiling on the hearth, the mantel breast above is crowded with the souvenirs of the generations who have lived in the house. It is the largest *trompe l'œil* of the school: eight feet high, five and a half feet wide. Called *Grandma's Hearthstone* (Fig. 137) (1890) (The Detroit Institute of Arts), it occupied Haberle for two years of work; involved transporting the fireplace and the surrounding section of wall from an old Massachusetts farmhouse to Haberle's studio in New Haven; and is a singular performance in every way. Such bravura represents, however, the taste of an exacting and ambitious patron who ordered the picture; Haberle's own taste is shown by his small, amusing, illusionistic tricks.

There were a large number of lesser still-life painters working around these men. The most interesting artistically are:

J. D. Chalfant (1856-1931), a cabinetmaker turned painter; he lived in Wilmington, Delaware, and did his best work in the eighties, following Harnett closely.

George W. Platt (1839-1899), son of a picture framer in Rochester, New York, was a draughtsman on geological expeditions in the Rockies and western plains; studied at the Pennsylvania Academy in the seventies, in Munich, and in Italy; and painted pictures in Chicago and Denver in the last two decades of the century.

Richard LaBarre Goodwin (1840-1910), a wandering portrait painter in western New York State, was inspired by Harnett's *After the Hunt* (1886) to emulate him: in the nineties and the first decade of this century he was perpetually on the move through the western part of the United States, painting portraits and large, illusionistic still lifes based upon Harnett's "cabin door" motive.

George Cope (1855-1929) spent his life in West Chester, a few miles outside Philadelphia. His art was based upon Harnett's; he carried the illusionistic style into the new century (as late as the nineteen-twenties when this type of painting was totally outmoded) and died poor and neglected.

The still-life painters of this movement spoke only the language of the eye. No critic, or wit, or other interpreter put into words what they were trying to do. In their own time they were neglected by sophisticated taste. Harnett and some of the other still-life painters sold their work at good prices to saloonkeepers or to unpretentious businessmen who enjoyed their pictures for their subject matter. Their patrons were outside the polite world of art, which considered their illusionism vulgar.

The Paris-schooled men were all trained as figure painters, yet one finds among them surprisingly little genre painting showing a shrewd eye or affectionate feeling for the life of their own country. Perhaps it was the fault of the cult of estheticism, persuading them that nothing in life was worth representing except the purely esthetic, that kept them from applying their observation to their own country, as the Impressionists did to Paris. Perhaps, as Isham suggested, the enormous fashion for the French, German, and Dutch nineteenth-century genre painters, whose works filled the New York dealers' galleries and were bought greedily at fantastic prices, made it impossible for the Americans to sell their work.

One has to turn to the magazine illustrations of the eighties and nineties to find a flourishing and popular art of observation of American life. Indeed, the story of objective realism would be incomplete without some account of the development of illustration, for the painter-illustrator was one of its distinctive features, and magazine illustration formed one of its most important points of contact with the public. Some of the painters already discussed were illustrators. Others, like Edwin A. Abbey, Howard Pyle, A. B. Frost, C. S. Reinhart, and Frederic Remington, applying the atmospheric technique of objective realism to magazine illustration, made the last quarter of the nineteenth century the golden age of this branch of American art.

Until the later 1870's the best wood block reproductions are to be found in books; the monthly magazines contain little of interest. *Harper's Weekly* was the leading illustrated periodical, publishing the work of Winslow Homer, Thomas Nast, Sol Eytinge, Jr., W. L. Sheppard, A. R. Waud, and Augustus Hoppin, but its wood block reproductions were, as has been said, coarse and hasty. Winslow Homer learned to draw with such largeness that his work came through the process fairly well.

But the man who seems to have been born for this period and medium was Thomas Nast (1840-1902), a child of German liberal refugees from Germany, who went to work at fifteen as an illustrator for *Frank Leslie's Illustrated Newspaper*. Nast learned his trade at work and by looking at the great English illustrators, Leech, Keene, and Tenniel. He found his true role during the Civil War and his true medium in *Harper's Weekly*. He joined that periodical as staff artist in the summer of 1862 and for many years thereafter he and *Harper's Weekly* were almost synonymous. The imaginative and enlightened Fletcher Harper saw Nast's natural gift and encouraged him to become an artist of ideas rather than an illustrator of events. Nast supported the Union cause with such fire that toward the end of the war Lincoln is reported to have said: "Thomas Nast has been our best recruiting sergeant." After the war, following his own inclinations and those of the editors, Fletcher Harper and George William Curtis, he made the magazine a strong liberal and reform influence. He found his mature graphic style in 1869, when he began to draw with a pencil instead of a brush. Pencil gave a hard, incisive line, easy for the wood engraver to reproduce, and perfect for the harsh, urgent eloquence of his ideas. His fierce attacks upon the corrupt "Tweed Ring" in New York city politics were perhaps the most effective editorial cartoons ever known in America; certainly they were the first to impress the whole nation and have never been surpassed in vitriolic intensity (Fig. 139). Nast was not only eloquent; he created types which have become lasting symbols: the Tammany tiger, the Republican elephant, the Democratic donkey, and other images of his invention are still alive today.

Nast left *Harper's Weekly* in 1886 when their editorial policy no longer gave him the freedom he required; thereafter, although he continued to work for various papers, his great days were over. Most of his life's savings were lost in the failure of the firm of Grant and Ward and he fell on evil days. In 1902 Theodore Roosevelt appointed the old man United States Consul at Guayaquil, Ecuador, where he succumbed to the climate within a few months. But between 1862 and 1886 Nast lifted his branch of American graphic art, the political cartoon, to a new level of influence and importance.

Toward the close of the seventies, the monthly magazines took the lead in the field of illustration. The short-lived *Appleton's Journal* (1869-1881), in which many of the illustrations of *Picturesque America* first appeared, was the first to set a new standard. Harry Fenn (1845-1911), a discovery of Appleton's, showed himself particularly skillful in landscape illustration. But on the editorial side it was Alexander W. Drake (1843-1916), art editor of *Scribner's Monthly Household Magazine* in the seventies and (after the name and ownership of the magazine were changed in 1881) of the *Century Magazine* and *St. Nicholas*, who exerted the greatest influence in raising American illustration to a new level. The illustrators had already begun to work in an atmospheric, luminous style. The engravers had been experimenting with means of rendering lights and broad tones and in 1877 there was perfected a style that made it possible to render the most subtle nuances of the painter's atmospheric tones. In the black-line engraving, forms were defined by the black ink line (made by the raised wood surface) against the white tone of the paper (where the wood block had been cut away). The new style was called the *white-line*, in contrast to the older *black-line* wood engraving. It abandoned the definition of form for a free creation of tone by using white lines, flocks or dots to suggest the painter's atmospheric colors and gradations of tone. Linton, in his *History of Wood-Engraving in America*, claims to have done white-line engravings for gift books issued by Scribner and Company as early as 1868-1870; [6] but some believe he exaggerated his own part in the change of style. Timothy Cole, afterward the most famous engraver of the new school, considered his unsigned engraving of *The Gillie Boy*, from a wash drawing by James E. Kelly, in *Scribner's Monthly*, August, 1877, the first woodcut executed completely in the new manner; however, F. Juengling, working on other illustrations by Kelly at the same time deserves perhaps as much credit. Kelly, afterwards a sculptor but at this time an illustrator and studio-mate of E. A. Abbey, had submitted to Drake some spirited wash drawings. Drake insisted that his engravers find a way to render every touch of Kelly's brush, rejecting Juengling's first plate and demanding that he cut a new block in search of perfect reproduction. The new style, once found, made possible the most brilliant period of American illustration, which lasted from 1877 until the literary monthlies were driven out of the field by a cheaper mass journalism at the end of the century.

Only a few illustrators can be mentioned out of the crowd of able men at work in the period. In the seventies C. S. Reinhart (1844-1896) was chief of the school. Trained in Munich, he returned to New York in 1870, just at the beginning of the great period; later he lived for a long time in Paris. He was an excellent draughtsman; had a good sense of character (the lack of which is the illustrator's most common weakness); and was successful also as an illustrator of travel books, such as George P. Lathrop's *Spanish Vistas* (1883), and Charles Dudley Warner's *Their Pilgrimage* (1887), a book on American watering places.

Arthur B. Frost (1851-1928) was a pupil of Eakins. He went to work for *Harper's* and, like Abbey, went to England in 1877. But he returned the next year: his talent and sympathies were so entirely American that England meant nothing to him. Frost was a keen observer and had a droll sense of comedy. His special gift was for drawing American rural life, showing a fidelity and freshness that retain their flavor instead of fading with the passage of time as so many clever illustrations do (Fig. 138). His best known illustrations are for stories by Mark Twain, Frank R. Stockton, and Joel Chandler Harris. For the last named he was the perfect illustrator, giving a wholly satisfying visual form to Uncle Remus and his genial world of animals, for Frost was endowed with both a gift of character and a gift of comedy.

In the eighties the great names were Edwin Austin Abbey and Howard Pyle. Both, however, were masters of the historical imagination and will be discussed in the next chapter.

[6] Linton, *op.cit.*, p. 37.

Then there was Frederic Remington (1861-1909) who made himself the recorder of the old West, of the open range, the cowboys, and the Plains Indians. Remington loved the out of doors and drew it with feeling and enthusiasm. He had also a most exact and conscientious sense of fact: if he painted a Sioux or an Apache, he really was a Sioux or Apache, not just "an Indian." His defect lay in his color sense, which was crude and raw. He is at his best in black-and-white (or in bronze, for he was also a clever and popular sculptor) rather than in his paintings.

Another of Drake's illustrators on the *Century* list was Joseph Pennell (1860-1926), famous for his bitter tongue (he left the Pennsylvania Academy, however, because he resented Eakins' trenchant tongue), whom Drake sent to Italy in 1883 to do the drawings for W. D. Howells' *Tuscan Cities*. From 1884 to 1912 Pennell made London his home. He was an ardent American, but his commissions were all for European subjects and he could not afford constant travel back and forth across the ocean. He and his wife, Elizabeth Robins Pennell, collaborated on many books of travel; Whistler chose them to write his biography. Pennell was a pen-and-ink draughtsman and etcher until 1895, when he became interested in lithography. Its soft granular blacks, which seemed to him an ideal medium for smoke or steam or industrial subjects, led him to visit the Panama Canal in 1912 (his lithographs of it appeared as *The Wonder of Work*, 1916) and then to settle again in America; thereafter he devoted himself to interpreting his native land. Pennell was, if not the first to observe, perhaps the most effective popularizer of the themes of American skyscrapers, New York harbor, and giant industry (Fig. 146).

Finally, one should mention the appearance of a fresh graphic humor in Peter Newell (1862-1924). His gently fantastic imagination might be called the first American appearance of the gentle humor of the absurd, which *The New Yorker* has subsequently developed to such a high point. Seeing one of his children looking at a book upside down, Peter Newell got the idea for his first book, *Topsys and Turvys* (1893), consisting of drawings which could be looked at either right side up or upside down; this was followed by *The Hole Book* (1908), *The Slant Book* (1910), and other works whose droll fancy can still give much pleasure.

There are also a few painters of easel pictures who belong in spirit to the illustrators. E. L. Henry (1841-1919) is one of this category. He was trained as a painter at the Pennsylvania Academy, and in Paris at Suisse's and under Gleyre and Courbet, yet he learned none of the French richness of pigments. His use of oil is drily naturalistic. His great interest and the source of his popularity in his own lifetime were in his ability to re-create the past of America in historical scenes of the eighteenth and early nineteenth centuries. Today we are apt to value more highly his studies from life, done on Long Island or in the Catskills around his summer home at Ellenville, which, though hard in style, still please by their homely fidelity.

Fidelity is also the word for the marine painter, Seth Arca Whipple (1855/56-1901) of Detroit, the son of a ship captain on the Great Lakes. He painted the Lakes and especially the ships that sailed or steamed through the famous strait of Detroit with the affectionate truthfulness demanded by his audience of ship owners and builders. But Whipple was not a naïve painter like the Bards. He used the atmospheric style of his time with a real if modest sensibility.

A faithful naturalism also marks the work of Conrad Wise Chapman (1842-1913), son and pupil of the romantic painter, John Gadsby Chapman. A fiery southern partisan, when the Civil War broke out Chapman returned from Italy to fight for the Confederacy. While on duty at Charleston he painted a series of small, precise, luminous sketches of great interest, now preserved in the Valentine Museum, Richmond. After the war he was "unreconstructed" and lived a long time in Italy and Mexico (where he painted some panoramic landscapes in the manner of the great Mexican landscapist Velasco) before returning as an old man to die in Virginia.

These independents all used light as a medium; yet they are not Impressionists. Homer's images of roaring seas or northern forests were constructed in light and a rich chromatic scale of tone. Light burns duskily like an inner radiance in Eakins' warm, shadowy canvases; shines from Harnett's lamps and tin horns and sheets of music; glows from the soft paint of Peto's innocent inventions. But unlike the painters of Paris (and those who followed them), these independents never sacrificed resonance of tone to brilliance of hue: their palettes kept the broad scale of light and dark that the old masters had shown (and, indeed, all Western painting down to 1860). Their pictures, hung among the French or American Impressionists, seem almost as warm and deep-toned as those of the seventeenth century. To their own time, which identified modernity with bright, blonde color, their depth of tone was a grievous fault; so was their lack of the clever, sweeping brush stroke, so much admired in Sargent, Boldini, and Zorn. Compared to the suavity and sweetness of the American Impressionists, their style seemed rugged, harsh, displeasing. They might have said, in the words of Edward Hopper, that what they were interested in was *an art of intense reality*. But intense reality was disagreeable. Only in magazine illustration was an intense interest in subject matter allowable: there it did not seem to conflict with the fashionable avoidance of anything but the esthetic in life. Even today the independents' works are too dark, too sober, too rough; above all, too real for conventional tastes, and their fame has never spread beyond the United States. But with time the force of their achievement has made itself felt. Winslow Homer and Thomas Eakins are now accepted as two of the greatest names in our art.

CHAPTER 12

THE WORLD OF HISTORY, MEMORY, AND DREAM

IDEALISM, THE APPEAL OF THE UNIVERSAL IN THOUGHT AND THE GENERALIZED in feeling, did not altogether disappear during the decades of objective realism. The other side of our minds may retire into the shadow when the shining globe of consciousness revolves, but it always exists: the dreamers exist in a period of realism, the realists in a period of idealism, each playing their part in the infinitely complex flow of Western culture.

It is striking, in fact, to see what tremendous effort was put forward in the last three decades of the nineteenth century by thinkers, artists, scholars, religious leaders in every country of the West, to find a new form of ideal thought or rekindle an old one. In every country there were painters who strove to create a monumental and ideal art on the model of the great mural cycles of the fourteenth and fifteenth centuries; there were other brooding, meditative artists, in whom we can find the origins of the subjective and expressionist tendencies which burst into life early in the twentieth century. In America there are three important figures of this later idealism: LaFarge, who made the old imagery of classical and Christian culture live again and founded a new enthusiasm for mural decoration; Ryder, who created an ideal world out of his dreams; and Vedder, who created a strange kind of ancient mythology all his own.

Although the second half of the nineteenth century saw such spectacular advances made by the physical sciences, that, if there had been war between science and religion, one might expect science to have driven its antagonist from the field, the same period saw a striking growth of the more mystical and liturgical Christian churches, notably the Roman Catholic and Episcopal. If someone may object that the first was largely fed by immigration, this was not true of the second which, from a disorganized and unpopular group after the Revolution, rose to a strong, wealthy denomination in the late nineteenth century, actively building churches and cathedrals and offering the best

American artists a new opportunity for monumental art. Also, as the population grew and early governmental buildings were outgrown, a whole series
of new federal, state, county and city buildings were erected. The desire for
monumental decoration, which began with the churches, widened to include
these governmental structures and other new architectural expressions of the
community such as the public library, the art gallery, the university. If this
movement degenerated at the end into insipid sentimentality in men like
Blashfield and Kenyon Cox and is today largely ignored or discounted, it
seemed at the time one of the serious and hopeful movements of American art;
and I believe it was.

The great figure of this movement was John LaFarge. LaFarge was an
artist with a mind: his art is the expression of a wide-ranging, acute, and
subtle intelligence. He is one of the remarkable group of the friends of Henry
Adams (with whom he traveled to the Orient and the South Seas in 1886)
which included, besides LaFarge: H. H. Richardson, the architect; Augustus
Saint-Gaudens, the sculptor; John Hay, the statesman. Adams, the philosopher of the group, has given in his writings (*The Education of Henry Adams*,
1907, and *Mont-Saint-Michel and Chartres*, 1904) an acute analysis of the
dilemma of minds born to deal with life in terms of ideas and ethics, who
found themselves living in the United States of the reconstruction period. The
tide was setting strongly against them: it was the age of the mechanistic philosophy of Herbert Spencer and the materialistic determinism of Marx; of the
cynical power-worship of Bismarck; the corruption of American civic and
national life. Adams' *Education* offers a picture of a philosophic mind finding
eighteenth-century rational humanism ineffective to explain such a world, in
search of a new philosophy. He speculated with two hypotheses—that the
development of life was governed by the mechanical principles of science
(the second law of thermodynamics) or by the power of emotion (the Virgin of *Mont-Saint-Michel and Chartres*). But what ground was there to stand
on to relate these two? At the end he seems to have remained an agnostic.

Adams gives a vast, discursive, subtle panorama of the spiritual dilemma
of his age, yet he throws over it a somewhat misleading air of artificiality
and frustration. He himself saw only the decadence of all he believed in and
failed to find another positive philosophy to take its place. Yet when one
looks at the artists of his circle, it is evident that they were anything but
frustrated or decadent. Never have American artists of major talent had
greater influence or occupied a greater national position than did they.

John LaFarge (1835-1910) was one of the old New York French colony: his father, an officer in Napoleon's army, was a refugee from Santo
Domingo; his mother was the daughter of Binsse de Saint-Victor, a refugee
from the Terror. Though passionately American, he was also proud of his
French heritage; growing up as the child of two traditions prepared him
later to have a sense of kinship with all culture. His family sent him to Eu-

rope in 1856 to become acquainted with his French relatives, the Saint-Victors. There he saw something of French painting: he met Chassériau and spent a few weeks drawing in Couture's studio, more with the idea of enriching his education than of studying professionally. It was after his return to America that, under the influence of William Morris Hunt, he turned to painting as a profession.

His first efforts show the strong vein of naturalism that ran through his life's work. He began as an independent, intensely faithful observer of nature and of light. Of *Paradise Valley, Newport* (ca.1866-1868) (Miss Mary B. Lothrop), the most important of these early studies, he said, "I wished to apply principles of light and color of which I had learned a little. I wished my studies from nature . . . to be free from *recipes*, and to indicate very carefully in every part, the exact time of day and circumstance of light." This faithfulness to an exact moment and place gives the picture its character: it is a portrait of the unity of light flooding a little featureless hollow among the moor-like fields near Newport. He painted other landscapes; did book illustrations; made studies of flowers, curiously real and curiously poetic at the same time; and still lifes, like the *Greek Love Token* (Fig. 141) (1866) (Washington, National Collections of Fine Arts), which have the factual mystery of a *trompe l'œil*.

It was H. H. Richardson, the great pioneer architect, who plunged him headlong into mural painting. Richardson settled in Boston at a time when New England was turning away from the austere tradition of its past. The passionate eagerness with which Mrs. Jack Gardner collected the art of the most splendid, the most articulate, and most mystical of centuries, Byzantine, Gothic, Renaissance, Baroque, is a symptom of the thirst with which the descendants of the Puritans now turned to the past for something of splendor and mystery to feed their souls. Richardson's rich, massive, vital, monumental architecture was the first great artistic expression of the new spirit. Buildings like Trinity Church, Boston, are creations of such emotional warmth that organic decoration in sculpture and mural painting was necessary to give them completeness. With acute discernment, Richardson turned to John La-Farge to decorate the great somber inner space of Trinity Church. The problem was to create an atmosphere of solemnity, which would wipe away the everyday mood from those entering and prepare the mind for meditation and worship. LaFarge rose to the challenge. With little time or preparation, he and a group of young assistants produced the first artistically successful treatment of a great interior by an American painter.[1] The completion of these decorations on January 13, 1876, marks the beginning of the second great wave of mural painting in America.

The walls of Trinity seem, however, but a beginning compared with

[1] Francis Lathrop was LaFarge's chief helper. Lathrop, Millet, Maynard, and Kenyon Cox, among other helpers, later became mural painters themselves.

some of his later work: the *Athens* (Fig. 142) in the Walker Art Gallery, Bowdoin College (1898); the *Ascension* in the Church of the Ascension, New York city; the *Four Aspects of the Law* in the Supreme Court Chamber of the Minnesota State Capitol; or the lunettes of the *Law Givers* in the Baltimore Court House. LaFarge was a colorist. Instead of following the example of Puvis de Chavannes, who toned down the richness of oil colors with white in order to emulate the flat, cool effect of mediaeval frescoes, LaFarge worked his way to the same conclusion as Delacroix, that mural painting should be fully realized in form and in luminous, atmospheric color. American painting thus returned once more to the example of the Venetians.

Mural decoration differs from easel painting not only in scale but in purpose. It is a *public* art: that is, its measure of success is not that it expresses the artist's personal feelings well but that it embodies a subject of general interest and an emotion that has meaning for all. The late nineteenth century lacked the common faith that had given the mediaeval artists their themes; it lacked the education in classical literature that furnished the imagery of the Baroque. LaFarge was nevertheless remarkably successful in choosing out of the growing sense of world culture in his age vivid images from the poetry of Greece and Rome, from the Bible, from the history of Europe and of Asia, and making these seem both effective and convincing.

His weakness was a naturalism, in harmony with his time, that made him approach these themes with a factual technique: there is often a certain fussy insistence on small detail, in draperies and accessories, that is disturbing. He thus reveals in his own way the conflicting ideal and factual tendencies of his age, with which Henry Adams was struggling. He is an uneven artist; sometimes greatly successful, sometimes failing lamentably. But in the best of his murals LaFarge achieved a noble solemnity and great richness of feeling.

He was unique, moreover, in his sense of ensemble. At Trinity Church, Boston, he did a whole interior. Next he did the chancel of St. Thomas' Church in New York city, an ensemble of stained glass, painting, carving, and inlay; the reredos was a high relief by Saint-Gaudens, on either side of which were two large paintings by LaFarge. He consciously revived the workshop tradition of the arts, employing many young artists as well as artisans; he was both able and prepared to execute anything from a large altarpiece for a church to the decoration of a music room for Mr. Whitelaw Reid (with two large paintings by the head of the workshop) or of an interior for Mrs. Cornelius Vanderbilt without paintings.

Yet it is perhaps not in these works on a great scale—portentous though they were—but in his small studies and drawings that one comes closest to the complex, subtle, and reflective mind that fascinated Henry Adams (Fig. 145).

About the time of the completion of Trinity Church, he began experimenting also with stained glass, which became in his hands a second, more

Fig. 146. Joseph Pennell: *Riveters at Night, Detroit* (lithograph, 1917). (Courtesy of the Library of Congress.)

Fig. 147. Howard Pyle: *Merry Robin Stops a Stranger in Scarlet*. (From *The Merry Adventures of Robin Hood*, Charles Scribner's Sons, 1883.)

333

Fig. 148. John Sloan: *The Wake of the Ferry*
(1907). (Courtesy of the Phillips Collection,
Washington, D.C.)

Opposite page, bottom: Fig. 150. Jerome
Myers: *The Children's Theatre*. (Courtesy
of The Detroit Institute of Arts.)

Fig. 149. Maurice Prendergast: *The East River* (1901). (Courtesy of The Museum of Modern Art, New York, gift of Mrs. John D. Rockefeller, Jr.)

Fig. 151. William J. Glackens: *Chez Mouquin* (1905). (Courtesy of The Art Institute of Chicago, Friends of American
Art.)

Opposite page, bottom: Fig. 153. Louis
Michel Eilshemius: *Niagara Falls*. (Private Collection, Detroit.)

Fig. 152. George Wesley Bellows: *Introducing John L. Sullivan.* (Courtesy of Mr. and Mrs. John Hay Whitney, New York.)

Fig. 154. Rockwell Kent: *Horn Island*. (From *Voyaging Southward from the Strait of Magellan*, G. P. Putnam's Sons, 1924.)

Fig. 155. Arthur B. Davies: *Along the Erie Canal*. (Courtesy of the Phillips Collection, Washington, D.C.)

Fig. 156. John Marin: *Maine Islands* (1922).
(Courtesy of the Phillips Collection, Washington, D.C.)

Fig. 157. John Marin: *Sea Piece* (1951). (Courtesy of Mr. and Mrs. Lawrence A. Fleischman, Detroit.)

Fig. 158. Charles Demuth: *Acrobats* (1919). (Courtesy of The Museum of Modern Art, New York, gift of Mrs. John D. Rockefeller, Jr.)

Opposite page, top: Fig. 160. Marsden Hartley: *Log Jam, Penobscot Bay*. (Courtesy of The Detroit Institute of Arts.)

Fig. 159. Georgia O'Keeffe: *American Radiator Building*. (Courtesy of the Stieglitz Collection, Fisk University, Nashville, Tennessee.)

Below: Fig. 161. Charles Sheeler:
Modern Classic (1931). (Courtesy
of Mrs. Edsel B. Ford, Detroit.)

Fig. 162. Joseph Stella: *The Bridge* (1920-1922). (Courtesy of The Newark Museum.)

Fig. 164. Stuart Davis: *Garage
Lights* (1931). (Courtesy of The
Rochester Memorial Art Gallery.)

Fig. 165. Ivan LeLoraine Albright:
*That Which I Should Have Done I
Did Not Do* (1941). (Courtesy of
The Art Institute of Chicago.)

Fig. 166. Charles Burchfield: *The Sphinx and the Milky Way* (1946). (Munson-Williams-Proctor Institute, Utica, N. Y.)

Fig. 167. Mark Tobey: *San Francisco Street* (1941). (Courtesy of The Detroit Institute of Arts.)

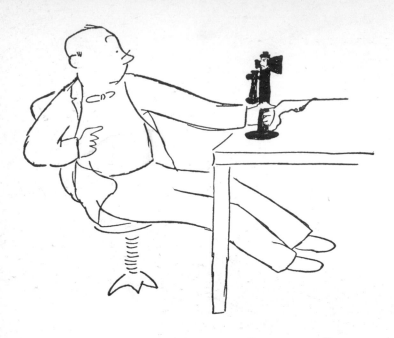

Fig. 168. James Thurber: *Psychiatrist about to Phone his Wife.* (From *Let Your Mind Alone!* Harper & Brothers, 1937.)

Fig. 170. Grant Wood: *American Gothic* (1930). (Courtesy of The Art Institute of Chicago.)

Opposite page, bottom: Fig. 169. Franklin C. Watkins: *Thomas Raeburn White* (1940). (Courtesy of Mr. and Mrs. Thomas Raeburn White, Penllyn, Pennsylvania.)

Plate XV. Albert P. Ryder: *The Tempest*. (Courtesy of The Detroit Institute of Arts.)

specialized form of mural painting. Noticing the iridescence on a commercial soap dish, he thought that there must be qualities of reflected and shimmering color in glass that had not yet been realized. From this suggestion sprang his own experiments. As he succeeded, and his colored glass became more and more a splendid and diffused richness, he eliminated the leads as far as possible, so that the whole window becomes a composition in the glow of light. His glass was a personal achievement. No one else could handle it with artistic success; and he left no successors, unless one can call Tiffany glass such.

LaFarge was also an articulate artist and set a high standard both as writer and lecturer. He was a man of great culture, experience, and sympathy; no one, perhaps, represents the breadth of interest and of inspiration of the period with greater dignity.

Albert Pinkham Ryder (1847-1917) lived in a world as private and enclosed as that of LaFarge was spacious. Born in New Bedford, Massachusetts, he had the sea in his background; but when he was twenty-one, his family moved to New York. He studied with a romantic painter, William E. Marshall, and in 1871 at the National Academy of Design; but he was essentially a self-taught artist, developing his own style from his experience as a painter of decorative screens and lacquers; and his own imaginative world out of his walks at night about New York, his memories of the sea, his love of music. In the midst of New York city he lived the life of a solitary, his studio a picturesque confusion of dusty piles of newspapers and magazines, empty cereal boxes, dishes, and an accumulation of rubbish that left only a path from the door to his easel and chair—a studio that has become a legend. His art matured slowly. He exhibited at the National Academy of Design first in 1873, and from 1878 to 1887 in the Society of American Artists also, but without attracting much attention. It was Daniel Cottier, the picture dealer, who first recognized the distinction of his work and interested a few collectors, notably Col. C. E. S. Wood, Thomas B. Clarke, and Sir William Van Horne. In 1893 Cottier the picture dealer, Olin Warner the sculptor, and Ryder went abroad together. Ryder did not enjoy travel; of the European galleries he said only, "We all like our own songs the best." He preferred to walk by the sea on Cape Cod or in Central Park at night; it is said that he made several voyages to London and back with a sea captain friend, only to stay on deck all night long to watch the moonlight and moving water. His most productive years were from about 1880 to 1900. After this he tended to work over his old pictures, repainting and altering, not always for the better. His production was small, approximately one hundred and fifty works (there came later to be ten times as many forgeries as originals) and of these only a small number can be said to represent him at his best.

Yet Ryder has come to have a great position in American art. The brooding, dreaming element which runs through our imaginative life—in All-s̤on and Hawthorne, Whistler and Poe, Page and Emerson—found exceptional expression in his few, small, eloquent pictures with their pigment like warm enamel in which a soft light seems to linger.

In a famous letter to a friend he described his own art:

Have you ever seen an inch worm crawl up a leaf or twig, and then clinging to the very end, revolve in the air, feeling for something to reach something? Thats like me. I am trying to find something out there beyond the place on which I have a footing.

This sense of eloquent mystery fills even his pictures which are based most directly on nature, like *The Dead Bird* (Phillips Memorial Gallery, Washington) or *The Hunter's Rest* (collection Mr. and Mrs. Lawrence A. Fleischman, Detroit); it is embodied also in the dramatic visionary pictures drawn from Shakespeare or Wagner, *The Tempest* (Plate XV) (The Detroit Institute of Arts), *Macbeth and the Witches* (Phillips Memorial Gallery, Washington), *Siegfried and the Rhine Maidens* (Fig. 143) (Washington, National Gallery of Art, Mellon Collection); it haunts his images of a boat flying over the moonlit waves of the sea. These pictures form a silent commentary upon the torrent of ambition and pleasure, power and material wealth, that roared about his studio on Fifteenth Street in New York; for him, it had only this meaning.

Elihu Vedder (1836-1923) was a descendant of the early Dutch settlers of the Hudson Valley; his family were of old Dutch stock from Schenectady, although the artist was born in New York city. He studied painting with Tompkins H. Matteson, the genre painter, in Sherbourne, New York, and with Picot in Paris. It is impossible to find any relation between either of these teachers and his later development. After living abroad in Paris, 1856-1861, he returned to New York city. The Civil War occupied all minds. He found it impossible to sell serious work and existed by doing hack work—comic valentines, sketches for *Vanity Fair*, diagrams of dumbbell exercises for a teacher of calisthenics. (The standard of comic valentines must have fallen off sadly when Vedder went back to Europe.) It was while doing this potboiling, living in a room on Beekman Street, that he conceived the strange, haunting ideas which he embodied in *The Questioner of the Sphinx* (1863) (Boston, Museum of Fine Arts), *The Lair of the Sea Serpent* (Fig. 144) (1864) (Boston, Museum of Fine Arts), *The Lost Mind* (1864-1865) (The Metropolitan Museum of Art). These are all storytelling pictures; and storytelling is out of fashion today. But they reveal a strange mind at work, a power of imagination capable of conceiving most unexpected and haunting images.

In 1866 he was able to return to Europe and settled in Rome, which became his home from 1867 until his death in 1923. He liked to roam about in the remote villages of the Campagna and the mountains. Some of his best works are small landscape sketches done on these expeditions, warm, dusky little pictures, painted in tone and simple, luminous colors, like an early Corot. He continued to paint imaginative fantasies, like the *Ideal Head* (Fig. 140) (1872), the *Cumaean Sibyl* (1876) (Wellesley College Art Museum), or *The Pleiades* (1885) (The Metropolitan Museum of Art), of an eloquent strangeness, although his style gradually changed. His later paintings are notable for their intricate and very interesting movement of line; but his color becomes chalky, pale, and ultimately very bleak. The masterpiece of his later style is, in fact, not a painting at all, but a series of more than fifty black-and-white illustrations for the *Rubáiyát of Omar Khayyam* (1884). During the enthusiasm in the nineties for mural painting he turned to that field, doing a large lunette, *Rome* (1894), in the Walker Art Gallery, Bowdoin College; and five wall paintings and a mosaic (1896 and 1897), for the Library of Congress, Washington. By this time, however, his style had become a cold, repellent mannerism; and these late works created a distaste for his work that has injured his reputation and concealed his real significance.

Vedder was a literary artist. His mind was intellectual rather than sensuous. The ancient mysteries and terrors which he imagined, or the melancholy hedonism and exotic splendor of the *Rubáiyát*, which were so congenial to his temperament, presented themselves to him in clear, intellectual images; they are unlike either the neurotic expressionism of our time or the world of shadows one finds in Ryder. He fits into no category and has therefore been ignored; but he is a master of subject matter, in a vein entirely his own.

In addition to these three there were a few other artists born to deal with general ideas or subjective images. Albert Blakelock (1847-1919), painter of woodland sunsets and trees silhouetted in the moonlight, was a painter of pictorial ideas rather than of observation. His work is kept alive by his tragic story. Able to sell his work only with the greatest difficulty, he was treated with such callous brutality by an art dealer who wished to beat down his price that he went mad and was put into an asylum for the last twenty years before his death; almost as soon as he became insane his pictures began to bring high prices, without any benefit to the poor, mad painter in his cell or to his poverty-stricken wife and children.

Henry O. Tanner (1859-1937), a Negro pupil of Eakins, who preferred to live in Paris to escape the prejudices of his own countrymen, was a painter of deep and eloquent religious feeling, as may be seen by his *Annunciation* (1895) (Philadelphia Museum of Art, The Wilstach Collection).

Abbott Thayer (1849-1921) was famous, in the nineties, for the virginal purity of his white-robed women. He expressed a mood of rapturous idealization of women which placed them symbolically on an angelic pedestal. With the coming of the twentieth century, the virginal and angelic pose ceased to be a way in which the American woman cared to be thought of;

and Thayer's sweet, idealized pictures now seem a little silly.[2] He was also passionately interested in animals and birds. His studies of protective coloration in animals, leading to what came to be called Thayer's law, "that animals are painted by nature darkest on those parts which tend to be most lighted by the sky's light, and vice versa," embodied a useful observation and bids fair to outlive his pictures.

The two famous illustrators who emerge in the eighties, Edwin Austin Abbey and Howard Pyle, also show the same hunger for the past.

Abbey (1852-1911) was born in Philadelphia and studied at the Pennsylvania Academy about the time Eakins began to assist Schussele. His real teachers were the illustrations in English books by artists like Millais, Rossetti, Houghton, Keene, which he saw in Philadelphia bookstores and antique shops. He worked first in New York for *Scribner's Monthly* and *Harper's Weekly;* in 1878, the latter sent him to London. England was thereafter his physical home, as it was already his spiritual home. Abbey was born with a natural antiquarian taste and with an instinctive sympathy for the English seventeenth and eighteenth centuries. His illustrations for Herrick's poems, for Goldsmith, for *Old Songs*, and many of his illustrations for Shakespeare are little jewels of impressionist pen drawing and of happy sympathy for his subjects. In 1890, the trustees of the Boston Public Library commissioned a decoration from him and he turned to the monumental scale for *The Quest of the Holy Grail* (completed in 1902). This has always been an immensely popular work; yet neither this nor his later murals in the Pennsylvania State Capitol (1902-1911) are so satisfying artistically in harmony of scale and style as are his small pen and ink drawings.

Howard Pyle (1853-1911) had the same instinctive love of the past, the same passion for antiquarian accuracy. His range was wider than Abbey's; he used all media successfully but was at his best in pen and ink. He illustrated many books on American history which re-create with great vividness the people and scenes of the early days of America. But his reputation rests most firmly on his books for children. He wrote and illustrated a long series of children's books beginning with *The Merry Adventures of Robin Hood* in 1883 (Fig. 147). Pyle combined the suppleness and ease of a gifted observer, in the spirit of objective realism, with a passion for historical research. His figures are alive and convincing; every detail of costume and setting is based upon careful research. In his power to make the past come alive and in his charm of style, Pyle was extraordinary. Later in life, inspired by his friend Abbey, he turned to mural painting, doing the stirring *Battle of Nashville* (1906) (Minnesota State Capitol) and other commissions. Realizing, however, that he was only making illustrations large and determining to achieve a more monumental, less illustrative style, he went to Italy to study the old masters. But

---

[2] The idealization of woman was so popular a theme in our art in the nineties that it struck foreign observers as something peculiarly American.

burnt out by decades of intense work, he died in Florence at the age of fifty-eight.

LaFarge's career as a mural painter was the beginning of a movement that became more and more widespread. During the eighties only some rather sporadic mural work was done, chiefly in New York hotels and clubs; also in a few churches. In 1890 the trustees of the Boston Public Library gave commissions to Abbey and Sargent for decorations in their imposing new building facing Trinity Church. In 1892, Francis D. Millet was placed in charge of mural decoration in the neoclassic buildings of the World's Columbian Exposition, Chicago; he recruited a small army of painters whose work was a popular feature of the "White City." Then, in rapid succession, came a series of notable mural projects: the Walker Art Gallery of Bowdoin College, decorated by John LaFarge, Kenyon Cox, Abbott Thayer, and Elihu Vedder; the Library of Congress, elaborately decorated by Henry O. Walker, Elihu Vedder, E. H. Blashfield, Robert Reid, John W. Alexander, and others; the New York Appellate Court building, by Kenyon Cox and E. E. Simmons; the Pierpont Morgan Library, by H. Siddons Mowbray; and a succession of murals for neoclassic state capitols, courthouses, and libraries, stretching down into the nineteen-twenties.

The Columbian Exposition popularized not only mural painting but the neoclassic style of architecture of its "White City", so that most of these subsequent murals were installed in the lunettes, wall panels, or ceiling vaults of neoclassic buildings. It is true that niches and lunettes, in this type of building, call for sculpture or painting and are rather absurd without it. Nevertheless the painters did not seem able to make their panels appear at home in these buildings. They appear always rather isolated in the architecture, a little pasted on; so that in addition to their thinness of subject, they are not very good decorations. This was a fault that H. Siddons Mowbray, at least, avoided in the Morgan Library, where the painted panels are not only small, but form part of an over-all scheme including color, modeling, architectural ornament, and paintings, all designed to fit the shape of the vaulting; all conceived and executed harmoniously by one man. The Walker Art Gallery, Bowdoin, contains, in LaFarge's *Athens*, perhaps the most impressive mural painting of the nineties. Yet even there the four lunettes are placed rather awkwardly under the shallow dome, are poorly lighted and, having been executed as four separate works, bear little relation to one another in tone, and less to the surrounding architecture.

One comes back, therefore, to the Boston Public Library decorations as perhaps the best example, after all, of what the mural movement of the nineties achieved. Puvis de Chavannes' decoration in the stairhall, a work of the great Frenchman's old age and done without seeing the building, does not fit very happily in its place. E. A. Abbey gave his room of Arthurian legends at least a rich, decorative continuity and an atmosphere. But for an interior space, conceived as a decorative unity and given a powerful, dramatic atmosphere by means of wall paintings, I find to my surprise that Sargent's much criticized and highly unpopular room must be given honors that our period may be reluctant to grant.

This is not a universal opinion, by any means. Sargent's decorations were much criticized at the time, for not staying flat on the wall plane, as Puvis de Chavannes had said a mural should do—but the history of art is full of great wall paintings that contradict Puvis' dogma. They also seem, to some tastes, overdramatic; and this, one must allow, they are.

But the requirements of the mural are, that it must be:

(1) monumental enough to be an enrichment of the building rather than an insertion, or patch, upon its fabric;

(2) harmonious enough to be seen as a unit;

(3) dramatic enough to give the room a life and atmosphere of its own; and,

(4) complex enough to be seen again and again (for the room must be used and lived in), yet still reveal new details or suggest new thoughts. If these points are valid, Sargent's work, although executed in an outmoded manner and open to criticism in detail, succeeds in one respect, at least, better than any others of the decade—it creates a unified and effective whole.

The room was difficult and unrewarding, being nothing more than a narrow, barrel-vaulted hallway over a staircase. Sargent's theme was the history of the Jewish and Christian religions. The outline of his various passages (as given in the Library's synopsis) is an exact, systematic outline of religious history and dogma such as might have been drawn up by an intellectual group of medieval monks for the guidance of their stonemasons: but Sargent himself drew it up. Its treatment of the subject, in consequence, is not didactic, as a medieval artist would have made it, but esthetic. The qualities which Sargent saw in man's search for the divine were overwhelming splendor and mystery: in color, impact, mood, the room is rich in tone; monumental in decorative harmony; and massively dramatic (or overdramatic, if you will) in impact. The effect of this narrow, overwhelming space is a parallel to the sense of the overwhelming splendor and profusion of the past, which is the dominant tone of his friend, Mrs. Jack Gardner's, interpretative work-of-art, Fenway Court. This is a very surprising work, indeed, to come from the cool, objective mind of Sargent.[3]

[3] Sargent's later decorations in the dome of the Museum of Fine Arts, Boston (1916-1925), are conceived in an entirely different style: light, clear, and airy in tone, as befits a dome; and very skillful; but chilly in feeling, and with somewhat the effect of a number of cutouts, inserted into an inert setting.

LaFarge's four lunettes in the Supreme Court Chamber of the Minnesota State Capitol should also be mentioned as very effective, dramatic decorations in a neoclassic building. This room has, however, lost some of its unity of tone, owing, I suspect, to ill-considered repainting of the architectural surroundings.

That artists as different as LaFarge and Sargent should, in the nineties, spend their best efforts on these large, ideal, dreamlike visions of the past is significant. The discovery of the arts of the past and of the past through the arts was one important way in which the imagination and sensibility of artists (and of those in close sympathy with them—friends, collectors, writers, dealers) responded to the vast horizons of time and space laid open before men's eyes by the discoveries of the nineteenth century.

There occur sometimes among those who use the arts, as well as those who create them, individuals of a kind of genius. They have the imagination and the need to create an ensemble out of the works of others, which seems to us, coming after, to be a work of art in itself and an expression of its age. Jefferson created in Monticello a symbol of the lucidity and perspective of the Age of Reason. Washington Irving left us in Sunnyside a little masterpiece of romantic sentiment. The discovery of the past, at the end of the century, found a collector of such genius in Isabella Stewart Gardner, whose work of art was the museum-home she created in Boston. Although her friends among the painters were men like Whistler, Sargent and Zorn rather than the painters of ideal subjects, her own work of art illustrates, better than any other ensemble, the intoxication with the poetic and ideal past felt by her generation. The tone of her collection was formed in the nineties, when many of its greatest works of art were acquired; and the building that houses it was completed by 1903: that strange, inward-facing construction that presents so blank an exterior to the bleakness of the Fenway. Within it is an embodiment, not so much of the gaiety of Venice that was her model, as of her own burning thirst to taste the splendor and mystery of the past. The austere tradition of the Puritans, the sober reasonableness of nineteenth-century Boston, to her were meaningless. Instead she surrounded herself with the profuse creativity of the most splendid, the most opulent, the most mystical centuries of the past—Gothic, Renaissance, Baroque. There is much there that is trivial and dead, mingled with some of the greatest works of art in our hemisphere. It expresses all the better the spirit of the period. Although this is the work of an *animateur*, one who arranges the works of others, rather than an artist herself, it is nonetheless a remarkable and significant creation of the age's passion for the past, its hunger to re-create on New World soil the ancient riches of tradition.

One should close one's survey of later idealism with this strange and eloquent construction rather than with the inept murals which the movement drags behind it, like a long and bedraggled train stretching down into the nineteen-twenties. For unfortunately, although after LaFarge and Sargent the life went out of the revival of mural painting, the influence of the World's Columbian Exposition of 1893 marched on. For decades after, wherever there was a neoclassic public building, someone was likely to paint a mural. The men who produced these decorations were apparently convinced that the secret of mural painting was to represent a vaguely pretty woman in a long white robe. Standing with the Duomo and the Ponte Vecchio behind her, she represented Florence; seated or standing with appropriate emblems, she was Law, Fate, the Pursuit of Learning, the Telephone, or the Spirit of Ceramic Art; walking with Bible clasped in her hands, eyes upturned, the Pioneers crossing the Plains. (Needless to say, all these were actually painted, with many more of equal ingenuousness.) To us today, the Genius of Silliness seems to have been the muse most often consulted by these painters. What a waste of opportunity!

CHAPTER 13

THE TWENTIETH CENTURY:
THE FIRST GENERATION

As WE REACH OUR OWN CROWDED AND CONFUSING CENTURY, LET US LOOK ONCE again at the tendencies we have thus far considered permanent traits of painting in America that have served as it were as the warp threads of our story. Under the impact of novel influences and new problems in the twentieth century, these traits will seem to change greatly on the surface without, I believe, altering fundamentally underneath. These are:

(1) The double perspective of our civilization: so gifted in observing and exploring the outer world of nature; so rich in memories and subtle in introspection; giving us the two categories of the imagination for which I use the terms, the real and the ideal; the work of art carved out of the experience of nature, and the work of art spun out of memories, traditions, literatures, dreams. As the direction of attention changes, the weight of emphasis swings from one to the other, but no generation is without artists of great talent to express each of these Janus-faces of our minds.

(2) The double nature of the arts: art, and craft; unpredictable creativity, and disciplined skill; imaginative discovery, and practical livelihood; the ever fresh eye, and the traditional technical problems and traditional means of solving them.

(3) The two poles of attraction: the life of our own country, so varied and interesting, yet so new, diffused, and raw; the tradition of our civilization, represented by Europe, so profuse in talents, concentrated and dense in flavor as a rich old wine; giving us the two tendencies—the cosmopolitan artist, drawn toward Europe and the traditional centers of art; the independent or nativist who wants above all to find the meaning of America and of the spot where he was born.

(4) The effect upon the craft of painting of the wilderness continent

359

and the advancing frontier of settlement, stretching the population so thin that many born to be artists grew up far from the skilled practice of art, thus giving us the phenomenon of the *untrained professional*.

The nineteenth century closed with the cosmopolitan tendency in the ascendant. The conspicuous effort from 1875 to 1900 had been to link our painting with that of Europe, and to make American talents part of the international life of art.

There were notable artists at work in the year 1900—Whistler, Sargent, Homer, Eakins, LaFarge, Ryder were all still active. But they were old now. The tone of painting was set by the younger generation. The century closed on the pale, quiet note of the Ten American Painters and their contemporaries, who, in search of refinement, had excluded all but the purely esthetic from their attention. In style a watered-down combination of Sargent's brushwork and French Impressionism prevailed. This gentle, overrefined art was rudely challenged shortly after the turn of the century by a new generation of native talents from within, and from without by the furious explosions of Fauvism and Cubism in Paris, Expressionism in Germany, and Futurism in Italy, whose reverberations quickly reached our shores.

The painters were not alone in their attitude of genteel imitation. The country was in an imitative mood. In education, Germany was the model; at Harvard, Johns Hopkins, Yale, Princeton, Chicago the transformation of the American college was undertaken on German lines, and the system of the Ph.D. fastened like a vise upon the academic world. In social life, England was the model. The nineties and early nineteen hundreds were the period of international marriages between the new American industrial millionaires' daughters and the sons of impoverished European nobles, which delighted and scandalized American public opinion. Life in the ring of suburbs springing up around each of our big industrial cities was modeled as closely as possible upon English society. In literature, a similar imitativeness prevailed. Mary Colum, the Irish poet and essayist, coming to New York from the self-confident activity of the Irish Revival, observed:

I think that the beginning of the twentieth century and the end of the nineteenth were intellectually America's most colonial periods. On the eastern seaboard one could meet people who hardly ever read an American book; in fact I myself was more familiar with American literature than many of my American friends. In those days, certainly praise from London was the badge American authors sought. When they could afford it, they took the boat over and called on London editors, publishers, reviewers and authors. Between the period of Emerson, Poe, Whitman, and the second decade of the twentieth century, there had been little poetry that was not an imitation of the well-known English poets, in fact the American poetry that reached Europe was for a long time without any particular character, as a lot of Irish poetry before Yeats was. It seemed as if both American and Irish writers were, for the most part, not conscious enough, not critical enough, at the end of the nineteenth century, to know that they were imitation English.[1]

In the third quarter of the nineteenth century painting had been a popular and flourishing craft, practiced in every corner of the land and surrounded by its related and supporting crafts of illustration and engraving. By the end of the century, as Isham observed sadly, a man could no longer expect to earn a living by painting, no matter how hard-working or talented he might be. Portrait painting, the useful, bread-and-butter craft that had supported painters for two hundred years, was gone. Photoengraving had killed the beautiful craft of wood engraving that had flourished in the monthly magazines in the eighties and the decline of illustration had begun. Painting, without a staple product that society wanted, had become an insecure, impoverished pursuit whose rewards were at the mercy of fashion and the shifting breezes of reputation.

At this moment, when the loss of its craft foundation had struck it a heavy blow, painting was overwhelmed by a flood of displaced talents. The special kind of concrete, figurative imagination that produces a painter has always been rare. Even in the greatest and most productive ages of art, in fifteenth-century Florence, or eighteenth-century France, for example, painters were numerically a small group compared with the numbers engaged in the handcrafts and in applied design: one to fifty, perhaps, in proportion to the silversmiths, cabinetmakers, wood carvers, potters, weavers, stone carvers, gilders, bronze casters, and all the other formal and beautiful skills that once flourished.

The rise of nineteenth-century technology and machine production had worked devastation in the handcrafts. The men and women born to be craftsmen, displaced from their proper fields of skill and applied design, now came crowding into painting; though not suited to their gifts, it was the only outlet left to them. In the twentieth century we have had fifty painters to one worker in applied design. Painting thus became diluted with talents that did not belong to it; while the important task of the designer and craftsman—shaping and giving order and harmony to the whole setting of life—was abandoned to unguided machine production. Even if the result had been an enormous increase in the number of good painters, the vulgarization of all the objects that form the setting of our daily lives would have been a heavy price to pay: while it is very questionable if the inflation of numbers in painting has made the truly original and gifted artist any more common.

Not only the poverty but, I believe, some of the restlessness of painters and painting in our time is connected with this change. Something of the regular rhythm of modern painting from revolt to rapidly hardening convention to renewed revolt is connected, in my opinion, with the want of balance

[1] *Life and the Dream* by Mary Colum. Copyright 1947 by Mary Colum. Reprinted by permission of Doubleday & Company, Inc., New York.

in the arts caused by the destruction of the handcrafts. Nothing could be more overcrowded, insecure, and underpaid than the craft of painting in our times. All the more remarkable the daring, the invention, the stubborn devotion that have marked it as an art.

One would suppose that when the last free land in the West was occupied, about 1890, and the frontier became a vanishing element in American life, the primitive note lent by the untrained professional would disappear also. "The American [primitive] artists," as Flexner put it in *The Light of Distant Skies*, "had evolved their primitive decorations without conscious intent, as a result of experimentation forced on them by ignorance."

But new sources of stylized and antinaturalistic forms now arose out of a revolt against scientific rationalism and from the new world-wide horizon of the arts produced by travel, by the camera, by archaeology, and the museum. The revolt from reason to intuitive and emotional bases of life had made itself felt in an increasing subjectivity before 1900. In the new century it exploded in a thousand forms, in neoprimitivism, and in the exploration of the unconscious, led and symbolized by the name of Freud.

The revolt against the pale estheticism of second-generation Impressionism was touched off, first, by an exhibition of Eight American Painters, who showed together at the Macbeth Gallery, New York, in 1908. The Eight were united only by their friendship, for there was no common point of view of style; and they exhibited together only this once.[2] Yet the impact of the exhibition was such as to make it a landmark. Its significance lay in the fact that these artists were warm, courageous human beings who restored self-confidence and joy of life to American painting.

The leader of the Eight was Robert Henri (1865-1929), born in Cincinnati, trained first under Anshutz at the Pennsylvania Academy, then at Julian's and the Ecole des Beaux-Arts in Paris. In 1891 he returned to Philadelphia (to teach at the School of Design for Women) and began to show his magnetic quality. There were four young newspaper illustrators then working for the *Philadelphia Press*, William J. Glackens, George Luks, John Sloan, and Everett Shinn, whose talents Henri recognized and whom he encouraged to go on from newspaper illustration to painting. After further travels and independent work abroad in 1895-1897 and 1899, Henri settled in New York in 1900 to begin a long career, primarily as a teacher. His funda-

[2] The exhibition was held at the Macbeth Gallery in February, 1908. The Pennsylvania Academy asked for the exhibition and afterward circulated it to eight other museums over a period of more than a year. Seven paintings were sold from the exhibit—four to Gertrude Vanderbilt Whitney, who was to play a notable part as friend and patron of independent artists in the next two decades. The best descriptions of the group and the exhibit are to be found in the catalogs of two retrospective exhibitions, *The Eight*, by John I. H. Baur, The Brooklyn Museum, 1943-1944, and *John Sloan*, by Lloyd Goodrich, The Whitney Museum of American Art, 1952.

mental principle as a teacher, as Sloan said later, was "the importance of *Life* as the primary motive of art." By this, rather than his style of painting, Henri challenged the whole prevailing mood of imitative estheticism. A friend described him, in 1906, in these words:

At present he is the patriarch of the Café Francis crowd, a number of young painters, illustrators and *liberati* who believe in the poetical and pictorial significance of the "Elevated" and the skyscrapers, of city crowds and rows of flat houses. To these men Henri expounds his theories of art, and he seems to take these monologues over his entrée or *café noir* as seriously as his brush performances. And perhaps they are equally important, for it is Henri's personality first of all that has made a mark in our American life.[3]

These were prophetic words, for time has agreed that his inspiring, magnetic warmth as a teacher (enshrined in his book, *The Art Spirit*), his reawakening of the love of life and self-confidence in American painters, were his great contribution. His own paintings are direct, rather sketchy portraits, done in a style that reflected his admiration for Hals, Velasquez, and Manet, but marred by hasty and careless handling.

In 1907, the jury of the National Academy of Design, intolerant toward the younger generation, rejected the work of Henri's friends, George Luks, John Sloan, and William Glackens. Henri, in disgust, withdrew his own pictures from the exhibition. Arthur B. Davies had been exhibiting at the Macbeth Gallery, founded in 1892 as the first New York picture dealer's gallery devoted to contemporary American art. In 1908 this gallery asked Davies to arrange an exhibition of some of the younger painters that interested him. Davies selected eight painters: Henri, Glackens, Luks, Sloan, Shinn, Davies, Prendergast, and Lawson. The first five were realists. They had all studied at the Pennsylvania Academy of the Fine Arts and absorbed Eakins' tradition of realism, as carried on by Anshutz. Sloan, Luks, Glackens, and Shinn had worked as pictorial reporters for the *Philadelphia Press* before coming to New York. There they continued to earn their living as illustrators for magazines or newspapers. The predominant element was thus a revolt of lively young painter-illustrators against a milk-and-water estheticism. The humorous street scenes of New York's crowded slums contributed by John Sloan seemed to have shocked the reviewers most: at least he was, of the group, the one who for years after found it most difficult to sell his work. It is hard to believe now that the swift, sure brushstroke and gaiety of color of William Glackens' *Chez Mouquin* (1905) (Fig. 151) (Art Institute of Chicago), which was in this exhibit, can have seemed disagreeable at that time: yet even Ernest Lawson, a pleasant but far from exciting decorative Impressionist landscape painter, was accused of emphasizing the ugly in his landscapes.

[3] S. H. in *International Studio*, XXX (1906), 182-183.

The revolt of the Eight was not one of style or of the brush but of the heart: it was a reassertion of self-reliance, in the tradition of Emerson and Whitman, against an atmosphere of imitativeness and timid estheticism. It had its parallel in literature in the appearance of Dreiser, Frank Norris, and later of Sinclair Lewis to assert the importance of American life and daily experience as themes of art.

Of all the Eight, John Sloan (1871-1951) left the largest and most consistent achievement. Before coming under Henri's influence, in his newspaper period he was a successful black-and-white artist working in a clever, somewhat bookish *art nouveau* style. Henri turned his interest outward to the vivid actualities of life about him. His removal to New York from Philadelphia in 1904 gave him his great subject. He loved New York. He loved to walk its streets and watch the movement of the city; he loved the warm, rich flavors of human life in its great masses of people, on the streets, in their places of enjoyment, at home; his paintings were direct, spontaneous reports of what struck his keen and humorous eye (Fig. 148). As Lloyd Goodrich said, "His art had that quality of being a direct product of the common life, absolutely authentic and unsweetened, that has marked the finest genre of all times." [4] Sloan always drew with vitality and pungency. His color sense was not so sure as his sense of tone, so that his best work is to be found either in his drawings and etchings or in his early oils, painted in low-keyed, dusky tonal harmonies which he used with skill and richness.

Strangely enough, when he was approaching sixty Sloan again turned away from life and began to draw his inspiration from pictures, as he had in his *art nouveau* youth. His last years were an attempt to find through bright, hard color the art of classical form he admired in the old masters—alas, a vain attempt. The thirty years devoted to the mellow observation of New York are his enduring achievement.

William Glackens (1870-1938) also studied at the Pennsylvania Academy and worked for the *Philadelphia Press*. In 1895 he went to Paris for a year of independent work and, on his return, settled in New York, working as an illustrator for newspapers and monthly magazines and doing humorous drawings for *Life* and *Judge*. Other painters greatly admired his skill as a draughtsman: Guy Pène du Bois, the painter, who served for a time as art critic for the magazine *Arts and Decoration*, called him (September, 1914): "The best eyes in American art." Glackens first painted in the warm tonality that all these painter-illustrators adopted, partly out of admiration for Manet, partly in revolt against the sugar-and-cream palette of the American Impressionists. Later, under the influence of Renoir, he adopted a bright, sharp color that does not please the eye as much as his early, darker but more harmonious work. As an observer, Glackens showed a cooler temperament than Sloan; his pictures are those of a gay but rather detached observer (Fig. 151).

[4] *John Sloan*, Whitney Museum of American Art, 1952.

George Luks (1867-1933), on the contrary, was one of those roaring, gusty painters who become legends in their lifetimes, but of whom very little is left when their vital personality is gone. He had great love of life and fantastic humor and, as his friend Shinn said, he was "a great actor and a fascinating liar. . . . Only George Luks's great ability as a painter could excuse his weaknesses." After the Pennsylvania Academy, Munich, and the *Philadelphia Press* he moved to New York in 1896, where he drew a comic strip for the *New York World*—how far from the code of genteel estheticism! —and about 1902 turned to painting in a style inspired by his love of Frans Hals.

Everett Shinn (1876-1953), the youngest of the group, was a clever illustrator whose best work has grown out of his love of the theater and his love of Paris, both of which he has painted with gaiety and charm.

The other members of the Eight show the diversity of inspiration that was to be an outstanding characteristic of twentieth-century painting.

Ernest Lawson (1873-1939), a pupil of Twachtman, was a decorative Impressionist; but from love of the massive richness of oil paint he developed his own style in which the image of the thing painted seems sunk, still visible but partially obliterated, in the spongy depths of the paint.

Maurice Prendergast (1859-1924) was the only member of the Eight from outside New York. He grew up in Boston, traveled and painted abroad a good deal, and moved to New York only in 1914. He was a pioneer of the impulse (apparently latent in all Impressionism) to turn its medley of small brushstrokes into a pattern and thus to stylize nature into a two-dimensional color mosaic. Nature interested Prendergast only as a point of departure: his goal was a tapestry-like composition of fresh, luminous, happy colors. Older than the others, he had already developed in highly personal water colors, in the nineties, his art of cheerful, multicolored pattern (Fig. 149). It is a question in my mind whether his later oils, delightful in color but monotonous in subject and composition, represent any actual advance over the early water colors.

Arthur B. Davies (1862-1928) was, on the other hand, a painter of idyllic visions and reveries, in the tradition of Allston and Ryder. Unlike Ryder, Davies was not a recluse; he was, on the contrary, a man of culture and wide knowledge, whose paintings were fed by memories of poetry and of the past. The frieze-like designs of nude figures and rhythmic colors which form his mature style (Fig. 155) might have made better mural paintings than most of those being done by the mural specialists of that time; but Davies, with rare exceptions, preferred the idyllic and intimate to the monumental. At the end of his life, however, he turned to tapestry design for which his art was most suitable, and had his designs woven at the Gobelins factory in France.

The Eight thus brought forward not only the realism of a fresh generation of painter-illustrators but the interest, characteristic of the new century, in stylized forms and two-dimensional color patterns, which was being given powerful expression at the same moment in France by the Fauves, and in Germany by the painters of Die Brücke.

As one looks back at the period 1900-1914, however, it is obvious that the painter-illustrators of the Eight were by no means an isolated phenomenon. The first decade of the century was filled with efforts to break away from the decorative direction that Impressionism had taken, and to adapt its luminous colors and strongly emphasized brushstrokes to a new realism and zest for life.

Some of the artists who took part in this new movement of realism worked in New York. George Bellows (1882-1925) was an artist who preferred the strong, hearty, pungent flavors of life—prize fights, religious revivals, New York's swarming streets, or the drama of the great rivers that surround Manhattan. Time has not sustained Bellows' contemporary fame, which was based in part on big, violent pictures of boxing matches that seemed at the time very bold and exciting (Fig. 152). He was a rapid and slashing rather than a fine draughtsman, and his color was often bad, so that he was at his best, probably, in his lithographs. Perhaps his energy and gusto might have matured artistically had he not died prematurely at forty-three; but his surviving work, marred by careless handling and coarse color, seems now faded and, worse still, mediocre.

Rockwell Kent (born 1882) also began as a painter of landscapes and marines, working in a dark palette close to that of the Eight. Later he turned to book illustration in black-and-white. He was a wanderer by temperament, who lived in Maine, Newfoundland, and Alaska; explored Tierra del Fuego and the Straits of Magellan in a small boat; and wrote of his travels in books illustrated by himself. His *Wilderness* (1920) and *Voyaging Southward* (1924) (Fig. 154) are visually about the best American books of their period in their balanced harmony of text and illustrations. His admiration for William Blake helped shape his dramatic black-and-white style: ideal rather than realistic; marked by tall, slender, generalized figures, whose flowing sweep of line and contrasts of tone often give eloquent expression to moods of loneliness and tension.

Jerome Myers (1867-1940) was, like Sloan or Bellows, a painter of New York's streets and slums; but he created out of this subject matter an art with neither Sloan's warmth nor Bellows' violence. Instead, his pictures are tender and darkly luminous little canvases, idyllic or sometimes gently fantastic in feeling (Fig. 150). His is a personal art, handsome in color, and too generally overlooked today in the silence that always falls after a generation's passing.

Guy Pène du Bois (born 1884), another painter-illustrator, made the night life of New York his theme. He is a witty, intelligent man and a good critic; but like Forain, his contemporary in Paris, he fell into a painting formula that quickly grew wearisome.

This is not the place to discuss Edward Hopper, although by date of birth he belongs in this generation. Slow-growing as an oak, he matured late and is better considered with the artists of the twenties and thirties.

By 1900, New York city had reached the peak of its dominance as the center of American painting. There also took place then the first attempts to break away from it, not by the process of other cities reasserting their vitality and attraction, but by the creation of artists' colonies. This was a novelty in American life. The aim of an artists' colony, presumably, is to create a congenial, stimulating atmosphere for artistic production—which is not always what is achieved. It was originally also an impulse of realism, a desire to paint something of great character and interest in the American land that led to the formation of the famous colonies. The fact that they, too, rose out of the new realism of the beginning of the century is not often remembered. (Woodstock, which had its origin in the nineties, growing up around the summer school of the Art Students League, then directed with great success by Birge Harrison, is a special case; it always seems less a colony than an offshoot and summer residence of New York.)

It was Joseph Sharp (born 1859) who discovered the beauty of Taos pueblo in New Mexico, and led some fellow pupils of Duveneck, Oscar Berninghaus (1874-1952), and Ernest Blumenschein (born 1874) to settle there on their return from Paris. The Taos colony was in existence by 1900. Irving Couse (1866-1936), Walter Ufer (1876-1936), and Victor Higgins (1884-1949) were other well-known painters of the colony, who settled there early in the century. The compelling impulse of these men was a desire to paint the Indians, the noble landscape, and the burning sun of New Mexico as something uniquely American and rich in artistic significance. They found their subject in Taos as the painter-illustrators of the Eight found theirs in New York city.

Provincetown, at the tip of Cape Cod, was another place of attractive pictorial character where a colony sprang up. Charles W. Hawthorne (1872-1930), after studying with Chase and painting independently in Venice, settled at Provincetown about the time of his marriage in 1903. The swarthy Portuguese fishermen among their nets and fish, in their yellow oilskins, and their dark-eyed wives and daughters were the pictorial material that drew Hawthorne there. The art colony grew up around the influential painting class he established.

A third colony sprang up in the rich, idyllic landscape of the middle Delaware Valley at New Hope, Pennsylvania, where a group of landscapists—William L. Lathrop (1859-1938), Edward W. Redfield (born 1869), Robert

Spencer (1879-1931), Daniel Garber (born 1880)—settled in the first years of the century.

And by about 1904 in California a group of writers and artists had settled among the pines of Carmel. This colony was largely literary in origin, however, and has always been stronger in writers and philosophers than in painters.

All these colonies grew out of the desire to break away from New York or Europe and to find new subject matter in the American scene. Each group of painters made its appearance as a novelty in American art, lent a note of fresh interest briefly to exhibitions and faded. Or so it seems to us. It is always dangerous to attempt to estimate how lasting are the achievements of artists of our own time—or still worse, of artists of forty or fifty years ago. Our eyes, it may be, are dazzled and fatigued by the successive forest fires of other, newer enthusiasms across which we must look to see these events of the first decade of our century. Technically, however, the founders of these colonies had in common a desire to adapt the long, bold brushstroke and the bright colors of Impressionism to the American landscape and people. Time has made only too evident certain weaknesses in many of them—graceless handling of the brush, muddy or greasy color, or that obviousness in point of view that is the beginning of boredom.

It is evident as one looks back at all these realistic movements of the early twentieth century that American painters, coming from a style of warm, tonal luminism, found it hard to master the Impressionist system of cool, bright, variegated hues, used without strong contrasts of tone. The best paintings by Sloan, Glackens, and Luks are their early works, in the deep-toned palette adopted, at first, in opposition to Impressionism. Pop Hart (1868-1933), the genial wandering water colorist, and Jerome Myers were both successful in color and both worked in dark tonalities. It should be said, however, that some of the portrait painters like Eugene Speicher (born 1883), W. Wayman Adams (born 1883), Charles Hopkinson (b. 1869), and Adolph Borie (1877-1934) made a pleasing and effective instrument of the Impressionist technique.[5]

[5] One group of painters, indeed, tried to develop in the opposite direction from Impressionism. Closely related to the quietism of Tryon and Dewing, they worked toward an even deeper, warmer tonalism and an even more elegiac mood. Buried beneath the avalanche of subsequent movements, this movement is today completely forgotten. Even their names—J. Francis Murphy (1853-1921), Bruce Crane (1857-1937), Ben Foster (1852-1926), Henry W. Ranger (1858-1916) were some of the best known—hardly awaken an echo in the memory. Yet Christian Brinton mentioned these "tonalists" as he called them, in the catalogue of the exhibition of American painting sent in 1910 to Berlin as among the leaders of contemporary painting. One can hardly find their works, so out of fashion is their movement—the only one with whom I feel familiar is the delicate pastellist Lendall Pitts (1876-1938) of Detroit and Paris—so that one can do no more than record the existence of an attempt to go in the direction of deeper tone, rather than brighter hue, and that it was popular in the first decade of the century.

As one might expect, some impetus from the good period of American illustration continued into this generation. When the wood engraving process of the seventies and eighties vanished before the introduction of halftone photoengraving, the fine harmony of engraving and typeface went with it. But the period was still rich in notable talents that, either as observers or satirists, left their mark on the American consciousness.

One of these, Charles Dana Gibson (1867-1944) at the height of his popularity from 1890 to about 1910, became something like a national institution. Today we may prefer the more subtle humor of Oliver Herford or the more vigorous observation of the painter-illustrators, Sloan, Glackens, Luks, or Kent.

In social and political satire the two great names were Boardman Robinson (1876-1952) and Art Young (1895-1944). Robinson was a powerful and expressive draughtsman who moved from newspaper cartoons, to book illustration, to painting. Art Young, as cartoonist for the *New Masses*, brought the Nast qualities of passion and eloquence to bear on the stormy period of early twentieth-century social unrest.

N. C. Wyeth (1882-1945) continued the tradition of Howard Pyle with emphasis upon historical accuracy in detail and dramatic action.

The revolt of the realists against academic Impressionism filled the years before the 1914 war. The revolt of the idealists began at the same time but gathered momentum more slowly and became the dominant force after the war, giving shape and élan to the painting of the twenties. The impulse to paint the images of the inner mind took many forms in the new century. Like Proteus, it changed so rapidly that one must hold fast to its essential nature or its multiplex forms will elude one.

There were, as always, certain transition figures and tendencies pointing the way toward an intuitive and stylized art.

Louis Michel Eilshemius (1864-1941) had exhibited at the National Academy of Design as early as 1887; but so far as his work has a chronology, his best work seems to have been done in the early years of this century (Fig. 153). The recognition of his naïve spirit and tender, lyrical color came through the broadened sympathies of this generation expressed in the Independents Show (as the exhibitions of the Society of Independent Artists were always called), founded by John Sloan in 1917 to open the door to all the clamoring voices of the new century. At the beginning of our century, which was to produce so many and such incessant changes, the general attitude toward change was one of solid and entrenched dislike. There were fewer opportunities for painters to exhibit than there are today; and exhibition juries were dominated by an older generation frankly hostile to change. The attitude of friendly, eager curiosity to discover new talents, which has now become so common that it even brings disadvantages (for the youthful promise of a new talent is much more eagerly sought for than the maturity of a great one)—was created in the American art world by the generation of the Eight.

There was an urge in the air to simplify and concentrate painting into rhythmic patterns of color. We can see it in Davies and Prendergast; it appears also in the mural painter, Augustus Vincent Tack, another independent (1870-1949). Tack married the daughter of George Fuller and studied with LaFarge. He was an artist of the same kind of dream world as his father-in-law; but his color and his love of two-dimensional pattern belong to a new age (*Storm*, in the Phillips Memorial Gallery, Washington).

What is the source of this urge to stylize and conventionalize, to simplify nature into flat, glowing areas of color and bold patterns of line, that sprang up everywhere in the first decade of this century? The popular impression is that it represents the influence of the Armory Show, which introduced "modernism" (as the influence of French Post-Impressionist painting is called) into America. This is, however, far too easy an answer. All the original American artists who seem now to deserve remembrance were already moving toward an ideal, stylized art before the Armory Show; the painters whose modernism dates from it are the derivative figures who have been forgotten.

The reaction from objective realism to the unrealistic styles of twentieth-century art—in which drawing and color are released from any necessity to represent what the eye sees in nature, expressing instead formal harmonies of the mind's invention—was in part one of those alternating tides in the direction of attention that are normal in our history. We are the heirs not only of Greek rationalism and centuries of disciplined observation of the outer world of nature but of the inwardness of the Orient, whose great representative is Christianity, to which the wisdom of this world is foolishness. Our intellectual and artistic history is a succession of alternating tides of these impulses, realistic and idealistic, objective and subjective.

After the scientific rationalism of the late nineteenth century came a reaction to the emotions, to intuition and dream. Not merely a reaction: an active cultivation of the unreal, the irrational, the primitive. For into this alternation of reason and instinct, logic and intuition, came an influx of ideas from outside the Western tradition.

The white race had begun the nineteenth century still confined, with the exception of a few merchants and sailors, to the small peninsula of Europe jutting off from the land mass of Eurasia, while the United States consisted of five million souls (three and a half million white) of whom all but a few hundred thousand were within a hundred miles of the Atlantic shore. When the century ended, the white race had spread its dominance over most of the globe. Western culture had been carried over the earth, acting as an apparently irresistible solvent upon all other cultures. In the twentieth century the return tide of influence from the discovery of so many alien and brilliant traditions came flooding back into Western art.

The artists of neoclassicism, revolting in the later eighteenth century against the Rococo, looked backward into history for another inspiration: but how simple their perspective was, compared with that of 1900. They saw their own immediate tradition stretching back to the Renaissance, and the past of our own civilization stretching back to Rome and Greece. Beyond this, only the legendary heroes of Homer gleamed in the darkness of time. Since then the new-born science of archaeology had doubled the length of recorded history. Egypt, Assyria, Babylon had been added to our consciousness. Then, with hardly a pause, archaeology went on to the discovery of preclassical Greece; the civilizations of Mycenae and Crete; the Persians; the Sumerians; the Hittites; Europe's dark, unwritten mysterious past in the cave paintings of Stone Age man; Neolithic man's mysterious standing stones; the beautiful whorled bronzes of the Celts; the arts of the barbarian invasions; of Ostrogoths and Visigoths; and of the Vikings in their beaked ships. Meanwhile, other whole worlds of art had been brought back from China and Japan; from India and the South Seas; and from the lands of modern primitive men. These arts were collected in Western museums. One by one their qualities were recognized by Western scholars and artists. The cultures from which they came might be dead or dying at the touch of Western life; but at the moment when their own creators ceased to believe in them the West fell in love with them and began to imitate them.

These ancient and non-European arts sprang from bases wholly different from our tradition: they were radically different, both in style and attitude of mind, from the vision that Western artists had created. From 1850 onward Western artists, especially in Paris, experimented with and adopted a succession of forms from the non-European arts. With the twentieth century, the stream of influence from outside the Western tradition became a roaring flood. An artist like Picasso is typical of our times: he has roamed through the history of art, borrowing suggestions from Negro sculpture, from late Greek vase painting, from Visigothic sculpture in Spain, from the arts of New Guinea, and, it may be, from the newspaper comic strip, and with demonic energy and eclecticism has invented one new style after another of extraordinary brilliance. The major part of the twentieth-century artists' revolt against the nineteenth century has been shot through with inspirations from ancient, primitive and, almost always, non-European forms of art.

Thus, as artists turned again toward an ideal art, a great wave of influence from exotic, mystic, and irrational arts outside our civilization fell heavily against the swinging pendulum. If one were to read only esthetic theory it would seem that Western art had now completed a circle and returned to the position of Winckelmann and neoclassicism—that beauty was to be found not in the face of nature, but only in the inner world of the mind. In practice, however, nothing now seemed more boring to artists than the classical Greek or Roman art admired by Winckelmann's contemporaries. Japanese prints, Persian pottery, mediaeval stained glass, Negro masks and fetishes, South Sea idols, Egyptian sculpture were to this generation what the Roman marbles of the Vatican Gallery and the Louvre had been to the neoclassicists.

This movement first found expression in the most highly self-conscious centers of painting, Paris, Berlin, and Vienna. The French created the clear, logical styles of Fauvism and Cubism, the Germans and Austrians an emotional expressionism. Knowledge of these movements was brought to the United States by a generation of Americans who studied in Paris in the decade 1900-1910. Lloyd Goodrich called their roll recently in an interesting, retrospective exhibition at the Whitney Museum of American Art, called *Pioneers of Modern Art in America* (1946). The men who went to Paris from 1900 on and felt the impact of Fauvism and Cubism were Alfred Maurer (who went to Paris in 1897); Bernard Karfiol (1901); Samuel Halpert (1902); Maurice Sterne (1904); Max Weber (1905); Abraham Walkowitz (1906); and after these, Walter Pach, Charles Demuth, Morgan Russell, Stanton Macdonald-Wright, Thomas Benton, Arthur Dove, Andrew Dasburg, Morton Schamberg, Charles Sheeler, Marguerite and William Zorach, Joseph Stella, Arthur Carles, Marsden Hartley.

The years from 1905 to 1908 in Paris saw the great retrospective exhibitions of Cézanne and Gauguin as well as the birth of Fauvism and Cubism. Most of the American students came to know the Parisian leaders of painting, Matisse, Derain, Braque, Picasso, and plunged ardently into their new movement—the liberation of color from natural appearance and the construction of ideal rhythmic harmonies instead of the depiction of the outer world. Gertrude Stein's Saturday night receptions formed a meeting place for some of the Americans in Paris and became a center of propaganda for the new movement. "Young man," she said to one young poet who had submitted his work for her opinion, "I am afraid your poetry means something." Within a few years two young Americans, Morgan Russell and Stanton Macdonald-Wright, with the quick adaptability of the American temperament, even founded an *avant-garde* movement of their own in Paris, in opposition to the earth colors of Cubism. They called it Synchromism and equipped it with all the apparatus of dogmatic creed, public manifestos, and challenges both to the public and to other artistic rivals, which had become the way to launch new forms of art. Everyone soon forgot about Synchromism, including its creators.

If the public and juries were hostile to John Sloan, it may be imagined how difficult it was for the disciples of the newest movements to show their work when they returned home. The first gallery open to them was the Photo-Secession gallery, owned by Alfred Stieglitz, which became famous as "291," its street number on Fifth Avenue. Stieglitz was a formidable personality and controversialist, a passionate defender of the artists he believed in, and an autocrat in his own circle. He exerted a strong influence on public opinion.

But the public at large was introduced to the new movements by the Armory Show of 1913. The exhibition was the project of a group of liberal-minded artists. All but one of the Eight were involved in it, as well as Bellows, Du Bois, Myers, Walt Kuhn, Allen Tucker, and a dozen more. Arthur B. Davies was president of the group, and with the aid of Walt Kuhn and the assistance of Walter Pach in Paris, organized the international section of the exhibition. Its purpose was twofold.

The first and main aim of the Armory Show was to carry on the revolt of the Eight against the intolerance of their own profession. There was a great deal of new talent which could not gain a hearing in the big, national, salon-type exhibits—Philadelphia, Chicago, Pittsburgh, the Corcoran, the National Academy of Design—where at that time an artist's reputation was made. The one-man exhibition at a key dealer's gallery has since become the gateway to success; but nothing then existed comparable to the batteries of contemporary galleries in New York city and elsewhere, eager for contemporary novelties. There was need of a place where the younger artists could show their work, and the catalogue of the Armory Show lists 1,112 works by 307 American artists (although others were added until the total is said to have been 1,600 pictures).

But the part of the exhibition that attracted most attention was the international section, which offered the first full representation in America of Cézanne, Gauguin, Van Gogh, and the living artists of Paris. The "shock" of the exhibition was Marcel Duchamp's *Nude Descending a Staircase*. Although called international, this section consisted almost exclusively of the school of Paris. For a long time after this American artistic opinion remained unaware of the vigorous experimental movements in Germany, Italy, and England.

The uproar over the Armory Show was prodigious. The eye is a conservative organ. Most people do not use their eyes intensively, and the thought patterns connected with the sense of sight are few and rudimentary. Americans, as a matter of fact, had then little opportunity to see contemporary painting. New York had drained away the best contemporary talent from the rest of the country, and the few strong artists outside New York lived largely in isolated colonies. Without a vigorous artistic life in most parts of the country it is no wonder that public taste was sluggish. But if there was small public for good painting—or painting of any kind—there was a huge and clamorous newspaper press that filled the country with the noise of this distant war and popularized the Cubist joke. After the exhibition closed in New York its international section was shown in Chicago where the students at the Art Institute school burnt a Matisse in effigy. The time was soon to come when, if an American painter did not choose to follow the lead of Paris, he had better learn to eat grass.

For a cultural change as great and abrupt as this a price must be paid, as Toynbee would say. Among the American converts to Fauvism and Cubism were many who exhausted their energies in breaking away from their background and had no vitality to create something of their own. Cubism in its strict form—the keen, logical analysis and re-creation of form, as practiced by Picasso, Braque, and Gris in the heroic days of the movement—was never followed or even understood in America. The wave of imitations of Cézanne or the Fauves (also ill-digested enough) also soon passed. What took root in America was a love of more rigorous and stylized ways of painting than had been practiced before, an interest in rhythmic pattern, and a use of free simplifications of the image of nature to emphasize either the construction of the picture or the artist's mood.

The most consistently strong and productive original artist in America was John Marin (1872-1953), the dominant figure of the twenties, who lived long enough to become the patriarch of American painters and to produce some of his finest work in his fifth decade of painting.

Marin was an architect for four or five years before he began to study painting at the Pennsylvania Academy under Anshutz (it is remarkable how many of the best of the early twentieth-century Americans came out of Anshutz's classes) and later at the Art Students League. In 1905 he went abroad and stayed until 1910. The luminism of Whistler was then his model. His main medium during those years was etching. He etched many European city views, inspired by Whistler: subtle studies of shimmering light and atmosphere upon the face of Venice, or Paris, or Amsterdam. Absorbed in his own problems, he was unaware of the *avant-garde* movements of Paris until he came in touch with them after his return at Stieglitz' gallery in New York. But an oil painting of 1903 (*Weehawken* in the Lawrence Fleischman Collection, Detroit) shows that even at this early date his interest lay in simplifying landscape into harmonies of pure, radiant color. The water colors done in Europe before his return to New York show his first, tentative attack upon the central problem of his art: how to translate the light and movement of nature into an architectonic construction of shimmering, fresh, radiant colors.

New York city and the American landscape seemed very exciting to him when he returned to America. He began to paint his great subjects—New York's skyscrapers and the coast of Maine—trying to convey that excitement. "These [my] works," he wrote in 1928, "are meant as constructed expressions of the inner senses, responding to things seen and felt." Color became an explosive, graphic language for the heroic poetry of rocks, and sun, and sea, for the drama of skyscrapers and elevated, for mountains and clouds. The phrase "pertaining to," in the title, was often his way of expressing this oblique relation to things: *Pertaining to Deer Isle; Pertaining to Stonington Harbor*. However abstractly expressed, his paintings aimed to express the poetry of the actual things of nature: but nature was transposed to a new plane of excitement, and described in a coloristic shorthand (Plate XVI).

His major medium, for the quarter-century after his return to America, was water color. He used it in a staccato, dynamic style that was new, yet with the same finality and authority one sees in Winslow Homer's use of the medium. Several of his technical devices—the self-enframing image; the breaking of the vista into several separate but related compartments; the emphasis on both depth and the flatness of the picture plane at the same time (so different from Matisse's way of doing it) were very original graphic inventions (Fig. 156). In the twenties he again turned back to oils, which he used much like water color—emphasizing transparency of color and the dry, dragged stroke of the brush.

In pictorial language Marin has been one of the inventive painters of his age. It is a pictorial language, not of formal harmonies, but of lyrical expression; and a lyrical expression, not of the studio world of objects on a table or a model posing on a stand, but of the expansive, joyful poetry of earth, and sun, and sea (Fig. 157).

Marin was always an independent, in the modern movement but apart from it. Charles Demuth (1883-1939), whose home was in the beautiful, staid, provincial city of Lancaster, Pennsylvania, surrounded by rich farms and the sober elegance of eighteenth-century brick architecture, by contrast loved the life of the art centers—Paris, Greenwich Village, Provincetown, then at the height of their bohemian effervescence—and was in temperament very much part of the world of *avant-garde* estheticism. But his cool, watchful, aloof personality and his jewel-like style, precise and elegant as a print by Utamaro, were highly original.

Demuth, like Marin, studied at the Pennsylvania Academy of the Fine Arts under Anshutz, and lived in Paris in 1904 and again in 1910-1914. His art came to maturity about 1915, his most productive period following in the next few years. After 1920 his health began to fail. Some of his best work was done in the twenties, however, and he continued painting until shortly before his death in 1935.

Like Marin, Demuth used water color with great distinction. His style was a combination of clear, sharp, pencil outline with wet, free, color washes of eggshell translucence; the effect is a combination of delicacy and strength (Fig. 158). In the years 1915-1919 he did many illustrations, not for actual publication, but to re-create for himself in his own pictorial terms the writing that interested him—Henry James's horror stories, Zola, Wedekind, Poe. He showed a special fondness, also, for vaudeville and café and bar life. Andrew Ritchie calls these latter the "distillations of that period of esthetic bohemianism that flowered during the first two decades of this century and whose roots were in Paris, London and Berlin. . . . No other American has given us by implication so sensitive and so subtle an account of the cynicism and disillusionment that marked the years before and during World War I." [6] But if these scenes of *vie de bohême* are part of a general mood at this time, they are treated with a cool, formal detachment, as if seen through a window of quartz through which no warmth could penetrate, that is entirely personal with Demuth.

Demuth was interested in many kinds of subject. He painted the provincial American Palladian architecture of Provincetown or Lancaster, translating its formal severity into new harmonies suggested by Cubism; he discovered classical monumentality in the newly invented, grandiose, industrial architecture in concrete; on the other hand he painted flowers and fruit delightfully, in his cool, elegant, jewel-like way.

One of his entertaining inventions was what he called the poster portrait. These were in oil and were characteristically oblique, symbolic portraits of a few of his intimates like Georgia O'Keeffe, Arthur Dove, Marsden Hartley, and John Marin. The portrait of the poet, William Carlos Williams, *I Saw the Figure Five in Gold* (1921) (The Metropolitan Museum of Art), is outstanding, a bold, strong, interesting picture which could be the product only of a highly individual mind and eye. It illustrates also Demuth's tendency to draw inspiration from the geometric shapes of architecture and modern technology. It seems odd, yet characteristic, that this elegant esthete should have been one of the first to discover the cold beauty of the machine.

The touch of Cubism seems to have stimulated many Americans. In France the first enthusiasm for intellectual analysis of form gave way, about 1915, to a second phase in which the medium of oil paint—its colors, textures, and brushstrokes, spots, stripes, stripplings, its scrapings and grainings, its effects of mass and thinness—became both the medium and the subject of pictures. In France, this second phase was to produce a new period of decorative invention. In the United States, on the contrary, the effect of Cubism was to produce a heightened awareness of form, a love of clean lines and architectonic shapes; and these were turned outward into a new approach to nature. Demuth illustrates this development very clearly; and so does Charles Sheeler (born 1883). Like so many other good painters of this generation, Sheeler was born in Philadelphia and studied at the Pennsylvania Academy; but after a visit to Europe in 1909, which brought him in touch with the school of Paris, he settled in New York. In 1912 he took up photography for a living, a fact which was to have an influence on his painting. After a period of experiment with Cubist analysis of form, he turned in the twenties toward an objective art based on careful observation. With a deep feeling for American traditions and sources, he discovered qualities of clean, strong form in Shaker

---

[6] Andrew C. Ritchie, *Charles Demuth*, New York, Museum of Modern Art, 1950.

buildings and craftsmanship; in the stone barns of Pennsylvania; in New York skyscrapers; in the gigantic new concrete and steel industrial architecture. By translating this discovery into painting, he was able to reinterpret eloquently to Americans their own native setting. Sheeler's series of paintings and photographs, made in 1927 and 1930, of the River Rouge plant of the Ford Motor Company, probably more than any other work opened the eyes of his generation to the severe beauty of functional engineering design (Fig. 161).

Preston Dickinson (1891-1930), another significant figure of the twenties, found in the bridges and industry of the Harlem River or the ramparts and stone houses of Quebec subjects for paintings of an austere, intricate beauty of plane and line in oil or pastel.

Lyonel Feininger (1871-1956) had gone to Europe in 1887 at the age of sixteen, and lived in Germany until the rise of the Nazis drove him back across the Atlantic in 1937, fifty years later. His art thus belongs to the story of painting in Germany, rather than in America. But it is curious to find him developing, in Berlin, along lines parallel to those we have been tracing—adapting the Cubist language of line and plane to the poetry of light and nature.

Joseph Stella (1879-1946) was born in Italy and came to New York at the age of twenty-three. After working for some years as a magazine illustrator, he returned to Italy for study in 1909. There he came in touch with the Futurist movement and in 1911 with French Cubism. Returning to New York, he too turned to the bridges and lights of New York for large, dramatic, and highly personal pictures of the beauty of technology (Fig. 162).

When one remembers the eclectic suburban architecture of the nineteen-twenties, rearing its atrocious Olde Englishe or neo-Spanish from Bar Harbor to Los Angeles, the need for the eye-training offered by these artists in the beauty of clean, severe forms is evident.

For some reason the impact of Fauvism on American colorists was not so immediately helpful as Cubism had been to the American sense of form. Marsden Hartley (1877-1943) was a born colorist who, after studying with Chase in New York between 1900 and 1910, had worked his own way toward the liberation of color and the stylization of nature. In Berlin, where he spent much of the time from 1912 to 1915, he found himself for the first time in huge, abstract still lifes. His *Portrait of a German Officer* (1914) (Metropolitan Museum of Art) in glowing, clangorous, primary-color-notes, red, white, yellow, green, and black, on a black ground, has all the color-eloquence of a great Fauve painting. He was not to do anything so personal and strong again for twenty-five years.

Hartley was always very susceptible to influences and, after his return to America in 1915, spent a long time groping through a rather arid and imitative estheticism—much of the time in the twenties he was trying "to take up where Cézanne left off"—and it was not until the end of his life, when he had returned to his native state of Maine, that he found himself again. Then, in a style of glowing color and massive paint, filled with a peculiar sense of leaden weight, he painted the beautiful still lifes of rocks and ropes, shells and dead sea-birds, the landscapes, and the figure subjects (which are also still lifes) on which his final reputation as a painter rests (Fig. 160).

There were other gifted colorists in this generation: Walt Kuhn (1880-1949); Max Weber (born 1881); Arthur Dove (1880-1946); Arthur B. Carles (1882-1952); Clayton S. Price (1874-1950); yet not one can be said to show a steady, sustained, self-confident activity. A restless series of experiments with new manners, or an esthetic thinness, a meagerness of production haunts them all. Who can say what Max Weber really is, for example, out of all the manners he has tried? To me he is an admirable still-life painter; and a good figure painter when interested in his subject, as when for a time he turned to themes of Jewish traditional life that meant much to him as a human being: but he has been so much else!

This eclectic group of colorists was not confined to New York. Carles worked in Philadelphia. Price, an old cowboy artist in solitude out in the Pacific Northwest, groped his way toward an expressionism of pure color that was more important for its influence on younger artists in that region than for itself. But none of these colorists developed such a pure, individual voice, speaking from the heart, through color and brushstroke, as did the little-known Canadian painter, Emily Carr, in her solitude at Vancouver.

The exhibition of the Eight at the Macbeth Gallery in 1908 is the accepted symbol of the first artistic movement of the twentieth century, the revolt of the realists against the estheticism of the nineties. I have tried to show that it was a momentary grouping within a much large movement. Early twentieth-century realism included Bellows, Kent, Jerome Myers, and Guy Pène du Bois in New York, who did not exhibit with the Eight; it included other painters who revolted against New York and settled at Provincetown or Taos or New Hope.

Through them all runs an underlying note of what in the nineteen-thirties would have been called regionalism. They were men in love with their subjects—the crowded life of New York, the Portuguese fishermen of Provincetown, the Indians and fierce sunlight of New Mexico, or the landscape of the Delaware Valley. Their revolt was in their gusto and enthusiasm toward life rather than in style. Perhaps the Ten American Painters were more influenced by Monet, and the realists more by Manet or Renoir: but these differences of style were not an impossible gulf; were, in fact, far less important than differences of imaginative tone. By 1914 one finds Bellows, Henri, Glackens, Walter Ufer, Hawthorne, Garber, Redfield, not only accepted but figuring prominently in the annual exhibitions where painters' reputations were then made and measured—the Pennsylvania Academy, the Carnegie International at Pittsburgh, the National Academy of Design, the Corcoran Gallery, and the Art Institute of Chicago. By 1914, one may say, the point of view of the realists had won its place and been absorbed into the stream; by 1920 its stimulus was gone.

But the vital movement of the times was not realistic. The direction of attention was surging away from nature toward the lyrical and subjective imagination, toward a formal and stylized art. The various forms of idealism took shape at the same time, between 1900 and 1914; but men like Marin or Demuth, who began at the same time as the realists, had to wait until the nineteen-twenties for a hearing. The first two decades of the century were years of struggle and obscurity for them, marked by confused battles of ideas and personalities which were by no means clarified by the Armory Show of 1913.

The Armory Show has become something of a Sacred Cow in the public mind, which is under the impresison that it created modern painting in America. On the contrary, it is important to emphasize that the artists who were to emerge as the strong, original figures of this movement in America were on their way before the Armory Show.

What the Armory Show created was an enormous interest in the Post-Impressionist artists of France. It gave a new direction and fresh impetus to the enthusiastic collecting of French painting. The ferment aroused may have been stimulating also to the general public interest in painting. It produced a certain amount of Neo-Fauve, Neo-Cubist, and Neo-Primitive painting, which, being wholly derivative, is already forgotten.

But the important American painters of the movement had to wait another decade for recognition. In the years between the close of the 1914 war and the great depression, reinforced by some able recruits from a still younger generation, they won recognition and gave a new shape to the imaginative life in the United States. That period, however, is partly the story of the next chapter, for two brilliant generations met in the art of the twenties.

Gradually collectors appeared to support the new taste: John Quinn, advised by Walt Kuhn; Miss Lillie Bliss, advised by Arthur B. Davies; Albert C. Barnes, introduced to the new taste by Glackens; Frederic Clay Bartlett, the painter, whose collection in the Art Institute of Chicago exerted an early and very potent influence; and most personal of all, Duncan Phillips, who in 1918 founded in Washington the Phillips Memorial Gallery, the first public institution devoted to twentieth century taste. Finally, the Museum of Modern Art was founded in 1929 in New York city, with the primary support of Mrs. John D. Rockefeller, Miss Lillie Bliss, Mrs. Cornelius Sullivan, and A. Conger Goodyear. Its first series of exhibitions: *Cézanne, Van Gogh, Gauguin, Seurat; Painting in Paris;* and *Modern German Painting and Sculp-*

ture, selected and interpreted with superb taste and eloquence by Alfred Barr, presented European Post-Impressionism and twentieth-century developments with an éclat that roused immense popular support the nation over.

The first three decades of this century also brought great changes in the opportunities to see the range and height of the art of painting. The art museums of the chief American cities, though founded twenty-five years before, in 1900, were still in their infancy. Their collections were small. The perspective offered by them upon the range and greatness of the arts was spotty and of indifferent quality. The twentieth century was to change all this. A period of tremendous collecting set in, more ambitious and more discerning than had ever existed before in this country.

It is characteristic of the change in atmosphere that collecting now turned to the mystical ages of art. Admirable collections were formed of the glorious ranges of mediaeval art: in Boston, Cambridge, New York, Cleveland, in the John G. Johnson Collection in Philadelphia and the Walters Collection in Baltimore. The unequalled collections of Asiatic art were formed in Boston, in the University Museum, Philadelphia, and the Freer Collection, Washington. The wonderful Egyptian and Greek collections of Boston and New York took shape. Rich collections of primitive arts and pre-Columbian archaeology were formed in the University Museum, Philadelphia, the American Museum of Natural History and the Museum of the American Indian, New York, and in the Peabody Museum in Cambridge. Great panoramas of European painting were the aim of all ambitious museums. In forming these, a notable emphasis was put on the mediaeval centuries of painting, which had been weakly represented in American collections before 1900. The new directions of attention among artists were thus paralleled by new interests among historians and scholars.

It was also an age of great private collectors whose enthusiasm and taste enriched the country by their purchases, which have now for the most part passed to public institutions: Henry C. Frick, J. P. Morgan, Benjamin Altman, Henry Walters, Martin A. Ryerson, John D. Rockefeller, Jr., Henry O. Havemeyer, John G. Johnson, Collis P. Huntington.

One should not overlook the influence of notable antiquaries like Joseph Brummer, Dikran Kelekian, A. Kevorkian; and of great firms of picture dealers such as Knoedler, Wildenstein, Seligmann, Rinehart, Drey, Duveen, who established themselves in New York and, continuously importing works of art of first quality for their American clients, in their own way exerted a great and creative influence upon taste. New York city became an important depot of the international art market. And, as it became an art dealing center, news magazines of New York exhibitions appeared: *The Art News* (founded 1902) and *The Art Digest* (founded 1926). *The American Magazine of Art* (1908) was founded by the American Federation of Arts as a journal of popular education, a function which *Art and Archaeology* (1908), published by the Archaeological Institute of America, undertook for the ancient, mediaeval, and primitive arts.

Thus a world horizon was created for the arts in America; and for the first time the great inheritance of the human race was brought together here for study and reflection.

CHAPTER 14

THE TWENTIETH CENTURY:
THE SECOND GENERATION

IN 1920, AS THE AMERICAN PEOPLE SANK BACK WEARILY FROM THEIR SURGE into international politics, it did not seem that American painting was about to enter a brilliant period. Other arts were flourishing. Architects were piling up skyscrapers which boldly expressed American business' awakened pride and self-consciousness. An outburst of talented writers in the early twenties gave us a vigorous, imaginative, national literature and theater. The motion picture had won a world-wide audience.

But the fogs of imitativeness and snobbism described by Mary Colum still hung over large provinces of the arts and polite life. The 1914 war had, in fact, given a fresh impetus to the lack of self-confidence and the expatriate temper that the Eight had fought against. It seemed, in 1920, that the revolt of the realists had failed and that the feeble eclectic temper of 1900 had returned with renewed force.

Nothing shows this more plainly than the neopicturesque, neoantique suburbs which were built in the nineteen-twenties around American cities. In the ring of residential towns around New York, Chicago, and every other Eastern and Midwestern city, an eclectic revival spirit governed domestic architecture as absolutely as it had when Richard Morris Hunt built French chateaux on Fifth Avenue—although to do Hunt justice, he set a higher architectural standard than prevailed in the welter of suburban architecture in the twenties. It seemed as if the fashionable and well to do of America felt the need more than ever to clothe themselves in the borrowed splendors of Europe's past, or in something that might pass for them. The decorations in vogue in these suburban houses were chiefly paintings by the fashionable English eighteenth-century portrait painters: but the motive of collecting, subsequent events were to show, was not to acquire loved and appreciated works of art, but to achieve a fashionable decor. As soon as the fashion

PLATE XVI. John Marin: *Lower Manhattan* (1920). (Courtesy of Philip L. Goodwin, New York; color plate courtesy of Coward - McCann, Inc.)

PLATE XVII. Charles Burchfield: *Black Iron*
(1935). (Courtesy of Mr. and Mrs. Lawrence A.
Fleischman, Detroit; color plate courtesy of the
Archives of American Art.)

changed in interior decoration, pictures for which fantastic prices had been paid became a drug on the market.

Among the intelligentsia, the urge to escape from the world of George F. Babbitt took another form. It was the great expatriate period when, for hosts of writers and painters, Paris seemed the only possible place to live. This in itself is no crime: Paris is delightful. But it was the dogma of these Americans of the Left Bank, loudly and freely expressed, that the United States was a spiritual desert in which no self-respecting artist would attempt to live.[1] A transatlantic version of this dogma was boomed across the land, like the sounds of a furious brass band, by H. L. Mencken and George Jean Nathan in *The American Mercury*. Their version was that America south or west of the Hudson River was the domain of the Boobocracy, a sour mass of vulgarity and stupidity (Dean Swift had called them Yahoos) and that the further south or west you went, the worse it got. The Middle West was a term of hissing, and the prairie states across the Mississippi something one did not allow one's self to think of. A few little spots where artists gathered, in Greenwich Village or another colony, might try to reproduce a bit of transplanted Left Bank atmosphere here and there. But on the whole, in the opinion of the intelligentsia, America was hopeless.

In the midst of these fogs of self-doubt, the best of the painters who had appeared before 1914 were still struggling for a hearing. They were gradually to win recognition in the twenties, when a vigorous second generation began to come forward and reinforce their ranks.

As I write of the nineteen-twenties, however, so near and yet as remote and dead as the moon, I realize again only too forcibly that there are no chapters except in books. Life goes on its way, a continuous, multitudinous tumult, now amusing, now boring, now noble, now stupid, now climbing to heights, now stumbling and falling in the mud. Each decade, each year, has its own flavor; each season has its own exhibitions and enthusiasms and discoveries; each artist has his own year, advancing or falling back; talents blossom and fade. In fact, each year the big national survey exhibitions show hundreds of paintings in a vain attempt to represent what is going on in this vast country. How can we compress into a chapter what required twenty-five crowded years of life to experience? How can we mention all the artists who have done good work in our own time? It is an ungrateful, indeed an impossible task. All we can do is to mention certain people and events which may offer us a kind of thread to follow through the maze.

In the nineteen-twenties two groups of artists stood out in New York city. One was the circle around Alfred Stieglitz—John Marin, Marsden Hart-

---

[1] "The trouble with the United States," said Gertrude Stein in the thirties, explaining to someone why there was no landscape painting in America, "is that it has no sky."

ley, Arthur Dove, and a new recruit whose first exhibition of drawing was arranged by Stieglitz in 1917, Georgia O'Keeffe—and other painters, like Demuth, who were intimates of that circle. (Demuth and Preston Dickinson exhibited first at the Daniel Gallery which, for a time, exerted a strong influence.) The other group was younger on the whole and mostly products of the Art Students League; they found a haven in the Whitney Studio Club.

One of the earliest, kindest, and most generous supporters of New York artists was Gertrude Vanderbilt Whitney, a good sculptor in the neoclassical tradition and a lover of art and artists, who began to help artists by buying their work as early as the exhibition of the Eight. At first she merely bought a picture for fifty or a hundred dollars to help an artist friend pay his studio rent or grocery bills. Her interest in helping American artists took more definite shape in 1914 when she acquired a secretary, Juliana Force, to help her in the Whitney Studio Club. The Club was a place for informal gatherings and exhibitions of unknown or struggling artists; gradually these exhibits grew more important (Alexander Brook was for a time assistant director of the Club) until, in 1931, they evolved into an institution, the Whitney Museum of American Art, with Juliana Force as its first director. The policy of this institution, in all stages of its evolution, was to encourage artists and especially, of course, the New York artists on its own doorstep. John Sloan, Alexander Brook, Peggy Bacon, Yasuo Kuniyoshi, Eugene Speicher, Edward Hopper, and many others benefited by this haven in the nineteen-twenties. Many although not all of this group also exhibited at the Rehn Gallery.

This leads us to speak of a new phenomenon, the rising influence of the art dealer in contemporary art. In the nineteenth century the American artist had looked to annual exhibitions, modeled upon the Salon in Paris and the Royal Academy in London, as the gateway to recognition and professional success. When the twentieth century opened, the old, long-established exhibitions of the Pennsylvania Academy of the Fine Arts and the National Academy of Design had been supplemented by others in Washington, Pittsburgh, Chicago, and elsewhere. As numbers increased and changes of style grew more frequent the control of taste shifted. The large, rather miscellaneous national surveys continued, but beginning with the exhibit of the Eight at the Macbeth Gallery in 1908, the small group or one-man exhibition at the New York gallery of an astute art dealer became more and more the means by which reputations were made and paintings were sold. Macbeth, Stieglitz, Daniel, Rehn, Kraushaar, Edith Halpert were pioneers of a new relation between artists and public in the story of American painting.

Another new factor was a higher level of the journalism of art. *The Dial*, transferred in 1916 from Chicago to New York, was a highly articulate and intelligent force acting upon taste in America. In 1920, Hamilton Easter Field, with the financial help of Mrs. Whitney, founded *The Arts*. Field was a critic of broad culture, quick sensibility, and the independent mind of his Quaker heritage, who made *The Arts* the best periodical of the kind that we have yet produced. Field had collected Winslow Homer when Homer could not sell a group of ten watercolors for $300. He had lived six years in Paris and understood well the advancing spirit of the French artists. He saw the merit in the most diverse kinds of art and was a critic who would praise the qualities of Matisse, Arthur B. Davies, or Joseph Stella to conservatives or, with equal readiness, point out the merits of Bouguereau to undisciplined young modernists. A passage in his critique of a now forgotten group is typical of his hatred of esthetic dogmatism:

The one shadow that hangs over the . . . school is the shadow caused by the artists themselves. They do not love life as the greatest masters loved it. When you cease to love life with all your heart, the tempter comes in and his form is that of the theorist and he pulls life up by the roots and shows you its technique. You begin to analyze life and art. Joy flies out at the window as the theorist comes in at the door.

American art was well served by Field until his untimely death in 1922, after which Forbes Watson, assisted by Lloyd Goodrich, continued *The Arts* in the same tradition of broad interests and intellectual independence until it died in 1931.

In the 1920's the Stieglitz circle received a distinguished addition in Georgia O'Keefe (born 1887); for a time, indeed, the honor of American painting was felt to rest upon the triumvirate of Marin, Demuth, and O'Keeffe. Her paintings of American architecture (her *American Radiator Building* is one of the best things ever done to the vastness and mystery of New York city) (Fig. 159) and of landscape, her giant-sized flowers, her austere paintings of bones and skulls helped to create in us the love of disciplined line and clean proportion that has since permeated (and how much for the better!) the arts of applied design and architecture. In her art, loneliness, silence, the inner world of contemplation became a new form of poetry of unmistakable eloquence and personal accent. Perhaps a somewhat puritanic disregard of the sensuous quality of oil paint works against her today, when the splash and texture and glow of the medium itself have become the subject of so much contemporary painting. But hers was one of the voices that helped in the twenties to reawaken this country to the imaginative richness of its own life.

Stieglitz was a passionate believer in his artists and a masterful propagandist for them. Much of his early energy went also into interpreting the stylized and emotional forms of expression developing in Europe. But this group, if very influential, was small. Many good painters working along similar lines were not a part of it.

Stuart Davis (b. 1894) was the son of the art director of the *Philadelphia Press* who had employed Sloan, Luks, Glackens, and Shinn, and been a friend of Henri back in the nineties. But the elder Davis moved to the *Newark Evening News* about the time the painters moved to New York; and the son grew up to enter Henri's class in New York in 1910. Davis was schooled, however, on modern French painting, which he saw in the Armory Show and in New York Galleries: the decisive influence upon his development was the late, color-rich phase of Cubism, out of which he created his own poster-like style of composition. He uses highly simplified but still recognizable objects in flat brilliant colors with much amusing use of lettering, to form compositions of great decorative warmth and gaiety. Davis's work has freshness, a personal accent, and wit (a quality very rare in our painting) (Fig. 164).

Karl Knaths (born 1891), like Stuart Davis, was one of the first of the new generation to accept Cubism as a new basis for painting. Unlike the earlier colorists influenced by Cubism, whose work was changeable and uncertain, Knaths has evolved a consistent, personal style, a balanced harmony of geometry and soft, radiant color. He has worked by himself (since 1919 his home has been in Provincetown) and stands alone (Fig. 163).

The influence of the school of Paris was a discipline through which a great many other painters passed, between 1910 and 1930, who later developed in quite other directions. It brought also a new discovery, or perhaps one should say a new sympathy. The creators of the stylized, emotional art of the twentieth century, the most advanced and self-conscious artists of Europe, discovered an unconscious echo of their own interests at the other pole of artistic consciousness in the naïveté of children, artisans, and peasants. Fauvism and expressionism made the discovery of folk art and popular art, the art of untutored levels in our own society.

The first people in America to become interested were, so Holger Cahill tells me, artists who had studied in Europe and seen the interest which the Fauves in France, the Brücke and Blaue Reiter artists in Germany showed in the arts of primitive peoples, peasant art, and the art of children. Some discerning collectors appeared in the twenties: Holger Cahill himself, Hamilton Easter Field, Mrs. Isabel Carleton Wilde of Boston, Juliana Force, Elie Nadelman, and a few others. Henry Schnakenburg, the painter, arranged the first exhibition of "American Folk Art," as it was called, in 1924 at the Whitney Studio Club. Field's collection at Ogunquit roused the interest of other artists such as Robert Laurent, the Zorachs, and Kuniyoshi. Their interest led up to the American Folk Art Exhibitions arranged by Holger Cahill at the Newark Museum in 1930 and the Museum of Modern Art in 1932, and one arranged by Lincoln Kirstein for the Harvard Society for Contemporary Art in 1930, which introduced this enthusiasm to a wider taste. Then came the great collections of Mrs. John D. Rockefeller (now united at Williamsburg; but once also part of the Museum of Modern Art and The Metropolitan Museum of Art), Mrs. Webb at Shelburne, the collections at Cooperstown and Old Sturbridge Village, the Garbisch Collection in the National Gallery of Art —to name only those now in public institutions; while at Winterthur Mr. H. F. du Pont, although collecting with a different goal, acquired some of the finest early examples.

The conjunction of the Museum of Modern Art and American naïve and artisan art of the eighteenth and nineteenth centuries is significant. The date of that exhibition, 1932, may be taken as marking the triumph of a new taste and a new way of seeing. Stylized design and emotional (rather than intellectual or literary) expression were now what was expected and admired not only by artists but by the most discerning and sympathetic members of their audience.

Eilshemius' works came into their own.

When a Pittsburgh carpenter and housepainter named John Kane (1860-1932) in 1927 submitted a picture to the jury of the Carnegie Exhibition, it was accepted for exhibition and hung among the works of the skilled, self-conscious professionals. From that time Kane's landscapes of Pittsburgh—memory pictures painted in low quiet tones, of a simple, childlike affection for the city in which he had spent his life—were widely exhibited and much enjoyed.

The naïve memory-landscapes of Joseph Pickett (1848-1918), a carpenter-shipbuilder of New Hope, Pennsylvania, who painted as a hobby, suddenly began to please more than did the famous professionals of the New Hope artists' colony.

Horace Pippin (1888-1946), an unschooled Negro of West Chester, Pennsylvania, unfitted for labor by a war wound, turned to painting. "Pictures just come to my mind," he explained, "and I tell my heart to go ahead," an explanation of his innocent art which needs no further comment. His discovery and exploitation as a painter in 1937 did not change his art, although it was too much for him as a human being.

The same was happily not true of the delightful old lady of Eagle Bridge, New York, who has become known as Grandma Moses. Her success as a painter, which has made her a beloved national character, has not altered in the least either her gaiety or her attractive, simple humanity.

A large proportion of the artists who made their names in the twenties first exhibited their work at the Whitney Studio Club. John Sloan had his first one-man show there; so did Edward Hopper, Reginald Marsh, Guy Pène du Bois, Henry Schnakenburg, Andrew Dasburg, Molly Luce. The early group exhibitions at the Club, before 1920, showed all of the Eight, as well as Bellows, Kent, Winthrop Chanler, Eugene Speicher, Maurice Sterne, Samuel Halpert, Henry McFee, Stuart Davis, Paul Berlin, and Louis Bouché; later Ernest Fiene, John Carroll, Arnold and Lucile Blanch, David Burliuk, Glenn Coleman, Georgina Klitgaard, Henry Mattson, Kenneth Hayes Miller, Pop Hart, John Steuart Curry, and many others who were significant in the artist-life of New York. Three painters only must serve to represent here this large and influential group.

One of the first of the younger generation to get a hearing was Alexander Brook (born 1898), at one time assistant director of the Studio Club, who was given his first exhibition in 1920 by the great antiquary, Joseph Brummer. Brook had studied the touch and luminous color of Cézanne (who was to painting in the twenties what Picasso became in the forties, the almost universal god of the studios), yet he painted with his own style and delicate poetry of perception. In the nineteen-twenties and -thirties Brook was a leader in the protest against too slavish a following of Paris; and his warm human sensibility and subtle style were, and remain, sensitive and refreshing. The lyrical charm and rich color of a still life like *A Number of Things* (1935) (Boston, Museum of Fine Arts), or the Tanagra-like grace of the figure called *Ann* (1935) (The Metropolitan Museum of Art) are admirable, although in the kaleidoscopic changes of taste they have now come to be considered old-fashioned because based upon nature.

Peggy Bacon is a satirist whose shrewd and caustic observation expresses itself both in words and graphic images. If I had to select one typical example of her shafted wit, I think it would be the drawing of Childe Hassam in her volume of portraits in words and black-and-white, called aptly *Off with Their Heads* (1934).

Yasuo Kuniyoshi (1893-1953), born in Japan but receiving his artistic education in America, accepted the stylized drawing and color of the twenties. He created first a somewhat drab and edgy style, but interesting in its quality of outline and amusing amalgam of Japanese and Western conventions. After a visit to France in the late twenties, he became aware of the beauty of Western oil paint and developed a subtle coloristic style that led him at last to achieve intense luminosities. Kuniyoshi was a stylist rather than an artist of wide sensibility or thought. He does not interest you by his observations or by the flavor of his mind, but by a painting style that pleases and delights. He was perhaps only a studio artist, yet his color, his touch, his luminosity were a personal vision.

These New York painters of the twenties did not form into tight little groups and evolve programs of esthetic dogma as the painters of Paris did. They developed as individuals, trusting in their own intuitions, forming their own style out of the influences and ideas boiling in the teeming atmosphere of New York studios and exhibitions. Their subjects were not novel or un-usual. They used traditional themes—posed figures, still lifes, and landscapes—but brought to them an expert and disciplined grace of style. They continued the American tradition of independence, experiment, and intuitive rather than theoretical approach to painting and to life; and they succeeded at last in absorbing the lessons of Post-Impressionist color. To this degree they can be said to have completed the work of the Eight.

There was one field, however, where the emphasis upon expression and the freedom of drawing of the twentieth century was quickly accepted and became a popular art in the best sense of the words. That field was humor. Many of the painter-illustrators of the first generation made drawings for *Life* and *Judge*. Glackens, Sloan, Luks, and Shinn all had a vein of pleasant humor. But the illustrative technique of the Charles Dana Gibson era, around 1900, was pen-and-ink drawing which was not particularly suited to the freer pictorial vision developed by the new century. During the 1914 war Sloan, Bellows, Glackens, and Art Young all made drawings for the *New Masses* and substituted for pen-and-ink the freer, more atmospheric line and tone of pencil or crayon. Forty years before, Nast had created a linear style for the newspaper cartoon, suited to the woodcut process of reproduction then in use. Now, the painter-illustrators of the twentieth century—among whom Boardman Robinson also takes an important place—created a new free-dom of light and shadow suited to the photoengraving processes of reproduc-tion that were now universal. The way was opened for a revolution in the style of graphic humor and satire, beginning in the second and triumphing in the third decade of the century.

Rollin Kirby (1875-1952) introduced the use of crayon and pencil into the newspaper cartoon. He first spent a decade (1901-1910) in New York as a magazine illustrator before turning to newspaper work. In 1914 he be-came political cartoonist for the brilliant, liberal *New York World*. The somber complexities of postwar international politics and the spirit of bigotry and repression in America during the postwar reaction called out his fiercest drawings. One of his most effective inventions—which three times won the Pulitzer Prize in the twenties—was the long, lank, sour, black figure of the Bluenose, the spirit of prohibition.

D. R. Fitzpatrick (born 1891), who has been the political cartoonist of the *St. Louis Post Dispatch* since 1913, is also an admirable, biting draughts-man who knows how to make effective use of the broad, sweeping line and somber tones of the crayon.

The postwar period was one of great social tensions, as the United States underwent the greatest revolution in manners of its entire history. John Held (born 1899), without special distinction as a draughtsman, nevertheless created an image of the flapper and the jazz age which enabled the nation to bring the new manners into some kind of focus.

The magazine *Vanity Fair*, in the twenties, under the editorship of Frank Crowninshield, also was important graphically. Chiefly it popularized modern French art and a new standard of photography. But it found in the Mexican artist Miguel Covarrubias, and the man-about-town dandy and wit, Ralph Barton (1891-1931), two draughtsmen who were able to express the light-hearted mockery of the times; Gluyas Williams (born 1888) became there another voice of the period.

The foundation of *The New Yorker* in 1925 gave the new school of graphic humor its greatest medium. The irreverence of the twenties, gradually mellowing into an urbane sense of life's absurdities, and the new, freer, expressive, economical, graphic style produced a whole garden full of notable graphic humorists: James Thurber (born 1894) (Fig. 168); Constantin Alajalov (born 1900); Alan Dunn (born 1900); Helen Hokinson (1893-1949); Peter Arno (born 1902); Richard Taylor (born 1902); and more recently Robert Day (born 1900); Richard Decker; Whitney Darrow, Jr.; and Charles Addams form a remarkable school of expressive draughtsmanship. Their popularity is so great that no description or comment is necessary, except to emphasize that their work is art as well as humor.

The same can be said of the transplanted Austrian, Ludwig Bemelmans (born 1898), whose work both as writer and artist has added a new note to the charm of life.

To Norman Rockwell (born 1894) we must be grateful for rescuing the magazine cover from the endless repetition of insipid girls' faces and making it a medium for the humors of everyday life.

The comic strip had been a feature of American newspapers since the nineties, supplying an unpretentious form of broad, low comedy. It was a true twentieth-century popular art, too familiar to be noticed, until George Herriman (1881?-1944) in 1911 developed the figure of Krazy Kat. Herriman made the comic strip the expression of a curious, highly personal drollery. His society of animals, Krazy Kat, Ignatz the mouse, Officer Pup, and their neighbors who lived among the fantastic deserts and mesas of Kokonino Kounty became living characters in a little imaginary world of their own with something of the reality of a folk tale. Herriman had a great following among artists and intellectuals as well as among less self-conscious readers. Woodrow Wilson, it is said, used to read Krazy Kat with delight during the 1914 war, as Lincoln had read Artemus Ward.

The graphic humor of the twentieth century has been extremely individual, varied in style, pungent in flavor—a popular art of the first caliber.

On the serious and self-conscious levels of American culture, however, in spite of the vitality of many artists who seem to us now in retrospect to have made the twenties a remarkably interesting period, it would be hard to describe, to those who did not themselves experience it, the subservience of American polite taste in that decade to foreign leadership. We like to think of ourselves as a shrewd, hard-headed, businesslike people, and perhaps we are: but we are also creatures of enthusiasms so volatile and sentimental vogues so overwhelming that reason, perspective, and good sense are bowled over like ninepins. Between the enthusiasms of those who paid fantastic prices for eighteenth-century English portraits on the one hand, and those who thought nothing was art if it was not modern French on the other; between the loud contempt of the Parisian expatriates for everything on this side of the Atlantic, and the contempt of the New York intelligentsia for the Middle West; the mockery of the debunkers of the American past and the uproar of the young in general revolt against their elders, the twenties were filled with sound, for the most part unflattering to all we had ever done, or were doing. Calvin Coolidge spoke for a majority opinion when, on receiving an official invitation to send an American representation to the *Exposition des arts décoratifs*, held in Paris in 1925, he replied that America had no art to send.

A reaction against these extremes of cultural subservience and expatriate temper was inevitable. At its best, the reaction came quietly. Certain artists appeared who had something of their own to say, which, being deeply original, gave voice to the thoughts and emotions of their own land and people.

In general it can be said that a nation's art is greatest when it most reflects the character of its people. . . . The domination of France in the plastic arts has been almost complete for the past thirty years or more in this country. If an apprenticeship to a master has been necessary, I think we have served it.

These words, spoken by Edward Hopper (born 1882 at Nyack on the Hudson River, of mingled Dutch and English ancestry) might be taken as a keynote of the thirties. Hopper was no flag-waving nationalist. His first exhibition at the Whitney Studio Club in 1920 was of paintings done in Paris. But during his long, slow development he had matured a point of view in diametric opposition to the rising tide of the "international modern." Hopper's personal vision contradicted the strongest trends of the day: "Instead of subjectivity, a new objectivity; instead of abstraction, a reaffirmation of representation and specific subject matter; instead of internationalism, an art based on the American scene." [2] He felt the need which Eakins had felt fifty years before, to create an art of intense reality out of his own world. He found himself first in etching, more slowly in water color and oils: he was fifty before he found both his style and his audience. His subject matter was the face of the American city and countryside. People are only an incident in

[2] Quoted from Lloyd Goodrich's admirable essay, *Edward Hopper Retrospective Exhibition*, Whitney Museum of American Art, 1950.

his works: light is the theme and the means by which his art is built. To achieve his personal vision, he lived in a self-enforced isolation in the midst of New York city almost as complete as Ryder's was. A brooding spirit of loneliness and the light-bathed, objective poetry of architecture, which man has built and in which his life is embodied, fills his work (Fig. 172).

With Hopper the independent, native trend of Winslow Homer reasserted itself in the midst of the clamorous studio world of New York city. And, as if the time had come in the thirties to reassert the life and the diversity of this vast country, other independent voices appeared. They were not a group, nor a school; they had individual points of view and developed individual manners. But they showed that the long period of assimilation was over and a nationwide development beginning again.

Something of the urbane spirit of Franklin still lingers in Philadelphia: it is an old city, yet unself-conscious; very native and yet at home in the world. Franklin Watkins (born 1894) created an art in that same easy, urbane, yet individual spirit. His art springs from a broad culture and knowledge of the whole tradition of painting, from the Middle Ages to Post-Impressionism; his sensitive, handsome, coloristic style is both very knowledgeable and very personal. Perhaps partly because the studio life of Philadelphia is not such a deafening and self-enclosed world as that of New York city, Watkins has shown himself more adventurous in subject matter than the New York painters. He is interested in human personality and is one of the great portrait painters of our time (Fig. 169); he is a painter of enchanted and refreshing still life; and he has a mind which has found material for fresh imaginative studies in the ancient themes of life and death. Some years ago (in 1950) when his large decorations of *Death* and *Resurrection,* executed for the music room of Mr. Henry P. McIlhenny of Philadelphia, were shown at the Museum of Modern Art in New York, they were rather ill received by New York studio opinion. A painter, it was felt, should not be interested in such themes in the twentieth century; or, if interested, should paint them in one of the accepted modern European styles, Expressionist, or Surrealist, perhaps. This reaction was a curious instance of how readily contemporary movements of revolt harden into new conventions: it was Watkins' individuality, his refusal to fit accepted patterns, that was complained of. What impressed me about these pictures was not so much their great subjects and scale, or their freedom from traditional symbolism and imagery (though these are sufficiently unusual), but their eloquence and their extraordinary luminous color harmonies, of a clear soft radiance yet monumental power. They are the work of a highly personal imagination expressing itself in an exceptionally gifted style.

The Erie Canal, which opened the interior of the continent, had its western terminus at Buffalo on the Great Lakes. The Middle West begins there—a region of fertile plains bordering the Lakes, sprawling towns built in the late nineteenth century, a land of factories and cornfields. It is a region of different character from the East.

Charles Burchfield (born 1893) grew up in an Ohio town called Salem, settled originally by Quakers. In his boyhood it was a town of about 8000. It had a few small factories along the railroad line, a main street with stores to serve the townspeople and nearby farmers, and quiet streets of small wooden houses each set on its own plot of ground with trees and a lawn. These small midwestern towns are one of the norms of American life. Farming, the village and the factory meet in them. Architecturally undistinguished, culturally belonging to the lingering simple rural life of the past, they are also through their factories and stores linked to the mass production world of today.

To H. L. Mencken and to the expatriates of the twenties, these towns typified everything they hated, everything that they said made it impossible for an artist to live or breathe in America. To Burchfield they are beautiful; they are home. He has never been able to live away from these small towns, this rolling midwestern plain as endless as the sea, and he has created out of this hated and rejected material a grand, brooding, mysterious art whose aim, as he once put it, is "the big epic power of nature."

As a boy he studied art in Cleveland and tried, briefly, to live in New York, but the big city bewildered and utterly defeated him. He went back after a few weeks to Salem, took a job in a local factory, and began to develop his own art, in water color, painting on week ends or at night. His aim was to paint nature, "not invent a quasi poetry and try to fit the facts of nature around it." But his response to nature was so deeply emotional that his first independent work was an art of visionary fantasy.

He had little command of tone or color at this period but loved to play with the decorative and expressive qualities of line. To express the subject matter of the familiar scenes about him—the wooden houses, lawns and trees of Salem; the sun and moon; summer and winter; the sound of insects in summer, of winter wind in the trees, of the cawing of crows, the ringing of church bells—he invented a strange, calligraphic language of line.

In 1921 he moved to Buffalo, where he worked for some years as a designer of wall papers in order to support his family. He found a home in a little town outside the city, very like Salem. The countryside was the flat plain of the Great Lakes, but it was the same environment he had known, the same transition zone between nature and modern industry, the gray winters and burning summers of the midwest. Dissatisfied with the thinness of his early style, he settled down to master this world in terms of light and tone. His medium was water color but he came to use it with the power of oil. His art grew steadily more monumental, more objective and at the same time more deeply expressive, until he was able to paint, with great authority, the grandeur and power of modern industry in pictures like *Black Iron* (1935)

(Plate XVII) or express in his landscapes the poetry of the sun and the re-volving year.

The 1939 war, cutting off his free exploration of the countryside, threw him back upon his own inner self. He began to rework some of his early, visionary water colors, enlarging, revising, enriching them with the authority and monumentality of style gained in his middle period. *The Sphinx and the Milky Way* (1946) (Fig. 166) is such a picture, a vision of a night in sum-mer, heavy with stars and the scent of flowers and filled with the song of in-sects. A great moth in the foreground sips the honey of a pale ghostly flower. Such a subject is part of the ordinary, popular vision of the prettiness of na-ture—and Burchfield works best, always, with ordinary, familiar materials. But he has turned the subject into a vision of haunting mystery, filled with a sense of the elemental powers in nature.

In his most recent works, such as *Sun and Rocks* (1918/50, Albright Art Gallery, Buffalo), *Winter Moonlight* (1951), *Hot September Wind* (1953) or *An April Mood* (1946/55, Whitney Museum of American Art) this sense of awe-inspiring power and mystery in nature grows even stronger. Much of his most recent work strikes a note also of loneliness and chill. All his life Burchfield has had a vision of a phantom landscape. "Over the rim of the earth—to the North—lies the land of the unknown—it is windy, the ground is frozen, hard, barren—there is no snow—white wind clouds scud over a vast gray sky."[3] But whether he deals with the cold of March or November, or the heat of summer, Burchfield has created out of the typical, familiar, daily sights of his midwestern countryside a monumental, visionary art of "the big epic power of nature."

Chicago is also a Midwestern city but with the grand scale and drama of the mid-continent; Buffalo, by contrast, seems a small town. The lake front of Chicago lifts a fantastic panorama along Lake Michigan: but behind, huge grim factories and slums, and gray blighted miles of nineteenth-century wood and brick houses show the character of the Midwestern city translated to colossal scale.

In Chicago there was Ivan LeLorrain Albright (born 1897). In these strange sad cities of the Middle West, the element most interesting to the painter's eye is the beauty of decay. Burchfield has painted it often (in addi-tion to the Roman grandeur of industry) but he is a landscape painter, an observer of things in the large. Albright is a figure painter and one, moreover, whose vision is of the near and tangible. His style expresses a pin-point vision of fierce intensity, of people and of their possessions in whose dusty, hap-hazard accumulation is told (to the artist's eye) the story of times and lives now dead. Of his haunting, melancholy visions of the beauty of decay per-

---

[3] This and the previous quotations of Burchfield's own words are taken from *Charles Burchfield*, by John I. H. Baur, published for the Whitney Museum of American Art by The Macmillan Company, New York, 1956.

haps the most poignant, certainly the most famous, is the one called *That Which I Should Have Done I Did Not Do* (Fig. 165) (1941) (Art Institute of Chicago, lent by the artist), unique in subject, in style, and in a hallucinatory eloquence, as if of a vision in a dream.

Out on the Pacific Coast in the rain-beaten Northwest is a country of rain-forest and mountains and sea. It is old; for the West it has already a legendary past; yet very new, as all the Pacific states are: and it looks from its newness across the vast ocean to the old, old cultures of the Orient. The region has a character yet one feels that American life has not yet struck root deeply into its soil.

Mark Tobey (born 1890), one of the artists who has given a voice to that land, is characteristic, in a way, because he did not originate there. He lived in New York, moved to the Northwest in 1923, was in Paris 1927-1929, spent a long time in England and the Far East 1931-1938; Seattle really became his home only in 1939. Today he is the oldest of a group of painters who have made the states of Washington and Oregon important in contemporary painting; yet the country at large did not discover him until the forties after a younger artist, Morris Graves, who had learned much from Tobey, was already well known. Influenced both by European abstraction and by the Orient, Tobey developed in 1935 his "white-line" style, a personal kind of calligraphic brush writing, interweaving on the surface in ceaseless movement over dimly discernible patches of color beneath. In his earlier works suggestions of natural forms come and go in this maze (Fig. 167); but recently those have largely disappeared, and the dance of color and direction alone create their music for the eye. "I am accused often of too much experimentation," he said in 1951, "but what else should I do when all other factors of man are in the same condition. I thrust forward into space as science and the rest do."

These five painters show the geographical and imaginative diversity of a continental culture in the thirties. Some (Hopper and Burchfield) use objective images; others (Watkins, Tobey, Albright) subjective, to express strong emotion. Some searched for the meaning of the familiar world about them; others transformed human personality into strange images, into a floating smoke of color, or into reflections as intense as a loon's feathers reflected in a mirror. They are not "regional" artists but they give a voice to regions of experience.

Thomas Benton (born 1889) was a "regionalist," in the sense that the nineteen-thirties understood by the word: a conscious reaction to the expatriatism of the twenties. This reaction began in the twenties: but the Great Depression killed the expatriate movement. When dividends from America were cut off, the intelligentsia drifted reluctantly home from Paris in the early thirties. Only a few die-hards clung to the Left Bank. Those who returned found the United States, under the New Deal, a much more lively and interesting place than the prosperous and complacent country they had left. The decade of the thirties was a time when the imagination of artists turned suddenly again to the United States, stirred by the feeling of crisis, by the dramatic national leadership provided by Franklin Roosevelt, and by the sense of great events taking place in our own land. It was a time of rediscovery for the nation as a whole of the importance, the vastness, the picturesque variety of the life, people, and traditions of their own country. Some of those who had once tried hardest to cut themselves off from the dull familiar prose of home in order to turn themselves into Parisians were also the most vehement in reaction.

Thomas Benton had left Missouri as a young man for New York and Paris. He was one of the first group of American art students to rebel against late Impressionism and turn to abstraction. He went through a long period of groping, described in an illuminating autobiography called *Artist in America*. Benton's real interests were the American people, particularly the life and landscape of the South, and American history. Eventually he rebelled against a decorative abstraction alien to his vehemently positive nature, and turned first to painting historical murals, then realistic genre. His mural paintings in the library of the New School for Social Research, New York city (1930) and in the Indiana State Building at the Chicago World's Fair of 1932 (now at Indiana University, Bloomington, Indiana) mark the high tide of his revolt against abstraction in favor of native subject matter.

Benton's mural style was an interesting invention. He filled his walls with figures in active movement, one scene overlapping and penetrating another in ingenious fashion. The scenes were separated by wholly arbitrary moldings, somewhat as overlapping photographs are separated in the pictorial sections of the Sunday paper. It is an original device and was used with imagination and effect. Benton has never seemed to me quite so happy in his easel painting. In a small canvas the restless movement of his drawing seems too insistent and mannered.

Thomas Benton was not only a painter but a propagandist, as vocal and belligerent as his grandfather, the famous senator from Missouri. The revolt against the domination of French painting found in him and in the critic, Thomas Craven, two strident voices. Craven had followed, as a writer, somewhat the same course as Benton, from Kansas to Paris and back. Craven's eloquence, rather than any natural unity, grouped Benton and two other realists from the prairie states, Grant Wood from Iowa, and John Steuart Curry from Kansas into a noisy crusade under the banner of "The American Scene." He attacked not only the contemporary French painters but American expatriates, and tossed in New Yorkers for good measure: they were all iniquitous and effete, compared with the artistic renaissance taking place west of the Mississippi.

Craven undoubtedly greatly overpraised these painters (Wood and

Curry, at least, died unhappy, haunted by the contrast between Craven's claims of greatness for them and their own knowledge of themselves) and both he and Benton made many violently extravagant statements. Yet can one blame them? For a generation, smart young wits in New York had used "Middle Western" as an omnibus term of contempt for all that they despised in the United States. They had invented various mythical characters from there, like the Old Lady from Dubuque, as types of provincial imbecility against which they raised the gay trumpets of revolt.[4] I remember one instance of the sense of self-congratulation of the Easterner. It was in the twenties. A lecturer from New York, with a reputation as a wit, recited to his audience in a Midwestern city a verse which he said he had composed on the train, coming out to talk to them:

> O, pack my grip for a trip on a ship
> Where the scene at least is variable;
> For East is East, and West is West,
> But the Middle West is terrible.

Is it a wonder that the enraged natives of Kansas, Missouri, and Iowa, when their turn came, heaped insults upon the effete East and the colonials of the Left Bank, and claimed that art and virtue were to be found only in the prairies? In this war it cannot be denied that Craven and Benton showed a picturesque talent for vituperation.

Grant Wood (1892-1942) grew up in Cedar Rapids, Iowa, in circumstances of extreme poverty and barrenness. At first his struggle was to break away from Iowa to Paris and to paint like an Impressionist. After a few years he came back to Cedar Rapids and, while teaching art, received a commission for a stained glass window in the local legion post. Knowing nothing about the medium, he went to Munich to study this problem. There, among the early Flemish paintings and Gothic portraits of the Alte Pinakothek, the earnest, severe faces reminded him of his own people at home. It suddenly appeared to him that homely, simple things, seen with love and intensity, become both beautiful and important. He returned to Cedar Rapids determined to paint (if he could) his Iowan neighbors with all the fidelity and affection he admired in the pictures of the Alte Pinakothek. At first the fact that the memorial window commissioned for an American Legion Building had been made in Germany involved him in a hassle with the local forces. The window was rejected. The result was a memorable satirical picture, *Daughters of Revolution*. But the incident did not deflect him from his new purpose. Wood was a skillful and knowing figure painter, capable of the effective characterization

---

[4] The Middle West had already found its poets in Carl Sandburg and Vachel Lindsay. But while Lindsay's *Congo* or *The Chinese Nightingale* were enthusiastically received, nothing but silence greeted *The Golden Book of Springfield, Illinois*. The gloom and bitterness of Edgar Lee Masters' *Spoon River Anthology* was more to the taste of that day.

shown in the two portraits of *American Gothic* (Fig. 170) (1930) (The Art Institute of Chicago), which is perhaps his best work. He could paint the plain people of Iowa well. He was unsuccessful only in painting its landscape, for he tried to avoid the task of mastering the multitudinous forms of nature by using trivial stylizations borrowed from the landscapes in his mother's English china.

John Steuart Curry (1897-1946), born on a farm in Kansas, studied at the Art Institute of Chicago and the Art Students League, struggled for several years as an illustrator for pulp magazines, and managed to spend a year in Paris. On his return he settled in New York city where Mrs. Whitney gave him his first encouragement and support. His great ambition was to paint the life of his own state of Kansas, for he loved his native soil and wanted to make its prairie life a subject for art. He saw Kansas in a rather melodramatic way, choosing violent incidents—a tornado sweeping down on a farmstead, hogs fighting and killing a snake, or an emotional country baptism—and his melodrama helped to make his work popular. His weakness was that he really cannot be said to have mastered his medium: his drawing and color were weak and undistinguished; although his sincerity was unquestionable, that is not enough to make great art.

To the three painters of the Corn Belt Craven added a fourth master of the American scene, Reginald Marsh (1898-1954), who loved the tumultuous masses of humanity in lower Manhattan as Grant Wood loved his small-town Iowans. Marsh's pictures painted in the early thirties, showing depressed crowds in the Bowery and Union Square or exhausted sleepers on the Elevated, are the works by which he made his name; I am inclined to think they will also preserve it. They are somber pictures, grim in feeling, harsh in style, but they have emotion and power. He continued to paint the crowds on the streets of lower New York or at Coney Island; but his work showed an increasing coldness, so that ultimately his endless, teeming crowds came to seem like soulless automata writhing in the blast of some kind of mechanical twentieth-century inferno. This, too, may be called a vision of a sort, and perhaps Marsh may someday seem a kind of Fuseli of our times.

There are other painters whose subject is New York in this generation, chief of them, perhaps, Louis Bouché (born 1896), a painter of sharp eyes and witty intelligent mind; and Isabel Bishop (born 1902), whose world of New York shop girls is a little sad but well observed and truly felt.

Craven and the painters of the American scene made the greatest stir in the early thirties. They reaped a harvest of praise never given to Thomas Eakins, or the Eight, or to Burchfield and Hopper. But as I have tried to show, the mood of rediscovery of America was something wider, deeper, more pervasive and intangible in the whole country than this one shrill chauvinistic outcry. The early twentieth century had rediscovered Bohemia and had thought to build its new Republic of Art on the Left Bank of the Seine. The reaction of the thirties was not only against a colony of expatriates in Paris, but against all the exoticisms and Neo-Primitivisms that had so far inspired much of twentieth-century art, both in Europe and America. There was an awakening to the fact that the imagination's loftiest structures of art need, as their base, some experience that is long known and deeply felt. Instead of running away from home to Paris or even to New York, artists now wished to accept the mystery and challenge of their place of birth as the foundation of their art.

Promised, promised, promised, promised, promised, say the leaves across America. . . . And everywhere, through the immortal dark, something moving in the night, and something stirring in the hearts of men, and something crying in their wild unuttered blood, the wild, unuttered tongues of its huge prophecies— so soon the morning, soon the morning: O America.

This is not Walt Whitman, but Thomas Wolfe, whose novels of the soul's pilgrimage found many eager readers in the thirties; for Wolfe put into words not only a vast pageant of the young provincial's hunger for the magic city, the "Enfabled Rock" Manhattan, but the ultimate realization that this is not enough: that there is still something more.

Regionalism was a word of power. In writers of the South like Faulkner, Katherine Anne Porter, and the embattled southern Agrarians, in writers of California like Steinbeck and Saroyan, in writers speaking for the depressed classes in the northern cities like Farrell, or for the Negroes of the South like Wright, the whole country seemed to find voice. The state guide series of the Federal Writers' Project brought together a massive panorama of the nation such as had never before been assembled; and books like Carl Sandburg's *Lincoln* and Van Wyck Brooks's *The Flowering of New England* re-established for a wide public a sense of historical continuity.

The vital movement of the twenties had been to establish the new style of the century—the liberation of drawing and color from natural appearance, the creation of formal harmonies, and the expression of subjective emotions. The work of the thirties was to give form to a surge of national feeling which began to redress the balance between cosmopolitan and native strains in our culture, which had been out of balance for half a century.

The thirties did not create a "national" school of painting. Individualism is the core of American life and diversity its natural structure. (Our surface uniformities are the expression of our love of practical convenience and remain on that level.) There was a chorus of independent voices giving speech to the imagination in all parts of the country. The variety among the artists just mentioned—Hopper, Watkins, Burchfield, Albright, Tobey, Benton—is characteristic, then, of the decade: independent but not provincial; native, because deeply rooted in their own perspective upon life, but rarely chauvinist. The reawakening of the country to its own variety and wealth of imaginative material was, in the largest sense, the achievement of the thirties.

How large a part in this was played by the Federal Arts Project is difficult at this point to say. No adequate history of the New Deal's art projects has ever been written. Never popular with the general public, always severely criticized, they have never received the credit they deserved as a stimulus and training school for artists. What I can give here is not a history but an attempt to suggest the large, and I believe honorable, part the projects played in our artistic life in their time.

The federal government entered the field of painting in 1933 on an unprecedented scale, in the form of work relief for artists, organized as part of the Public Works of Art Project under the general direction of Harry Hopkins, relief administrator. The first work relief program had two aims. One was strictly to give relief to the unemployed, but at the same time to maintain the self-respect of artists by giving them work during a period of disaster. The second aim was to provide works of art to decorate public buildings. In 1935 the second program was transferred from the relief administration to a newly formed section of Fine Arts under Edward Bruce in the Treasury Department. Assistance to the artist on relief was reorganized as the Federal Arts Project, under Holger Cahill, within the Works Progress Administration.

Holger Cahill has already been mentioned as one of the pioneers in the discovery of the popular arts. Just previous to this time, he had spent eighteen months exploring the South for Mrs. John D. Rockefeller, Jr., collecting many of the objects now at Williamsburg. His interest in popular art gave the Federal Arts Project a fortunate direction. Painters and craftsmen, under his direction, were put to work in groups that suggested the vanished workshops of the handcraft period. They made posters, painted murals, circulated exhibitions, executed small decorative commissions, all on a basis of local needs and interests. People with old-fashioned skills were set to work using them. The national heritage of skilled crafts and popular arts was studied and recorded on a regional basis. Local art centers were established, local skills fostered, local traditions revived and honored.

As one might expect of a relief program, most of the work produced by what were called the "creative projects" was of only passing value. It is rather surprising, however, how many of our best talents today were either, as established figures, helped over a bad time by the WPA, or as young students were given their first opportunity to do uninterrupted work and to establish themselves as artists.

There were two other influential programs besides the creative projects. One was that of local art centers. At one time there were one hundred and three in operation, mostly in small communities, all over the nation. There is no question in my mind that these played a part in getting people all over the United States working in some medium—paint, wood, stone, textiles, clay—not as a livelihood but as a pleasant part of their daily lives. The second program was a historical research into our native inheritance of crafts and skills, which resulted in a monumental survey known as The Index of American Design.

The good that came from all this was an artistic activity diffused over the entire country in towns and cities where none had existed for two generations. Many young artists were given a start in their own communities who, in preceding decades, would have left home for New York or Paris, never to return. The interest in handcrafts was revived and refreshed, both by practice and historical study. If a greater degree of activity has been diffused all over the country since the thirties than had been since the romantic period, the bitterly criticized WPA art projects must be given their share of the credit.

Unfortunately for the reputation of these projects, the activity most in the public eye at the time was also the least successful. A nationwide program of mural painting was set up to decorate the federal buildings in Washington and the post offices, schools, and other public buildings rising all over the land. There were, among these murals, certain honorable exceptions to a general ineptitude. Boardman Robinson, Henry Varnum Poor, William Gropper, John Steuart Curry did creditable and pleasing works in the federal department buildings in Washington. Ben Shahn's mural of the dreams and hardships of the immigrant, in the community center at Roosevelt, New Jersey, has artistic quality, like all his work. In Colorado, Frank Mechau (1903-1946) discovered himself in this program. His best work was the fresco of *Wild Horses* in the inner court of the Colorado Springs Fine Arts Center, which shows not only an intelligent use of local subject matter but a happy wedding of mural painting and modern architecture, unfortunately without descendants.[5]

But in general the mural paintings done at this time amount to rather unsuccessful illustrations, pasted on the wall with little understanding of architectural effect. Perhaps we should not blame the artists too severely. If you leave a horse in the stable for years, then suddenly, without exercise or preparation, set him to run a race, it is not surprising that the poor old nag is tied into knots before getting halfway round the track. The mural painting

[5] Of the Treasury Department murals, the most successful as architectonic decorations seem, understandably enough, to have been the last: Siporin's and Millman's post office decorations in St. Louis and Anton Refregier's Rincon Annex post office decorations in San Francisco belong to the artistic history of the forties. Both these murals have been heavily attacked by people who do not like their somewhat morose tone.

The most successful mural paintings to come out of the whole movement, in the opinion of many, were the frescoes representing *The Story of the Land Grant College* executed by Henry Varnum Poor for the Pennsylvania State University at University Park, Pennsylvania (1940; 1948-1949).

program was much like this. Nonetheless, it was a disappointment that American painters, given such an opportunity, and in spite of the example of Mexican painters over the border, were unequipped either to achieve monumental form or to put themselves in large sympathy with their fellow men. Regionalism in mural painting became identified with sentimental home-town subject matter, presented in a horrid melange of ill-digested modernisms.

During the years that saw the great bubble of prosperity swell and burst, the United States became gradually aware of a new school of painting in Mexico. The Mexican people had emerged from their long colonial sleep in the sufferings and triumphs of the Obregon revolution. In the twenties they produced a national school of painting. Its artists were vehemently national in spirit. They made a virtue of national and local subject matter and believed in the artist's identifying himself in spirit with the mass of people around him. They revolted against the abstract estheticism of the twentieth-century painting and its cosmopolitan thinness and wished to create instead an art at once monumental, national, and heroic. American artists saw Orozco's power to express the smoldering unhappiness of mankind and admired Rivera's epic narratives of Mexican history. The effect was electric, for here was an art of *meaning* which at the same time embodied the stylistic discoveries of twentieth-century painting.

No one can understand the developments of the thirties without remembering the influence of Mexico both on the painters of social protest and upon the mural paintings done under the federal government projects. Rivera, Orozco, and Siqueiros all worked in the United States as well as in their own country. Orozco painted frescoes at Pomona College, at the New School for Social Research in New York city, and at Dartmouth College, filled always with a somber awareness of man's suffering and his inhumanity to his fellow man. Rivera first celebrated *California* in the San Francisco Stock Exchange; then made the first serious attempt by an artist of the twentieth century to make modern technology and mass production the theme of mural painting, in The Detroit Institute of Arts; and having found the positive side of twentieth-century American life in Detroit's industry, found its negative side in the frenetic atmosphere of New York, that inspired his ill-considered murals in Radio City (afterward destroyed).

The great depression brought bitterness and despair in its victims that found expression in a wave of sharp, satiric art. The Mexican Syndicate of Technical Workers, Painters, and Sculptors became the inspiration of the American Artists Congress and the American Artists Union. A few artists, for a time, marched in picket lines and debated Karl Marx. But the passion of social protest found a more valid artistic expression in painting, for the sympathies of the American artist in the thirties, as *Fortune Magazine* summarized the decade, were definitely on the side of the underdog. Much of the social satire painted or written in the thirties has been forgotten. Its work is done. The advantage of such plain speaking is that it helps the country adjust its thoughts to hard problems. When the problems begin to be solved, the work that was merely propaganda for the day is forgotten. But some of the painted satire and social protest had more enduring qualities.

Philip Evergood (born 1901) used the artist's new freedom from naturalistic drawing to achieve a vehement, angry expressionism. *My Forebears Were Pioneers* (1940), painted after the New England hurricane, was a cry of violent bitterness against what seemed the failure of the American dream. A witch-like old woman in black seated in a chair in front of a ruined mansion glares fiercely out of the canvas, seeming the very embodiment of the hatred of the past for the future.

William Gropper (born 1897) made the same use of dramatic exaggeration but, less gifted a painter than Evergood, did his best work in black-and-white.

Ben Shahn (born 1898) has now passed out of his stage of social protest. When he first made his appearance in 1932 he was a bitter, ironic draughtsman, a master of harshly expressive line, using color much as the colored comics do, to fill in areas with decorative tones. From 1935 to 1938 Shahn worked for the Farm Security Administration, as artist and photographer, traveling widely and learning to love the land to which he had come as an immigrant. In 1938-1939 he did a mural in the community center of Roosevelt, New Jersey, commissioned by the FSA, which is a vivid graphic statement, somewhat influenced in style by Rivera, of the contrasting facets of the immigrants' dreams of America and the hard struggles of reality.

In his later development Shahn's drawing has grown more subtle, his color more luminous and imaginative, his feeling for his fellow man warmer. He has become concerned with individuals rather than types, with individuals who were lost and alone in the terrible bigness of modern cities and modern society. The sad, dramatic poetry of his art is still today (1956) developing in new aspects and Shahn is now one of our most significant artists (Fig. 171).

While the American artists were suffering through the depression, another convulsion was spreading over Europe. The ferocity of the human race and the cruelties which men driven by fear or encased in a sense of superiority (whether of race, color, or economic theory) will perpetrate on other men have filled our time with horrors. In the thirties we began to receive refugee artists from Europe. George Grosz (born 1893) and Karl Zerbe (born 1903) fled from Germany to live in the United States. Feininger found Berlin no longer habitable and came back to New York. In the mid-thirties Pavel Tchelitchew (born 1898) and Eugene Berman (born 1899) came to America. Both had fled from Russia after the revolution and had attained fame as painters in Paris in the twenties. Amédée Ozenfant, the French painter and writer (born 1886), Kurt Seligman (Swiss, born 1900), and many others from Paris fled before or after the fall of France and sought refuge in New York; others, who survived the horrors of 1939-1945, came after the liberation. Some of these artists have remained and become a part of the artistic life of this country. George Grosz and Karl Zerbe, a gifted stylist, have become influential teachers, as have Ozenfant and Hans Hoffmann from Munich. George Grosz at first felt such a relaxation of tension after arriving in America that his work, once so savage, became mild and gentle until the onset of the war aroused him again to wild, hallucinatory fantasies in protest against its horrors. His autobiography under the title *A Little Yes and a Big No*, is one of his major works of art since coming to this country.

Transplanting to America has not affected the others so obviously. The mournful reveries of Tchelitchew and Berman found new subject matter during their stay here. Berman has added the Southwestern desert and Mexico to the inspirations of Italian landscape; Tchelitchew has studied the autumn colors of Connecticut and the world of medical science. Ozenfant has found the lighted city of New York at night a subject of poetry. All these men are essentially international in spirit. They have grown as artists and they enrich the artistic scene in America but their place of residence is the least aspect of their art.

The artistic tedium into which regionalism fell and the chauvinism of Craven and Benton were bound to provoke reaction. As Sinclair Lewis remarked somewhere, in America a pendulum is not a pendulum; it is a piston. In the later thirties the piston began to move again. The school of Paris had by this time passed into a new phase. The flat, decorative colors and stylized drawing of the twenties were being combined with fantastic imagination in the work of painters like Miro, Yves Tanguy and, above all, Picasso. Their works inspired a new wave of abstract and fantastic art in America. The Society of Abstract Artists was formed in New York in 1936. Later a number of Surrealists, mostly refugees from the war, held an exhibition, encased in a vast expenditure of string, in an old building on Madison Avenue. More and more American painters began to follow their lead, turning away from a regionalism now become sentimental and banal to an art without anchor in space or time; resting on nothing except the artist's own self-consciousness. Someone, with foot in mouth, christened the revival of abstraction "nonobjective painting" and the term was clumsy enough to become popular.

The trend away from realism received a strong recruit in Abraham Rattner (born 1895). He had studied at the Pennsylvania Academy but went to Paris as a soldier in the 1914 war and returned afterward to live there for more than twenty years until the fall of France finally brought him back to New York in 1940. Rattner, adopting the idiom of Paris, had poured into it the intensity and oriental richness of his Jewish heritage, creating an art of burning color and emotion.

The atmosphere of the 1939 war, with its international interests, and the awareness aroused in all men that they and their home towns were part of a continuum embracing the whole world, was seemingly favorable to the development of an abstract art. Many of the leaders of this second wave of abstraction and fantastic art were of the generation we are now describing, but they achieved recognition only with the postwar movement. Among those are Charles Howard (born 1899) of San Francisco, living recently in England, who has developed an eloquent art of color and moving shape: in New York there are Lee Gatch (born 1902), Bradley Walker Tomlin (1899-1953), Adolph Gottlieb (born 1903), Mark Rothko (born 1903), Clyfford Still (born 1904), Arshile Gorky (1904-1948), Balcomb Greene (born 1904), all painters of personal style. New York is the center of the movement and a second generation has come forward there since the war. Many of its best-known figures are painters now in their thirties or early forties, who fall outside the scope of this chapter.

CHAPTER 15

THE PRESENT

THE PAINTERS OF THE PRECEDING CHAPTER ARE THE GENERATION BORN BE-
tween 1885 and 1904, who have passed the boundary where youthful promise and early reputation give place to the harvest, or lack of harvest, of
maturity. It is usual to close a survey such as this by a chapter on the present,
formed of long lists of names of the younger artists of reputation at the moment of writing. But the perspective of the present changes from month to
month and only time can tell who will cross that dangerous border with success. In five years such lists of names, I notice, begin to go out of date; in ten
years they become sad. Rather than attempt to weigh living minds that are
still growing and developing, I shall try to draw the general outlines of the
present tendencies (mentioning names only if they are necessary to illustrate a main current) and shall speak of some new problems which painting,
as a craft and an organized element in society, now faces.

The war of 1939 to 1945 accentuated a tendency, already seen in the
thirties, for painters to turn away from the actual and to live in an ideal world
within the mind. Whether this is the result of pressure of events too great to
be easily grasped or faced; whether it is a reflection of the interest in exploring the unconscious, which, stemming from Jung and Freud, has become
both a new science and a popular fad in our day; whatever the reason, or
reasons, it is certain that a withdrawal from the objective world to one of inner fantasy has taken place on a massive scale. Since the close of the war abstract and fantastic elements have absorbed the imagination of American
painters more than ever before in our history. The populous republic of
painters in New York city—or, perhaps one should say, the large and entertaining anarchy—has been the principal center, San Francisco a lesser focus,
but the movement has been nationwide.

The ideal aspect of imagination has thus swung to the front, but, unlike the ideal art of the past, it is an idealism without memories, except from the unconscious. The vast, Greco-European heritage of religion and mythology, poetry and fable, which formerly supplied the subject matter of ideal painting, is gone. Greek mythology and the tragic poetry of the Bible, which were alive to artists as recent as LaFarge or A. B. Davies, have vanished. Ryder's Homeric dreams of sea and moon and cloud seem simple and objective compared with the visions of the dreamers of today. Artists have set themselves the task to create a wholly "nonobjective" world, without reference to any forms of nature. Alone with their self-consciousness, they try to make themselves understood (if they have not, as some have, abjured communication altogether) by muffled visions and unknown imagery from the subconscious.

Within this perspective certain strong tendencies make themselves felt.

As the observed world of nature has been eliminated from painting, the materials and textures of paint, the resources of the medium itself, its colors, its lights, its suggestions of movement, have grown more important. The inner, formal logic of the picture has become the subject matter of some painters.

With others, it is a desire to transcend reality, and to pulverize the vision of nature. In so doing, they pretend to reveal its essence.

The aim of another numerous group is to translate the tumult of the emotions directly into paint. Sometimes these painters use no suggestions of images but rely on the power of color and movement to express feeling; sometimes they use the associative power of imagery drawn from the primitive arts. The exploration of the irrational, the intuitive, the unconscious has brought to the surface fears and terrors which reason had tried to banish. Painting in the United States, since the close of the 1939 war, has been haunted by apparitions: the ghosts and demons of Stone Age man have risen to stalk into the twentieth century. It was only a coincidence, but a singular one, that while American soldiers fought a terrible war in the jungles of New Guinea, the demonic images of Papuan art rose from the museum cases and walked among the enthusiasms of the studio.

Another group of painters have revolted even against the logic and order of abstract art to work by a process akin to automatic writing. Their pictures, they say, paint themselves by suggestions to the artist's unconscious sympathies, beginning with random shapes and arriving at ends the artist cannot foresee.

Many of the leaders of this ferment of abstract and fantastic art belong, in generation, among the artists of the preceding chapter and have been mentioned there briefly, because these trends ripened late and belong to the postwar time. Others, including some of those I find most interesting, are in their thirties and forties: painters like I. Rice Pereira, Jackson Pollock, William Baziotes, Theodore Stamos, Lee Mullican, Charles Seliger, William de Kooning.

On the other hand, the qualities of memory, observation, and conscious selection from experience are basic traits of the human mind, and though rejected by one faction of art, are flourishing too. The subjective and objective imagination take various forms.

An art of lyrical fantasy has its center in the Northwest, in Seattle and Portland, where Mark Tobey and a number of younger painters make their home. Morris Graves and Kenneth Callahan are the most prominent of the younger men. Tobey's recent work has become wholly abstract, but Graves and Callahan are subjective, lyrical painters. Graves uses a haunted, moon-struck imagery of birds, flowers, and waves of the sea, as symbols to express a mystical imagination much influenced by both the art and the mysticism of the Orient. Callahan's dreamlike world, on the contrary, is a tumult of human figures, as if Michelangelo's *Last Judgment*, seen small through the wrong end of a telescope, obsessed his imagination.

There are other painters of lyric subjectivity at work all over the country, painters like Loren MacIver in New York, Margo Hoff and Julia Thecla in Chicago, Jacob Lawrence speaking imaginatively of the Negro, and too many others to mention. This is a very strong trend marked by subjectivity, eloquent expression of mood, a strong sense of pattern, and simplified statement.

The use of precise, sharp-focused detail to create a fantastic, subjective image is also an important trend. This showed itself in the generation of today as early as Peter Blume's *South of Scranton*, painted in 1931. Blume paints with extreme sharpness of detail but the large image of his picture is a melange of unreality and dream.

In contrast to abstraction, there has also been a sharp-focused naturalism, using bright local colors and obsessive detail, often with ominous overtones of hallucination or dream. Andrew Wyeth is a typical and gifted figure of this trend.

There is a large and interesting school of younger *trompe l'œil* still-life painters, in which Aaron Bohrod and Kenneth Davies are leading figures.

The objective poetry of nature and the atmospheric style of space and light which one sees in Hopper and Burchfield finds some younger painters to show that the riches of nature and the coloristic tradition of light and aerial tone are not exhausted. I shall mention only one, very close to me, Constance Richardson, who represents the tradition of the objective eye in this generation.

The forties contributed two notable recruits to the school of social satire. Jack Levine and Hyman Bloom, totally different in temperament, are alike in using an expressionistic style of profuse color and bitter, mordant emotion; another passionate and caustic satirist is Joseph Hirsch.

The school of American humorous draughtsmen continues to be enriched by lively younger talents. Saul Steinberg is an example.

But on the whole, abstraction, subjectivity, fantasy—the representation of the ideal world within the mind rather than of the stubborn actuality about us—have been dominant since the close of the 1939 war. Certainly the reaction against sentimental localism into which regionalism fell in the thirties has been complete. One would say that another move of the piston is due. But what it will bring only the artists and the future can tell.

As an organized profession in society, the craft of painting faces many problems in our decade, some old, some new. The war of 1939-1945 had one effect that deserves to be remembered. Between 1939 and 1945 the world had its mind upon other things than the arts. But toward the war's close the American artists fortunate enough to be alive and free to work at their art (of whatever shade of opinion) found that their pictures sold well. Such a thing had been unknown in America since the fifties and sixties of the last century. The explanation is, I believe, that our people were starved for something human and pleasant in a world laid waste by cruelty and grief. Deprived of their usual pleasures of sport and travel, unable to buy the complex and costly mechanical devices for the home that have first claim on the American family's income, people turned to works of art. This happy state for painters continued a year or more after the end of the war. Then normal civilian needs and pleasures returned and American painters resumed again their familiar position of poverty.

One may wonder, indeed, if one trend in domestic architecture continues, whether anyone will in the future be able to buy or use paintings. I met recently an old friend whom I had not seen since art school. He was now a prominent and successful executive in a great advertising agency. "What are you collecting now?" I asked him, knowing his keen interest in the crowd of painters and sculptors that churned around us. "Well," he said, "I am afraid I am not buying pictures. I am very much interested in modern architecture, too, you know. I have had X [naming an architect of international repute] build two houses for us. I have some of so-and-so's sculpture on the terrace but there is really no wall in either house where you could hang a picture." If the Medicis' architects had designed buildings in which their clients could find no place for a painting, the history of art would have been quite different.

The activity of the federal government as a patron of artists has also come to an end. The WPA art project was ended by Congress in 1939, the Treasury Department's project in 1943. The long tradition of Congressional indifference to the arts has, unfortunately, given way to a robust dislike.

Early in the war the Army began an ambitious historical program, planning to use artist-reporters in the field to record the world struggle. Scarcely had a number of good painters been recruited and sent to the various fronts than Congress heard of the project and at once put a stop to it. Fortunately for the painters, left stranded in Africa or Alaska, *Life Magazine* came to their rescue and employed them for a time. The Navy and Air Force were more discreet about their smaller programs of artist-reporting and were allowed to carry them through.

When the State Department in 1946 undertook as part of its information program to send an exhibition of American painting abroad, Congress again reacted with strong disapproval; the exhibition, then touring somewhere in central Europe, was abruptly withdrawn.

These are illustrations of a hearty and continuing prejudice. The reasons for it are complex but chief among them, probably, is the reaction which war brings with it of fear of intelligence, fear of the exploring quality of the human mind. Human beings, feeling and resenting the changes brought by a great war, seem to find the unusual or creative mind a convenient scapegoat: here is the too clever fellow who has done all the damage! Contemporary art, it must be confessed, makes on the whole few concessions to the layman's point of view, and easily gives the impression of being purposely mysterious or baffling.

Another and still more difficult problem is that of the physical growth of the nation. First, geographical diffusion. Since 1930, a steady increase in artistic activity has been notable throughout the entire country. New York city remains the largest center and contains the greatest number of painters. But there are good artists at work today in nearly every one of the forty-eight states. Much of this must be credited, I believe, to the Federal Art Program of the thirties; much of it also must be mere quantitative growth of population.

The establishment of museums and art schools has kept pace with this growth. There are now nearly a hundred active, significant art museums scattered over the United States. Local art centers have been established in uncounted numbers of smaller communities. Art schools are numerous.

The growth of the arts in college and university teaching has also been astonishing. Painters and sculptors as well as art historians are to be found on the faculties of most colleges and universities—over two thousand in number. The academic atmosphere has grave disadvantages for artists, because the best work in the arts rises from levels of consciousness that are not susceptible to academic testing in words. But the fact remains: the artists are there.

This great geographical diffusion is, I believe, a sign of health and vitality in the arts but it makes the artists' contact with their public an increasingly difficult problem.

A nation of 160,000,000 people spread across an entire continent presents a problem of organization different from that of a nation of five million, or even fifty million. In the last century, after the break-up of the Art Union, artists depended on local patronage and on annual exhibitions of painting of the Salon type for a national audience. The annual exhibitions of the National Academy in New York, the Pennsylvania Academy of the Fine Arts, the Corcoran Gallery in Washington, the Art Institute of Chicago, the Carnegie Institute in Pittsburgh, at the beginning of this century were able to offer representative national surveys. The annuals still go on but they no longer give a national survey. The country is too big and diversified. It contains too many artists. When The Metropolitan Museum of Art attempted a national survey of American painting in 1950 it was found necessary to have regional juries in various parts of the country before the final selection by a jury in New York. There were 9,000 entries; and the total cost of selecting, assembling, exhibiting, and returning the pictures is said to have been in the neighborhood of $75,000. Most museums have met this situation by abandoning the jury system; they invite a selected list of artists to exhibit. But who can make a personal inspection annually of the studios of this vast country in order to make a truly national selection? Many state and regional annual exhibitions are as large today and exhibit as high a level of professional skill as the national exhibitions of fifty years ago.

As the large national surveys grew ever bigger and clumsier, the small, one-man exhibit at a dealer's gallery in New York city became, in the twenties, the road to recognition. But this system too may be reaching saturation. New galleries in New York appeared in ever increasing numbers in the thirties and forties; there are now said to be over a hundred (1956). The number of fortnightly or monthly exhibitions has multiplied accordingly. Gallery goers, art critics, and reviewers in New York are now faced by more than 2,000 one-man exhibitions in an eight-month session. The task of seeing all these and retaining one's enthusiasm for talent, whether new or old, is beyond human capacity.

It is evident that once again, in mid-twentieth century, the painters of the country have outgrown their institutions and must find a new solution to their oldest problem.

Second, the problem of numbers, which is not one but two problems, each thorny and complex. There is the problems of numbers rising from the talents displaced from the destruction of the handcrafts in the nineteenth century. The tasks these varied talents of design should have been performing for us were to shape the whole environment of life, giving order and harmony to the setting of our lives, surrounding it with objects humane and gracious and pleasing. This task was not done: our cities and all the arts of the home fell in the early twentieth century into shapeless chaos. Today, at last, there seems the possibility that we are emerging from that chaos. Many brilliant talents have entered the fields of applied design and industrial design, and the situation there is now most interesting and promising. A revival of handcrafts is also taking place. It may be that the time has come when we shall master the machine age; when our cities, and homes, and machine-made products will regain their dignity and order. Yet a great redistribution of talents into the various fields of design must still take place before the arts find themselves in proper balance again.

The other problem of numbers is simply that the creative life of a nation of 160,000,000 people is too great to be brought into focus in one city, however active or strategically located that city may be. How then is new talent to be recognized in such a vast country? To find the answer to this problem is one of the great tasks of the second half of the century. I would say to those interested in contemporary art, as I heard one of our ablest art museum directors say to an audience not long ago: "You are not truly interested in contemporary art unless you are also interested in it locally."

These are problems of the craft of painting. This does not make them less worthy of attention. If I have told the story properly of how the subtle skill of painting was first brought to America in the brains and hands of men; how it was gradually established, took root, and developed a life of its own on this soil; how it slowly and painfully created, one by one, the institutions it required, no further proof is needed of the importance of the craft of painting. The problems that surround the craft of painting today—the vast increase in numbers; the economic insecurity of its members; their difficulties in finding a healthy relation to their public; external factors affecting the painter's opportunity to practice his art, such as the arbitrary rules promulgated by interior decorators, or the architects' hatred for this interloper upon their walls—all these are significant and vital since the craft must sustain the art of painting and keep it alive in human society.

Painting came to America first as a craft, serving practical purposes in the hands of the explorers, navigators, and soldiers; no less so in the hands of the missionaries who wished to show the images of Christian belief to the Indian. That is not the least curious part of our story—that first coming of the skills of drawing and painting to this continent and the rude life they led at first under the sky, on the decks of ships, on wilderness trails, in forts and missions in this far land.

What a subject painters had! When the weary sailors first looked across their bulwarks at the white lines of surf breaking on the thousand-mile beaches of this savage continent from which the sweet smell of the forest drifted out to enchant men tired of the sea, their eyes saw the dark, endless forests, into which each river was a road to the unknown, perhaps the western seas or China; brown, naked, painted men, swift and strong as wild animals, whose courage, endurance, and hunters' skills compelled the explorers' admiration, as their feckless, Stone Age ways, their dirt and thieving and childish whims aroused dismay. But the first painters who came here were simple craftsmen without the skill to tell that story—nor had the art itself achieved an imaginative perspective in which the interest and importance of all this could be seen.

Then came the first professional painters, trained in the studio practice of their homelands. They were simple craftsmen, too, capable of painting a good, honest likeness in pleasing colors and fashionable attitude, but with little impulse to do or see more. They brought their skill, however, and planted the practice of their profession.

The imagination began to work with the first native-born painters. They began to paint, not because there were men around them doing it, but because they were born with minds that felt a strange longing to paint. It was hard for them to learn the skills of it. To see pictures and learn the practice of a studio they had to leave these provinces and study abroad; the greatest and most ambitious of them had to remain abroad to find scope for their ambitions.

With independence came a vigorous search for a national expression. History, nature, sentiment inspired the artists; they found new subjects, new forms. They began to create the institutions of an artistic life. Thriving, popular crafts of portrait painting, engraving, and illustration formed an economic base for their profession; their work soon found an audience in their own people. The imaginative impulse was strong, sweet, and true. Only at the end of the romantic period was it invaded by the spirit of sentimental anecdote that haunted the mid-nineteenth century.

Beginning with the eighteen-seventies, the United States shared a great spiritual crisis in the Western world. A new technology, affecting every aspect of life, caused suddenly within the span of a single life changes in the structure of men's lives greater than had occurred since the invention of cities and the discovery of metals four thousand years before. It was a period of the rapid disappearance of old habits, the alteration of skills, a flood of new ideas, an overwhelming torrent of new impressions. Technological changes caused a major disaster to the craft of painting. Many other handcraft skills were destroyed, resulting in a great dislocation of the arts of design and migration of displaced talents into the field of painting, while that art, deprived of its old economic base in portraiture, was left impoverished and isolated.

In the United States, culture became self-conscious, imitative, eclectic. There were great but solitary imaginative achievements; but it was also a period of profound loss of national self-confidence in the imaginative life. The dramatic clashes of ideas, the alternating success and failure of the many movements that have filled the twentieth century are, from one point of view, to be seen as a struggle to repair the losses sustained in this spiritual crisis. How successful we have been let each one answer for himself.

From another point of view, however, the wonder is what vitality the art of painting has shown to meet the challenge. It is extraordinarily alive in our country; crowded with talents; immensely varied; ambitious; productive; undiscouraged by any obstacle—either poverty, overcrowding, war, the malice of decorators, the fury of architects, or the competition of all the protean amusements, distractions, and economic demands of the twentieth century.

But how could it be otherwise? This language of the eye, one of the noblest, most original, most ideal creations of Western man, has become part of our being; it is one of our instinctive forms of imaginative speech. In our branch of the Western world, in the United States of America, the mind and imagination are deeply stirred not only by the pressure of the terrible events and losses of our time but by passion to explore the whole world of sense and experience. The perceptive eye, the observing mind, the finely tuned emotions grow more, not less significant. The language of the eye has only begun to tell its story in our civilization.

The things to look for are imaginative force and intensity. Each age brings its own novelties of subject and style; yet these are not necessarily important or lasting imaginative creations. Each life feels the oldest experiences as if they were new: and indeed, they are new in each life. Creativity is part of the human spirit, and as varied, as manifold, as inexhaustible. It includes the daring mind grappling with the vast, new perspectives of our day and the Hopi Indian carving and painting the old, loved, unchanging image of his *katchina*. The novel and the traditional, the strange and the normal are equally its raw material. It proceeds by intensity of realization. The aim is freshness.

SELECTED BIBLIOGRAPHY

The bibliography given here makes no attempt to offer a complete documentation of 450 years of painting, nor to include all works of interest to the special student. It is intended to be useful to the general reader and the amateur, who wishes to go further than the present text can carry him—as it is the hope of both the author and the publisher that he will so wish. For those who desire to consult lists, many of the authors given below offer detailed bibliographies for their period. Among those most readily accessible, Virgil Barker's *American Painting: History and Interpretation* (1950); Flexner's *First Flowers of Our Wilderness* (1947) and *The Light of Distant Skies* (1954); and Larkin's *Art and Life in America* (1949) offer extensive and useful general bibliographies. Elizabeth McCausland's "Selected Bibliography on American Painting and Sculpture from Colonial Times to the Present" in the *Magazine of Art*, vol. XXXIX (November, 1946), pp. 329-349, is extremely useful. The *Dictionary of American Biography* does not always include the painters one wishes, but the biographies included give their own bibliographies. Finally, the Yale University Press has in process a new dictionary of American artists, to be published for The New-York Historical Society, which will be fuller and more accurate than Mantle Fielding's *Dictionary of American Painters, Sculptors and Engravers* (1926) and far more complete than the account of American painters given by any of the standard European dictionaries of artists.

The Archives of American Art, with its headquarters in The Detroit Institute of Arts, is engaged in a program of collecting the documents for the lives and activities of all American artists and craftsmen whom we can identify by name. (Only the anonymous household crafts and aboriginal arts are excluded.) It is not yet (1956) open to answer reference questions submitted by mail; but it will fill our need for a concentrated, national research institute.

The most extensive collection of photographs of American painting is in the Frick Art Reference Library, an institution to whose generous aid and hospitality the author, like every other student of art, is immensely indebted. The Waldron Phoenix Belknap Library of American Painting in the H. F. du Pont Winterthur Museum is also beginning a library of photographs, planned on the same noble scale but concentrated on the American field.

The aim of this selected bibliography is to offer current and easily available references. Special importance has therefore been laid on museum exhibition catalogs. In recent years, our knowledge has been advanced by many admirably thorough survey exhibitions and retrospective exhibitions of individual artists. Most of these catalogs are still in print and available from the museum that issued them, although not from general booksellers. The special student needs no guidance to the files of *The Art Quarterly* of which I have the honor to be one of the editors, to *Art in America*, the *Art Bulletin*, *The New-York Historical Society Quarterly*, the *Pennsylvania Magazine*, the *Journal of the American Antiquarian Society* and other similar journals; all periodical references are therefore eliminated.

No bibliography of American painting can, however, omit certain out-of-print but basic writers of the past, such as Dunlap (1834), Tuckerman (1867), or Isham (1905), whose work deserves our enduring gratitude and whose information cannot be replaced.

BIBLIOGRAPHY OF GENERAL SOURCES

Barker, Virgil, *American Painting: History and Interpretation*. New York, The Macmillan Company, 1950.

———, *A Critical Introduction to American Painting*. New York, published by W. E. Rudge for the Whitney Museum of American Art, 1931.

Baur, John Ireland Howe, *American Painting in the Nineteenth Century; Main Trends and Movements*. New York, Frederick A. Praeger, Inc., 1953.

———, *Landmarks in American Art, 1670-1950; A Loan Exhibition of Great American Paintings*. For the benefit of the American Federation of Arts, at Wildenstein, New York, Wildenstein and Company, 1953.

———, *Revolution and Tradition in Modern American Art*. Cambridge, Massachusetts, Harvard University Press, 1951.

———, *The Eight: Robert Henri, John Sloan, William J. Glackens, Ernest Lawson, Maurice Prendergast, George B. Luks, Everett Shinn, Arthur B. Davies*. New York, The Brooklyn Museum, 1943.

Benjamin, Samuel Greene Wheeler, *Art in America; A Critical and Historical Sketch*. New York, Harper & Brothers, 1880.

Bolton, Theodore, *American Book Illustrators; Bibliographic Check Lists of 123 Artists*. New York, R. R. Bowker Company, 1938.

———, *Early American Portrait Draughtsmen in Crayons*. New York, F. F. Sherman, 1923.

———, *Early American Portrait Painters in Miniature*. New York, F. F. Sherman, 1921.

Born, Wolfgang, *American Landscape Painting; An Interpretation*. New Haven, Connecticut, Yale University Press, 1948.

———, *Still Life Painting in America*. New York, Oxford University Press, 1947.

Boswell, Peyton, *Modern American Painting*. New York, Dodd, Mead and Company, 1939.

Brown, Milton W., *American Painting from the Armory Show to the Depression.* Princeton, New Jersey, Princeton University Press, 1955.

Burroughs, Alan, *A History of American Landscape Painting.* New York, Whitney Museum of American Art, 1942.

———, *Limners and Likenesses; Three Centuries of American Painting.* Cambridge, Massachusetts, Harvard University Press, 1936.

Cahill, Holger, *American Folk Art; The Art of the Common Man in America, 1750-1900.* New York, The Museum of Modern Art, 1932.

———, *Masters of Popular Painting. Modern Primitives of Europe and America.* New York, The Museum of Modern Art, 1938.

———, *New Horizons in American Art.* New York, The Museum of Modern Art, 1936 (WPA Art Programs).

Cahill, Holger, and Barr, Alfred H., jr. eds., *Art in America, A Complete Survey.* New York, Reynal and Hitchcock, 1935.

Christensen, Erwin O., *The Index of American Design.* New York, The Macmillan Company; Washington, D. C., National Gallery of Art, 1950. (Folk art.)

Clifford, Henry; Sloan, John; Shinn, Everett, *Artists of the Philadelphia Press.* Philadelphia, Philadelphia Museum of Art, 1946.

Dickson, Harold E., *Pennsylvania Painters.* University Park, Pennsylvania, Pennsylvania State University, 1955.

Dow, George Francis, *The Arts and Crafts in New England, 1704-1775.* Topsfield, Massachusetts, The Wayside Press, 1927 (Compendium of Newspaper Advertisements and Articles).

Drepperd, Carl William, *American Pioneer Arts and Artists,* with foreword by Rockwell Kent. Springfield, Massachusetts, Pond-Ekberry, 1942.

Dresser, Louisa, *Seventeenth-Century Painting in New England.* Worcester, Massachusetts, Worcester Art Museum, 1935.

Dunlap, William, *A History of the Rise and Progress of the Arts of Design in the United States,* 2 vols. New York, George P. Scott and Co., 1834. New Edition, edited by Frank W. Bayley and Charles E. Goodspeed, 3 vols., Boston, C. E. Goodspeed, 1918.

Fielding, Mantle, *American Engravers upon Copper and Steel* (a supplement to *American Engravers upon Copper and Steel by David McNeely Stauffer*). Philadelphia, printed for the subscribers, 1917.

———, *Dictionary of American Painters, Sculptors and Engravers.* Philadelphia, 1926.

Flexner, James Thomas, *America's Old Masters.* New York, The Viking Press, Inc., 1939.

———, *First Flowers of Our Wilderness, American Painting.* Boston, Houghton Mifflin Company, 1947.

———, *The Light of Distant Skies, 1760-1835.* New York, Harcourt, Brace & Company, 1954.

———, *The Pocket History of American Painting.* New York, Pocket Books, Inc., 1950.

———, *A Short History of American Painting.* Boston, Houghton Mifflin Company, 1950.

Ford, Alice, *Pictorial Folk Art, New England to California*. New York and London, The Studio Publications, Inc., 1949.

Frankenstein, Alfred, *After the Hunt: William Harnett and Other American Still Life Painters, 1870-1900*. Berkeley and Los Angeles, University of California Press, 1953.

Goodrich, Lloyd, *A Century of American Landscape Painting, 1800-1900*. Pittsburgh, Pennsylvania, Carnegie Institute, 1939; New York, Whitney Museum of American Art, 1938.

——, *American Watercolor and Winslow Homer*. Minneapolis, The Walker Art Center, 1945.

——, *Pioneers of Modern Art in America*. New York, Whitney Museum of American Art, 1946. (Early twentieth-century artists who studied in Paris.)

Gottesman, Rita Susswein, comp., *The Arts and Crafts in New York, 1726-1776: Advertisements and News Items from New York City Newspapers*. New York, The New-York Historical Society, 1938.

Grigaut, Paul L., *The French in America, 1520-1880*. Detroit, Michigan, The Detroit Institute of Arts, 1951.

Groce, George C., Jr., *1440 Early American Portrait Artists*. Newark, New Jersey, Historical Records Project, Works Progress Administration, 1940.

Hagen, Oskar, *The Birth of the American Tradition of Art*. New York, Charles Scribner's Sons, 1940. (From about 1670 to the revolution.)

Hartmann, Sadakichi, *A History of American Art*. Boston, L. C. Page, 1902; New Revised Edition, Boston, L. C. Page, 1932.

Haskell, Daniel Carl, *American Historical Prints*. New York, New York Public Library, 1927.

——, *American Historical Prints from the Phelps Stokes and Other Collections, 1497-1891*. New York, New York Public Library, 1932.

Heil, Walter, *Meet the Artist: An Exhibition of Self Portraits by Living Artists*. San Francisco, M. H. de Young Memorial Museum, 1943.

Hess, T. B., *Abstract Painting: Background and American Phase*. New York, The Viking Press, Inc., 1951.

Isham, Samuel, *The History of American Painting*. New York, The Macmillan Company, 1905; new edition with supplement by Royal Cortissoz, New York, The Macmillan Company, 1927.

Janis, Sidney, *They Taught Themselves; American Primitive Painters of the Twentieth Century*, foreword by Alfred H. Barr, Jr. New York, Dial Press, 1942.

M. and M. Karolik Collection of American Paintings, 1815 to 1865. Cambridge, Massachusetts, Harvard University Press, 1949, published for the Museum of Fine Arts, Boston.

La Follette, Suzanne, *Art in America*. New York, Harper & Brothers, 1929.

Larkin, Oliver W., *Art and Life in America*. New York, Rinehart & Company, Inc., 1949.

Lipman, Jean, *American Folk Decoration*. New York, Oxford University Press, Inc., 1951.

———, *American Primitive Painting*, New York, Oxford University Press, Inc., 1942.

Lipman, Jean, and Winchester, Alice, *Primitive Painting in America, 1750-1950, An Anthology*. New York, Dodd, Mead and Company, 1950.

Little, Nina Fletcher, *American Decorative Wall Painting, 1700-1850*. Sturbridge, Massachusetts, Old Sturbridge Village, in cooperation with The Studio Publications, Inc., New York, 1952.

Lorant, Stefan, *The New World: The First Pictures of America*. New York, Duell, Sloan and Pearce, Inc., 1946. (Explorer artists.)

McCausland, Elizabeth, "A Selected Bibliography on American Painting and Sculpture from Colonial Times to the Present." *Magazine of Art* XXXIX (November 1946), pp. 329-349.

McCausland, Elizabeth, and Williams, Hermann Warner, Jr., *American Processional, 1492-1900*. Washington, D. C., The Corcoran Gallery of Art, 1950.

McCracken, Harold, *Portrait of the Old West*, with a biographical check list of Western artists. New York, McGraw-Hill Book Company, Inc., 1952.

Mather, Frank Jewett, Jr.; Morey, Charles Rufus; and Henderson, William James, *The American Spirit in Art*. New Haven, Connecticut, Yale University Press, 1927 (Vol. XII in *The Pageant of America* series).

Miller, Dorothy C., *Americans, 1942: 18 Artists from Nine States*. New York, The Museum of Modern Art, 1942.

———, *15 Americans*. New York, The Museum of Modern Art, 1952.

Miller, Dorothy C., and Barr, Alfred H., Jr., *American Realists and Magic Realists*. New York, The Museum of Modern Art, 1943.

Monro, Isabel Stevenson, and Monro, K. M., *Index to Reproductions of American Paintings*. New York, H. W. Wilson Company, 1948.

Motherwell, Robert, editor, *The Dada Painters and Poets: An Anthology*. New York, Wittenborn, Schultz, Inc., 1951.

Murrell, William, *A History of American Graphic Humor*, 2 vols. New York, Whitney Museum of American Art, 1933/1938.

Neuhaus, Eugen, *The History and Ideals of American Art*. Stanford, California, Stanford University Press, 1931.

Pagano, Grace, *Catalogue of the Encyclopaedia Britannica Collection of Contemporary American Painting*. Chicago, Encyclopaedia Britannica, Inc., 1945.

Pearson, Ralph M., *Experiencing American Pictures*. New York, Harper & Brothers, 1943.

———, *The Modern Renaissance in American Art*. New York, Harper & Brothers, 1954.

Peat, Wilbur D. *Pioneer Painters of Indiana*. Indianapolis, Indiana, Art Association of Indiana, 1954.

Pleasants, J. Hall, *Four Late Eighteenth-Century Anglo-American Landscape Painters*. Worcester, Massachusetts, American Antiquarian Society, 1943, reprinted from The Proceedings of the Society for October, 1942. Contents: George and Mary Beck, William Groombridge, Francis Guy, and William Winstanley.

——, *Two Hundred and Fifty Years of Painting in Maryland*. Baltimore, Maryland, The Baltimore Museum of Art, 1945.

Prime, Alfred Cox, *The Arts and Crafts in Philadelphia, Maryland and South Carolina*. Topsfield, Massachusetts, The Walpole Society, 1929-1933; Series 1, 1721-1785; Series 2, 1786-1800.

Rathbone, Perry T.; Ravenswaay, Charles van; Leonard, H. Stewart, *Mississippi Panorama*. St. Louis, Missouri, City Art Museum of St. Louis, 1949.

Rathbone, Perry T.; Voelker, Frederick E.; Filsinger, Catherine; Eisendrath, William N., Jr., *Westward the Way*. St. Louis, Missouri, City Art Museum of St. Louis, 1954.

Read, Helen Appleton, *New York Realists, 1900-1914*. New York, Whitney Museum of American Art, 1937.

Richardson, E. P., *American Romantic Painting*. New York, E. Weyhe, 1944.

——, *The Way of Western Art, 1776-1914*. Cambridge, Massachusetts, Harvard University Press, 1939.

——, *The World of the Romantic Artist. A Survey of American Culture from 1800 to 1875*. Detroit, Michigan, The Detroit Institute of Arts, 1945.

Richardson, E. P., and Wittmann, Otto, Jr., *Travelers in Arcadia. American Artists in Italy, 1830-1875*. The Detroit Institute of Arts and The Toledo Museum of Art, 1951.

Ritchie, Andrew C., *Abstract Painting and Sculpture in America*. New York, The Museum of Modern Art, 1951.

Saint Gaudens, Homer, *The American Artist and His Times*. New York, Dodd, Mead and Company, 1941.

——, *Survey of American Painting*. Pittsburgh, Department of Fine Arts, Carnegie Institute, 1940.

Slatkin, Charles E., and Shoolman, Regina, *Treasury of American Drawings*. New York, Oxford University Press, 1947.

Soby, James Thrall, *Contemporary Painters*. New York, The Museum of Modern Art, 1948.

Soby, James Thrall and Miller, Dorothy C., *Romantic Painting in America*. New York, The Museum of Modern Art, 1943.

Stauffer, David McNeely, *American Engravers Upon Copper and Steel*, 2 vols. New York, The Grolier Club, 1907 (supplementary volume by Mantle Fielding, 1917).

Stokes, I. N. Phelps, and Haskell, Daniel C., *American Historical Prints, Early Views of American Cities, etc., from The Phelps Stokes and Other Collections*. New York, New York Public Library, 1933.

Sweet, Frederick A., *The Hudson River School and the Early American Landscape Tradition*. Chicago, Art Institute of Chicago, 1945.

Sweet, Frederick A., and Huth, Hans, *From Colony to Nation. An exhibition of American painting, silver and architecture from 1650 to the War of 1812*. Chicago, Art Institute of Chicago, 1949.

Taft, Robert, *Artists and Illustrators of the Old West: 1850-1900*. New York, Charles Scribner's Sons, 1953.

Tuckerman, Henry T., *Book of the Artists: American Artist Life*. New York, G. P. Putnam's Sons, 1867, 6th impression, 1882.

Walker, John, and James, Macgill, *Great American Paintings from Smibert to Bellows, 1729-1924*. New York, Oxford University Press, 1943.

Washburn, Gordon Bailey, *Old and New England: an exhibition of American painting of Colonial and Early Republican Days, together with English painting of the same time*. Providence, Rhode Island, Museum of Art of the Rhode Island School of Design, 1945.

Watson, Forbes, *American Painting Today*. Washington, D. C., American Federation of Arts, 1939.

Watson, Forbes, and Bruce, Edward, *Mural Designs, 1934-1936*. Washington, D. C., Art in Federal Buildings, Inc., 1936.

Wehle, Harry B., *American Miniatures, 1730-1850, with a Biographical Dictionary of the Artists by Theodore Bolton*. Garden City, New York, published for The Metropolitan Museum of Art by Doubleday & Company, Inc. 1927.

Wehle, Harry B.; Mayor, A. Hyatt; and Allen, Josephine L., *Life in America: a special loan exhibition of paintings held during the period of the New York World's Fair*. New York, The Metropolitan Museum of Art, 1939.

Weitenkampf, Frank, *American Graphic Art*. New York, Henry Holt & Co., Inc., 1912; new edition, New York, The Macmillan Company, 1924.

Wheeler, Monroe, *Twentieth Century Portraits*. New York, The Museum of Modern Art, 1942.

Wight, Frederick S., *Milestones of American Painting in Our Century*; introduction by Lloyd Goodrich. New York, Chanticleer Press, Inc., 1949.

Bibliographies Arranged by Artists

Washington Allston: Richardson, E. P., *Washington Allston, A Study of the Romantic Artist in America*. Chicago, University of Chicago Press, 1948.

Ezra Ames: Bolton, Theodore, and Cortelyou, Irwin F., *Ezra Ames of Albany, Portrait Painter, Craftsman, Royal Arch Mason, Banker, 1768-1836, and a Catalogue of his Works* by Irwin F. Cortelyou. New York, The New-York Historical Society, 1955.

John James Audubon: Ford, Alice, *Audubon's Animals: The Quadrupeds of North America*; New York, The Studio Publications, Inc., 1951. Ford, Alice, *Audubon's Butterflies, Moths and Other Studies*; New York, The Studio Publications, Inc., 1952. Peattie, Donald Culross (ed.), *Audubon's America, The Narratives and Experiences of John James Audubon*; Boston, Houghton Mifflin Company, 1940.

George Bellows: Boswell, Peyton, *George Bellows*; New York, Crown, 1942. Art Institute of Chicago, *George Bellows; Paintings, Drawings, Prints*; Chicago, Art Institute of Chicago, 1946.

Thomas Hart Benton: Benton, Thomas Hart, *An Artist in America*. New York, Robert M. McBride, 1937.

George Caleb Bingham: Christ-Janer, Albert, *George Caleb Bingham of Mis-*

souri; preface by Thomas Hart Benton. New York, Dodd, Mead and Company, 1940.

DAVID G. BLYTHE: Miller, Dorothy, *The Life and Work of David G. Blythe.* Pittsburgh, Pennsylvania, University of Pittsburgh Press, 1950.

CHARLES BURCHFIELD: Baur, John I. H., *Charles Burchfield.* New York, published for the Whitney Museum of American Art by The Macmillan Company, 1956.

MARY CASSATT: Sweet, Frederick A., *Sargent, Whistler, and Mary Cassatt.* Chicago, Art Institute of Chicago, 1954.

GEORGE CATLIN: Haberly, Lloyd, *Pursuit of the Horizon, A Life of George Catlin, Painter and Recorder of the American Indian.* New York, The Macmillan Company, 1948.

WILLIAM MERRITT CHASE: Peat, Wilbur D., *Chase Centennial Exhibition.* Indianapolis, John Herron Art Museum, 1949.

THOMAS COLE: Seaver, Esther I., *Thomas Cole.* Hartford, Connecticut, Wadsworth Atheneum, 1949.

JOHN SINGLETON COPLEY: Flexner, James Thomas, *John Singleton Copley;* Boston, Houghton Mifflin Company, 1948 (a completely revised and enlarged version of the biography of Copley originally published as part of the author's *America's Old Masters*). Parker, Barbara Neville, and Wheeler, Anne Bolling, *John Singleton Copley, American Portraits in Oil, Pastel and Miniature;* Boston, Museum of Fine Arts, 1938.

ARTHUR B. DAVIES: Phillips Memorial Gallery, Washington, D. C., *Arthur B. Davies: Essays on the Man and His Art.* Cambridge, Massachusetts, The Riverside Press, 1924.

CHARLES DEMUTH: Ritchie, Andrew C., *Charles Demuth.* New York, The Museum of Modern Art, 1950.

WILLIAM DUNLAP: Dunlap, William, *Diary;* New York, The New-York Historical Society, 1931. Phillips Academy, Addison Gallery of American Art, *William Dunlap Painter and Critic; Reflections on American Painting of a Century Ago;* Andover, Massachusetts, Phillips Academy, 1939.

GEORGE HENRY DURRIE: Cowdrey, Bartlett, *George Henry Durrie, 1820-1863, Connecticut Painter of American Life.* Hartford, Wadsworth Atheneum, 1947.

FRANK DUVENECK: Siple, Walter S., *Frank Duveneck.* Cincinnati, Ohio, Cincinnati Art Museum, 1936.

THOMAS EAKINS: Goodrich, Lloyd, *Thomas Eakins, His Life and Work.* New York, Whitney Museum of American Art, 1933.

RALPH EARL: Sawitzky, William, *Ralph Earl, 1751-1801.* New York, Whitney Museum of American Art, 1945.

LYONEL FEININGER: The Museum of Modern Art, *Lyonel Feininger . . . Marsden Hartley. . . .* New York, The Museum of Modern Art, 1944.

ROBERT FEKE: Foote, Henry Wilder, *Robert Feke, Colonial Portrait Painter;* Cambridge, Massachusetts, Harvard University Press, 1930. Whitney Museum of American Art, *Robert Feke;* New York, Whitney Museum of American Art, 1946.

WILLIAM GLACKENS: Watson, Forbes, *William Glackens*. New York, Duffield, 1923.

MORRIS GRAVES: Wight, Frederick S., *The Morris Graves Retrospective Exhibition*. Berkeley, University of California, 1956.

GEORGE GROSZ: Baur, John I. H., *George Grosz* (research by Rosalind Irvine). New York, published for the Whitney Museum of American Art by The Macmillan Company, 1954.

CHESTER HARDING: White, Margaret E. (ed.), *A Sketch of Chester Harding, Artist, Drawn by His Own Hand*, edited by his daughter, Margaret E. White, new edition with annotations by his grandson, W. P. G. Harding. Boston, Houghton Mifflin Company, 1929.

MARSDEN HARTLEY: McCausland, Elizabeth, *Marsden Hartley;* Minneapolis, University of Minnesota Press, 1952. The Museum of Modern Art, *Lyonel Feininger . . . Marsden Hartley. . . ;* New York, The Museum of Modern Art, 1944.

MARTIN JOHNSON HEADE: McIntyre, Robert G., *Martin Johnson Heade*. New York, Pantheon Press, 1948.

GUSTAVUS HESSELIUS: Brinton, Christian, *Gustavus Hesselius*. Philadelphia, Philadelphia Museum of Art, 1938.

EDWARD HICKS: Ford, Alice, *Edward Hicks, Painter of the Peaceable Kingdom*. Philadelphia, University of Pennsylvania Press, 1952.

WINSLOW HOMER: Cowdrey, Bartlett, *Winslow Homer: Illustrator, 1860-1875;* Northampton, Massachusetts, Smith College Museum of Art, 1951. Goodrich, Lloyd, *Winslow Homer;* New York, published for the Whitney Museum of American Art by The Macmillan Company, 1944.

EDWARD HOPPER: Goodrich, Lloyd, *Edward Hopper Retrospective Exhibition*. New York, Whitney Museum of American Art, 1950 (for a group of museums).

GEORGE INNESS: McCausland, Elizabeth, *George Inness, an American Landscape Painter, 1825-1894*. New York, American Artists Group, 1946.

JOHN WESLEY JARVIS: Dickson, Harold E., *John Wesley Jarvis, American Painter, 1780-1840, with a check list of his works*. New York, New-York Historical Society, 1949.

EASTMAN JOHNSON: Baur, John I. H., *An American Genre Painter, Eastman Johnson, 1824-1906*. New York, Brooklyn Institute of Arts and Sciences, 1940.

JOHN LA FARGE: Cortissoz, Royal, *John La Farge, A Memoir and a Study*. Boston, Houghton Mifflin Company, 1911.

JOHN MARIN: *John Marin Memorial Exhibition*, with a foreword by Duncan Phillips, appreciations by William Carlos Williams and Dorothy Norman, conclusion to a biography by Mackinley Helm; Museum of Fine Arts, Boston, 1955. *John Marin—Frontiersman* by Frederick S. Wight; Los Angeles, Art Galleries of the University of California, Los Angeles, 1955. *John Marin, Water Colors, Oil Paintings, Etchings:* "John Marin," by Henry McBride; "As to John Marin, and his Ideas," by Marsden Hartley; "John Marin—and Pertaining Thereto," by E. M. Benson; New York, The Museum of Modern Art, 1936.

SAMUEL F. B. MORSE: Larkin, Oliver W., *Samuel F. B. Morse and American Democratic Art;* Boston, Little, Brown and Company, 1954. Mabee, Carleton, *The American Leonardo: A Life of Samuel F. B. Morse;* New York, Alfred A. Knopf, Inc., 1943.

ANNA MOSES: Moses, Anna, *Grandma Moses; My Life's History*, edited by Otto Kallir. New York, Harper & Brothers, 1952.

WILLIAM SIDNEY MOUNT: Cowdrey, Bartlett and Williams, Hermann Warner, Jr., *William Sidney Mount, 1807-1868, An American Painter*. New York, published for The Metropolitan Museum of Art by Columbia University Press, 1944.

MOUNT BROTHERS: Cowdrey, Bartlett, *The Mount Brothers: Henry Smith Mount, Shepard Alonzo Mount, and William Sidney Mount*. Stony Brook, New York, The Suffolk Museum, 1947.

GEORGIA O'KEEFFE: Rich, Daniel Catton, *Georgia O'Keeffe*. Chicago, Art Institute of Chicago, 1943.

CHARLES WILLSON PEALE: Sellers, Charles Coleman, *Charles Willson Peale*, 2 vols.; Philadelphia, American Philosophical Society, 1947. Sellers, Charles Coleman, *Portraits and Miniatures by Charles Willson Peale;* Philadelphia, American Philosophical Society, 1952.

JOSEPH PENNELL: Pennell, Elizabeth Robins, *The Life and Letters of Joseph Pennell*. Boston, Little, Brown and Company, 1929.

MATTHEW PRATT: Sawitzky, William, *Matthew Pratt, 1734-1805*. New York, The New-York Historical Society, 1942.

MAURICE PRENDERGAST: Phillips Academy, Addison Gallery of American Art, *The Prendergasts; Retrospective Exhibition of the Work of Maurice and Charles Prendergast*. Andover, Massachusetts, Phillips Academy, 1938.

JOHN QUIDOR: Baur, John I. H., *John Quidor, 1801-1881*. New York, Brooklyn Institute of Arts and Sciences, 1942.

WILLIAM RIMMER: Kirstein, Lincoln, *William Rimmer*. New York, Whitney Museum of American Art and Museum of Fine Arts, Boston, 1946-1947.

ALBERT P. RYDER: Goodrich, Lloyd, *Albert P. Ryder Centenary Exhibition*. New York, Whitney Museum of American Art, 1947.

JOHN SINGER SARGENT: McKibben, David, *Sargent's Boston, With an Essay and a Biographical Summary and a Complete Check List of Sargent's Portraits;* Boston, Museum of Fine Arts, Boston, 1956. Mount, Charles Merrill, *John Singer Sargent, A Biography;* New York, W. W. Norton and Company, Inc., 1955. Sweet, Frederick A., *Sargent, Whistler, and Mary Cassatt;* Chicago, Art Institute of Chicago, 1954.

BEN SHAHN: Soby, James Thrall, *Ben Shahn*. New York, The Museum of Modern Art, 1947.

SHARPLES: Knox, Katharine McCook, *The Sharples, Their Portraits of George Washington and His Contemporaries*. New Haven, Yale University Press, 1930.

CHARLES SHEELER: *Charles Sheeler: Paintings, Drawings, Photographs*, with an introduction by William Carlos Williams; New York, The Museum of Modern Art, 1939. Wight, Frederick S., *Charles Sheeler, A Retrospective Exhibi-*

tion, with a foreword by William Carlos Williams and an appreciation by Bartlett H. Hayes, Jr.; Los Angeles, University of California Art Galleries, 1954 (for a group of participating museums).

JOHN SLOAN: Goodrich, Lloyd, *John Sloan, 1871-1951*. New York, Whitney Museum of American Art, 1952.

JOHN SMIBERT: Foote, Henry Wilder, *John Smibert, Painter*. Cambridge, Massachusetts, Harvard University Press, 1950.

GILBERT STUART: Flexner, James Thomas, *Gilbert Stuart; A Great Life in Brief;* New York, Alfred A. Knopf, Inc., 1955 (greatly expanded revision of the biography which appeared in the author's *America's Old Masters*). Morgan, John Hill, *Gilbert Stuart and His Pupils; Together with the Complete Notes on Painting by Matthew Harris Jouett from Conversations with Gilbert Stuart in 1816;* New York, The New-York Historical Society, 1939. Park, Lawrence, *Gilbert Stuart*, 4 vols.; New York, W. E. Rudge, 1926.

THOMAS SULLY: Biddle, Edward, and Fielding, Mantle, *The Life and Works of Thomas Sully, 1783-1872*. Philadelphia, M. Fielding, 1921.

ABBOTT H. THAYER: White, Nelson C., *Abbott H. Thayer*. Hartford, Connecticut, Connecticut Printers, Inc., 1951.

JEREMIAH THEUS: Middleton, Margaret Simons, *Jeremiah Theus, Colonial Artist of Charles Town*. Columbia, South Carolina, University of South Carolina Press, 1953.

COL. JOHN TRUMBULL: Sizer, Theodore (ed.), *The Autobiography of Col. John Trumbull;* New Haven, Connecticut, Yale University Press, 1953. Sizer, Theodore, *The Works of Colonel John Trumbull, Artist of the American Revolution;* New Haven, Connecticut, Yale University Press, 1950.

JOHN VANDERLYN: Schoonmaker, Marius, *John Vanderlyn, Artist, 1775-1852*. Kingston, New York, the Senate House Museum, 1950.

FRANKLIN WATKINS: Ritchie, Andrew C., *Franklin C. Watkins*. New York, The Museum of Modern Art, 1950.

BENJAMIN WEST: Marceau, Henri, and Kimball, Fiske, *Benjamin West, 1738-1820*. Philadelphia, Pennsylvania Museum of Art, 1938.

JAMES McNEILL WHISTLER: Pennell, Elizabeth Robins, *Life of James McNeill Whistler*, 6th edition, revised; Philadelphia, J. B. Lippincott Company, 1919. Sweet, Frederick A., *Sargent, Whistler, and Mary Cassatt;* Chicago, Art Institute of Chicago, 1954.

WORTHINGTON WHITTREDGE: Baur, John I. H. (ed.)., *The Autobiography of Worthington Whittredge*. New York, The Brooklyn Museum, 1942.

INDEX

NOTE: Italic page numbers indicate illustrations.